Christian Gerlach
Conditions of Violence

Christian Gerlach
Conditions of Violence

—

ISBN 978-3-11-156726-6
e-ISBN (PDF) 978-3-11-156873-7
e-ISBN (EPUB) 978-3-11-156901-7
DOI https://doi.org/10.1515/9783111568737

This work is licensed under the Creative Commons Attribution-NonCommercial-NoDerivatives 4.0 International License. For details go to https://creativecommons.org/licenses/by-nc-nd/4.0/.

Library of Congress Control Number: 2024941930

Bibliographic information published by the Deutsche Nationalbibliothek
The Deutsche Nationalbibliothek lists this publication in the Deutsche Nationalbibliografie; detailed bibliographic data are available on the internet at http://dnb.dnb.de.

© 2024 the author(s), published by Walter de Gruyter GmbH, Berlin/Boston
The book is published open access at www.degruyter.com.

Cover image: panic_attack/iStock/Getty Images Plus
Typesetting: Integra Software Services Pvt. Ltd.

www.degruyter.com

Contents

List of Abbreviations —— VII

1 Introduction —— 1

Part I: Mass Violence as Social Interaction

2 Festive Days of Killing: Enacting a New Social Order in Rwanda, 1994 —— 25

3 Sounds of a Massacre: Chuknagar, East Pakistan, 1971 —— 64

4 Crowd Violence in East Pakistan/Bangladesh 1971–1972 —— 88

5 Narratives of Suffering: Soviet Movies About World War II —— 111

Part II: Conditions of Violence

6 Famines and Imperialism: For a Different History of World War II —— 151

7 COVID-19 as Mass Violence —— 223

8 Conclusion —— 247

Acknowledgments —— 257

Bibliography —— 259

Index —— 285

List of Abbreviations

COVID	coronavirus disease
CPSU	Communist Party of the Soviet Union
EU	European Union
FAO	Food and Agriculture Organization of the United Nations
GDP	gross domestic product
GDR	German Democratic Republic
HIV	Human Immunodeficiency Virus
ICC	International Criminal Court
KESB	Kindes- und Erwachsenenschutzbehörde (Authority for the Protection of Children and Parents)
MDR	Republican Democratic Movement
MM	Mamoon, Muntassir, ed. *1971 Chuknagar Genocide*, second ed. Dhaka: University Press Publishers, 2014
MRND	Revolutionary Movement for National Development
NATO	North Atlantic Treaty Organization
n.d.	no date
NKVD	People's Commissariat for Internal Affairs
n.y.	no year
NGO	non-governmental organization
PA AA	Politisches Archiv des Auswärtigen Amtes, Berlin
POW	prisoner of war
RM	Reichsmark
RPF	Rwandan Patriotic Front
RTLM	Radio-Télévision Libre Mille Collines
Rwanda YCT	Rwanda Youth and Children's Testimonies
SS	Schutzstaffeln (Protective Squads)
UN	United Nations
UNRRA	United Nations Relief and Rehabilitation Administration
USSR	Union of Soviet Socialist Republics
WHO	World Health Organization

1 Introduction

This study pursues a social history of mass violence and analyzes the latter as social interaction. Based in large parts on the close-up view of witnesses and survivors, it shows how violence comes from people (not only abstract machineries and systems), from direct interactions between individuals, and how deeply rooted and firmly anchored it is in societies. The book demonstrates that indirect violence, too, is often not abstract and anonymous but rather produced by people in social exchanges that may be surprising because of their ordinariness. I take these approaches in the attempt to demystify violence. By rejecting the idea that the loss of some lives is greater than that of other lives, regardless of whether people were killed directly or indirectly, the book aims at working toward a non-racist history of violence.

This volume synthesizes my thoughts about the subject since the publication of my book *Extremely Violent Societies*, where I emphasized that mass violence is often participatory, multi-directional and multicausal. A variety of groups is attacked by people from various sections of society, along with state organs, for a multitude of reasons, based on different interests and attitudes. Violence originates not only from the state, but very much from the people. Often mass violence occurs in connection with a crisis of society with immense social and geographical mobility.[1] In the present book, I move in several ways further on the way to a social history of mass violence. First, I take a closer look at social interaction on the ground between groups as well as between individuals. Second, I explore how the tendency of groups and individuals to recklessly and forcefully pursue their own interests and ideas creates circumstances under which many people suffer and die in a matter of weeks, months or a few years in ways that were foreseeable and avoidable. I refer to this as "conditions of violence". Third, this book deals more than my previous work with multi-polar violence.

Two Concepts: "Mass Violence as Social Interaction" and "Conditions of Violence"

The two main concepts used in this book, "mass violence as social interaction" and "conditions of violence", are two ways of deepening one's understanding of the social roots of mass violence and its participatory character.

---

[1] See Christian Gerlach, *Extremely Violent Societies: Mass Violence in the Twentieth-Century World* (Cambridge et al.: Cambridge University Press, 2010), chapters 1 and 8.

"Life is precarious", writes Judith Butler, because it "relies fundamentally on social and political conditions"[2] – and on social relations, as one might add. Likewise, threats to life have a political and a social dimension. However, political history (or more broadly, scholarly inquiry into the political aspects of violence) dominates the field, whereas a social history of mass violence is rare.[3] Jutta Bakonyi and Berit Bliesemann de Guevara have proposed to understand violence as a "social [...] process".[4] More specifically, social interaction is not treated here as mere context, but simultaneously indicative and constitutive of violence. Exploring the social history of mass violence is essential for understanding its causes. In addition, understanding mass violence as social interaction also aims at a better understanding of the social situation at the time. This implies to understand violence as part of societal developments and de-emphasize discontinuity.

If mass violence is not only a matter of rogue regimes, it may be less extraordinary and more widespread than many people perceive it to be. By examining social interaction, this book also depicts in which ways mass violence is embedded in everyday life. This follows Ranajit Guha's argument that a full history needs to take into account everyday life and, by implication, ordinary people who have to be raised out of scholars' racist assignment of allegedly being "without history".[5] Just focusing on elites, in turn, often merges with political history. I came to think about this everydayness more systematically because of recent experiences, in particular the COVID-19 pandemic and the current international conflict involving Europe, North America and parts of Asia.

Understanding mass violence as being constituted by social interaction is an attempt to take all groups and individuals involved seriously. This is directed against any haughtiness toward 'victims' and 'perpetrators' alike, who are not 'evil', dumb, thoughtless, nor do they go 'like sheep to the slaughter', etc. People from all sides are to be scrutinized. Furthermore, accepting mass violence as social interaction leads to acknowledging, demonstrating and analyzing complexity.

Extremely Violent Societies was about interactions between social engineering (policies) and the activities of social groups. In inquiring about mass violence as

---

[2] Judith Butler, *Frames of War: When Is Life Grievable?* (London and New York: Verso, 2016 [first 2010]), 21.
[3] See some attempts in Christian Gerlach (ed.), *On the Social History of Persecution* (Berlin and Boston: De Gruyter Oldenbourg, 2023); Christian Gerlach and Clemens Six, eds., *The Palgrave Handbook of Anti-Communist Persecutions* (Cham: Palgrave Macmillan, 2020).
[4] Jutta Bakonyi and Berit Bliesemann de Guevara, "The Mosaic of Violence – An Introduction", Bakonyi and Bliesemann de Guevara (eds.), *A Macro-Sociology of Violence: Decyphering patterns and dynamics of collective violence* (London and New York: Routledge, 2012), 4.
[5] Ranajit Guha, *History at the Limits of World-History* (New York: Columbia University Press, 2002), 8 (quote), 94.

social interaction, large parts of the present book are no longer much concerned with policies and the state, but with the ways of functioning of social exchanges in times of mass violence. I dispute the notion that social history, in this context, is merely identical with a local history that shows little variation (whereas policies would be all that varies and is interesting) and that social history is only about how things are playing out on the ground and therefore does not matter.[6] Instead, I argue that social action shapes violence.

This is a different level of analysis, and therefore this study works with sources that reflect individual experiences and perspectives, which I found mainly in survivor and witness reports. Thus, sometimes the construction of memory becomes subject to an analysis of its own, particularly in chapter 5, which focuses on Soviet war movies.

How people commit violence often also tells something about the reasons behind the act. The way how violence is carried out is not only indicative of motivations for violence (through the symbolic content of actions), but also constitutive of these motivations. For example, racism, which often plays a role in mass violence, is not only a "social phenomenon",[7] or construct, but also a social practice that is shaped and manifests itself in social interaction. On several occasions, this book will demonstrate, as other examples, killers' feelings of (moral) superiority over their victims and other people, their sense of being cool and their insistence on their freedom to kill (in particular, chapters 2, 3 and 7).

It is important that the analysis does not stop there. Direct violence often captivates the attention of audiences, to regard mass violence as social interaction may be disturbing and the descriptions and explanations derived from it may appear illuminating. However, it should not be forgotten that indirect violence often causes more deaths than direct violence and the former deserves full consideration. To put it stronger, indirect violence requires comprehensive scholarly scrutiny precisely because it is less spectacular.

Thus, what I call mass violence requires further elaboration. Often, no blood is spilled even when people die in great numbers in what I call 'violent conditions', or conditions of violence. This is the second core concept in this book, which builds on the first. It is important to understand that conditions of vio-

---

6 This refers to remarks by Tomislav Dulić in a discussion at the conference "Destruction of Jewish Communities in South-Eastern Europe during the Second World War: Roots, Practices and Outcomes" at the University of Uppsala, May 9, 2023.
7 Jean-Loup Amselle calls "Whiteness" "a social phenomenon" in Souleymane Bachir Diagne and Jean-Loup Amselle, "On various contemporary questions", Souleymane Bachir Diagne and Jean-Loup Amselle, *In Search of Africa(s): Universalism and Decolonial Thought* (Cambridge and Medford: Polity, 2020), 137.

lence, too, are based on social interaction. Following Marx, according to whom humans "make their own history", they also make their own conditions, including those of violence – "but under circumstances existing already, given and transmitted from the past", within certain systems and collectivities, constructed by humans and then reproduced, modified or changed.[8] The processes in which this interplay between tradition, systems, social relations and social interaction occur are very complex, but they only seem to be impersonal. This is another aspect of how deep the roots of violence in societies are and how wide they are branching out.

The opacity of these processes lets conditions of violence appear quasi-natural, at the time they happen and later. This can be linked to what Ulrich Herbert described as the "disinterest" and indifference of Germans toward the millions of forced workers whom everybody met in the Reich during the Second World War. They did not recognize or acknowledge these workers' treatment as violence, although most were insufficiently fed, housed and dressed, verbally or physically abused and barred from using air raid shelters during bombings.[9]

Two characteristics of conditions of violence obscure the injustice that is present in them: their longevity and their everydayness. What I call conditions of violence can lead to death within a time period lasting between weeks and a few years. Moreover, they either appear normal, as in the cases of misery and poverty, or are set in everyday life, as in the case of the COVID-19 pandemic (see chapter 7).

These properties of conditions of violence facilitate that they are frequently written out of history, although the fact that they are overlooked is only one reason for their marginalization. Scholars' work often serves to legitimize the very social systems in which conditions of violence were produced while delegitimizing other violence (and systems), which leads them to construct, and neatly distinguish, between good and bad violence (or bad and not so bad violence). The fact that many of those suffering under conditions of violence usually belong to a lower class such as workers, peasants, colonial subjects and illiterates who often speak 'non-Western' languages makes it easier for scholars to ignore or deny the violence against them through a process of othering. This is part of what Judith Butler describes as the "ungrievable lives" of those who live in a "lost and destroyed zone" where no people who matter live.[10]

---

8 Adapted from Karl Marx, *The Eighteenth Brumaire of Louis Bonaparte* (1852), in https://www.marxists.org/archive/marx/works/1852/18th-brumaire/ch01.htm (accessed March 31, 2023).
9 See Ulrich Herbert, "Arbeiterschaft im 'Dritten Reich': Zwischenbilanz und offene Fragen", *Geschichte und Gesellschaft* 15 (1989): 352.
10 Butler, *Frames*, xix, see also xxii.

Conditions of violence frequently lead to forms of suffering and dying that include starvation; forced labor; exhaustion through work, coerced marches or flight (for example, refugees after expulsion); internment under miserable conditions; being exposed to cold; willful or neglectful exposure to deadly diseases; and denial of medical treatment. Often, conditions of violence become apparent through hunger, which indicates that the people affected can no longer cover their elementary needs and have lost their access to resources, either because they were poor from the beginning and vulnerable to economic changes or because of displacement/internment. In many cases, conditions of violence are a collective experience or one that people have in masses although in isolation from each other (for example, starving and freezing at home). Despite any collective character, it is difficult to resist such conditions because of the complex social relations at their root.

Some argue that it is normal that victims of indirect violence do not count as much and do not receive as much attention as those of direct violence. That this is incorrect and that conscious deliberations are behind assigning different values to the deaths and suffering of certain groups can be shown with the following: nobody will contest that the hundreds of thousands of Jews who starved to death and succumbed to related diseases in concentration camps and the Warsaw ghetto under the Germans were murdered. But it is very much contested that Soviet prisoners of war (POWs) were murdered, although they died under similar conditions and because of the same causes in German internment camps and mostly at the same time. Moreover, mass hunger can be put at the center of national histories of suffering from violence, as it has been done in a variety of ways in Ireland, India and Ukraine.[11] Whether this kind of narrative takes center stage or not depends on the circumstances of memory production.

Conditions of violence have originators, and the violence has a direction, or directions. Conditions of violence are created to affect certain groups, or it is known or foreseeable that these conditions will harm certain people. This typically targets groups rather than specific individuals. Many survive. People are exposed to conditions of violence in large numbers, but with such unequal chances that it seems too narrow to call all of those who endure survivors (for example, during the COVID-19 pandemic, see chapter 7). Considering conditions of violence thus blurs the line between the oft-used categories of 'victim' and 'bystander'.[12]

---

[11] This refers to Ireland in the 1840s, Bengal in the 1940s and the Soviet famine in the 1930s.
[12] See Raul Hilberg, *Perpetrators, Victims, Bystanders: The Jewish Catastrophe 1933–1945* (New York: Harper Perennial, 1992).

Conditions of violence are imposed on certain people, but often in complicated ways. Therefore a state-centered analysis falls short of providing a reasonable understanding of the processes that ensue. Famines are a case in point. If their occurrence is blamed on somebody it is usually governments ('evil regimes').[13] These (including occupiers and colonialist regimes) may indeed create difficult conditions by setting low rations, restricting some people's mobility, extracting and redistributing resources, failing to aid those affected, or besieging or 'sanctioning' enemies; however, other agents are involved in a famine, too. Merchants are hoarding and charging high prices; surplus food producers also profit from high prices; big landowners take the opportunity to cheaply buy land of poor peasants; neighbors buy movable possessions of people in misery (and sometimes even buy their children) for next to nothing; rich farmers take advantage of urbanites in similar ways; entrepreneurs exploit people in misery through minimal wages and expand their business, etc. Therefore, a famine is more than a political crime, it is a social process ridden by conflict and highly unequal outcomes – who die are mostly poor people.[14] In this sense, virtually all famines involve indirect violence. But the conditions of violence have multiple originators.

Conditions of violence differ from another concept that is often referred to as structural violence. The former is different from the latter and not supposed to replace it. Unlike structural violence, which is meant to be anonymous and abstract,[15] conditions of violence are produced by identifiable historical agents – groups, organizations, individuals – regardless of how indirect the violence is, and although it may be generated through a system and in a division of labor within society, which can involve the state or not. Second, conditions of violence denote something more dynamic and acute, although often medium-term, than the very long-term, "static" character that structural violence implies.[16] The point where the notions of conditions of violence and structural violence overlap is that in both, violence can be defined as "avoidable" harm and exists in inequality of power, in the "distribution of resources" and "unequal life chances".[17] Johan Galtung, who coined the term "structural violence", perceived imperialism as

---

[13] See Stephen Devereux, ed., *The New Famines* (London: Routledge, 2006).
[14] This draws from Amartya Sen, *Poverty and Famines* (Oxford: Clarendon, 1981).
[15] According to Johan Galtung, "structural violence" has no "actor that commits the violence" and is of a "more abstract nature". Johan Galtung, "Violence, Peace and Peace Research", *Journal of Peace Research* 6, 3 (1969), 170 and 187, note 12.
[16] According to Galtung, "structural violence [. . .] is essentially static". Ibid., 173.
[17] Ibid., 169 (first quote), 175 (second quote), 171 (third quote).

often being connected to structural violence and so it is with conditions of violence (see chapter 6 about the Second World War).[18]

Some scholars have used terms similar to "conditions of violence" to denote other things than meant here. Similar to Galtung, Emma Laurie and Ian Shaw attribute what they dub "violent conditions" to social injustice in general and its consequences, and, thus, stable conditions of life.[19] Of course, these are of great importance, but that is not what I mean by conditions of violence. Nor is the German literal equivalent of conditions of violence, *Gewaltverhältnisse*, the same what I mean because it has been used in reference to long-lasting problem zones like gender/family violence, and often came close to what structural violence depicts.[20]

No Struggle Between Good and Evil

The two concepts outlined thus far are different from 'genocide', among other things from its normativity. Genocide studies produce comforting stories of good and evil. They tell the tale of evil political systems, evil and absurd ideologies that inspire them, political radicals who drive them, evil individuals who govern and manipulate them, and regime change that removes these evils. This serves as the legitimation of their own political systems (namely, bourgeois democracy) through their supposed contrast to genocidal ones. It also leads authors and their middle-class audiences to thrilling, uplifting feelings of superiority over violent historical agents that are marked as decisively different through a process of othering. And many educators demand clear lessons from historians so they can tell simple stories of good and evil.

I reject the notion of evil. So do other authors, such as Mahmood Mamdani, who wrote that his "preoccupation is not with the universal character of evil [. . .]".[21] As a social historian, I do not believe in the discontinuities that such tales suggest. As an atheist, I refuse to let a discourse of religious origin be imposed upon

---

18 Johan Galtung, "A Structural Theory of Imperialism", *Journal of Peace Research* 8, 2 (1971), 81, 85.
19 See Emma Laurie and Ian Shaw, "Violent conditions: The injustices of being", *Political Geography* 65 (2018), 8–16.
20 See Regina-Maria Dackweiler and Reinhild Schäfer (eds.), *Gewaltverhältnisse: Feministische Perspektiven auf Geschlecht und Gewalt* (Frankfurt a.M. and New York: Campus, 2002); Otthein Rammstedt (ed.), *Gewaltverhältnisse und die Ohnmacht der Kritik* (Frankfurt a.M.: Suhrkamp, 1974).
21 Mahmood Mamdani, *When Victims Become Killers: Colonialism, Nativism, and the Genocide in Rwanda* (Princeton: Princeton University Press, 2001), 228.

me.²² (This may distance me from many readers.) The most important reason, however, is that the notion of 'evil' blocks a thorough analysis. Thinking along the lines of 'evil' leads to a mystification of violence, demonization and, thus, the dehumanization of the perpetrators; it indicates a low level of analysis – in fact, a refusal to analyze.²³

Many scholars have used the notion of 'evil' upfront, such as Hannah Arendt in her concept of the "banality of evil" and Samantha Power in 'A Problem from Hell'.²⁴ "Axis of evil"-politicians like George W. Bush could build on their work. Other genocide scholars, despite being more reflective of the term, insisted on speaking of 'evil' and marketed their books with titles like *The Roots of Evil* and *Becoming Evil*, offering elaborate explanations that they did not mean to refer to evil as an immutable, mystic force.²⁵ Claudia Card, a philosopher who claimed to offer a secular "theory of evil", was ambivalent regarding the demonization of perpetrators.²⁶ At the very least, this indicates that the concept is prone to misunderstandings.

But there is more to it. The political history of mass violence (or more broadly: the political inquiry into it) instills an uplifting sense of moral and political superiority in many people which is deeply *felt*. The attitude of 'How *could* they?' is a sign of ignorance, and, often, arrogance, from people who choose to overlook the violence of or by their own society (often directed against other peoples) and fail to realize or acknowledge how widespread mass violence is historically and contemporarily. People from ruling classes, or dominant nations, frown upon direct violence with a pleasant shiver but belittle conditions of violence that they may produce themselves.

---

22 For the impact of religion on the concept of evil, see Claudia Card, *The Atrocity Paradigm: A Theory of Evil* (Oxford et al.: Oxford University Press, 2002), 4; James Waller, *Becoming Evil: How Ordinary People Commit Genocide and Mass Violence* (Oxford et al.: Oxford University Press, 2002), 10.

23 According to Card, *Atrocity Paradigm*, 23 and 28, such concerns are not uncommon among scholars.

24 Hannah Arendt, *Eichmann in Jerusalem: A Report on the Banality of Evil* (New York: Viking, 1965, revised ed.); Samantha Power, *"A Problem from Hell": America and the Age of Genocide* (New York: HarperCollins, 2003). As a result, Arendt's analysis is intellectually weak. For further information on this, see Christian Gerlach, "The Eichmann Interrogations in Holocaust Historiography", *Holocaust and Genocide Studies* 15, 3 (2001): 428–452.

25 Ervin Staub, *The Roots of Evil: The Origins of Genocide and Other Group Violence* (Cambridge et al.: Cambridge University Press, 1989), xii, 126; Waller, *Becoming Evil*, 10–18.

26 "'Evil' may seldom mark monsters. But often enough it marks monstrous deeds", as she wrote, and there is a subchapter "The Reality of Diabolic Evil"; Card, *Atrocity Paradigm*, 23, 211–213; see also ibid., 7.

By rejecting the notion of a struggle between good and evil, I must have disappointed the expectations of many readers. And those of publishers, because writing about 'evil' augurs good business and using words such as 'Holocaust' (burnt sacrifice, a term serving mystification) leads to higher sales.

I also have profound doubts about the alleged forces of 'good', said to be victorious over the forces (and system) of 'evil', whether this concerns the Rwandan Patriotic Front or the Allies in the Second World War, a point scrutinized in chapter 6. This leads me to a broader issue: genocide studies (or: the prevalent political history of mass violence) have difficulties in accounting for multipolar violence, as in the case of a civil war. If there was a civil war in a historical situation, conventional studies tend to downplay its significance, marginalize it and focus on one target group of violence, fading out others.

It is necessary to move beyond a Manichean world view to be able to understand mass violence as being based on conflict, as it often is. The complex backgrounds and dynamics of multipolar violence that play a major role in this volume are not easily grasped. What I mean is not 'mutual violence' because it is often directed at civilians who neither directly attacked other people nor participated significantly in creating conditions of violence for others. However, violence comes from among both sides (or all sides) and those who are attacked on the other side are often vulnerable. (Notably, these vulnerable people are often *men*.)

Some scholars have tried to account for multipolar violence. For example, Mahmood Mamdani, in his book *When Victims Become Killers*, attempted to explain the mass murders in Rwanda in 1994 in part through Hutu's "fear of a return of servitude" and what they saw as their own victimization.[27] Wendy Isaacs-Martin explored the multiple and complex violent conflicts in the Central African Republic in the 2010s in an attempt to correct the dominant image of a binary religious conflict.[28] Notable here is the proposal by Musa Adam Abdul-Jalil, Jon Unruh and others to carefully record "grievance narratives" by people involved on all sides in the Darfur conflict and then mobilize them for peace building, work for it through traditional courts and mediation mechanisms and, in this context, pay great attention to competing claims to land.[29] This most significant ap-

---

27 Mamdani, *When*, 233.
28 Wendy Isaacs-Martin, "Political and Ethnic Identity in Violent Conflict: The Case of Central African Republic", *International Journal of Conflict and Violence* 10 (2016): 25–39.
29 Jon Unruh and Musa Adam Abdul-Jalil, "Constituencies of conflict and opportunity: Land rights, narratives and collective action in Darfur", *Political Geography* 42 (2016): 104–116, 104; see also Jerôme Tubiana, Victor Tanner and Musa Adam Abdul-Jalil, *Traditional Authorities' Peacemaking Role in Darfur* (Washington: United States Institute for Peace, 2012). And see Matthew

proach is based on the idea that all suffering matters rather than the notion that the suffering of one party is superior and that of the other is irrelevant because it is on the 'evil' side. In all three cases, social inquiry brought to light how questionable the prevailing simple narratives were, although most did more to explain conflicts than to solve them.

A Non-Racist Framework?

"Extremely violent societies" was also meant as a non-racist and non-imperialist framework. The latter was necessary because genocide studies, from which it split, have in origin and substance been wedded to liberal imperialism. To work toward a social history of mass violence was also a means to resist the politicization of the field (including Holocaust studies) and conduct fundamental research while avoiding a political instrumentalization of the research findings. The social history of mass violence may even have the potential to undermine simplified political narratives about the topic.

By contrast, most work in genocide studies and related fields consists of scholarly inquiry into political systems to fulfill the field's political function of supporting interventionism and legitimizing political liberalism. Financial support by funding institutions is allocated accordingly. In this study, I argue that some scholars' avoidance of social history is quite conscious.

As regards mass violence, liberal imperialists after the Second World War (and perhaps before[30]) have followed the following maxim in international fora: Declare 'our' norms universal, make the laws, man the courts. And write the history. This way, they condemned certain kinds of violence while distracting from others, for example preventing that their starvation blockades became a crime.

Genocide studies were arguably founded in the USA in 1944 by Raphael Lemkin, who denounced Axis rule in Europe at a time when the USA were claiming moral superiority over their enemies, demanded their total surrender and started to erect military bases in states around the world.[31] It is well documented that the

---

Allen, *Greed and Grievance: Ex-Militants' Perspective on the Conflict in the Solomon Islands, 1998–2003* (Honolulu: University of Hawai'i Press, 2013), set in a different context.

[30] See Daniel Marc Segesser, *Recht statt Rache oder Rache durch Recht? Die Ahndung von Kriegsverbrechen in der internationalen wissenschaftlichen Debatte 1972–1945* (Paderborn: Ferdinand Schöningh, 2010) For starvation blockades, see Mulder and van Dijk, "Why".

[31] See Raphael Lemkin, *Axis Rule in Occupied Europe* (Washington: Carnegie Endowment for International Peace, 1944). For indirect hints of Lemkin's ideas being compatible with imperialism, see Dirk Moses, *The Problems of Genocide: Permanent Security and the Language of Transgression*

great powers tailored the 1948 UN Convention on the Prevention and Punishment in ways that were to exclude their own past (and in part, future) mass violence – political, colonial and other types –, defining away some sorts of mass violence while denouncing others.[32] Genocide studies became a big thing academically and politically in the 1990s, being spread from North America to Western Europe and then to other parts of the world. It expanded as an instrument of bourgeois triumphalism and liberal imperialism; in other words, it serves an aggressive ideology. Allegations of genocide through governments and mass media served as a rationale for North American and Western European attacks during the wars of Yugoslav succession and the Second Iraq War. This resulted in the prolonged, and indeed colonial, foreign occupation of several countries and severe losses of human life.[33] The 1990s also saw the rise of political impositions of various kinds (from 'good governance' to gender issues and environmental aspects) as part of 'aid' conditionality by North Americans and Western Europeans.[34]

The rise of genocide studies in the 1990s also took place during a period when there was an upsurge of nationalism and ethnic polarization and the sanctification of the homogeneous nation-state. It was a time when some multiethnic states split up, or were split up, in Eastern Europe, West and Central Asia. This resulted in the foundation of many small to medium nation states, whose founding narratives sometimes incorporated stories of genocide. Leading industrial capitalist states, which robustly supported this disintegration and its rationales but which are multiethnic themselves, were not split up, such as Britain, Spain, the USA and France. Of course, nobody dared to intervene there. But given that most states in the world are multi-ethnic, industrial nations' policies of supporting ethnic separatism threaten peace and stability globally.

Genocide studies reached their peak during the high tide of the new colonialism in the 2000s and early 2010s. During that period, the "responsibility to protect" principle was adopted in the United Nations in 2005; Samantha Power,

---

(Cambridge et al.: Cambridge University Press, 2021), 166–168, and for direct hints, ibid., 404. For U.S. mass violence against non-combatants in World War II, see chapter 6 of this current study.

32 See Douglas Irvin-Erickson, *Raphaël Lemkin and the Concept of Genocide* (Philadelphia: University of Pennsylvania Press, 2017), 152–196; Moses, *Problems*, 223–231, 237.

33 For the connection between genocide studies and 'Western' imperialism, see also Moses, *Problems*, 455–462, 491–495, 499–509. To some extent, I disagree with Moses when he writes: "Ironically, and fatally, condemning illiberal permanent security [and, thus, violence] with the language of transgression often initiates a dialectic that leads to liberal permanent security [and, thus, violence]" (Moses, *Problems*, 39). There is no irony in this. The purpose of the condemnation of illiberal mass violence, its *raison d'être*, for many liberals is to commit own imperialist acts of violence.

34 See Olav Stokke, ed., *Aid and Political Conditionality* (London: Frank Cass, 1995).

author of a well-known pro-interventionist book in genocide studies,[35] was appointed to the U.S. National Security Council in 2009 and advocated the U.S. military attack on Libya in 2011, along with British and French forces, invoking the "responsibility to protect";[36] and the French Ambassador to the UN, Jean-Maurice Ripert, advocated an armed intervention in Myanmar in 2008 when it rejected industrial countries' 'help' after a devastating cyclone.[37] Not incidentally, this was also a time of institutional growth: programs in genocide studies were founded in universities in many industrial and some other countries and several new journals in genocide studies were being established.

Then, however, the new multilateral colonialism[38] entered a crisis in the late 2010s, which became manifest in the problems of the U.S. forces in Iraq, the end of the foreign occupation of Afghanistan in 2021 and in the French retreat from Mali. More broadly, it turned out that the new imperialism can destroy but not control countries; foreign powers did not bring peace and stability but more violence, like in Iraq, Afghanistan, Syria and Libya (in part because they did not resolve but often aggravate socioeconomic issues, one cause of the violence); and that imperialist powers of today are incapable of controlling political developments even in neighboring regions, occupied or not, be it the USA in Mexico or Haiti; Russia in Ukraine; the EU in Libya; or Saudi Arabia in Yemen. Simultaneously with this crisis, the growth of genocide studies stalled (and the field called Holocaust studies is in decline). In connection with this process, these fields congealed and increasingly follow the logic of memorialization and indoctrination rather than inquiry, marked by many new laws that prohibit certain statements about mass violence, such as in France, Ukraine, Russia, Belarus, Rwanda, Turkey and China; the most far-reaching restrictions are now in place in Germany.[39] It remains to be seen what kind of effects the most recent international tensions and conflict will have on this academic field.

This points to a close connection between political power, the intelligentsia (or large parts of it) and the legal system. Many scholars serve to uphold the national and international political system, thus cooperating with national and in-

---

35 Power, "A Problem".
36 From 2013 to 2017, Power was U.S. Ambassador to the United Nations and since 2021 she has been Director of the U.S. Agency for International Development.
37 In this context, I left the *Journal of Genocide Research* as a co-editor in 2011 in disagreement over an editorial on the NATO's bombings of Libya. The *Journal of Genocide Research* is part of imperialist genocide studies.
38 See James Mayall and Ricardo Soares de Oliveira, eds., *The New Protectorates*, New York: Hurst, 2011.
39 For Germany, see article 130 paragraph 5 of the German Criminal Law, https://www.gesetze-im-internet.de/stgb/__130.html (last accessed November 12, 2023), passed in 2022.

ternational courts. Where this leads, and where it comes from, becomes obvious after taking a brief look at the history of the International Criminal Court. Until 2015, all cases of this institution that reached the level of "investigation" were against Africans. The first non-Africans targeted (in 2016) were South Ossetian allies of Russia. At the point of this writing (April 2024), all official investigations have been against individuals from non-industrialized countries (eight in Africa, four in Asia and one in Latin America), except for one country: Russia. All of the 50 defendants have been Africans, except for three men from South Ossetia. At present, the president of the court is from Japan and the lead prosecutor is from Britain; except for one, the ten biggest financers are industrial countries.[40] Not only U.S. citizens but also those from NATO countries will hardly be put on trial in The Hague because *both* are covered by the American Service-Members' Protection Act of 2002, which authorizes the U.S. President to 'liberate' them by any means, apparently including military ones (in or against a country that happens to be allied with the USA).[41] Make the rules; man the courts. The ICC is but one example of the racism of the 'rules-based world order', with the proud involvement of many intellectuals.

If you think that I exaggerate, read John Rawls, the favorite philosopher of many contemporary liberals. In his book, *The Law of Peoples*, Rawls distinguished between five types of societies, including "liberal peoples", "decent hierarchical peoples" and three other types, "outlaw states", "societies burdened by unfavorable conditions" and "benevolent absolutisms".[42] Noting that "outlaw states" violating human rights "in grave cases may be subjected to forceful sanctions and even to intervention", Rawls argued:

> As we have worked out the Law of Peoples for liberal and decent peoples, these peoples simply do not tolerate outlaw states. This refusal to tolerate these states is a consequence of liberalism and decency. If the political conception of political liberalism is sound, and if the steps we have taken in developing the Law of Peoples are also sound, then liberal and decent peoples have the right, under the Law of Peoples, not to tolerate outlaw states. [. . .] Outlaw states are aggressive and dangerous; all peoples are safer and more secure if such states change, or are forced to change, their ways.[43]

---

[40] "International Criminal Court", https://en.wikipedia.org/wiki/International_Criminal_Court#Investigations_and_preliminary_examinations (last accessed April 15, 2024). See also "51 Defendants", International Criminal Court, https://www.icc-cpi.int/defendants (last accessed April 15, 2024). One defendant appears twice on the list.- South Ossetia is a small republic that split from Georgia and is not recognized by most states, but supported by Russia.- The International Criminal Court (ICC) should not be confused with the International Court of Justice (ICJ).
[41] U.S. Public Law 107–206 of August 2, 2002, Sec. 2008, a) and b), (1) and (2).
[42] John Rawls, *The Law of Peoples* (Cambridge and London: Harvard University Press, 1999), 63.
[43] Rawls, *Law*, 81.

I have difficulties to decide what is most remarkable about these thoughts: their circular logics, the question of who is included in the 'we',[44] the brutality of its liberal hybris, the selectivity of "rights" or the fact that it assigns – and denies – decency and worthiness of belonging to a "Society of Peoples" not only to states but also to peoples.[45]

If it comes to mass violence, a non-racist framework means that every civilian life has the same value.[46] At the time of this writing, during the Israel-Gaza war of 2023–2024, this is being repeated over and over by many politicians and public intellectuals from not-so-powerful countries around the world, but they are characteristically rarely quoted in European bourgeois media. If every civilian life has the same value, it follows that no victim group is more important than the other and no victimization is a proper rationale for attacking other civilians. If every civilian life has the same value, Palestinian lives are worth as much as Israeli lives; male and female; young and old; white, black and brown; Hutu and Tutsi; Hindu and Muslim; religious and atheist; and Axis and Allied citizens and subjects. Every life counts, and every experience counts. Sounds obvious but is in fact hugely controversial.

The problem of how to act responsibly in the field, i.e., without an endorsement of liberal imperialism, raises difficult questions, and in fact it is not easy to avoid racism.

Non-racist scholarship is not straightforward. Building on Souleymane Bachir Diagne's remarks on the universal, one could call it "a goal to be aimed at", a thing of the future, and the way to it is onerous.[47] Of course, I cannot be sure that I do not hold racist views on an unconscious level and against my will. My approaches are supposed to be non-imperialist; but are they, in an epistemic sense? After all, these are frameworks proposed by a person considered as white and intended to be applied to all sorts of contemporary societies, including some in Asia, Africa and Latin America, and my position allows me to export them. I do not think that every idea developed by a 'white' person is automatically contaminated. If there are no biological races among humans and race is just a social conception, one can possibly rise above it, like over one's class or nation. But is there anything in substance in my approach that is an imperialist imposition?

---

[44] With the word 'we', Rawls does not merely refer to himself.
[45] See also the criticism of parts of this excerpt in Zhao Tingyang, *Alles unter einem Himmel: Vergangenheit und Zukunft der Weltordnung* (Frankfurt a.M.: Suhrkamp, 2020), 194.
[46] In addition to civilians, this also applies to other unarmed non-combatants that are subject to this volume such as prisoners of war.
[47] Souleymane Bachir Diagne, "On the universal and universalism", Bachir Diagne and Amselle, *In Search of Africa(s)*, 39 (quote), 44.

That societies pass through phases of multi-directional mass violence can occur in industrialized and non-industrialized countries; this is meant in a non-essentialist manner. Similar to my work in the past, the case studies in this volume deal – if one may use these categories – with countries dominated by whites and countries dominated by others: East Pakistan/Bangladesh and Rwanda, the Soviet Union and (by point of emphasis) Central Europe in the COVID-19 pandemic and the Allies in World War II.[48]

Scholars of unrelated heritage have made important contributions to the study of mass violence through their sober external perspectives and new approaches, such as Christopher Browning for the persecution of Jews and Hilmar Kaiser for the destruction of the Armenians. Nonetheless, their findings have often clashed with nationalist narratives wedded to the genocide approach in some kind, and so did mine in the past, whether in Belarus, Hungary, Turkey, Bangladesh or Indonesia, because a common world historiography does not exist and it disaggregates into national and other particularistic narratives.[49] What is more legitimate, national or international perspectives, is an open question. In any case, I avoid using the word 'we' in this study. I am afraid there is no 'we'.

Moreover, to lay open all kinds of mass violence against all sorts of groups and point to the manifold people who committed it, including multipolar violence, can be regarded as a controversial, reckless and brutally frank concept. This contradicts cultural norms in many non-European countries that emphasize polite restraint, avoid open confrontation and prefer "silence after violence"[50] over outspokenness.[51] Also, what I propose includes distinctly historical thinking; it may only be possible after many years to face all of the mass violence that has taken place in a country.

It is part of my approach to take into account violence against all sorts of civilians in a given area or historical situation and analyze them on equal terms.[52] By implication, this is a non-racist framework, and at the same time it is not blind to the skin color and ethnicity of those who were attacked. It is compatible with

---

48 However, much – though not all – of my past work was either about Axis countries in World War II or violence in societies outside Europe (at other times than in World War II). *Both* could be misunderstood as uplifting stories proving one's own assumed superiority, because both Axis powers and violent regimes in non-European countries have often been portrayed as alien, although, as I would claim, not by me.
49 This is not to say that non-heritage scholars are free of particularistic outlooks.
50 See *Silence after violence*, special issue of *Acta Academica* 47, 1 (2015), edited by Anja Henebury and Yehonatan Alsheh.
51 See also Zhao's criticism of Jürgen Habermas' demand that a discourse must be "candid". Zhao, *Alles*, 193.
52 See Gerlach, *Extremely Violent Societies*, chapter 1.

the "principle of assigning equal value to [all] historical sufferings" from violence that Charlotte Wiedemann pleads for.[53] Already in my dissertation work (which dealt with the German occupation of Soviet Belarus in World War II) I had looked at violence against all major victim groups in one country.[54]

This means rejecting the hierarchies among unarmed victims prevailing in so many studies, whether they are based on the ways of killing or on the group to which those who suffer violence belong. These hierarchies are highly problematic, all the more because the argument behind them frequently has to do with affected people's descent. All lives matter equally.[55] To assign different values to the death of people from different groups and to do so on the basis of skin color or ethnicity, to create rankings in which premature losses of life of certain 'others' are less valuable and deserve less attention, is racist. To publish such ideas means spreading racist ideology.

In this context, this book may appear confusing to some. Who were the bad guys, Bangladesh or Pakistan? After all, chapter 3 depicts Pakistani atrocities but chapter 4 predominantly describes Bangladeshi violence, also against unarmed civilians, in 1971. And do I condemn the Soviet Union or not? Chapter 6 argues that the Soviet Union in the Second World War was an imperialist power like others which, supported by many of its people, used massive violence against foreigners and many of its own citizens, often with racist undertones, but chapter 5 shows that many postwar Soviet movies about the Second World War had tragic antiwar narratives instead of such of victory. What may appear contradictory to readers actually reflects some of the complexities involved in the social process that mass violence is.

Methods

To reach these goals, I take several different approaches in this book: sound history, participatory observation, but also film history and, in one case, a critique

---

53 Charlotte Wiedemann, *Das Leid der anderen verstehen: Holocaust und Weltgedächtnis* (Berlin: Propyläen, 2022), 201 ("prinzipielle Gleichrangigkeit historischer Leiderfahrungen"). See also ibid., 9.
54 Christian Gerlach, *Kalkulierte Morde: Die deutsche Wirtschafts- und Vernichtungspolitik in Weissrussland 1941–1944* (Hamburg: Hamburger Edition, 1999). But this was still a piece of political history.
55 This does not mean to criticize the Black Lives Matter movement in the USA. Its slogan made only sense if understood as countering the practice that black lives do *not* matter and deaths of 'black' people caused less public concern than others, doubtlessly an accurate assertion.

of existing scholarship and its narratives, confronting them with facts of social history. What links these approaches is the attempt to grasp the experience, and action, of people on the ground. In none of the chapters in this volume is the inquiry primarily policy-oriented (chapter 6 differs from this to some degree). This book is much less about intellectual history than practice. Perhaps one cannot say that the case studies are concerned with everyday life because they deal with people in extraordinary situations, but they do describe practice on some kind of everyday level, and search for overarching patterns in highly localized experiences. Compared to *Extremely Violent Societies*, this volume makes less of a political economy-related argument, with the exceptions of chapters 2 and 6, which focus on Rwanda and on the Second World War; see also chapter 7. Nonetheless, this volume strives for a people's history of violence, defined as a history from below.[56] For this I try to demonstrate what mass violence as social interaction entails and how conditions of violence work. This does not at all mean to idealize the masses or people from the lower classes – a common criticism of history from below – because it implies that they participated in shaping or influencing violence one way or another. It is not accidental that chapter 4 analyzes crowd violence in which, along with armed troops, many women and children were killed.

Sound history, which is used as a tool in chapters 2 and 3, brings readers to the level of direct exchanges surrounding violence and on-the-ground experience. Here, the historian listens in on past events and agents. This is not harmless and unproblematic; rather it is indiscrete and somewhat merciless. Noises have special qualities. I concur with Deborah Kapchan's argument that listening leads to "in-between" places and into "an acoustic space of ambiguity and paradox, a shifting ground wherein preconceived ideas have not yet overdetermined either the subject or the interpretation".[57] Listening produces more bodily and emotion-charged ways of knowledge than other avenues of perception.[58] In research about times of mass violence, attention to sound is of special significance because one can say that sound, and especially voice, embodies life as such since it is close to breathing.[59]

---

56 Examples for such an approach are E. P. Thompson, *The Making of the English Working Class* (New York: Penguin, 1968); Moritz Feichtinger, *"Villagization": A People's History of Strategic Resettlement and Violent Transformation: Kenya and Algeria 1952–1962*, Ph.D dissertation, University of Bern, 2016.
57 Deborah Kapchan, "Listening Acts: Witnessing the Pain (and Praise) of Others", Deborah Kapchan, ed., *Theorizing Sound Writing* (Middletown: Wesleyan University Press, 2017), 288.
58 Deborah Kapchan, "The Splash of Icarus: Theorizing Sound Writing/Writing Sound Theory", in Kapchan, *Theorizing*, 2–3.
59 For this thought in general, see Don Ihde, *Listening and Voice: Phenomenologies of Sound* (Albany: State University of New York, 2007, second rev. ed.), 3.

For the most part, the soundtrack is an untapped layer of information in the accounts of historical witnesses. Noises have been neglected by most historians, and by other scholars as well,[60] which is unfortunate. The core of the matter is that sounds – and larger "soundscapes" – can express power, rule and conflict, social relations, hierarchies, practices and social change, gender roles, religious practice, collective action, community ties, group identity and the use of technology.[61] The inquiry into sounds thus aims at much more than noises themselves. Sounds and hearing have also been associated with emotion, which corresponds to physical characteristics of sound that consists of waves that permeate the entire human body, which gives sound a special impact.[62] Hearing has a certain sense of existentiality to it and, working multidirectionally, the ear is the organ of alarm.[63] Sounds may not always be produced intentionally, but they are always communication.

Taken together, these qualities make it appear rewarding to inquire into what people heard in times of conflict, social upheaval and violence. In fact, sounds can *be* violence, used to intimidate or paralyze opponents.[64] However, except for the role of music and aerial bombings, almost no histories of sounds in mass violence exist, an article by Vannessa Hearman being the most notable exception.[65]

---

[60] See Jan-Friedrich Missfelder, "Der Klang der Geschichte: Begriffe, Traditionen und Methoden der sound history", *Geschichte in Wissenschaft und Unterricht* 66, 11/12 (2015): 633–649. For a fuller treatment of the potential of sounds for the history of mass violence, see Christian Gerlach, "Echoes of persecution: Sounds in early post-liberation Jewish memories", *Holocaust Studies* 24, 1 (2018): 1–25.

[61] See R. Murray Schafer, *The Soundscape: Our Sonic Environment and the Tuning of the World*, 2nd ed. (Rochester: Destiny, 1994), esp. 3, 29, 35, 71, 184, 237; Alain Corbin, *Village Bells: Sound and Meaning in the Nineteenth-Century French Countryside* (New York: Columbia University Press, 1998); Horst Wenzel, *Hören und Sehen, Schrift und Bild: Kultur und Gedächtnis im Mittelalter* (Munich, 1995), esp. 143–146.

[62] Jean-Luc Nancy, *Zum Gehör* (Zurich: diaphanes, 2010), 19, 23–24; Don Ihde, *Listening and Voice: Phenomenologies of Sound*, 2nd ed. (Albany: State University of New York Press, 2007), 79; Holger Schulze, "Bewegung Berührung Übertragung", in: *Sound Studies*, ed. Holger Schulze (Bielefeld: Transcript, 2008), 147.

[63] Hans Werner, *Soundscape-Dialog: Landschaften und Methoden des Hörens* (Göttingen: Vandenhoeck & Ruprecht, 2006), 79.

[64] For this point, see Schafer, *Soundscape*, 50–51, and in particular Steve Goodman, *Sonic Warfare: Sound, Affect, and the Ecology of Fear* (Cambridge and London: MIT Press, 2010), esp. xvii, 155, 189.

[65] See Vannessa Hearman, "Hearing the 1965–66 Indonesian Anti-Communist Repression," *A Cultural History of Sound, Memory and the Senses*, eds. Joy Darmousi and Paula Hamilton (New York and London: Routledge, 2017), 142–156, and several other contributions in the same volume; and Gerlach, "Echoes".

Whereas much of 20th-century related sound history focuses on media, music and city noise and is often based on technically recorded sounds and sound observation (like, for example, many anthropological studies as well), chapters 2 and 3 reconstruct sounds from written texts, which is an established practice in histories of earlier periods.[66]

Rather than merely setting up an inventory of sounds, aural observations shall be used here as a point of departure for further thoughts, as an approach that uncovers otherwise "neglected aspects of human experience".[67] Memories concerning dramatic, existential experiences seem to be especially rich in recollections of noises of mass violence.[68] However, to realize this, it is necessary to go beyond music, technically mediated sounds and city noise. Instead, all kinds of noises can be equally meaningful and must be subject to analysis, including modulations of the human voice, which the witness reports describe very often.[69]

Thus, rather than government documents, the primary material that forms the basis of this book are accounts of survivors and witnesses of violence from large collections that were compiled in unrelated contexts. The fact that most earwitnesses do not pay much attention to sounds, and to telling about sounds, is a problem, but it also bears a potential. Many sounds may have been forgotten and/or omitted. But narratives about past sounds, if they are based on unconsciously made remarks, may also reveal undercurrents in memories and deep structures in social interaction. In this respect, one could speak of hidden transcripts.[70] This is why statements of such persons who were not asked questions about their aural experience appear especially valuable.

Accounts by survivors and witnesses of violence are the basis of chapters 2 and 3, which use sound history, and of chapter 4 which deals with crowd violence in East Pakistan and Bangladesh, respectively, from 1971 to 1972, and sporadically in chapter 6. In a way, the perspective of people who endured violence is also

---

66 For example, Corbin, *Village Bells*; Wenzel, *Hören und Sehen*; Mark Smith, *Listening to Nineteenth-Century America* (Chapel Hill and London: University of North Carolina Press, 2001).
67 Such an approach was demanded by Jan-Friedrich Missfelder, "Period Ear: Perspektiven einer Klanggeschichte der Neuzeit", *Geschichte und Gesellschaft* 38, 1 (2012): 33.
68 See Gerlach, "Echoes".
69 This follows the approach pioneered by Schafer, *Soundscape*.
70 I use the term of 'hidden transcripts' more in the sense that Mark Greengrass has made of it than in the sense that James Scott used it, because for Scott, unlike Greengrass, the term indicates *conscious* collective strategies of expressing opposition and dissent. See Mark Greengrass, "Hidden Transcripts: Secret Histories and Personal Testimonies of Religious Violence in the French Wars of Religion" in Levene and Roberts, *Massacre*, 69–88, esp. 75; James Scott, *Domination and the Arts of Resistance: Hidden Transcripts* (New Haven and London: Yale University Press, 1990), esp. xii, 4, 20, 27, 120 and 134.

prominent in chapter 5, which operates through a different approach, film history, concentrating on film plots and narratives as forms of memory production; but these were in many cases constructed or enacted by people who had lived through some of the Second World War's most violent episodes. For all of these four chapters, I have read these personal accounts with critical distance and concentrated on finding general patterns of behavior of people from all sides, rather than on individual stories, often told long after the event. Using the term 'oral history' for such witness and survivor reports could lead to the misunderstanding that what they say *is* history and to be taken at face value, which is not the case.

Chapter 7 drives this focus on drawing from personal experiences further because it is partially based on participatory observation. This approach is problematic on several counts, particularly from a historian's perspective; this includes a possible lack of critical and temporal distance from the events as well as the narrower limits of what can be said for personal and legal reasons. My lack of experience with participatory observation is no help either.

Chapter 6 stands out in this volume because it is essentially a meta-study of existing scholarship, with one focus on famines, and a critique of mainstream narratives (of World War II). However, it does look at commoners' experiences of violence, or conditions of violence, which is something that ties all chapters in this volume together, although chapter 6 also poses the question of who created these conditions.

Structure of this Book

This volume consists of two main parts. The first examines mass violence as social interaction (but not conditions of violence) in different contexts and ways: through the sound history of the mass murders in Rwanda in 1994 (chapter 2) and of one Pakistani army massacre in East Pakistan in 1971, for which there are many survivor reports (chapter 3); through the history of one form of aggression (crowd violence) during the East Pakistan/Bangladesh conflict in 1971–1972 (chapter 4); and through the inquiry into memory production by way of scrutinizing plots and narratives in Soviet films about World War II from the 1940s to the 1980s (chapter 5).

While the first part of this volume is about direct violence, the second part mostly deals with indirect violence. This second part turns to look at the genesis and consequences of conditions of violence in two contexts: the Second World War, uncovering masses of forgotten victims, especially in famines, through a much more global perspective than usual (chapter 6), and by considering the COVID-19 pandemic in large parts as mass violence with many avoidable deaths, which occurred because of certain types of behavior. Chapter 7 on COVID-19, the only one in this book to work with both concepts (mass violence as social interaction and conditions of violence), shows through this combination of research perspectives how lethal violence can become socially hegemonic and normalized. This is absolutely crucial for the arguments made in this book. Finally, chapter 8 offers some conclusions, including naming some topics to which the concepts of this book, and conditions of violence in particular, could be applied in future research.

Part I: **Mass Violence as Social Interaction**

2 Festive Days of Killing: Enacting a New Social Order in Rwanda, 1994

Mass murder is a loud process, but the case of Rwanda is special. From April 6 to early July 1994, between 500,000 and 800,000 Tutsis were killed under the Rwandan state (80 percent of all Tutsis in the country), along with tens of thousands of Hutus, and another 30,000 to 50,000 civilians killed by the victorious Rwandan Patriotic Front (RPF) rebels.[1] The mass participation in the brutal slaughter of Tutsis is notorious.

This chapter links this violence with the social situation and trends in Rwanda. It analyses the soundscape in the months of the massacres, which was dominated by various loud noises from persecutors, and argues that it expressed the new social order that they strove for. The emotions surfacing in these sounds are telling, but the chapter also deals with audible challenges to this new order and the associated conflicts. Contrasts in religious practice provide particularly powerful evidence. By primarily drawing from survivor accounts and placing less emphasis on political leadership and technology than on social interaction between ordinary people and on human voice, I try to help overcome the hegemonic political history in the field and shed more light[2] on the question of why and how many people participated in the violence and how they related to those they attacked.

By limiting the analysis to 'Hutu power'-related killings, I mean in no way to condone the mass violence committed by RPF-led forces in Rwanda in 1994 and especially in the neighboring country of Zaire/Congo in the second half of the 1990s and later, which may have caused as many or even more victims than the 1994 killings but is less often cited. Much more research on this other kind of violence is sorely needed.

---

[1] Alison Des Forges, *Kein Zeuge darf überleben: Der Genozid in Ruanda* (Hamburg: Hamburger Edition, 2002), 34–35; Philip Verwimp, *Peasants in Power: The Political Economy of Development and Genocide in Rwanda* (Heidelberg et al.: Springer, 2013), 1–2; Philip Verwimp, "Death and survival during the 1994 genocide in Rwanda", *Population Studies* 58, 2 (2004): 235; Lee Ann Fujii, *Show Time: The Logic and Power of Violent Display* (Ithaca and London: Cornell University Press, 2021), 141–151.

[2] I use this metaphor in lack of a better one. Most metaphors in the language of research are from the visual sphere and few from the aural one.

The State of Research

Rwanda is a small, hilly landlocked country in East Africa that had a population of eight million in the early 1990s, 95 percent of which lived in the countryside. Unlike many African countries, it was very densely populated and had long traditions of a tight-knit administration. Most people were very poor, and many became poorer in the late 1980s and early 1990s as the result of a deep economic crisis that involved a decline in the price of coffee – the most important export product – and several refugee waves. Agricultural land ownership was relatively, and increasingly, unequal, and landlessness was on the rise.[3] Between 1984 and 1993, life expectancy declined dramatically (reportedly from 49.9 years to 26.7 years), and there was a famine in the south.[4] Average personal income stagnated and then declined especially in 1993 and 1994.[5]

The socioeconomic crisis went hand in hand with political upheaval and civil war.[6] The refugee waves had to do with ethnicized social conflicts between the so-called Hutus and Tutsis. Up to the 19th century, divisions had emerged between a social elite (with livestock being a marker of wealth and status) named Tutsis, and a mass of peasants living in semi-serfdom named Hutus. Although transitions across this status line always occurred, these groups were solidified and ethnicized from the 19th century onward, a process that was intensified under German and Belgian colonialism from the 1880s to the 1950s.[7] To a degree, Hutu and Tutsi remained fluid concepts, and the number of intermarriages was sizable, though limited.[8]

---

[3] See Peter Uvin, *Aiding Violence: The Development Enterprise in Rwanda* (West Hartford: Kumarian, 1998), 111–113; Jean-Paul Kimonyo, *Rwanda's Popular Genocide* (Boulder and London: Lynne Rienner, 2016), 69; Des Forges, *Kein Zeuge*, 72, 159, 313, 363; Florent Piton, *Le génocide des Tutsi du Rwanda* (Paris: La Découverte, 2018), 53; Michel Chossudowsky, "Economic Genocide in Rwanda", in *Economic and Political Weekly* 31, 15 (1996): 939–941; Saskia van Hoyweghen, "The Urgency of Land and Agrarian Reform in Rwanda", *African Affairs* 98, 392 (1999): 356–357.
[4] Kimonyo, *Rwanda's Popular Genocide*, 66–67; Uvin, *Aiding Violence*, 54, 111–112; Verwimp, *Peasants*, 65, 102–116.
[5] Verwimp, *Peasants*, 61.
[6] With strong social and geographical mobility intertwined with political conflict, Rwanda was a classic case of an extremely violent society. See Gerlach, *Extremely Violent Societies*.
[7] For a sketch, see Des Forges, *Kein Zeuge*, 55–93; see also Richard Benda, *The Test of Faith: Christians and Muslims in the Rwandan Genocide* (Ph.D dissertation, University of Manchester, 2012), 41.
[8] Kimonyo, *Rwanda's Popular Genocide*, 196–200, 318–320; Scott Straus, *The Order of Genocide: Race, Power and War in Rwanda* (Ithaca and London: Cornell University Press, 2006), 128.

A movement demanding power for the Hutus as an oppressed majority took power during decolonization in 1959–1962 (unlike in neighboring Burundi), in part through violent means, and their authoritarian regime stayed in power until 1994, governed by the Revolutionary Movement for National Development party (MRND) since 1975. Hundreds of thousands of Tutsis fled Rwanda after 1959, mainly to Uganda, and repeatedly tried to return and seize power again with military means. From 1990 to 1994, another such attempt by the RPF led to a civil war that coincided with economic misery and violent Rwandan party politics that developed after a multi-party system was introduced under the robust influence of foreign industrial countries and domestic political pressure. Rwanda was also destabilized by repeated large inflows of refugees from Burundi between 1972 and 1993, who fled violence against Hutus and were frustrated by economic marginalization in Rwanda. In addition, up to one million domestic refugees arrived from the north of Rwanda where the RPF operated.[9] Several thousand Tutsi civilians were killed in 1990–1993.[10] After Rwanda's president Juvenal Habyarimana and Burundi's president Cyprien Ntaryamira were killed when their plane was shot down near Kigali on April 6, 1994, the 'Hutu power' pro-government forces argued that all Tutsis were enemies in the civil war, and most were slaughtered. In July 1994, the RPF won the civil war and has ruled ever since. Up to one million refugees (mainly Tutsis) from earlier decades entered Rwanda, two million (mostly Hutus) fled in 1994, and 1.3 million of them returned later, forced by Rwandan military violence in Zaire and as a result of diplomatic pressure on Tanzania. Many refugees perished in Zaire.[11]

In independent Rwanda, Tutsis were largely excluded from politics and the "state class" (or administration) until 1994, including the military. Most were in fact peasants, but Tutsis continued to hold important social positions, which were often related to advantages in education. For example, they constituted the majority in lower and middle ranks of Catholic clergy; had a strong presence among teachers, medical staff and university students; a lower birthrate than Hutus; and were overrepresented among the urban population, which was, on average, wealthier than rural dwellers.[12] Gérard Prunier has stated that "there was no contradiction between the ethnic and the social aspects of the killing since, in Kigali

---

9 Des Forges, *Kein Zeuge*, 145, 175, 427, 510, 834.
10 Des Forges, *Kein Zeuge*, 119.
11 Van Hoyweghen, "Urgency", 354, 362–363.
12 See Uvin, *Aiding Violence*, 115, 207 (quote); Des Forges, *Kein Zeuge*, 30, 34, 70, 503, 561; Verwimp, *Peasants*, 47 and for Tutsi agriculturalism 55. For Hutu propaganda with exaggerated portrayals of the Tutsi position, see ibid., 56, and Des Forges, *Kein Zeuge*, 106–107.

at least, the Tutsi tended to be better off than the Hutu".[13] However, there is little specific evidence available in support or against this claim,[14] neither in terms of income nor land ownership.[15] In any case, most Rwandan Tutsis were poor, as were most Hutus.

During the 1994 mass murders, Tutsi men and women were killed in similar numbers (the Hutus killed were usually men). Over half of Tutsi victims were children under 15, some of whom were killed by male adolescents.[16] The murder of most of the Tutsis took place within a few weeks in April.[17] The biggest section was killed in large massacres in places where many refugees had assembled such as church compounds, sports stadiums and health centers, but many others died in their homes, in their neighborhoods or at roadblocks.[18] From the beginning, observers were amazed by the level of active mass participation in the violence,[19] which far exceeded the often-cited radical killing formations called "Interahamwe", a name under which many witnesses subsumed all attackers.[20] Scholarly estimates of perhaps 200,000 perpetrators were surpassed by determinations in gacaca (traditional) courts, which found more than 400,000 people guilty of killings or severe physical violence, and more than 1.2 million of looting in a country of eight million.[21] This mass participation was also reflected in the main methods of killing: only 14.8 percent received their death from firearms, 37.9 percent from *pangas* (a kind of machete), 16.8 percent were killed with *masus* (nail-

---

[13] Gérard Prunier, *The Rwanda Crisis: History of a Genocide* (London: Hurst & Company, 1995), 232.
[14] Uvin, *Aiding Violence*, 209.
[15] For some contradictory clues concerning the question whether Tutsis still owned more land on average than Hutus in the early 1990s, see Jean Bigagaza et al., "Land Scarcity, Distribution and Conflict in Rwanda", J. Lind and K. Sturmon, eds., *The Ecology of Africa's Conflicts* (Pretoria: Institute for Security Studies, 2004), 66–70; see also Verwimp, *Peasants*, 48, 75–76.
[16] Hélène Dumas, "Enfants victimes, enfants tueurs: Expériences infantines (Rwanda, 1994)", *Vingtième Siècle* 122 (2014): 75–86, esp. 77, 84; see also Piton, *Génocide*, 118.
[17] Piton, *Génocide*, 106, 112; Verwimp, "Death", 240–241; Straus, *Order*, 55–62; Scott Straus, "What Is the Relationship between Hate Radio and Violence? Rethinking Rwanda's 'Radio Machete'", *Politics and Society* 35, 4 (2007): 621. Thereafter killings were continued in a more tightly controlled way: Des Forges, *Kein Zeuge*, 337–349.
[18] Verwimp, "Death", 236; Piton, *Génocide*, 153 offers other figures.
[19] See Kimonyo, *Rwanda's Popular Genocide*, esp. 353 and title; Mahmood Mamdani, *When Victims Become Killers: Colonialism, Nativism, and the Genocide in Rwanda* (Princeton: Princeton University Press, 2001), 199; Uvin, *Aiding Violence*, 206; Adam Jones and Nicholas Robins, "Introduction: Subaltern Genocide in Theory and Practice", Nicholas Robins and Adam Jones, eds., *Genocides by the Oppressed* (Bloomington and Indianapolis: Indiana University Press, 2009), 6.
[20] See Straus, *Order*, 27.
[21] Piton, *Génocide*, 198.

fortified clubs) and 8.7 percent with hoes; 4.2 percent were drowned, 3.7 percent thrown into latrines and 2.3 percent were burned to death.[22] Some ways of killing and torturing people, but also responses of those persecuted, resembled the 1972 mass killings against Hutus in the neighboring country of Burundi.[23]

Early scholarship emphasized ethnic hatred, tight and centralized organization, long-term preparation and radio propaganda as causes for the mass murders in Rwanda.[24] During a wave of revisionism, in studies often based on interviews with persecutors, Scott Straus instead offered a war/civil war situation, insecurity and "group pressure", together with "ethnic categorization" in a tightly organized state, as explanations.[25] Mahmood Mamdani and Omar McDoom added the factor of fear to the equation, further emphasizing Hutu persecutors' defensive outlook.[26] Constructing a "social interaction argument", Lee Ann Fujii found "local ties and group dynamics", including not only friendship between persecutors but also between Hutu and Tutsi, which she considered crucial for the violence.[27]

Many have argued that the mass murders of 1994 were propelled by misery and land pressure.[28] Existing research has established that although most Hutu killers were peasants, technical professionals, administrators and those working in the service sector were overrepresented among them, as were those with a higher education than average.[29] A large group among the persecutors was land-poor but more than the average population was involved in off-farm economic

---

22 According to a 2004 Rwandan government report, which Piton, *Génocide*, 127 refers to.
23 Liisa Malkki, *Purity and Exile: Violence, Memory, and National Cosmology among Hutu Refugees in Tanzania* (Chicago and London: University of Chicago Press, 1995), esp. 89–92, 95–96, 108. See Christopher Taylor, "The Cultural Face of Terror in the Rwandan Genocide of 1994", Alexander Laban Hinton, ed., *Annihilating Difference: The Anthropology of Genocide* (Berkeley et al.: University of California Press, 2002), 140–141.
24 The best among the early studies is Des Forges, *Kein Zeuge* (published in English in 1999).
25 He also found correlations between early killings and the strongholds of the leading party, the MRND: Straus, *Order*, 7–9, 60–62, 136, 139, 155, 245 (quotes); see also Charles Mironko, "'Ibitero': Means and Motive in the Rwandan Genocide", Susan Cook, ed., *Genocide in Cambodia and Rwanda: New Perspectives* (New Brunswick and London: Transaction, 2006), 163–189.
26 Mamdani, *When Victims*, esp. 191, 231; Omar Shahabudin McDoom, "The Psychology of Threat in Intergroup Conflict: Emotions, Rationality, and Opportunity in the Rwandan Genocide", *International Security* 37, 2 (2012): 119–155.
27 Lee Ann Fujii, *Killing Neighbors: Webs of Violence in Rwanda* (Ithaca and London: Cornell University, 2009), 185, 187. In some ways, Hélène Dumas, *Le génocide au village: Les massacres des Tutsi au Rwanda* (Paris: Seuil, 2014) is similar.
28 Kimonyo, *Rwanda's Popular Genocide*, 6, 143–167, 215–263; Uvin, *Aiding Violence*, 206.
29 Straus, *Order*, 104–108; Philip Verwimp, "An economic profile of peasant perpetrators of genocide: Micro-level evidence from Rwanda", *Journal of Development Economics* 77 (2005): 307.

activities, including wage labor and small businesses.[30] In this light, it was argued that there were some wealthier people among persecutors who had something to lose and many poor who had something to gain.[31]

Scholarship dealing with cultural patterns of the 1994 mass murders has concentrated on the visual realm such as violations of the body and the sexual imaginary. Christopher Taylor identified them as a "massive ritual of purification".[32] Fujii pointed to performative aspects of the violence[33] while Hélène Dumas identified local "investment of popular intelligence" in the murders.[34] By contrast, there has been little analysis of aural aspects.[35]

This chapter attempts to link socioeconomic and cultural aspects by pursuing a social history of the mass violence in 1994 with sound history as its tool. The sources mainly consist of published accounts by approximately 250 witnesses and survivors. Its core is a collection of early statements (1994–1995), compiled by Rakiya Omaar and Alex de Waal from the London-based NGO African Rights.[36] Two volumes by Jean Hatzfeld with excerpts from extensive and telling interviews pertaining to events in one local rural area in Rwanda, one of which included persecutor statements, and three smaller collections, including one published by Samuel Totten and Rafiki Ubaldo, complement the material used.[37] The compilation by African Rights has the advantage of presenting accounts from all parts of Rwanda, made very early after the killings (most were collected between May and July 1994) and, thus, with little interference by memory politics and movies, which is important for sound history. But that publication also has its downsides as it presents interview excerpts, and occasionally just snippets, and although people from all walks of life were interviewed, the intelligentsia (in a wide sense)

---

30 Verwimp, "Economic profile", 307–308, 318.
31 Verwimp, "Economic profile", 319.
32 Taylor, "Cultural Face", 137–178, quote 139.
33 Fujii, *Killing*, esp. 12; Fujii, *Show Time*.
34 Dumas, *Génocide*, 241.
35 Dumas, *Génocide*, 45–46; Des Forges, *Kein Zeuge*, 902.
36 African Rights, *Rwanda: Death, Despair and Defiance* (London: African Rights, 1995, second revised edition).
37 Jean Hatzfeld, *Nur das nackte Leben: Berichte aus den Sümpfen Ruandas* (Giessen: Haland & Wirth and Psychosozial-Verlag, 2004); Jean Hatzfeld, *Zeit der Macheten: Gespräche mit den Tätern des Völkermords in Ruanda* (Giessen: Haland & Wirth and Psychosozial-Verlag, 2004); Samuel Totten and Rafiki Ubaldo, eds., *We Cannot Forget: Interviews with Survivors of the 1994 Genocide in Rwanda* (New Brunswick: Rutgers University Press, 2011); Rwanda Youth & Children's Testimonies, University of Southern Florida, http://genocide.lib.usf.edu/taxonomy/term/1435 (accessed September 5, 2018; cited: Rwanda YCT); Aimable Twagilimana, ed., *Teenage Refugees From Rwanda Speak Out* (New York: Rosen, 1997).

is overrepresented and peasants underrepresented. The book, produced in a feverish effort, has also been criticized for lack of proper scholarly documentation and part of the interviews having been produced in cooperation with the RPF and, consequently, possibly echoing an RPF narrative.[38] In some ways, the analysis of the accounts' 'soundtrack' does not support the latter claim. However, any study based on survivor narratives must take into account that Rwandans' dealing with deceased family members focuses not on a "cult of the corpse" but on a careful construction of remembrance.[39]

Noisy Killers, Festive Behavior

Persecutors in Rwanda made many loud sounds. This appears dysfunctional if one thinks within categories of deception, surprise attack, and military discipline and professionalism. Here, I am referring to loud, open threats and announcements when attackers would come to kill individuals or large groups. But the longer I thought about it, the more I wondered whether one should be content with musing about the function of noises for the killings or whether one should instead start to ask questions about the function of the mass murders, judging from the sounds.

In many cases, large groups of Tutsis (usually refugees) were attacked by people in great numbers, described as crowds, rural dwellers, villagers or neighbors, usually without marching formation.[40] They were often accompanied by various types of militias, and sometimes by military soldiers. According to accounts by persecutors and persecuted, crowds of attackers approached noisily so that they could be heard over long distances, singing, shouting, and using musical instruments.[41] They were agitated and agitated each other by shouting murderous

---

[38] Luc Reydams, "NGO Justice: African Rights as Pseudo-Prosecutor of the Rwandan Genocide", *Human Rights Quarterly* 38, 3 (2016): 547–588, esp. 561, 566–567, 569–570. See also Alex de Waal, "Writing Human Rights and Getting It Wrong", *Boston Review*, June 6, 2016, http://bostonreview.net/world/alex-de-waal-writing-human-rights/ (last accessed September 22, 2018). Reydams is ambiguous about the authenticity of the interviews gathered in the African Rights volume but does not substantiate any claim that they were not. See Reydams, "NGO Justice", 549, 576; Luc Reydams, "Protesting Too Much: A Response to Linda Melvern et al.", *Human Rights Quarterly* 40 (2018): 472.
[39] Fujii, *Show Time*, 143.
[40] Then most Rwandans lived in dispersed settlements, not necessarily villages.
[41] Accounts by Cassius Niyonsaba, Angélique Mukamanzi, Innocent Rwililiza, Berthe Mwanankabandi and Claudine Kayitesi, Hatzfeld, *Nur*, 17, 77, 92–93, 167, 182; account by Alphonse Hitiyaremye, Hatzfeld, *Zeit*, 264; accounts by Mathias Habimana, Félicitée Mukabashima, Claver

phrases and slogans, thus drawing in residents to join.[42] In some places, the hills resounded with calls to assemble and move against the Tutsis.[43] When crowds or groups closed in on Tutsis, who were, for instance, hiding in swamps, they yelled death threats and matching slogans in many variations,[44] and this frightened those who were targeted.[45] They were noted to be "singing in excitement",[46] bellowing at hidden people to come out and sometimes banging on doors.[47] They also shouted at people trying to protect those they had come to kill,[48] while other onlookers, on the contrary, shouted at the militias to kill Tutsis.[49] Loud insults and threats were also frequently heard at roadblocks.[50]

Singing and the use of sound devices were reported from the countryside. People recalled that the attackers used a variety of musical instruments when they approached them, including drums, tins, empty jerricans and whistles (for more on whistles, see below).[51] Drums were employed to call upon people to gather and attack.[52] Drumming rhythms were at times still used as their own language for this purpose.[53] Drums were also used for misleading public announcements that "peace had been restored" and persecuted people should gather at a

---

Munyandinda, a staff member of Nkanka health center and Egide Kayitore, African Rights, *Rwanda*, 187, 434, 444, 503–504, 531; accounts by "Umulisa" and "Ruberwa", Totten and Ubaldo, *We*, 52, 147–148; Des Forges, *Kein Zeuge*, 387, 390.

42 Account by Pancrace Hakizamungili, Hatzfeld, *Zeit*, 235; account by Emmanuel Karemera, African Rights, *Rwanda*, 518–519; Fujii, *Killing*, 155; Kimonyo, *Rwanda's Popular Genocide*, 242; account by "Emmanuel Murangira", Totten and Ubaldo, *We*, 88; Des Forges, *Kein Zeuge*, 407.

43 Account by Charlotte Mupenzi, African Rights, *Rwanda*, 597.

44 Account by Berthe Mwanankabandi, Hatzfeld, *Nur*, 167; accounts by Albert Majaro, Valentine Mulisa, "Pascasie" and Marguerite Karuhimbi, African Rights, *Rwanda*, 216, 266, 484–485, 1057; account by "Edith Muhaza", Totten and Ubaldo, *We*, 131.

45 Accounts by Marie-Gorette Mukalinda and Augustin Mubiligi, African Rights, *Rwanda*, 321, 957.

46 Account by Josephine Uwamahoro, African Rights, *Rwanda*, 830.

47 Accounts by Diane Muyebwayire, Joram Mugwaneza and Sister Ernest [sic] Nyiramuganga, African Rights, *Rwanda*, 314, 618, 924; account by "Edith Muhaza", Totten and Ubaldo, *We*, 129.

48 Account by Edith Uwanyiligira, Hatzfeld, *Nur*, 153.

49 Account by Marie-Gorette Mukalinda, African Rights, *Rwanda*, 322.

50 For example, account by Josephine Mukandori, African Rights, *Rwanda*, 1042–1043; account by "Kwibuka", Totten and Ubaldo, *We*, 102; Des Forges, *Kein Zeuge*, 549.

51 Account by Angélique Mukamanzi, Hatzfeld, *Nur*, 77; Fujii, *Killing*, 172; Des Forges, *Kein Zeuge*, 440, 566.

52 Accounts by Gaëtan Kabanda and Egide Kayitore, African Rights, *Rwanda*, 466, 531; Des Forges, *Kein Zeuge*, 526.

53 Account by Athanase Hodari, African Rights, *Rwanda*, 479.

specific location.⁵⁴ What the attacking crowds sang was described as traditional songs,⁵⁵ but they also also intoned improvised songs that called for killing.⁵⁶ There were chants of "Power, power!" (in Kinyarwanda: pawa, pawa), a slogan by the radical pro-Hutu party Republican Democratic Movement (MDR).⁵⁷ Elements of this music resemble historic battle music in its often popular character, rhythmic structure and purpose to create collectivity. But in other ways, both differed. In Rwanda, many participants had had no military training which involved music; in most cases it was neither linked to organizational structure nor did it instill discipline; and it was not used to overcome any impulse to run away out of fear.⁵⁸

Massacres, as such, were very loud due to the shouts made by killers against their victims, to encourage each other or instruct each other in the use of arms. The intense sounds of blows and slashes, shots, and screams of those under attack were also often described.⁵⁹ The same (i.e., that there was noise all around) was said about killing scenes involving smaller groups of people.⁶⁰ Some murderers taunted and mocked individuals and hurled abuses at them (which some found "refreshing") before killing them,⁶¹ and they also screamed that they would kill the Tutsis while doing it.⁶² An exceptional report stated that the attackers started killing people "without saying a single word",⁶³ and killers came silently out of the Ntar-

---

54 Accounts by Félicitée Mukabashima and Cômes Kayinamura, African Rights, *Rwanda*, 432, 436; Des Forges, *Kein Zeuge*, 312.
55 Account by Ignace Rukiramacumu, Hatzfeld, *Zeit*, 16; Des Forges, *Kein Zeuge*, 55.
56 Dumas, *Génocide*, 231; Kimonyo, *Rwanda's Popular Genocide*, 339; Des Forges, *Kein Zeuge*, 246, 313; anonymous account, Totten and Ubaldo, *We*, 71.
57 Account by Françoise Nyirasabera, African Rights, *Rwanda*, 956 (quote); Fujii, *Killing*, 172; Des Forges, *Kein Zeuge*, 313, 522, 566.
58 For battle music, I draw from an excellent presentation by Morag Josephine Grant, "What did battle music sound like – and why?", keynote at the workshop "Sound and Music in War from the Middle Ages to the Present", University of Fribourg, November 12, 2018.
59 Account by Christine Nyiransabimana, Hatzfeld, *Nur*, 127; accounts by Pancrace Hakizamungili and Alphonse Hitiyaremye, Hatzfeld, *Zeit*, 40, 245; accounts by Consolée Gwizimpundu, Félicien Bahizi, Odette Mukaranakusi and a staff member of Nkanka health center, African Rights, *Rwanda*, 418, 459, 469, 504; Dumas, *Génocide*, 245.
60 Account by Pancrace Hakizamungili, Hatzfeld, *Zeit*, 25.
61 Accounts by Adalbert Munzingura, Fulgence Bunani and Elie Mizinge, Hatzfeld, *Zeit*, 142 (quote), 143, 155; account by "Isa", African Rights, *Rwanda*, 817 (this killing was called off).
62 Accounts by Jean Paul Gashegu, Paulin Ndagijimana, African Rights, *Rwanda*, 277, 510.
63 Account by Egide Kayitore, African Rights, *Rwanda*, 538 (church of Shangi).

ama church after the massacre.[64] When Tutsis still put up resistance, there was, as it was called in one instance, a "thundering stone-throwing match".[65]

If murders were more selective, soldiers, gendarmes or militia called out lists of names of people from among the crowds of refugees that should report to them, usually to be killed.[66] Rape attempts led to laughter in many incidents, whether it be persecutors mocking a colleague trying to do it or to abduct a female or rapists laughing at their victims.[67] Rape itself was accompanied by insults hurled at the female victims.[68]

Sometimes, large enthusiastic crowds watched the killings and shouted encouragement for the murderers, providing hints regarding where Tutsis might be hiding. This happened during large massacres[69] as well as the slaughter of a few individuals.[70] In one village, the Tutsis who were caught were dragged to the center and then tortured to death in the presence of onlookers. "There were shouts from all sides. These were noisy popular festivals, very rare, but well attended."[71]

People accused of being Tutsi were loudly threatened by their neighbors, or neighbors of those who were hiding them.[72] Hutu children "were running around repeating the threats they heard from their parents".[73] Many survivors described scenes such as that of Gloriose Mukakanimba's escape: "Everywhere neighbours were screaming: 'Here she is, here she is.'"[74] In Bweyeye, Cyangugu prefecture, "[t]he population were chanting: 'Hand him [a priest] over to us, we will kill him.'"[75] Refugees reported witnessing many diatribes and insults from residents

---

64 Account by "Emmanuel Muhinda", Totten and Ubaldo, *We*, 120.
65 Account by "Chantal", African Rights, *Rwanda*, 514.
66 Accounts by Deus Ndayishimiye, Jacqueline Nyiranzeyimana, Gorette Uwimana, Salvador Nshimiyimana and Théodore Nylinkwaya, African Rights, *Rwanda*, 501, 526 and 529, 692, 715, 729.
67 Account by "Juliana", African Rights, *Rwanda*, 752, 754.
68 Accounts by "Beata" and "Alexia", African Rights, *Rwanda*, 791–792, 794.
69 Account by Christine Nyiransabimana, Hatzfeld, *Nur*, 127, 129; account by "Isaïe", African Rights, *Rwanda*, 556.
70 See Fujii, *Show Time*.
71 Account by Clémentine Murebwayre, Hatzfeld, *Zeit*, 144.
72 Account by Christine Nyiransabimana, Hatzfeld, *Nur*, 131; account by "Isa", African Rights, *Rwanda*, 816.
73 Account by Philomène Cyulinyana, African Rights, *Rwanda*, 995.
74 African Rights, *Rwanda*, 591. See also accounts by Marthe Mukamurenzi and "Caritas", African Rights, *Rwanda*, 678, 759; account by Evariste Habimana, Rwanda YCT.
75 Account by Anglican priest from Banda parish, Belancille Muhimrundu, African Rights, *Rwanda*, 890 (quote), 1037 (in Rurana, Cyangugu prefecture, people demanded with shouts that somebody be arrested). See also account by "Edith Muhaza", Totten and Ubaldo, *We*, 129.

being directed against Tutsis.[76] When killers searched in vain for specific people to kill, they occasionally also voiced their anger.[77]

Some Hutu neighbors, often in groups, had already voiced loud public threats in the months and years before April 6, 1994, which included death threats. Survivors described some as having been in a good mood.[78] With this intimidating behavior, they occupied the streets acoustically. Militias (often subsumed in the reports under the term "interahamwe") were loud and verbally aggressive, especially in and around bars.[79] Neighbors and teachers had also started to call Tutsis "inyenzi" (cockroaches) in the years before 1994.[80] Some cursed Tutsis all day, also in private.[81] A few survivors also alluded to frequent arguments between Hutus and Tutsis.[82] Singing was customary at public political party meetings and Interahamwe gatherings before April 1994,[83] in celebration of *kubohoza* (enforced changes of political party),[84] and especially during or after *umuganda* (mandatory communal work).[85]

When they returned from massacres, killers were said to have been tired but chatting.[86] In the evenings, they held parties,[87] where they would invite each other and sing loudly near private homes or in bars,[88] shouting and boasting of their misdeeds and occasionally joking about the behavior of their victims in what one murderer called later a "cheerful mood".[89] "It was the most exciting

---

[76] Account by Edith Uwanyiligira, Hatzfeld, *Nur* 154; account by "Rosalie", African Rights, *Rwanda*, 743 (Red Cross staff).
[77] Account by Evergiste Habihirwe, Hatzfeld, *Zeit*, 107.
[78] Accounts by Cassius Niyonsaba, Francine Niyetegeka, Odette Mukamusoni and Claudine Kayitesi, Hatzfeld, *Nur*, 15, 37, 141, 181; account by Innocent Rwililiza, Hatzfeld, *Zeit*, 50.
[79] Account by Jean-Baptiste Munyankore, Hatzfeld, *Nur*, 67; accounts by Clémentine Murebwayre and Evergiste Habihirwe, Hatzfeld, *Zeit*, 36, 103, 106; account by "Mugabo Arnaud", Totten and Ubaldo, *We*, 179.
[80] Accounts by "Angelique Isimbi", "Mugabo Arnaud", Totten and Ubaldo, *We*, 157, 178–179.
[81] Account by Clémentine Murebwayre, Hatzfeld, *Zeit*, 36.
[82] Account by Cassius Niyonsaba and Jean-Baptiste Munyankore, Hatzfeld, *Nur*, 15, 67.
[83] Account by Jean-Baptiste Murangira, Hatzfeld, *Zeit*, 195.
[84] Des Forges, *Kein Zeuge*, 420.
[85] Darryl Li, "Echoes of violence: considerations on radio and genocide in Rwanda", *Journal of Genocide Research* 6, 1 (2004): 23.
[86] Account by Angélique Mukamanzi, Hatzfeld, *Nur*, 77.
[87] Emmerence Mujawamariya reported about a party by dignitaries and functionaries held *before* the massacre at the parish of Nyange: African Rights, *Rwanda*, 409.
[88] Account by Innocent Rwililiza, Hatzfeld, *Nur*, 93; account by Alphonse Hitiyaremye, Hatzfeld, *Zeit*, 89, 100; Des Forges, *Kein Zeuge*, 526, 568.
[89] Account by Marie-Louise Kagoyire, Hatzfeld, *Nur*, 129; account by Clémentine Murebwayre, Alphonse Hitiyaremye, Hatzfeld, *Zeit*, 69, 264; account by Egide Kayatore and "Odette", African Rights, *Rwanda*, 532, 781. Quote: account by Pancrace Hakizamungili, Hatzfeld, *Zeit*, 101.

feast that you can imagine," said another.⁹⁰ Rwandan and Burundian folk and pop music would play through looted radios and cassette recorders.⁹¹ As one witness put it: "They became never tired of killing, jeering, drinking, laughing and celebrating."⁹² Often, they sat near to fireplaces where meat would be grilled. The smell of barbecue lingered on the hills of the Rwandan countryside. People ate meat from slaughtered cows formerly owned by Tutsis and drank alcohol. Before the weeks of killing, most had only eaten meat on special holidays, but now some did so every evening and a few during breakfast as well.⁹³

These cows deserve some consideration. Most cattle in Rwanda were the property of Tutsis (who were traditionally more involved in animal raising than farming) and killed.⁹⁴ Calixte Nzabonimana, a MDR politician and Minister for Youth and Cooperatives, called men to kill Tutsis by saying that their cows waited to be slaughtered, and in Nyakiza, Burundian refugees received cattle as promised after they massacred Tutsis.⁹⁵ Along with regarding cattle as the "material/ symbolic capital necessary to the social reproduction of human beings",⁹⁶ many Hutus also judged them as a source of Tutsi wealth and Hutu misery and as a symbol of Tutsi lifestyle. In addition, cows had been a source of petty trouble between farmers and pastoralists because they sometimes trampled agricultural fields.⁹⁷ One murderer later said that after he would be released from prison, "compromises between farming and husbandry" would need to be made.⁹⁸ But with this, he may also have referred to the distribution of land use. After all, the number of bovines in the country had increased significantly between 1959 and the 1980s, to reach approximately 800,000 head of cattle.⁹⁹ At the same time, the

---

90 Account by Alphonse Hitiyaremye, Hatzfeld, *Zeit*, 100.
91 Account by Clémentine Murebwayre, Hatzfeld, *Zeit*, 102.
92 Account by Clémentine Murebwayre, Hatzfeld, *Zeit*, 103.
93 Accounts by Angélique Mukamanzi and Marie-Louise Kagoyire, Hatzfeld, *Nur*, 77, 129; accounts by Pancrace Hakizamungili and Adalbert Munzingura, Hatzfeld, *Zeit*, 13, 64; Fujii, *Show Time*, 61; Verwimp, *Peasants*, 229.
94 Taylor, "Cultural Face", 164; account by "Kwibuka", Totten and Ubaldo, *We*, 105.
95 Des Forges, *Kein Zeuge*, 325–326, 436.
96 Taylor, "Cultural Face", 164.
97 This is alluded to in the accounts by Alphonse Hitiyaremye and Adalbert Munzingura, Hatzfeld, *Zeit*, 206, 235. For popular historical narratives, see Malkki, *Purity*, 68–70. See also Christopher Taylor, *Milk, Honey, and Money: Changing Concepts in Rwandan Healing* (Washington and London: Smithsonian Institution Press, 1992), esp. 7. The fact that many Rwandan proverbs refer to cattle can be taken from Pierre Crepeau, *Parole et sagesse: Valeurs sociales dans les proverbes du Rwanda* ([Brussels:] Musée Royal de l'Afrique Centrale, 1985).
98 Account by Pancrace Hakizamungili, Hatzfeld, *Zeit*, 208.
99 Uvin, *Aiding Violence*, 194.

cropped area had expanded at the expense of pastures.[100] Hutus killed not only Tutsis as competitors for land ownership, but also their cows because after their death, some pastures could be converted into cropland in a country with great land scarcity.

Despite the many chases for Tutsis and opponents, I see less importance in hunting metaphors of persecutors than some other scholars do,[101] although one killer also remembered that the Tutsis had been like prey and, for him, had lost their human status.[102] But hunters wait in silence for the prey or, in a drive hunt, use noise to trick animals so that they start running away and become visible targets to be easily shot, whereas in Rwanda in 1994, the persecutors used noise in relation to intimidate, overwhelm and paralyze their victims (as known from war cries).

However, the sounds they made served not only to facilitate the killings but also for communication which went far beyond this purpose. The killers showed enthusiasm and passion, an emotionality which was a sign of a new social order in itself. The feelings expressed by their noises were joy, happiness, anger and hatred; these were no sounds of fear.[103]

Feelings of joy and happiness were, for the most part, associated with the carefree life of modest prosperity that seemed to begin through the plunder of furniture, bikes, radios, other electrical appliances, corrugated metal sheets and windows.[104] "It was like a fest", said a witness about the looting of movable possessions after a massacre.[105] Killers spoke to each other about the "promising times that had started" and the "new life that would begin now".[106] Above all, their exaltation had to do with the hope gaining land, which will be discussed below.

---

100 Verwimp, *Peasants*, 60–61.
101 For such scholarship, see Mironko, "'Ibitero'", 180; Jeannie Burnet, *Genocide Lives in Us: Women, Memory, and Silence in Rwanda* (Madison: University of Wisconsin Press, 2012), 230 note 2. For a survivor statement under the same impression, see account by a staff member of the Nkanka health center, African Rights, *Rwanda*, 503.
102 Account by Elie Mizinge, Hatzfeld, *Zeit*, 51.
103 Mamdani, *When Victims*, 191, 233, argues that fear drove the Hutu attackers.
104 See Hatzfeld, *Zeit*, 64–69, esp. account by Alphonse Hitiyaremye, ibid., 64, 102. See also Des Forges, *Kein Zeuge*, 553.
105 Quoted in Des Forges, *Kein Zeuge*, 442 (quote retranslated from German, C.G.).
106 Accounts by Alphonse Hitiyaremye, Hatzfeld, *Zeit*, 100, 264.

Murderers in Costumes

In many cases, the killers' festive mode included some form of masquerade. It seems worthwhile to dwell on how they were dressed and where this happened, although this requires deviating from sound history as an approach. The fact that some attackers wore costumes is not new to scholarship but has not been discussed in detail.[107] Masquerade was observed in different parts of the country, but most available reports on this are from the south. In most cases, survivors and witnesses reported that their assaulters wore banana leaves, sometimes specified as dried ones.[108] Those with such costumes were either described as local villagers, people from another commune or group of leaders.[109] Sometimes banana leaves were combined with painting one's face with chalk and/or ash.[110]

In other cases, the attackers put manioc leaves in their hair,[111] wore leaves of tea or coffee plants if these were widely grown in their region,[112] a woman killer was described as having been "dressed in straw",[113] or assaulters wore jingles on their legs and arms.[114] These differences contradict the assumption that wearing costumes had been centrally ordered from Kigali.[115]

Attackers dressed for the occasion. Nearly all available reports regarding this were related to big massacres, all of which happened in April 1994. As the costumes document, many people must have made some preparations, and the dressing style hardly suggests any reluctance from them.

Observers have interpreted these dressing choices very differently. Undecided, Lee Ann Fujii characterized them as "costume or 'disguise'".[116] Alison Des Forges

---

[107] See in particular Des Forges, *Kein Zeuge*, 281, 285, 382, 402, 446–447, 463, 521, 526, 558, 693 and also Kimonyo, *Rwanda's Popular Genocide*, 250; Timothy Longman, *Christianity and Genocide in Rwanda* (Cambridge: Cambridge University Press, 2010), 6.

[108] Accounts by Second Twagirumukiza and Vestine Nyirafurere (parish of Kibeho) and Ignace Ruzindana (Butare), African Rights, *Rwanda*, 292, 297–298, 341; Des Forges, *Kein Zeuge*, 382 (Kaduho), 402 (Gikongoro), 521 (two communes in Butare prefecture), 556 (Butare town); McDoom, "Psychology", 149; a witness account is in Verwimp, *Peasants*, 229.

[109] For leaders, see for example account by Felicien Bahizi, African Rights, *Rwanda*, 459 (parish of Nyamasheke); for people from another commune, see Des Forges, *Kein Zeuge*, 382.

[110] Account by Josephien Mukandori (Butare) and "Catherine" (Massaka, a suburb of Kigali), African Rights, *Rwanda*, 355, 769; Des Forges, *Kein Zeuge*, 526 (Ngoma).

[111] Account by Cassius Niyonsaba, Hatzfeld, *Nur*, 17. See also account by Berthe Mwanankabandi, ibid., 169.

[112] Des Forges, *Kein Zeuge*, 281.

[113] Account by Marie-Gorette Mukalinda, African Rights, *Rwanda*, 322.

[114] Account by Alphonsine Undimwana, Rwanda YCT.

[115] This assumption is in Des Forges, *Kein Zeuge*, 285.

[116] Fujii, *Killing*, 172.

noted that during the change of political party enforced by groups of violent men in early 1990s Rwanda (known as *kubohoza*), some attackers wore banana leaves and had whitened their face with chalk.[117] So, wearing costumes was known from political conflict situations. She argued that the masquerade in 1994 was intended to make attackers recognizable so that they would not hurt each other.[118] People at the time were unsure about the meaning of the costumes. Some survivors felt reminded of traditional performances such as the *intore* dance (a traditional war dance with strong Tutsi connotations), *kubandwa* practices (used in the *ryangombe* cult, a Hutu tradition)[119] and the "Imparamba Dancers".[120] To one survivor it appeared that the first attackers in Butare, dressed in banana leaves, were not fully convinced of what they were doing; to him, they appeared as if they were playing a sort of game.[121] Another stated: "I did not know what the [banana] leaves meant because this was the first time seeing such a thing"; the person thought this attire was for "camouflage" because they all looked the same.[122] This, however, was unlikely because banana leaves worn across the upper body, as some reported,[123] did not make people unidentifiable. Another survivor said that the killers were dressed as devils.[124]

The fact that some killers were dressed in banana leaves was so widely known that some Tutsis fleeing across the countryside wore them as well after someone had advised them that this would make them look like "Interahamwe" rather than potential victims and, thus, protect them.[125]

In any case, masquerades are another confirmation of the festive character of the killings. The agricultural symbolism of the dresses was commensurate with the mindset of Hutu peasants. Drawing from different cultural and political traditions, aggressive people invented their own, special festivity. At least temporarily, this replaced others: "During the [time of the] killings only one wedding was cele-

---

117 Des Forges, *Kein Zeuge*, 86.
118 Des Forges, *Kein Zeuge*, 281, 285. See also account by "Emmanuel Murangira", Totten and Ubaldo, *We*, 83.
119 See the statement by a survivor who was on his way to the Burundian border in Des Forges, *Kein Zeuge*, 463. For general information on the *intore* dance (known for grass wigs worn) and *kubandwa* (painting face and body), see Julius Adekunle, *Culture and Customs of Rwanda* (Westport and London: Greenwood, 2007), 92, 117–118, 139, 141–142.
120 Account by Second Twagirumukiza, African Rights, *Rwanda*, 292.
121 See Des Forges, *Kein Zeuge*, 693.
122 Account from Kigembe, prefecture of Butare, quoted in Kimonyo, *Rwanda's Popular Genocide*, 250.
123 See Des Forges, *Kein Zeuge*, 387, 446, 463, 558.
124 Account by Berthe Mwanankabandi, Hatzfeld, *Nur*, 169.
125 Account by "Ruberwa", Totten and Ubaldo, *We*, 140; Des Forges, *Kein Zeuge*, 576.

brated, no baptism took place, no football game was played, no church service held, for example on Easter. Nobody was interested any more in such festivities", said a former killer, who added that the latter appeared to them as "inanities" at the time.[126]

After giving it some consideration, I do not find it appropriate to call this carnivalesque. Rwandans do not celebrate carnival,[127] and although the assaulters in 1994 tried to invert the existing social order and used elements known from carnival like masquerade, the suspension of the separation between performers and audience, collective singing, dancing, going on a rampage and getting drunk in the end, they did not mean to do that only in a temporary, passing manner, as customary in a carnival.[128] Carnival is especially widespread as momentary liberation and outlet of emotions in predominantly Catholic environments,[129] but what happened in Rwanda in 1994, even though the majority religion was Catholicism, was totally opposed to the national habit of strict discipline and self-control. The new order was meant to last, and with it, new customs.

Conflicts Among Persecutors: Property and Other Issues

There were two situations during which loud conflict arose between persecutors. The most common one involved arguments about the possessions of their victims, such as furniture.[130] This was no coincidence because pillaging was widespread, with over a million people later being convicted for it. Other conflicts between Hutus often had to do with robbery among them and sometimes with the murder of Tutsi wives of Hutus.[131]

---

[126] Account by Alphonse Hitiyaremye, Hatzfeld, *Zeit*, 101.
[127] Amanda Carlson and Courtnay Micots, "Carnival in Africa: Join the Party!", *African Arts* 55, 4 (2022): 17 note 10 (the article provides a survey of carnivals in Africa); see also Daniel Crowley, "The Sacred and the Profane in African and African-Derived Carnivals", *Western Folklore* 58, 3–4 (1999): 223–228; Taylor, *Milk*, 23 and 233 note 1.
[128] Early on, Gérard Prunier called the killings in Kigali a "dark carnival". Prunier, *Rwanda Crisis*, 232.
[129] Scholarly concepts of carnival are in Mikhail Bakhtin, *Problems of Dostoevski's Poetics* (no place: Ardis, 1973), 100–106; and, on political crowds in a carnivalesque mode, in Jeffrey Verhey, *Der "Geist von 1914" und die Erfindung der Volksgemeinschaft* (Hamburg: Hamburger Edition, 2000), 50, 144–155.
[130] Account by Marie-Louise Kagoyire, Hatzfeld, *Nur*, 115. See also Des Forges, *Kein Zeuge*, 355; account by "Emmanuel Murangira", Totten and Ubaldo, *We*, 84.
[131] See Des Forges, *Kein Zeuge*, 492–498, 657–662.

The struggle for the land of those killed was the most heated, loud and at times violent.[132] Hutu men hunted for certain people to murder them and take over their parcels of land.[133] Or they even tried to kill even the last potential heir for the same purpose.[134] In one instance, a man stabbed his immediate neighbor and then danced on his corpse while singing.[135] One persecutor, a functionary in charge of changing land titles, later stated that Tutsis were killed "primarily by people wanting their land".[136] This confirms the descriptions already provided by Alison des Forges. Since the murderers claimed the land of their victims but other locals did too, local administrations tried to register vacant land and created various regulations for distributing it to new users. People who had personally committed murders apparently had an advantage, and they were probably among those who simply occupied the land.[137] Valuable land robbed from murdered Tutsi was sometimes divided among several Hutus.[138] On the other hand, acoustic evidence from villages does not support that Hutu peasants murdered Tutsis in defense of their own land, businesses or possessions.[139]

Lee Ann Fujii has argued that looting and stealing had been unthinkable before "war and genocide", became "a radically new way of relating to one's neighbors"[140] and, thus, a sign of a new social order. However, similar things had happened during the violence in 1959, 1962 and 1973, and Kimonyo has pointed to the "striking rise of the level of violent crime at the grassroots level [in the last years] before the genocide caused by hunger and intense land pressure".[141] The social crisis had been brewing over several years, but the acoustic evidence described so far supports Kimonyo's (and Fujii's) thesis that Rwanda's Hutu masses acted out of a desire for social change in the early 1990s and the mass murders constituted a revolt of the rural poor though not the poorest[142] albeit this seems to have been rarely expressed as in the words of the crowds screaming from the

---

132 Accounts by Elie Mizinge, Adalbert Munzingura and Pancrace Hakizamungili, Hatzfeld, *Zeit*, 88, 92–93, 101; Des Forges, *Kein Zeuge*, 407.
133 Account by Pancrace Hakizamungili, Hatzfeld, *Zeit*, 130; Kimonyo, *Rwanda's Popular Genocide*, 246.
134 Account by Joséphine Kampire according to Dumas, *Génocide*, 296.
135 Account by Angélique Mukamanzi, Hatzfeld, *Nur*, 78.
136 Kimonyo, *Rwanda's Popular Genocide*, 340–341.
137 See Des Forges, *Kein Zeuge*, 289, 355–356, 407, 409, 474, 498, 666, 669.
138 Account by "Mugabo Arnaud", Totten and Ubaldo, *We*, 172; Des Forges, *Kein Zeuge*, 669.
139 This claim was made by Mandani, *When Victims*, 231.
140 Fujii, *Show Time*, 61.
141 Kimonyo, *Rwanda's Popular Genocide*, 6 (quote), 143–167, 215–263.
142 Kimonyo, *Rwanda's Popular Genocide*, 356, 358; see also Verwimp, "Economic profile".

hills of Kivuru sector, "'The Hutu revolution has begun'".[143] The persecutors of 1994 may have committed mass murder in defense of the prevailing political order, but in social terms, many killers rather went for a new order in an attempt to overturn the existing conditions and make gains.[144]

As for other conflicts among persecutors, part of those returning from killings were generally described as aggressive, menacing and hollering even among Hutus so they had to be calmed down,[145] although many seem to have stopped short of physical violence against each other.[146]

Reports about women's behavior varied. Because of the promise of quick prosperity through plunder, "one did not hear them [i.e., wives] complaining anymore", according to one murderer,[147] while other women agitated and hurled insults against Tutsi women or argued about the loot.[148] But one was scolding her husband for being a too-eager perpetrator.[149]

It has to be noted that loud arguments also arose in cases of disagreement concerning a certain case of murder.[150] If this was about whether entire massacres should go on, those in crowds who opposed murders were said to have been less loud than those cheering for them, although this was not always the case.[151] Moreover, those manning roadblocks sometimes argued among themselves,[152] often about what to do with a suspect.[153] The question of whether a woman or a girl should be raped or not could also lead to an argument.[154] This means that at least some killings and rapes were not uncontroversial among Hutus and that

---

143 Quoted in Kimonyo, *Rwanda's Popular Genocide*, 244.
144 This matches Adam Jones' claim that "genocides by the oppressed" seek a new, just order and a world turned upside down. See Adam Jones, "On the Genocidal Aspects of Certain Subaltern Uprisings", in: Robins and Jones, *Genocides*, 52. Contemporary Rwandan propaganda was divided on whether people should seek a new order or defend the old, i.e., whether "feudalism" (or serfdom) was still to be abolished or had already been terminated after 1959 and its return was to be prevented: see, for example, Des Forges, *Kein Zeuge*, 108–109; Mamdani, *When Victims*, 233.
145 Accounts by Jean-Baptiste Murangira, Alphonse Hitiyaremye, Fulgence Bunani and Clémentine Murebwayre, Hatzfeld, *Zeit*, 53, 55, 100, 121.
146 Account by Jean-Baptiste Murangira, Hatzfeld, *Zeit*, 42.
147 Account by Ignace Rukiramucumu, Hatzfeld, *Zeit*, 68.
148 Account by Jean-Baptiste Murangira, Hatzfeld, *Zeit*, 118.
149 Account by Fulgence Bunani, Hatzfeld, *Zeit*, 116, 118.
150 Account by "Edith Muhaza", Totten and Ubaldo, *We*, 130.
151 Account by Christine Nyiransabimana, Hatzfeld, *Nur*, 127, 129; account by Hamidou Omar, an Angelican priest from the parish of Banda and Belancille Muhimrundu, African Rights, *Rwanda*, 560, 889, 1037; Dumas, *Génocide*, 206–207, 211.
152 Account by François Xavier Nsanzuwera, African Rights, *Rwanda*, 723.
153 Accounts by "Pascasie" and "Catherine", African Rights, *Rwanda*, 484, 772.
154 Account by "Pascasie", African Rights, *Rwanda*, 482.

some Hutus could loudly, and occasionally successfully, object to them, apparently without fear of severe negative consequences for themselves. Society is complex, and even among armed Hutu men, attitudes were not unanimous. Violence was hegemonic but not uncontested.

Arguments could also be hierarchical. In some cases, leaders of groups that attacked people yelled abuses toward men who were late or, in their view, showed too little murderous effort.[155] Only those who protested loudly against taking part in killings received punishment such as fines; consequently, few people objected openly.[156] Those hesitant to kill were mocked and berated.[157] This indicates what was predominant but also, once more, that there was a great variety of behavior.

Confronting Noise with Quiet Dignity: a Last Statement of Social Superiority

Some victims countered the noise in an unlikely manner. When being hacked to death, Jeannette Ayinkamiye's mother only muttered "Holy Cecily" but did not lament.[158] Similar behavior was occasionally even reported about children.[159] Several survivors said that during the big massacre at the church of Nyamata, those under attack remained silent, in contrast to the noise of shouting and machete blows all around.[160] Some of the accounts by relatives of victims where this is conveyed are slightly contradictory in themselves,[161] but they emphasize the discipline, composure and dignity of the dying. Besides, such accounts are confirmed by several statements made by attackers.[162] The group of killers extensively interviewed by Jean Hatzfeld were irritated, even worried, and discussed in the eve-

---

[155] Account by Pancrace Hakizamungili, Léopord Twagirayezu, Fulgence Bunani and Ignace Rukiramacumu, Hatzfeld, *Zeit*, 13, 17, 67, 76.
[156] Accounts by Ignace Rukiramacumu, Adalbert Munzingura and Pio Mutungirehe, Hatzfeld, *Zeit*, 76, 78, 81.
[157] Account by Alphonse Hitiyaremye, Hatzfeld, *Zeit*, 245.
[158] Account by Jeannette Ayinkamiye, *Nur*, 27–28.
[159] Account by Innocent Rwililiza, Hatzfeld, *Nur*, 96; account by Pio Mutungirehe, Hatzfeld, *Zeit*, 155.
[160] Accounts by Cassius Niyonsaba and Janvier Munyaneza, Hatzfeld, *Nur*, 17, 49; account by Valentine Muslisa, African Rights, *Rwanda*, 266.
[161] Also, one account speaks of screams of fear among those attacked in the church of Nyamata: account by Christine Nyiransabimana (a Hutu onlooker), Hatzfeld, *Nur*, 127.
[162] Account by Léopord Twagirayezu and Alphonse Hitiyaremye, Hatzfeld, *Zeit*, 31, 153; account by "Mashimangu", African Rights, *Rwanda*, 853.

nings among themselves why it was that many Tutsis did not ask them for mercy, protest and did not even talk to them in the moments before and during their killing; instead, they either prayed or said nothing at all, and a few even suppressed any screams of pain.[163]

Some killers placed their blows in ways intended to make their victims scream and drew pleasure when those whom they hunted down asked for mercy.[164] Not all of them did so; gendarmes told Théophile Zigirumugabe "to say nothing and above all not to ask for mercy" before they deliberated on his fate, and spared him.[165] Elsewhere, leaders instructed killers to hit the victims in ways so that they would not scream.[166]

In addition, many Tutsis reputedly stopped moving before the deadly blows, according to one murderer.[167] This finds confirmation in forensic evidence from the church in Kibuye, the site of another big massacre, where "few bodies showed any defensive wounds" and people thus had not tried to "ward off blows".[168]

Survivors offer several explanations for the silence with which some victims met their deaths, suggesting that those under attack were too "stunned" to scream,[169] exhausted, or thought that resistance made no sense anymore.[170] However, one important root of this near-incredible composure lay in the Rwandan custom of exercising restraint, discipline and emotional control, which was already taught to children and all the more valid for adults. This custom also entailed that people, particularly men, should not cry in public, even while mourning.[171] Often, this kind of demeanor

---

[163] Accounts by Elie Mizinge, Pio Mutungirehe and Léopord Twagirayezu, Hatzfeld, *Zeit*, 155–156, 253.

[164] Accounts by Adalbert Munzingura and Alphonse Hitiyaremye, Hatzfeld, *Zeit*, 140, 264.

[165] African Rights, *Rwanda*, 303.

[166] Account by Léon Mukihira, African Rights, *Rwanda*, 606.

[167] Account by Pio Mutungirehe, Hatzfeld, *Zeit*, 41.

[168] Fujii, *Show Time*, 140.

[169] Account by Spéciose Mukayiraba, African Rights, *Rwanda*, 217.

[170] Account by "Ruberwa", Totten and Ubaldo, *We*, 147.

[171] See Crepeau, *Parole*; Déogratias Bagilishya, "Mourning and Recovery from Trauma: In Rwanda, Tears Flow Within," *Transcultural Psychology* 37, 3 (2000): 337, 341, 347–348; Prosper Harerimana, "Death and Life after Death in Rwandan Culture", 2009, https://deathinafrica.word press.com/2009/05/02/death-and-life-after-death-in-rwandan-culture-by-prosper-harerimana-hare prosyahoofr/ (last accessed February 21, 2019); Fujii, *Killing*, 34; Fujii, *Show Time*, 111; Andrea Mariko Grant, "Noise and Silence in Rwanda's Postgenocide Religious Soundscape," *Journal of Religion in Africa* 48 (2018): 47; Benda, *Test*, 37. See also Gerard van't Spijker, *Les usages funéraires et la mission de l'église: Une étude anthropologique et theologique des rites funéraires au Rwanda* (Kampen: Uitgeversmaatschappij, 1990); Claudine Vidal, *Sociologie des passions: Côte d'Ivoire, Rwanda* (Paris: Karthala, 1991).- Similar observations have been made recently. See Patrick Im-

has been especially attributed to Tutsis who had the reputation to act in more formal, emotionally restrained, sober and polite ways than Hutus, who were sometimes collectively characterized as "frank" and "impulsive".[172] Internationally, it is not uncommon that the norms of an elite come to shape those of a country. By refusing to beg, scream and wail, and by meeting their death in silence, Tutsis not only tried to keep their personal dignity but also performed their class. They made a final statement not only of their own moral superiority but also of social superiority, negating the social order that their attackers sought.

Emotional Responses

Others under persecution were forced into behaviors that displayed emotions and contradicted tradition. They occasionally challenged the forces of violence by shouting provocatively at them, sometimes even if they were previously undiscovered,[173] pleading to kill them too,[174] and screaming loudly while attempting a counterattack to scare them off.[175]

Except for some summary remarks, I will not detail here the sounds made by dying people, which are frequently mentioned in accounts. They were as could be expected from any people in such a terrible situation. Given the great pain and slow death that attacks with *pangas* and *masus* inflicted on them, many vocal expressions were described as groans, screams and howls. It may have been because of severe loss of blood, stunning head injuries, paralysis or emotional restraint that the noises heard afterward from those in agony were often described as being in a low voice or subdued.

What does require more consideration is the act of crying. General scholarship has established that weeping is not pure emotion and not simply a natural reaction to certain events but is influenced by gender roles, age, social norms, political expectations, cultural values and religion; moreover, it is subject to educa-

---

hasly, "Wo ist das Gewusel Afrikas?", *Neue Zürcher Zeitung*, July 17, 2022, 14 ("Loud music, and noise more generally, are being frowned upon in Rwanda"; my translation).

172 Crepeau, *Parole*, 183; Des Forges, *Kein Zeuge*, 140 (citing Théoneste Bagosora, a leading organizer of the mass murders; quotes); accounts by Francine Niyetegeka (a Tutsi) and Christine Nyiransabimana, Hatzfeld, *Nur*, 40, 135. For a similar colonial perception, see Piton, *Génocide*, 28.
173 Accounts by Laurent Ngonkoli and Caritas Kabagwiza, African Rights, *Rwanda*, 231, 429; accounts by "Rose Marie Mukamwiza" and "Ruberwa", Totten and Ubald, *We*, 50, 143.
174 In this case, the person was not killed. Accounts by Liberata Mukasakindi and "Odette", African Rights, *Rwanda*, 625, 780.
175 Account by "Emmanuel Murangira", Totten and Ubaldo, *We*, 83.

tion as well as historical change. Crying is a form of communication.[176] Here, it is of interest to note what practices of crying say about emotional regimes and, through this, social relations and norms.

Generally, many people under persecution were said to be crying, although killers' narratives omitted this fact.[177] Survivors reported having wept out of fear when they were under attack, threatened with death or in the act of fleeing,[178] under stress when their spouse was abducted by attackers,[179] dealing with the impact of a recent attack on them,[180] in pain due to physical injuries[181] and in horror when they found corpses, especially if they were found naked.[182] Women cried during attempts of rape or after they were raped.[183] Children were often crying bent over their dead parents' bodies, a sight unforgettable to witnesses, or if a parent was severely injured or missing.[184] Some adults also cried about the death of their relatives.[185] What survivors remembered most distinctively were the cries of children dying, facing immediate death, or walking around "sobbing and calling out for their parents", as well as the "sobbing whispers" of babies.[186] Child survivors were also haunted by memories of the death of their relatives or close friends who had been injured and crying, feeling guilty that they had not been able to help.[187]

---

[176] For example, see Tom Lutz, *Crying: the natural and cultural history of tears* (New York: W.W. Norton, 1999).
[177] See Hatzfeld, *Zeit*.
[178] Accounts by Théophile Zigurumugabe, Emmerence Mujawamariya, Claudien Kanamugire, Chantal Uwimana, Mamerita Uwamariya and an anonymous nun, African Rights, *Rwanda*, 301, 411, 471, 810, 947, 1042; anonymous account, Totten and Ubaldo, *We*, 70; Jean Louis Mazimpaka, "I survived the Rwandan genocide", *Guardian* online, 18 July 2009; Des Forges, *Kein Zeuge*, 577.
[179] Account by "Mugabo Arnaud", Totten and Ubaldo, *We*, 184.
[180] Account by "Yvette", African Rights, *Rwanda*, 310.
[181] Account by "Kwibuka", Totten and Ubaldo, *We* 103.
[182] Account by Francine Niyitegeka, Hatzfeld, *Nur*, 37
[183] Account by "Pascasie", "Juliana", "Odette" and "Beata", African Rights, *Rwanda*, 483, 753, 781, 792.
[184] Accounts by Spéciose Mukayiraba, Emile Karuranga, Oreste Incimatata, Beatrice Mukandinda, Immaculée Mukeshimana and Célestin Mukeshimana, African Rights, *Rwanda*, 217, 346, 384, 857, 936, 962; account by Jacqueline Hagenimana, Rwanda YCT.
[185] Account by "Annonciata", African Rights, *Rwanda*, 813; account by "Kwibuka", Totten and Ubaldo, *We*, 103.
[186] Accounts by Second Twagirumukiza, Marie-Gorette Mukakalinda, "Emmanuel" (quote, from a scene in the church of Murambi), Eugène Busa and Marthe Mukamurenzi, African Rights, *Rwanda*, 293, 321, 386, 563, 678; account by "Emmanuel Murangira", Totten and Ubaldo, *We*, 87.
[187] See Sara Brown, *Gender and Genocide in Rwanda: Women as Rescuers and Perpetrators* (New York: Routledge, 2018), 68–69 and account by "Ruberwa", Totten and Ubaldo, *We*, 144.

Many persecuted children also cried from hunger or stress, which could attract killers.¹⁸⁸ At one roadblock, the guards were slapping children who cried, and some murder gangs tried to deceive children who were being led to their execution to avoid making them cry.¹⁸⁹ In another scene, three girls crying in front of a crowd before they were murdered made some people call for mercy on their behalf, although others were left indifferent and still others mocked them.¹⁹⁰ Some female Hutu students complained that the babies of a crowd of Tutsi refugees disturbed their sleep.¹⁹¹ To prevent them from making noises, children of refugees were given sleeping pills by their mothers or instructed not to cry. Often, they purportedly obeyed, as in the case of a child of eighteen months who spent an entire night alone hidden in a closet.¹⁹² At massacre sites, murderers sometimes used tear gas or pepper gas to find survivors of any age among the bodies by inducing crying and sneezing.¹⁹³

Those who cried included women, children and men, and they tended to weep more often when they were in a group or in front of others than when they were alone. Survivors also wept a lot in memory of their murdered relatives¹⁹⁴ or because of their own suffering. In contrast, people crying out of relief when they were reunited with their families was very rare.¹⁹⁵ Those who were weeping included some who were not under persecution. A Hutu relative of a Tutsi mother also cried when explaining that he felt that he could not save her child because it "looked very Tutsi",¹⁹⁶ while a Hutu man wept when he succeeded in bringing a group of children to their mother.¹⁹⁷ A man from Zaire cried while watching kill-

---

188 See account by "Chantal", Lidie Utagoma and "Vestine", African Rights, *Rwanda*, 512, 618, 785; account by "Rose Marie Mukamwiza", "Emmanuel Murangira", Totten and Ubaldo, *We*, 29, 85; Des Forges, *Kein Zeuge*, 458.
189 Account by François Xavier Nsanzuwera, African Rights, *Rwanda*, 723; Dumas, *Génocide*, 251–252.
190 See Dumas, *Génocide*, 211 and for a similar scene 263.
191 Account by "Yvette", African Rights, *Rwanda*, 308. For Hutu complaints about Tutsi refugees in general being too noisy, with the implication that they should be removed or killed, see accounts by Marie-Gorette Mukalinda and Jerôme Banyingana, African Rights, *Rwanda*, 320, 448.
192 Accounts by "Caritas" and Thérèse Mukarusagara, African Rights, *Rwanda*, 758, 1032.
193 See accounts by Louis Rutaganira, Elia Gashi and Françoise Nyirasabura, African Rights, *Rwanda*, 421, 446, 956.
194 Accounts by "Ruberwa" and "Murorunkwere", Totten and Ubaldo, *We*, 140, 175.
195 Account by Jean Paul Birmavu, African Rights, *Rwanda*, 570; account by "Ruberwa", Totten and Ubaldo, *We*, 140.
196 Account by Mamerita Uwamariya, African Rights, *Rwanda*, 821.
197 Account by "Mugabo Arnaud", Totten and Ubaldo, *We*, 182.

ings at the Rwandan border,[198] and priests also wept when they left or abandoned Tutsi refugees in a parish.[199]

What most of this suggests is that many Tutsis did openly show emotions like fear, pain and sadness by crying, which was in violation of traditional social norms. While some of this may have been instinctive and involuntary, in other cases – and through collective, public weeping in particular – crying served to strengthen community ties among those who were still there and signaled the need for help to others. Self-control gave way to loud expressions of emotion to garner social support or express one's authentic personality.

Religious Practice

Rwanda is the only case of mass violence that I have examined through sound history where religious practice played a major role. Praying, having mass and reciting religious songs are acts that are often mentioned in survivor accounts. This contrast to other cases requires an explanation. The strength of organized religion in Rwanda is only part of it. The circumstances matter, too – whether these practices were individual or collective, supervised by clergy or not, and occurred on church grounds or elsewhere. (The other cases that I examined include Chuknagar, East Pakistan, in 1971; the murder of European Jews and German mass killings of Belarusian villagers in the course of anti-partisan warfare in World War II; Indonesia in and after 1965; and Hiroshima and Nagasaki after the nuclear attacks.[200])

Research on Rwanda thus far has concentrated on the role of the clergy in the violence and emphasized that the Christian churches – and the Catholic church in particular – waited a long time before condemning the 1994 mass murders (if they did at all), rather than justifying or concealing the massacres as before. Owing to a close relationship between church leaders and the leading party, MRND, large parts of the clergy did little to support the faithful, especially foreign and Hutu priests, when church and monasterial compounds were crowded with refugees desperately looking for help. Moreover, many Tutsi clergy were mur-

---

[198] Des Forges, *Kein Zeuge*, 541.
[199] Anonymous account and account by Sicolas Mukarugaba, African Rights, *Rwanda*, 461, 489.
[200] For Chuknagar, see chapter 3 of this study; otherwise, see Christian Gerlach, "Echoes of persecution: sounds in early post-liberation Jewish memories," *Holocaust Studies* 24, 1 (2018): 1–25; and idem, "Indonesian Narratives of Survival in and after 1965 and Their Relation to Societal Persecution", in: Christian Gerlach and Clemens Six, eds. *The Palgrave Handbook of Anti-Communist Persecutions* (Cham: PalgraveMacmillan, 2020), 441–458.

dered by attackers, and so were most refugees at Christian compounds in some of the biggest massacres during the 1994 killings.[201] More than 60 percent of Rwandans were Catholic and about 90 percent were Christians. The indifference of the clergy is supported by the fact that I could only find one account in which a church bell was rung in alarm.[202] But my analysis differs from earlier ones in that I am focusing on religious practice rather than political action as well as on the behavior of lay people rather than the clergy.

Many survivors tell stories of piety, strength of faith and martyrdom, often through drastic examples. When attackers burned down the church in Kibeho and children inside screamed while burning or suffocating, a group of adults in the building sang a Kinyarwanda song that translates to "We were created for heaven. That's where all shall be happy for ever [sic]."[203] Another group of students at the same parish prayed together when being surrounded.[204] When militias burned down a private house near Nyamata which had ten refugees inside, those inside rushed out with burns when the silence indicated that the attackers had left and one woman shouted "Jesus is alive!"[205] Inside the infamous church of Nyamata, people were singing from the start of the attack, one of the bloodiest in Rwanda's history, "Onward, Christian soldiers", without putting up a fight.[206] Nuns in Nyapubuye assembled refugees for holding mass, praying the rosary and singing hymns until their death.[207] According to the reports, these practices were mostly for emotional in-group community building and in preparation for death and hardly intended to include, and thus appease, attackers.

On the other hand, when facing those who were about to kill them, some Tutsis abstained from praying.[208] At the health center in Nkanka, many people "prayed to god for help" before the attack, but during it many were reportedly "unable to pray" despite being in the center's chapel.[209] One of the Tutsis who

---

201 See Longman, *Christianity*.
202 Account by Egide Kayitare, African Rights, *Rwanda*, 533 (parish of Shangi).
203 Account by Vestine Nyirafurere, African Rights, *Rwanda*, 298. Spelling as in the original.
204 Account by "Yvette", African Rights, *Rwanda*, 309.
205 Account by Pélagie Mukashema, African Rights, *Rwanda*, 631.
206 Account by "Emmanuel Muhinda", Totten and Ubaldo, *We*, 119. For a similar scene from Shangi, see account by Egide Kayitare, African Rights, *Rwanda*, 538.
207 Account by Ernest [sic] Nyiramuganga, African Rights, *Rwanda*, 903.
208 Account by Pio Mutungirehe, Hatzfeld, *Zeit*, 155; see also account by Félicien Bahizi (a seminarian), African Rights, *Rwanda*, 459 for a crowd of refugees where some took to praying and others did not.
209 Account by a staff member by the Nkanka health center, African Rights, *Rwanda*, 504, 505.

spent weeks and months in hiding reported that the refugees either lost their faith or forgot to pray after a while.[210]

According to an official Rwandan study, close to 40 percent of all Tutsi victims were killed at church compounds.[211] People went there because the many who had taken refuge in churches in the previous sprees of violence in Rwanda had been spared. This part of the 1994 killings is central to many survivor accounts, which is why many cases of religious practice described in them also occurred in or near churches. Some people who were under persecution also said that they went to a church to say their prayers together;[212] others (including Christians) fled to mosques, just as some Muslims fled to churches, where they too were murdered.[213]

As several of the aforementioned examples show, even in consecrated spaces not everybody who turned to audible religious practice collectively did so in the presence of clergy. On rare occasions, priests were reported to have held a last mass with refugees or conducted other rites, but some of these men were depicted as dishonest.[214] In the church of Gishamvu, a priest baptized children among the refugees and gave other people the last sacraments.[215] Mass services held for murdered people were exceptional as there seemed to be not enough time or energy for them.[216] The same goes for individual prayers for those who had been killed.[217] Most victims stayed without proper burial and rites, a constant concern for many survivors.[218] In the parish of Nyamasheke, as in many other places, the believers were abandoned by the priests (in this case, a bishop). As the peasant Gaëtan Kabanda recounted: "We tried to organize ourselves. But all we

---

210 Account by Janvier Munyaneza, Hatzfeld, *Nur*, 52.
211 Dumas, *Génocide*, 58.
212 Accounts by Emerithe Uwinera and Jeanne Kanyana, African Rights, *Rwanda*, 269, 282
213 Account by Fréderic Mutagwera, African Rights, *Rwanda*, 226. Muslims have often been praised for mass abstention from the killings and protecting persecuted people, although there were prominent cases of the opposite so that their faith did not immunize members from becoming violent. See the paper Kristin Doughty and David Moussa Ntambara, *Resistance and Protection: Muslim Community Actions During the Rwandan Genocide* (Cambridge, 2005), and the cautionary thoughts in Benda, *Test*, 127–152.
214 Longman, *Christianity*, 287; for dishonesty, see account by Jean-Baptiste Sibomana, African Rights, *Rwanda*, 327.
215 Account by Zayasi Kanamugere, African Rights, *Rwanda*, 353.
216 Account by "Consolata", African Rights, *Rwanda*, 1046. They also contradicted the Rwandan customs of mourning in silence and privately: Harerimana, "Death".
217 Allan Thompson, "Introduction", in Allan Thompson, ed., *The Media and the Rwandan Genocide* (New York: Pluto, 2007), 3.
218 Burnet, *Genocide*, 95. For the context, see Bagilishya, "Mourning,", 347.

could do was pray. It felt like the end of all our lives." After the killers left, the survivors were "praying throughout the night".[219]

There were also many instances of *individual* audible religious practice, more often elsewhere than in church areas. People often said last prayers alone when being wounded and facing their death or while hiding during an attack or in the fields[220] and also during rape.[221] Sometimes, this made persecutors revise their decision to kill, as in the case where a mother started singing a hymn after two men came to pick up her family to murder them. The men changed their minds and told the family before leaving: "Be quiet". But after a while, the family loudly praised God.[222]

On some occasions, it was the persecutors who told the victims to say their last prayers.[223] The fact that groups prayed and sang Christian songs together when facing their attackers is less frequently mentioned.[224] In one case, a Tutsi family took turns praying day and night while hidden at home.[225]

In the weeks of the mass murders, the attackers did not make religious utterances. During massacres, they desecrated and destroyed many churches, and occasionally their anti-Tutsi slurs were openly heretic in terms of religious dogma, as observed in the church compound of Murambi, where they shouted: "The God of Tutsis is no longer around", "There is only the God of the Hutus remaining!"[226] At home and in public, they either did not pray or only for their own sake, in part out of fear.[227] One murderer claimed that in the months of the slaughter, the radio no longer broadcast Sunday mass or sermons, and religious songs were put on the air only a few times.[228] Another murderer from the same area added that no local church services were held in these months.[229]

---

[219] African Rights, *Rwanda*, 465, 467.
[220] Accounts by Théophile Zigirumugabe, Léon Mukihira, Laetitia Ugiriwabo, "Isa" and Joseph Sibomana (a retired bishop), African Rights, *Rwanda*, 302, 607, 808, 816, 883; account by "Ruberwa", Totten and Ubaldo, *We*, 145.
[221] Account by "Alexia", African Rights, *Rwanda*, 794.
[222] Account by "Pierre", African Rights, *Rwanda*, 575; another case is mentioned in Brown, *Gender*, 65, and see account by "Umulisa", Totten and Ubaldo, *We*, 53.
[223] Account by "Edith Muhaza", Totten and Ubaldo, *We*, 129.
[224] Accounts by Félicien Bahizi and "Pascasie", African Rights, *Rwanda*, 460, 481.
[225] Account by "Umulisa", Totten and Ubaldo, *We*, 50.
[226] See account by "Emmanuel Murangira", Totten and Ubaldo, *We*, 83.
[227] See above; for praying, see accounts by Alphonse Hitayaremye and Léopord Twagirayezu, Hatzfeld, *Zeit*, 153 (also for desecration), 157, 159.
[228] Account by Elie Mizinge, Hatzfeld, *Zeit*, 158.
[229] Account by Alphonse Hitiyaremye, *Zeit*, 101.

Along with religious activities, people also took up regional traditions that transcended ethnic groups. Hutus in Burundi who were facing their murder in 1972 were also said to have done "nothing but praying and singing only".[230] That said, some aspects of the behavior demonstrated in 1994 are noteworthy. Often, Christians who prayed, chanted and sang religious songs, whether individually or collectively during the persecution, were not under the instruction of clergy. This displayed quite an individualized, quasi-protestant relationship to God, foreshadowing the turn to Protestantism in a broad sense (although most post-1994 converts were Hutus) and the surge of piety after 1994.[231] Religious practice in the months of mass killings can therefore be understood as popular action and social activity.

It is significant that, according to the accounts accessible to me, persecuted Tutsi would only sing religious songs during that time, in contrast with the secular ones that were all what persecutors were singing (and secular music was also most of what they listened to from the radio and cassette players): folk music, political songs, improvised hate chants and African pop music.[232] With this, the former claimed universal values and social inclusion (though, in a Rwandan context, with overtones of foreign colonial domination – while secular songs and ethnic connotations, including with past Tutsi splendor, were missing) whereas the latter took the justification for their exclusionist particularism of the majority from political discourse and past and present popular struggles with connotations of a lower-class perspective and not from their religious creed. This audible difference between religious vs. non-religious practice shows the wide social gap between these groups and their different concepts of society. With the Catholic church, aggressive Hutus challenged or attacked the social order and some social norms ascribed to Catholicism, like silent composure and passive obedience to traditional elites.

Sound Technology and Social Situation

Of course, the emergence of this new order was not without inner contradictions, as one piece of sound equipment proves. Whistles were reported as having served various purposes, most frequently for organizing killings. They were command-

---

230 Malkki, *Purity*, 100.
231 For both developments, see Anne Kubai, "Post-Genocide Rwanda: The Changing Religious Landscape", *Exchange* 36 (2007): 198–214, and Grant, "Noise", 35–64.
232 See above. One killer claimed that Hutus and Tutsi still sang chorals together in Nyamata on 7 April 1994. Account by Adalbert Munzingura, Hatzfeld, *Zeit*, 152.

like blown to mark the beginning and the end of killings and searches for victims.[233] This points to the existing hierarchies as well as, together with a recurrent daily schedule in some places, also a work-like attitude.[234] Scholars have already pointed to persecutors likening their killings to work,[235] reminiscent of the rural labor which the MRND regime had propagated.[236] In fact, some killers later complained about having been disciplined this way, as one peasant described: "We were not used to work, march and return according to whistle signals."[237] This was less of a culture shock for the many rural dwellers who were already used to day labor or employment in service jobs.

There were also other aspects of organization and mobilization in the ways whistles were used. In many places, groups or crowds were called using whistles to assemble for the hunt for Tutsis.[238] Sometimes they served to attract people to join a murderous crowd on the way spontaneously.[239] Whistles were apparently also used by persecutors to exchange signals during chases and on guard, day or night,[240] or as start signal for an attack on crowds.[241] Or they were instrumental to tell others what to do, such as signaling Hutus to leave a place where many Tutsi had gathered, or to wake up local residents in the morning.[242]

But their carriers adopted whistles also for purposes other than hierarchical organization, such as during celebrations of the killings of the day[243] or to make

---

[233] Accounts by Janvier Munyaneza and Claudine Kavitezi, Hatzfeld, *Nur*, 51, 183; account by Innocent Rwililiza, a survivor, or Elie Mizinge, Hatzfeld, *Zeit*, 51.
[234] Account by Angélique Mukamanzi, Hatzfeld, *Nur*, 77. But whistles were hardly proof of central national organization, as Des Forges, *Kein Zeuge*, 285, argued.
[235] For example, see Des Forges, *Kein Zeuge*, 178 note 126; Taylor, "Cultural Face", 169.
[236] See Philip Verwimp, "Development ideology, the peasantry and genocide: Rwanda represented in Habyarimana's speeches", *Journal of Genocide Research* 2, 3 (2000): 325–361.
[237] Account by Fulgence Bunani, Hatzfeld, *Zeit*, 67 (quote translated from German). See also account by Ignace Rukiramacumu, ibid., 16. Taylor, "Face", 169 argued that persecutors rather used metaphors of labor to allude to their alleged service to the nation and make a claim to state compensation.
[238] Account by Charlotte Mupenzi, African Rights, *Rwanda*, 596; account by Justin Karangwa, Rwanda YCT.
[239] Kimonyo, *Rwanda's Popular Genocide*, 245; Des Forges, *Kein Zeuge*, 383.
[240] Accounts by Spéciose Mukayiraba, "Cathérine", Claudine Muyebwayire and eyewitness from ICRC hospital, Kigali, African Rights, *Rwanda*, 216, 218, 772, 828, 938; account by "Kwibuka", Totten and Ubaldo, *We*, 102; Des Forges, *Kein Zeuge*, 440.
[241] Account by Célestin Mazimpaka, African Rights, *Rwanda*, 373; Des Forges, *Kein Zeuge*, 460.
[242] Account by Théophile Zigirumugabe, African Rights, *Rwanda*, 300; account by "Rose Marie Mukamwiza", Totten and Ubaldo, *We*, 25.
[243] Account by Adalbert Munzingura, Hatzfeld, *Zeit*, 100; Des Forges, *Kein Zeuge*, 528.

intimidating noise with various instruments.²⁴⁴ Whatever their use, whistles were often remembered and mentioned by survivors because they always constituted a menacing sign, and a symbol of the new order.

Most types of electric sound equipment surface less frequently in the accounts, and they once again indicate organized action by the persecutors. This includes the honking horns of trucks and buses loaded with militias²⁴⁵ and loudspeaker announcements by officials (in some cases, the witnesses were perhaps also referring to megaphones), which were often misleading,²⁴⁶ or transmitting names of persons among a crowd of domestic refugees who were supposed to surrender to the killers.²⁴⁷

While loud instruments used by persecutors, and especially their leaders, dominated the Rwandan soundscape over these months, a less loud and more concealed acoustic tool was used by people under persecution (both Tutsis and Hutus): the telephone.²⁴⁸ However, back then, only the upper classes had access to phones. These were usually members of the intelligentsia in a broad sense (politicians, civil servants, military and gendarmerie officers, clergy, school directors, medical staff, lawyers, journalists, 'aid' workers and foreigners), mostly male, and more likely to live in urban than rural areas. They used their phones to ask for help for themselves and/or their families or for refugees,²⁴⁹ to gain information about the violence happening and share it with family, friends and colleagues,²⁵⁰

---

244 Accounts by Egide Kayitare, "Cathérine" and Marguerite Karuhimbi, African Rights, *Rwanda*, 531 (the men were also beating drums), 769 (the men were also beating tins), 1057; account by "Emmanuel Murangira", Totten and Ubaldo, *We*, 83; account by Jacqueline Hagenimana, Rwanda YCT; Des Forges, *Kein Zeuge*, 390, 440, 522.
245 Account by Fulgence Bunani, Hatzfeld, *Zeit*, 13.
246 Accounts by Jean Muragizi and "Catherine", African Rights, *Rwanda*, 621, 769 (loudspeakers installed on the roofs of cars), accounts by Sébastien Garsana, Virginie Musabyemariya, Christine Uwanyirigire and Mamerita Uwamariya, ibid., 477, 541, 842, 1094; Des Forges, *Kein Zeuge*, 312, 439. See also Carrie Sperling, "Mother of Atrocities: Pauline Nyiramasuhuko's Role in the Rwandan Genocide", *Fordham Urban Law Journal* 33, 2 (2006): 649.
247 Des Forges, *Kein Zeuge*, 251.
248 Soldiers, but also persecuted civilians, are sometimes also depicted of having used walkie-talkies: accounts by François Xavier Nsamzuwera, Hamidou Omar, Léon Mukihira and Mariette Kabanda, African Rights, *Rwanda*, 232, 561, 605, 836.
249 Account by "William Jean-Robert", Twagilimana, *Teenage Refugees*, 44; accounts by Pierre Claver Rwangabo, Catherine Kanyundo, Jacqueline Nyiranzeyimana, François Xavier Nsanzuwera and Médecins sans Frontières employee, African Rights, *Rwanda*, 181–182, 523, 525, 721, 975; Des Forges, *Kein Zeuge*, 572.
250 Accounts by Marc Rugenera, Pierre Claver Rwangabo, Joseph Nsengimana, Kamoso Pie, Jean Népumucène Nayinzara, Médard Rutijanwa, Gaspard Karemera, Spéciose Mukayiraba, Fréderic Mutagwera, Ismail Amri Swed, Nkonko health center staff member, Marie Leimalda Munyakazi,

to warn people[251] and to report to others about the situation.[252] Officials called politicians and the military, but this was mostly in vain if they asked for support to restrain the murderers.[253] Thus, information exchange was the single most important reason for making calls. What is less often reported are instances of threatening phone calls[254] or instructions provided by phone to assist in the persecution.[255]

These activities were hampered by individual phone lines being interrupted or connections between prefectures or within regions breaking down.[256] If people had their phones cut off, this indicates authorities' awareness that phones were often used to evade or locally stop the violence and thus utilized by people under persecution or those opposing the murders. However, with phones, people could only undermine the new order but not openly challenge it. Even undermining it usually did not work, as most calls were made in the early period of the mass murders; the callers eventually gave up, lost their access to phones or left the country. Nonetheless, phone lines constituted an elite network that was relatively often used with success to gain protection or exit opportunities, a chance that most peasants or day laborers did not have.

The most cited acoustic medium in the Rwandan mass murders is the radio, and its uses illuminate the social situation. According to the standard narrative in scholarship and courtrooms, the organizers of the 'genocide' steered, instructed and manipulated perpetrators nationwide using radio propaganda, namely through *Radio-Télévision Libre Mille Collines* (RTLM), a private station founded in 1993 by Rwandan business leaders and politicians that is known for its interactive format, informal and flexible style, fashionable music mix, and radical content.[257] Many

---

anonymous African missionary, Mamerita Uwamariya and Paul Rusesabagina, African Rights, *Rwanda*, 179, 181–182, 184–185, 190, 194, 196, 204–205, 215, 225–226, 234, 503, 674–675, 874, 947, 1001.
251 Account by Gaspard Karemera, African Rights, *Rwanda*, 205, in addition to some other calls referenced in the previous footnote.
252 Des Forges, *Kein Zeuge*, 251.
253 Accounts by Kamoso Pie, "Luc", "Monique", Célestin Mazimpaka, Félicien Bahizi, anonymous parishioner, Maurice Kalisa, Paul Rusesabagina and Beatrice Uwamwezi, African Rights, *Rwanda*, 191, 368, 370, 373, 375, 457, 459, 461, 478, 719, 849–851; Des Forges, *Kein Zeuge*, 390.
254 Des Forges, *Kein Zeuge*, 512, 547; nurse from university hospital in Butare, African Rights, *Rwanda*, 945.
255 Accounts by Paul Rusesabigana and Emmanuel Sagahutu, African Rights, *Rwanda*, 719, 1020.
256 Des Forges, *Kein Zeuge*, 375 (Gikongoro prefecture), 393 (Kivu area), 514 (various prefectures); individual cases: accounts by Marc Rugenera, Joseph Nsengimana, "Marianne", Léon Mukihira and Paul Rusesabigana, African Rights, *Rwanda*, 180, 184–185, 239, 605, 719.
257 See, for example, Des Forges, *Kein Zeuge*, 98–100. Straus, "What", 610, 612–614 sums up the dominant narrative.

scholars found radio to be of enormous importance to the mass murders in a country where 34 percent of the people over the age of six were illiterate in 1994 (and, thus, many adults).[258] Existing research has concentrated on RTLM and broadcasts' contents.[259] RTLM focused on a defensive war narrative and often implied that all Tutsi were the enemy (even though it rarely said so openly and unequivocally).[260] Some studies revised the standard narrative to an extent, stating that although RTLM informed and influenced persecutors' actions, it did not determine or remote-control them; that the peak of killings did not correlate with inciting broadcasts; that RTLM's content was more contradictory than is often portrayed, including calls for stopping violence broadcast alongside more frequent and fervent demands for violence; and that the radio was not a decisive factor in the mass murders.[261] Even a field survey commissioned by the Senate of the Republic of Rwanda found that 34 percent of respondents considered the "media" to be the major tool for mobilization in the 1994 mass murders, a sizable but limited percentage,[262] while the International Tribunal for Rwanda found a direct impact of RTLM airings was only proven in a few cases.[263]

In this context, the operations of the official and rather rigid Radio Rwanda have been neglected. The same goes for the station installed by the RPF, *Radio Muhabura* (Beacon), but because of its dogmatic and radical style, even some RPF soldiers preferred to listen to RTLM.[264] It has to be added that most scholarship has inquired into what persecutors heard, with most attention paid to urban areas. Therefore, examining survivors' experiences adds some crucial aspects and helps modify earlier findings.

One such insight pertains to the places where RTLM was heard. About 27 percent of rural households in Rwanda and 59 percent of urban ones owned a radio

---

[258] Des Forges, *Kein Zeuge*, 96.
[259] For example, see Thompson, *Media*; McDoom, "Psychology", 141–143, 146–147, 151–152.
[260] See also Dumas, *Génocide*, 117–128.
[261] Straus, "What", especially 611, 622–628, 630; Li, "Echoes", 9–27; Charles Mironko, "The Effect of RTLM's Rhetoric of Ethnic Hatred in Rural Rwanda", Thompson, *Media*, 134; Mary Kimoni, "RTLM: the Medium That Became a Tool for Mass Murder", in: Thompson, *Media*, 120. See also Piton, *Génocide*, 93; Des Forges, *Kein Zeuge*, 247–248, 318, 339, 342, 346; Balthasar Grüter, *Aufstachelung zum Massenmord? Das Radioprogramm von Radio Télévision Libre des Mille Collines in Ruanda von Juli 1993 bis Juli 1994*, Master's thesis, University of Bern, June 2016.
[262] Republic of Rwanda, Parliament, The Senate, *Rwanda: Genocide Ideology and Strategies for Its Eradication* (Kigali: Senate, 2006), 85.
[263] "Summary Judgment of the Media Trial" (ICTR-99-52-T, 3 December 2003), Thompson, *Media*, 277–306.
[264] Des Forges, *Kein Zeuge*, 98; Li, "Echoes", 8; Prunier, *Rwanda Crisis*, 189.

in 1991.[265] Accordingly, people from Kigali reported more often that they listened to the radio than those from the countryside.[266] Usually, radio sets were battery-driven and often in the form of boom boxes with integrated cassette players. Outside Kigali, survivors, who talked of Radio Rwanda more often, rarely listened to, or received, RTLM. A few did so in the western prefectures of Kibuye and Cyangugu, but also in Kibungo, Gikongoro and Butare.[267] This matches Charles Mironko's findings that RTLM was received throughout the country – although more often in Kigali – better than Scott Straus' that it reached only Kigali and parts of central and western Rwanda.[268]

Unlike in most cases of mass violence that I have studied where it played only a marginal role,[269] listening to the radio is an important feature in survivor accounts from Rwanda. This requires explanations. In the following discussion, I distinguish among three functions of radio broadcasts: information, organization and agitation/incitement, starting with the latter.[270] Radio propaganda was a factor that some persecutors strongly emphasized, arguing that they had been manipulated into killing.[271] Many survivors also referred to the rabble-rousing in the broadcasts.[272] More than a few reported that this baiting had already been going on in the early 1990s, and most of it was thus done through Radio Rwanda.[273] During the 1994 massacres, radio stations also spread misleadingly calming informa-

---

265 Des Forges, *Kein Zeuge*, 96; Adekunle, *Culture*, 61 note 15; McDoom, "Psychology", 138. Straus, "What", 616 suggests that it was less than ten percent, based on UNESCO data.
266 For Kigali, see African Rights, *Rwanda*, 179–239.
267 Elie Mizinge, Hatzfeld, *Zeit*, 102; accounts by "Luc" (Kibungo), Emmanuel Nsabimana and Nelson Nsengiyumva, African Rights, *Rwanda*, 368 (Kibungo), 400 (Kibuye), 612 (Cyangugu), see also 588 (Kibuye); accounts by "Rose Marie Mukamwiza", "Emmanuel Murangira", "Angelique Isimbi", "Mugabo Arnaud", Totten and Ubaldo, *We*, 24–25 (Butare), 82 (Gikongoro), 158 (Butare), 179 (Cyangugu).
268 See Mironko, "Effect", 126–127; Li, "Echoes", 25 note 2; and McDoom, "Psychology", 139–140, opposing Straus, "What", 617.
269 See chapter 3 of this study; Gerlach, "Echoes"; and idem, "Indonesian Narratives".
270 Des Forges, *Kein Zeuge*, 28, 301–304.
271 Accounts by Adalbert Munzingura and Pancrace Hakizamungili, Hatzfeld, *Zeit*, 55, 76, 98, 235, 239–240, 246; Kimonyo, *Rwanda's Popular Genocide*, 340. In another defense strategy, other persecutors strongly claimed ignorance of RTLM; see Mironko, "Effect", 129–134.
272 Accounts by Innocent Rwililiza and Christine Nyiransabimana, Hatzfeld, *Nur*, 103, 130; accounts by "Umulisa", anonymous, "Emmanuel Murangira", "Emmanuel Muhinda", "Angelique Isimbi" and "Mugabo Arnaud", Totten and Ubaldo, *We*, 48, 68–69, 82, 116, 158, 179; two examples are in Brown, *Gender*, 46–47.
273 Account by Jean-Baptiste Munyankore, Hatzfeld, *Nur*, 67; account by Nelson Nsengiyumva, African Rights, *Rwanda*, 614; accounts by "Umulisa" and anonymous, Totten and Ubaldo, *We*, 42–43 and 45, 65 and 68. As for persecutors, see accounts by Joseph-Désiré Bitero, Elie Mizinge and Pancrace Hakizamungili, Hatzfeld, *Zeit*, 192, 194, 238.

tion that was obviously intended to lure Tutsis out of hiding or refuge, such as a speech by President Sindikubwabo.[274]

However, propaganda and incitement are mentioned more often in accounts made years after the event, probably because the interviewers asked specific questions about it, than in the early reports in the collection of African Rights, where people rather emphasized the radio's role in informing.[275] Some of these early accounts, in turn, accused Radio Rwanda of having aired misleading or inciting propaganda and called for it to be held accountable.[276] Within that radio station, employees organized a "witchhunt" against other colleagues, some of whom fled to the Hotel "Mille Collines" in Kigali.[277] Moreover, the initial prefects of Gikongoro and Butare warned citizens to evaluate what they heard on the radio critically.[278]

RTLM was also accused of having helped organize concrete killing operations.[279] It named people who should be apprehended (or killed)[280] and pointed to places where many refugees (mostly Tutsis) had gathered as alleged security risks, warned that the crowds included infiltrators, and openly told people to attack them.[281] Some persecutors and people manning roadblocks reported hearing such broadcasts.[282] But, unlike some foreigners, of the many survivors who mentioned roadblocks, almost none said anything about guards listening to the radio, let alone RTLM.[283] All things considered, there is little evidence in these sources

---

[274] Account by "Joseph", African Rights, *Rwanda*, 1005; accounts by "Umulisa" and anonymous, Totten and Ubaldo, *We*, 51, 69.

[275] For political agitation via the radio mentioned in African Rights, *Rwanda*, see accounts by Kamoso Pie, "Marianne", "Luc", Félicien Bahizi and "Isaie", 191, 239, 368, 457 and 460, 555.

[276] Accounts by Reine Munyantore, Caritas Kabagwiza, Félicien Bahizi, "Isaie", Apolonia Mukandamage, "Juliana" and an African missionary from Gitarama, African Rights, *Rwanda*, 267, 428, 457 and 460, 555, 658–659, 757–758, 1054; account by "Didier" (a son of the director of Radio Rwanda), Twagilimana, *Teenage Refugees*, 55.

[277] Account by Louise Kayibanda, African Rights, *Rwanda*, 362.

[278] Des Forges, *Kein Zeuge*, 517–518.

[279] Des Forges, *Kein Zeuge*, 46, 249–252.

[280] Account by Emmanuel Nsabimana, African Rights, *Rwanda*, 400. Already in April 1993, Radio Rwanda had suspected eleven school students from Nyanza of supporting the RPF and specified their names: account by "Angelique Isimbi", Totten and Ubaldo, *We*, 158.

[281] Accounts by Fréderic Mutagwera and Caritas Kabagwiza, African Rights, *Rwanda*, 226, 428, see also 566; account by "Emmanuel Muhinda", Totten and Ubaldo, *We*, 118; Des Forges, *Kein Zeuge*, 518.

[282] Account by François Bybarumwanzi, African Rights, *Rwanda*, 220.

[283] See African Rights, Rwanda, and the Rwanda YCT collection in contrast to Alison Des Forges, "Call for Genocide: Radio in Rwanda, 1994", Thompson, *Media*, 50 and Philippe Dahinden, "Information in Crisis Areas as a Tool for Peace: the Hirondelle Experiment", Thompson, *Media*, 381.

suggesting that this radio station was effective as a co-organizer of killings, except for rare cases.

By far, the most frequent way in which survivors spoke of the radio was as a source of information. Their accounts primarily mention the news about the plane crash and the death of President Habyarimana, often along with the curfew that followed.[284] Many specified that RTLM broadcast the news of the crash already in the evening of April 6, when Radio Rwanda merely switched to sending classical music, only to officially confirm the president's death the next morning while announcing the curfew.[285] (In fact, even a Tutsi journalist from Radio Rwanda recalled that she heard of the President's death only on April 7 despite having worked the evening shift the day before.[286]) Many survivors also spoke about the premonitions that they had upon hearing this news. During the following days, persecuted people listened to the news regarding the violence in Kigali and other parts of the country.[287] Sometimes they were also informed about specific political decisions.[288]

During the mass killings, information was vital, and listening to the radio was essential for getting it. Survivors from the capital as well as from the province clad this in terms like "I tried to follow things on the radio",[289] "[b]ecause of

---

[284] Account by Edith Uwanyiligira, Hatzfeld, *Nur*, 151; accounts by Albert Majaro, François Bybarumwanzi, Bernadette Kanzayire, Laurent Ngonkoli, Angelo Nkurunziza, Beata Niyoyita, Pierre Canisius Rutagengwa, Philipo Kayitore, Jeanne Kanyana, "Luc", Beatrice Uwamwezi, Jean Claude Karangumunwa, Anastase Nkinamubanzi, Félicitée Mubashima, Jerôme Bayingana, Gaëtan Kabanda, "Pascasie", "Claudine", anonymous journalist, Pierre-Simon Hitiyiza, "Pierre", Agnes Ndabubaha-Kansine, Nelson Nsengiyumva, Claver Mbugufe, "Jean", Gaston Nsengiyumva, Christian Kineza and Josephine Mukandori, African Rights, *Rwanda*, 210, 219, 221, 228, 238, 262, 268, 270, 281, 355, 368, 374, 377, 403, 431, 448, 463, 480, 486, 564, 567, 574, 599, 612, 664, 677, 682, 846, 1044; accounts by "Rose Marie Mukamwiza", "Umulisa" and anonymous, Totten and Ubaldo, *We*, 24, 47, 69. Some men said that at the time of the first news in the evening of 6 April 1994 they had watched a football match on TV: accounts by Denis Kaniwabahizi, Hamidou Omar and Frédéric Mutagwera, African Rights, *Rwanda*, 96, 195, 225.

[285] Account by Marc Rugenera, Pierre Claver Rwangabo, Joseph Nsengimana, Bonaventure Ubalijoro, Hamidou Omar, Gaspard Karemera, Frédéric Mutagwera, François Xavier Nsanzuwera, Ismail Amri Swed, Oreste Incimatata, Jean Paul Birmavu, Marthe Mukamurenzi, Jean Marie-Vianney Nkurunziza, Gorette Uwimana and Désiré Gashirabake, African Rights, *Rwanda*, 179, 181, 184, 189, 195, 204, 225, 232, 234, 381, 569, 678, 684, 689, 1029; account by "Beatrice", Twagilimana, *Teenage Refugees*, 31–33.

[286] Account by Louise Kayibanda, African Rights, *Rwanda*, 361.

[287] Account by Sylvie Umibyeyi, Hatzfeld, *Zeit*, 207; accounts by "Yvette" and "Chantal", African Rights, *Rwanda*, 306, 512; Mazimpaka, "I survived".

[288] Account by Jean Damascène Kayitesi, Jean Paul Biramvu and a nurse from Butare university hospital, African Rights, *Rwanda*, 333, 570, 945.

[289] Account by Bonaventure Niyibizi, African Rights, *Rwanda*, 697.

the curfew, we stayed at home and decided to follow events by radio",[290] and "We listened to RTLM because they would relate what was happening."[291] One survivor monitored broadcasts by RTLM, Radio Rwanda and *Radio Muhabura* "in order to try to figure out what was happening in the country".[292] Everything was about information – next to no survivor spoke about having listened to music after 6 April 1994 (unlike many persecutors).

This desire for factual orientation included efforts to recognize misinformation.[293] Some – particularly educated listeners in Kigali – found the information from RTLM unreliable,[294] whereas one, on the contrary, declared that whereas RTLM and also *Radio Muhabura* reported specific details, Radio Rwanda's broadcasts were not useful as they were vague and unspecific.[295] A nun said that radio information did not allow her to get an accurate picture of the situation.[296]

Relatively few people recounted programs by RPF's *Radio Muhabura*. A bishop warned school students in Kibeho against listening to it.[297] If this station praised a person, this endangered his life because Hutu-power advocates suspected him to be a foe.[298] To listen to foreign radio stations that could be received in Rwanda seems to have been a rare occurrence.[299]

Philippe Dahinden has argued that during the mass murders, refugees "had no real information", i.e., access to radio sets.[300] Some survivor accounts confirm that they lacked information from the radio while in hiding.[301] In rare instances, refugees did have a radio with them and listened to news about the killings while

---

[290] Account by a peasant family from Byumba, African Rights, *Rwanda*, 366.
[291] Account by "Mugabo Arnaud", Totten and Ubaldo, *We*, 180. See also account by "Jean-Hubert", Twagilimana, *Teenage Refugees*, 37.
[292] Account by "Umulisa", Totten and Ubaldo, *We*, 53. Verwimp, *Peasants*, 224 mentions a similar behavior by a Hutu-manned MDR group in 1992-1993, during the civil war.
[293] Account by Marc Rugenera, African Rights, *Rwanda*, 180 (he heard about his own death on an unspecified channel).
[294] Accounts by Gaspard Karemera (a journalist), Fréderic Mutagwera and Ismail Amri Swed, African Rights, *Rwanda*, 204, 225, 234.
[295] Account by "Umulisa", Totten and Ubaldo, *We*, 54.
[296] See African Rights, *Rwanda*, 239.
[297] See Burnet, *Genocide*, 174; account by "Umulisa", Totten and Ubaldo, *We*, 45, 53–54. For the bishop, see account by "Yvette", African Rights, *Rwanda*, 309.
[298] See Prunier, *Rwanda Crisis*, 259.
[299] Accounts by Béatrice Uzayizaba, Egide Kayitare and "Jean", African Rights, *Rwanda*, 492, 531 (both unspecified), 677 (BBC); Burnet, *Genocide*, 174 (BBC and Radio France International). For technical details, see Straus, "What", 612 and 634 note 14.
[300] Dahinden, "Experiment", 381.
[301] Account by Francine Niyitegeka, Hatzfeld, *Nur*, 39.

in hiding,[302] and this was certainly the case in places where hundreds or thousands of refugees had gathered in April 1994. Unlike before April 6,[303] listening to the radio had become a segregated practice, separating Hutus and Tutsis.

However, the main point is this: dominated as it was by power holders, the radio was not only an instrument for the persecutors, as discussed by scholars thus far, but also a tool in the hands of those under persecution (and other people). Survivors primarily describe the radio as a source of information. They were not passive victims, but actors. In order to find a way of survival, they tried to 'read' the persecution, its rules, means and local course. Thus, people under persecution were active and, for the most part, critical media consumers trying to monitor the situation, often switching channels to do so. RTLM in particular, with its participatory character, represented the new social order in which those under persecution had near unsurmountable difficulties in finding a place. At least in many early accounts, the propagandistic function of the radio appears secondary in terms of how often it was mentioned, and the co-organization of murder by radio stations seems marginal.

Among the reasons why many Tutsis soon lost their access to radio was that they were coveted commodity among murderers and looters.[304] One of the looters remembered his greed upon seeing "a neighbor riding a new bicycle or proudly brandishing a radio set".[305] Reportedly, *Interahamwe* members and soldiers received the first or best radio sets.[306] Looters also gave radios away as a gift or sold them, and their price dropped locally to ten percent of their earlier value.[307] In the evenings, these sets were used to play Rwandan or Burundian modern or traditional music at parties, which involved plenty of alcohol and raucous singing.[308] Unlike in earlier years, the sound of music was often heard around because people no longer thought they needed to save battery power.[309] This could be read as symbolic of a period of plenty and pleasure.

---

302 Account by Innocent Rwililiza, Hatzfeld, *Nur*, 103; account by Théodore Nyilinkwaya, African Rights, *Rwanda*, 726; account by "Emmanuel Muhinda", Totten and Ubaldo, *We*, 123. Hutus who fled from Burundi to Tanzania in 1972 also carried radio sets with them: Malkki, *Purity*, 108.
303 Account by Pancrace Hakizamungili, Hatzfeld, *Zeit*, 120.
304 Account by Alphonse Hitiyaremye, Hatzfeld, *Zeit*, 69; accounts by Spéciose Mukayiraba, Jean Paul Biramvu, William Rutaremara, "Eugenia" and an African missionary from Gitarama, African Rights, *Rwanda*, 215, 570, 644, 802, 1055; Des Forges, *Kein Zeuge*, 553.
305 Account by Adalbert Munzingura, Hatzfeld, *Zeit*, 90.
306 Account by Alphonse Hitiyaremye, Hatzfeld, *Zeit*, 88–89.
307 Des Forges, *Kein Zeuge*, 448.
308 Account by Clémentine Murebwayre, Hatzfeld, *Zeit*, 102.
309 Account by Elie Mizinge, Hatzfeld, *Zeit*, 102.

Conclusion

More could be said about the soundscape in Rwanda in the months of the mass killings in 1994, such as the fact that most survivors – at least among those interviewed early on – heard shots, which were often intended to intimidate rather than kill; there were a startling number of grenade explosions; and people in hiding often listened to menacing footsteps nearby.

In this chapter, I have argued that many Hutu attackers in 1994 sought a new social order, which had both socioeconomic and normative aspects. Especially the poor among the murderers were committing murder for a better life, agricultural land or to gain a few possessions. Not much in the available acoustic evidence speaks of their fear and insecurity, despite the ongoing civil war and scholarly claims that they defended the existing political order, as justified as these may be. The attackers acted passionately, often in a festive mode, expressing themselves in secular rather than religious terms, but not because of an "atheism of fear".[310] The use of violence became a matter of prestige, perhaps of male attractiveness; however, unlike in the Chuknagar massacre and the COVID-19 pandemic (see chapters 3 and 7), one could not describe it as a 'cool' or relaxed demeanor.

The acoustic evidence also points to broader, long-run social trends in Rwanda. Whether it be the struggles among Hutus for the loot or Tutsis praying and singing religious songs alone or with laypersons, both were signs of growing individualism. Loud religious practice, screams of fear and emphatic crying in public, as well as shouts of hatred, anger and joy, reflected a trend toward emotionalism in Rwanda, which violated the older social norms of exercising restraint, a trend that had already been fueled by early 1990s party politics and, presumably, the social crisis of the late 1980s and the early 1990s, and one which found one expression in new, noisy religious rituals shared by Hutus and Tutsis in several protestant churches in the 21st century.[311] Narrowing circles of private social interaction (outside the church)[312] were not only in response to an authoritarian government but also driven by a growing distrust in everyday life. All of this is to say that there were social currents that outlasted the political-military defeat of Hutu power policies and the RPF victory in 1994 and encompassed Tutsis and Hutus, and were also made by them.

In many ways, Rwandans in 1994 were children of their time. A fascination with private radio stations, an active role of women, a tendency toward individual-

---

310 This contradicts Benda, *Test*, 180 (quote).
311 See Grant, "Noise".
312 For example, see Dumas, *Génocide*, 86.

ism and extrovert emotionalism and the drive for mass consumption even if one could not afford it (as most items that were robbed were fashionable consumer goods) were internationally shared experiences that came here into play under horrific circumstances, and these tendencies influenced some of the events.

The new order was not only loudly announced, it was also noisy and emphatic in itself. No wonder, then, that some survivors shuddered years afterward from hearing unknown people talk loudly[313] and that many survivors moved from dispersed houses into densely settled villages – official post-1994 villagization programs mainly covered Tutsis – and/or spent less time with their neighbors than before the mass murders.[314] Some even refused to talk for some time, or periodically, or said that they initially lost their speech.[315]

Important elements of what became the new social order for some months in 1994 were later politically and legally suppressed. Therefore, threatening ways of behavior toward survivors in the years to follow were silent (in anonymous letters) or, if loud, only acted out at night, when people would stone houses, knock at doors and windows or scream and then run away to not be identified.[316] Demonstrating that some social forces opposed the post-1994 political order, this was menacing, but no longer overt, reminders that aggressive social claims still existed.

Dealing with a different time period and place, the following chapter will use sound history again to expose the complex social interaction involved in mass violence even in a case that appears straightforward at first sight.

---

313 Account by Berthe Mwanankabandi, Hatzfeld, *Nur*, 175.
314 Hatzfeld, Zeit, 200; Dumas, Génocide, 86; for resettlement programs, see Bigagaza et al., "Land Scarcity", 75–76.
315 African Rights, *Rwanda*, 846, and account by Fortunata Ngirabutware, ibid., 350; account by "Angelique Isimbi", Totten and Ubaldo, *We*, 166.
316 Accounts by "Angelique Isimbi" and "Mugabo Arnaud", Totten and Ubaldo, *We*, 166, 186–189.

3 Sounds of a Massacre: Chuknagar, East Pakistan, 1971

This chapter aims to develop a new understanding of a large massacre by analyzing what survivors and witnesses heard, according to their later statements. This massacre occurred on May 20, 1971, at Chuknagar, East Pakistan, a large village about 30 km west of Khulna. It was part of the violent attempt by the Pakistani military government to suppress the Bangladeshi autonomy movement and prevent a secession from March 25 to December 16, 1971. A small, unidentified unit of Pakistani troops entered Chuknagar, where a crowd of thousands of predominantly Hindu people had gathered on their flight to India, and shot a large number of people, probably thousands, with most of them being Hindu male refugees.[1] It was an unprovoked mass killing of unarmed fellow citizens.

Why analyze a massacre? This term, it seems to me, has had more of a political than a scholarly career. In the academic literature, there seem to be two distinct concepts of 'massacre', a narrow one and an encompassing one. The latter understands massacre – usually appearing in the singular in such studies – as a chiffre for mass murder in general, which can be supra-local and of a longer duration (and may even turn into a legal category),[2] coming close to what is being called 'genocide'.[3] However, this is not what I am referring to here. Much of the study of massacre in the narrow sense has been concerned with the memory of

---

[1] An early brief mentioning of the killing is in "Over one lakh killed in Khulna alone", *Bangladesh Observer*, February 4, 1972, putting the number of victims at "at least 3,000". The massacre was rarely discussed in scholarship until the year 2000. But see another journalistic account (of 1972?): Gouranga Nandi, "Killing Fields in Khulna", in: *Tormenting Seventy One: An Account of Pakistany army's atrocities during Bangladesh liberation war of 1971*, ed. Shahriar Kabir (Dhaka: Nirmul Committee, 1999), www.mukto-mona.com/Special_Event_126-march/shahriar_kabir/Tormenting71_1.pdf (last accessed March 9, 2007). Both articles mentioned in this note specify that the victims were refugees but not that they were overwhelmingly Hindus, framing them as "Bengalis" instead. More recent treatments are in Sarmila Bose, *Dead Reckoning* (London: Hurst & Company, 2011), 115–125 and Salil Tripathi, *The Colonel Who Would Not Repent: The Bangladesh War and Its Unquiet Legacy* (New Delhi: Aleph, 2014), 118–125.

[2] See, for example, the considerations with reference to Jacques Sémelin in David El Kenz, "Présentation: le massacre, objet d'histoire" in *Le massacre, objet d'histoire*, ed. David El Kenz (Paris: Gallimard, 2005), 7–23, here 9. Eric Wenzel, "Introduction: Le massacre dans les méandres de l'histoire du droit", ibid., 25–45 and some chapters in Eric Carlton, *Massacres: An historical perspective* (Aldershot and Brookfield: Scholar Press, 1994) seem to follow this line of argument.

[3] See Jacques Semelin, "In consideration of massacres", *Journal of Genocide Research* 3, 3 (2001): 377–389, here 379.

Open Access. © 2024 the author(s), published by De Gruyter. This work is licensed under the Creative Commons Attribution-NonCommercial-NoDerivatives 4.0 International License.
https://doi.org/10.1515/9783111568737-003

and public discourse on massacres.⁴ Although informed by these aspects, this chapter does not follow this course either.

My brief study is not primarily concerned with violence in general, but rather with a specific form of it. One particular characteristic of a massacre is arguably the "physical proximity" between perpetrators and victims. Characterized by the unity of time and place, massacres represent a special kind of dramatic collective violent interaction.⁵ In fact, they have been called "public, performative acts".⁶ A massacre implies direct violence and a physicalness and close interaction that lets an inquiry into sounds appear productive. Among the questions with which researchers usually approach single mass slaughters, one pertains to the degree of organization and state control.⁷ Historians – this author is one – have been looking for specific characteristics of individual massacres instead of constant features. The question of why *this* massacre should be studied can be answered as follows: because of the special course of action in the case of Chuknagar, there were many survivors and, thus, more people who could tell the story than usual. This analysis provides insights into the persecution in East Pakistan, but may also be useful to raise questions concerning other mass killings, which could be further discussed.

However, there are problems with and limitations to the attempt to 'read' a massacre in a semiotic sense.⁸ Although violence is always also a communicative act, it is also true that in a context of organized mass violence, different violent methods may be used against one target group and by one group of persecutors, and the same method may be used against different groups. Therefore, the method may not be characteristic of the relationship between perpetrator and victim.⁹ Moreover, one of the questions connected with massacres that are usually asked is about why people kill.¹⁰ But massacres may be decided upon by politicians or func-

---

4 El Kenz, "Présentation", 14–18.
5 Mark Levene, "Introduction" in *The Massacre in History*, eds. Mark Levene and Penny Roberts (New York and Oxford: Berghahn, 1999), 6; Philip Dwyer and Lyndall Ryan, "The Massacre and History", *Theatres of Violence: Massacre, Mass Killing and Atrocity throughout History*, eds. Philip Dwyer and Lyndall Ryan (New York and Oxford: Berghahn, 2012), xiii–xiv.
6 Dwyer and Randall, "Massacre", xviii.
7 Levene, "Introduction", 13; Dwyer and Ryan, *Massacre*.
8 One example is Christian Ingrao, *Hitlers Elite* (Berlin: Propyläen, 2012), 241–314.
9 See Christian Gerlach, *The Extermination of the European Jews* (Cambridge et al.: Cambridge University Press, 2016), 140.
10 Carlton, *Massacres*, 1–3, 167–177 discusses this and other possible questions. The question of motives is also central to Christopher Browning, *Ordinary Men* (New York: HarperCollins, 1993) and Daniel Goldhagen, *Hitler's Willing Executioners* (New York: Vintage Books, 1997), both dealing with German mass shootings of Jews in Poland on the basis of problematic material.

tionaries far away from the perpetrator units dispatched to carry them out, so studying the latter may do little to explain why people were killed. Studying the violent acts themselves, as many scholars suggest,[11] tells analysts more about the 'how' and performative aspects than the 'why'. Importantly, it is also telling of the experiences and responses of victims, survivors and witnesses.

This is remarkable because many studies of massacres concentrate on the perpetrator side.[12] However, the fact that Pakistan never acknowledged the slaughter at Chuknagar (which is telling about the state of Pakistani government and society), that there is no documentation by, and about, those who carried it out, and that there are no pictures, creates an opportunity to change perspectives, look at – or rather listen from – the direction of those under attack, inquire into their experiences and use their accounts in a novel manner.

This chapter uses the approach of sound history. It reconstructs sounds from written texts, as is an established historical practice. Who tapes the sounds of a mass killing anyway? Historians have to work in the absence of recordings of this kind. This, however, creates some problems. Narratives do not equal perception at the time, which may have been selective anyway; memory and representation are additional filters that may distort what once was the actual experience.

Given that sound history is used here to generate findings beyond noises, not all considerations in this chapter stay within the realm of aural experience. I ask what the noises of the massacre in Chuknagar are telling about its performative and communicative aspects; what the acoustic experience reveals about social interaction and relations between those involved, between and within groups; which emotions can be traced and how they were expressed or could not be expressed through sounds; what role religious practice played; and how community ties or their absence were audible. In addition, I consider what acoustic omissions there are in the narratives. In this manner, this chapter attempts to show how mass violence is constituted by social interaction and what characterized the social situation in Chuknagar on that day.

---

11 See Trutz von Trotha, ed., *Soziologie der Gewalt* (Opladen: Westdeutscher Verlag, 1997); Alexander Laban Hinton, ed., *Annihilating Difference: The Anthropology of Genocide* (Berkeley et al.: University of California Press, 2002).
12 See for example the research questions formulated in Jacques Sémelin, "Analyser le massacre: Reflexions comparatives", *Questions de Recherche* no. 7, 2012, 1–42, esp. 4, 32–33; Dwyer and Randall, *Massacre*.

Sources

The material this chapter is based on is a collection of 90 accounts by survivors and witnesses. This was the result of Bangladeshi researchers gathering such people in September 2000 and letting them provide public statements in Chuknagar and Khulna during a two-day event. Out of the 200 statements that were made, 90 were selected and published in a book in Bengali in 2001 that was translated into English in 2013.[13]

On the one hand, this material is highly valuable because it provides many angles of listening: by locals and refugees; Hindus and Muslims; men, women and children at the time; and people of different classes and trades. Unlike other recollections pertaining to the conflict in East Pakistan in 1971 (this is similar to many other cases of mass violence), the sample is not dominated by well-educated middle-class Muslim urbanites (but it is dominated by male accounts and includes only 25 women).[14] The selection of reports is special because it encompasses many poor, lowly educated people. Even beyond the conflict in East Pakistan, I am not aware of any massacre in history for which so many accounts are available, at least not in such a concentrated form.[15] In any case, this provides a rare opportunity.

On the other hand, the material is problematic in several respects. It was compiled 29 years after the events when peoples' memories had possibly faded or become distorted and many had probably already told their story many times. These are not sources in a strictly historical sense, but representations in retrospect. Further, most of the text of the printed statements, although grammatically first-person accounts, seems to consist of summaries, judging from occasional stretches of text put in quotation marks that seem to indicate word-by-word reproduction. The texts appear to be based on interviewers' notes and not tape recordings.[16] Many of the statements are laconic, being only a page long. Moreover, the text was – badly – translated from Bengali (a language that I unfortunately am not in command of) into English, a process through which nuances of sound description may have gotten lost. The procedure through which this material came about is also questionable, as there were introductory speeches condemning Pakistan and helpers of the Pakistani government of 1971, whether Bengali or from minorities; the organizers tried to frame the Chuknagar incident as the sin-

---

13 Muntassir Mamoon, ed., *1971 Chuknagar Genocide*, 2nd ed. (Dhaka: University Press Publishers, 2014). Quoted: MM.
14 16 persons in the sample appear to be Muslim.
15 This excludes Hiroshima and Nagasaki, if the use of the Atomic bomb there could be called a massacre.
16 See Hasina Ahmed et al., "Compilers' Note", in *MM*, 19–20.

gle biggest massacre during the entire conflict, calling it "Chuknagar genocide"; and the statements were made in front of groups of other locals.[17] As a result, many people may have felt inhibited about talking frankly and may have complied to certain narratives.[18] The "Chuknagar genocide" has been being used as part of a larger narrative of a Pakistani "genocide" against Bengalis in general. What survivors and also witnesses presented were narratives of pain, suffering, victimization and accusal.

Context: The Conflict and Mass Killings in East Pakistan in 1971

In March 1971 cultural and economic tensions between Pakistan and the especially poor, marginalized and geographically isolated eastern wing of the country (contemporary Bangladesh) erupted.[19] In late 1970, the Awami League, a political party with social-democratic rhetoric that spearheaded the autonomy movement in East Pakistan, won an absolute majority of seats in parliament elections for all Pakistan through a sweeping victory in the east where more than half of the country's population lived. Afraid of secession, West Pakistani elites, including the ruling military junta, delayed the lawful takeover of the Awami League. When President Yahya Khan announced the indefinite postponement of the opening of parliament in early March 1971, most East Pakistanis suspected betrayal, and the Awami League adopted a policy of non-cooperation in East Pakistan and controlled the administration and public life. Confrontations between Bengali civilians and Pakistani troops, police, West Pakistanis and so-called Biharis (i.e., non-Bengali speakers who were former refugees from India and collectively accused in 1971 of siding with the Pakistani regime) claimed several thousand lives within weeks in riot-like skirmishes. On 25 March 1971, the military started a crackdown to crush the autonomy movement, ruthlessly using tanks and fighter jets in their own country.

Within days, the relatively weak military units (less than 50,000 in a province with a population of 70 million) split between Bengalis and West Pakistanis and

---

[17] See reports about the event in *MM*, 175–191; and the critical appraisal by Bose, *Dead Reckoning*, 116.

[18] For some of the pressures involved in public statements about one's own persecution of 1971 in 1990s Bangladesh, with special reference to rape, see Nayanika Mookherjee, *The Spectral Wound: Sexual Violence, Public Memory and the Bangladesh War of 1971* (Durham and London: Duke University Press, 2015), 68.

[19] For the following two paragraphs, see Gerlach, *Extremely Violent Societies*, 123–176. See also chapter 4 in this volume.

turned to infighting. The pro-Pakistani troops, at first confined to a few large cities, defeated their opponents, taking control of the province within four weeks. They also killed civilians from the first night, including many intellectuals; Awami League functionaries; Hindus (a 15-percent minority in the province) who were collectively suspected of supporting India and, thus, autonomy or secession; and, increasingly, rural dwellers once guerrilla activity started. Among the troops, anti-Bengali and anti-Hindu sentiments were strong. In the complex conflict that ensued, mutual massacres between Bengalis and Biharis occurred, along with instances of violence by local pro-Pakistani militias, guerrilla attacks, Muslim neighbors turning against Hindus, looting and struggles for land, and widespread rape of women and girls by troops but also civilians. Ten million people (most of whom were Hindus) took refuge in India and up to 15 million (who were largely Muslims) fled within the province. Hundreds of thousands were killed, and many also died in a famine that primarily claimed the lives of small children and old people of rural poor in 1971 and 1972. In December 1971, an Indian invasion with the help of pro-Bangladesh fighters put an end of Pakistani rule within weeks, and the state of Bangladesh was founded.

The designer of the Pakistani re-conquest of the province was Lieutenant-General Amir Abdullah Khan Niazi. According to his scheme, the troops, after defeating the insurgents in cities and towns, should fan out in small units and rapidly advance radially toward the border to terrify the 'enemy' and cause them to flee.[20] The last phase of Niazi's plan involved "combing out the whole province" including the countryside.[21] In May, the time for it had come. It was a central point in Niazi's strategy to sow panic, to the point that he proposed to a superior in June 1971 to bomb a metropole like Calcutta, India.[22]

In April, informants to the West German consulate general in the area of Khulna and Jessore agreed that the army had searched cities systematically after the conquest and killed all Hindus that they found (to reiterate, Chuknagar is in the Khulna area).[23] A critical Pakistani journalist reported similar procedures for villages in the province of East Pakistan that he had visited in the spring of 1971.[24] During May, the U.S. consulate in Dacca called the fact that army troops entered

---

20 Gerlach, *Extremely Violent Societies*, 141–142.
21 A.A.K Niazi, *The Betrayal of East Pakistan* (Karachi et al.: Oxford University Press, 1998), 60.
22 Niazi, *Betrayal*, 65–66.
23 Deutsches Generalkonsulat Dacca, "Lage in Ostpakistan", April 17, 1971, Politisches Archiv des Auswärtigen Amtes, Berlin, B37/630.
24 Anthony Mascarenhas, *The Rape of Bangla Desh* (Delhi et al.: Vikas, n.y. [1971]), 117.

villages in East Pakistan to search for and kill Hindu men a "common pattern".[25] In the week between May 14 and 21, 1971 (which was right around the time when events in Chuknagar were occurring), army units destroyed Hindu villages near Nagari to the north of Dacca, killing and wounding many people, burning houses and producing thousands of refugees.[26] In June 1971, 'World Bank' officials also reported the large-scale destruction of housing by fire in villages in the areas of Khulna, Jessore and Kushtia.[27] The practice of army squads storming villages, killing Hindu men, looting and burning their homes appears to have continued in June.[28] Again, there must have been many survivors and witnesses.

During the counterinsurgency operations in the countryside, the most frequent pattern that was observed was that military units gathered villagers, separated men from women and children and killed all or part of the former and especially Hindu men.[29] But there were also reports of more chaotic scenes where soldiers shot down villagers running away in panic.[30] Such incidents took place during the Jinjira massacre where large crowds of displaced persons were shot with machine guns and shelled on April 1, 1971, with many women and children among the victims.[31] A recent survey study of 100 massacres in Bangladesh in 1971 found that 42 percent of the persons identified among those killed were Hindus, 3.55 percent were women, and 3 percent were minors under 16. Over 90 percent of those killed were men aged 16–60.[32] The events at Chuknagar were probably the army's largest attack on refugees, but other, smaller ones often happened closer to the Indian border.[33]

On May 20, 1971, thousands of refugees had gathered in the village of Chuknagar west of Khulna.[34] Many of them had come by boat through the river Bhadra

---

25 Archer Blood, *The Cruel Birth of Bangladesh* (Dhaka: University Press, 2002), 217–220, quote 217 from a telegram of May 14.
26 James and Marti Hefley, *Christ in Bangladesh* (New York et al.: Harper Row, 1973), 45–46.
27 *Thousand My Lais: World Bank Study on Bangladesh* (n.p., n.y. [1971]), 15.
28 See Sydney Schanberg, "East Pakistan: An 'Alien Army' Imposes Its Will", *New York Times*, July 4, 1971.
29 Gerlach, *Extremely Violent Societies*, 141–144.
30 Prabodh Chandra, *Bloodbath in Bangla Desh* (Delhi: Adarsh, n.y. [1971]), 159.
31 See Kalyan Chaudhuri, *Genocide in Bangladesh* (Bombay et al.: Orient Longman, 1972), 32–33; A. M. A. Muhith, *Bangladesh: Emergence of a Nation* (Dacca: Bangladesh Books International, 1978), 223.
32 See Shahid Kader Chowdhury, "Age, Gender and Religion of the Victims of the Bangladesh Genocide", *Jagannath University Journal of Arts* 11, 1 (2021).
33 Chaudhuri, *Genocide*, 93; Gerlach, *Extremely Violent Societies*, 138; for the treatment of Hindus ibid., 144–148.
34 This paragraph is based on *MM*.

to continue their flight to India on foot or on buses. They crowded a lowland area at the riverbank, as well as areas near the bazaar, a bus stop and some buildings in town. In the late morning, at around 10 or 11 a.m., a squad of Pakistani soldiers arrived near the bazaar on two to four trucks, dismounted and swiftly started shooting. They split up in several groups, one or two of which advanced to the river, whereas at least one other hunted for victims in the village, searching buildings. The troops were focused on killing Hindu males between the ages of 15 and 60 years. Hindu men, rather than being interrogated, were killed on the spot, which means what they had done or had not done hardly mattered. In cases of doubt concerning a man's identity, the soldiers checked whether he was circumcised (and, thus, presumably Muslim). Many were shot at short range. At the riverbank, the troops lined up male refugees in an improvised manner and tried to shoot them all.

However, then, as at other locations in Chuknagar, a panic set in, people began to run away screaming and tried to hide. The soldiers attempted to find Hindus in their hiding places and kill them at close range. Some, including people who were wounded, were bayonetted to death. Especially near the riverside, however, the perpetrators also shot at people from some distance in situations where they were running away, swimming in the river or trying to hide under water in ponds. As a result, aside from those who were killed, many were left wounded and women and children were hit in the process, too, some of them fatally. Many people, particularly children, also drowned. Several Muslims also ended up getting shot. Most victims were refugees, whereas most local residents, including Hindus, managed to evade the troops and hide. The massacre ended in the early afternoon, at around 3 or 4 p.m. The survivors describe horrible scenes, with corpses and dying people lying everywhere in great numbers, many of which had portions of their skulls blown away or their entrails falling out.

From a genocide studies perspective, this would appear as a clear case: a state-organized mass killing, selectively directed against a religious minority. It resembled, though not entirely, several smaller killings that took place in the same area on May 19 to 21, 1971.[35] However, an analysis of the sounds involved makes the event at Chuknagar appear more complex and less straightforward.

---

35 Possibly the same unit committed a smaller massacre against male Hindu refugees in Jhaudanga further west, closer to the border, in the early morning of the same day. Bose, *Dead Reckoning*, 117. A large mass shooting of a crowd of thousands of civilian refugees on the way to the border quite similar to that in Chuknagar seems to have happened at Dakra (about 50 km east of Chuknagar) on the following day. There, 20–25 razakars (pro-Pakistani militias) arrived on two boats and opened fire. See "Dakra massacre", https://en.wikipedia.org/wiki/Dakra_massacre (last accessed March 9, 2017). In Badantola, 40 km west of Chuknagar, persons described as "followers

Evidence: Behavior of Soldiers

Unsurprisingly, the sounds most frequently mentioned in the accounts came from the shooting. Many persons stated that they tried to locate the shots in space, recalling from which direction they heard them and how far away the shooting was. Some also said that it seemed to come closer.[36] Usually, the people identified the sounds as shooting, which is not a given[37] and testifies to the hearing competence and alertness of those present (except for one little boy who said that his family first mistook shots for another noise).[38] One local Muslim said that he had been afraid before that a shooting might happen.[39]

The shots were reportedly fired from semi-automatic weapons and LMGs. Many stated that they heard shots coming without interruption for a long duration. The witnesses (or interviewers) often described the Pakistani troops as firing "ceaselessly"[40] or "incessantly".[41] One stated: "We heard the firing like an incessant rain", a man who was 15 years old at the time referred to it as a "brushfire", while a man who was aged 31 in 1971 recalled: "In the torrents of bullets I started crying."[42] Sometimes, the shooting appeared inescapable, surrounding the person; one woman (then a girl of 16) spoke about "the noise of gunshots coming from every direction", one who was six years old at the time said: "Bullets were coming from all sides [. . .] Such a rain of bullets was it."[43] Even from a large distance, it was loud: "The Pakistani army came loaded in two trucks. 'They opened fired [sic!] the air was filled with tremendous noises. Every minute the noise was changing. I was about half a mile from the spot of [the] massacre and standing behind a tree watched the situation [sic!].'"[44]

---

of the pro-Pakistan Muslim League" massacred over 100 people, predominantly non-locals (presumably refugees), on May 19, one day before the slaughter at Chuknagar. Salil Tripathi, "Blood in the water: The contested history of one of Bangladesh's worst wartime massacres", November 1, 2014, http://www.caravanmagazine.in/essay/blood-water, last accessed November 2, 2017.

36 For example, account by Purno Chandra Roy, *MM*, 24.
37 For example, see James Lastra, "Reading, Writing and Representing Sounds", *Sound Theory, Sound Practice*, ed. Rick Altman (London and New York: Routledge, 1992), 68–69.
38 Account by Someer Biswas, *MM*, 162.
39 Account by Mohammad Sher Ali Sardar, *MM*, 42.
40 Accounts by Purno Chandra Roy and Kalidashi Mondol, *MM*, 24, 52.
41 Accounts by Horipodo Mondol and Ruhidas Chandra Roy, *MM*, 26, 51, see also account by Shorola Mondol, *MM*, 160.
42 Accounts by Atiar Rahman, Monoj Kanti Roy and Bolaj Goldar, *MM*, 87, 117, 149. Harendra Nash Gain in MM, 69, called it "incessant brush fire".
43 Accounts by Bukul Roy and Shorola Mondolin, *MM*, 113, 160; see also Shuvash Chandra Tarakder, *MM*, 158.
44 Account by Bolaj Krishna Kundu, *MM*, 33. Spelling as in the original.

By contrast, the sound of military trucks was mentioned very rarely[45] although several speakers were located close enough to hear them and described the scene of their arrival. This sound may have not been so remarkable because there was, for instance, a bus service in the village, so the sounds of big motor vehicles were normal. In fact, one survivor said that many had left Chuknagar on the morning of May 20 for India by bus.[46]

Genocide studies assign a great deal of importance to inciteful propaganda, usually spread through mass media, which is viewed as a crucial transmission belt between genocidal ideas and action. Some families in Chuknagar probably did have radio sets, and at least one refugee mentioned having listened to disquieting radio news about the Bangladesh conflict, "seeking the latest information".[47] However, none of the accounts from Chuknagar mentions the troops contributing to the propaganda, and none speaks about having heard Pakistani radio propaganda against Hindus or other groups.[48] This is all the more worth mentioning as I have made a similar observation concerning survivors' accounts of German violence against Jews and villagers in the course of anti-guerrilla warfare during World War II, as well as regarding survivors of the mass violence in Indonesia in 1965.[49]

The absence of another sound is notable. It seems that, for the most part, the Pakistani soldiers were not shouting in Chuknagar (which was, for instance, in stark contrast to many Germans persecuting Jews in the early 1940s[50]). Just one out of 90 accounts mentions that "one or two military men" ran to a house with

---

45 Account by Meena Gain, *MM*, 127.
46 Account by Shuvash Chandra Roy, *MM*, 78. See also Ashutosh Nandi, *MM*, 91.
47 The available information about the ownership of radio sets in East Pakistan/Bangladesh is contradictory. One source speaks of only 300,000 sets in 1974, but another mentions that 17.2 percent of all households owned a set in 1961, a percentage that had risen markedly by 1974, including in the district of Khulna where Chuknagar was located; see Ian Smillie, *Freedom from Want: The Remarkable Story of BRAC, the Global Grassroots Organization That's Winning the Fight Against Poverty* (Sterling: Kumarian, 2009), 35; M. A. Taiyeb Chowdhury, *Dimensions of Development and Change in Bangladesh, 1960–1980*, Ph.D dissertation, University of Western Ontario, 1988, 213, 216–218. Quote: account by Purno Chandra Roy, *MM*, 23.
48 For examples of Pakistani propaganda at the time, see Government of Pakistan, *White Paper on the Crisis in East Pakistan* (n.p., August 5, 1971); *Pakistan News Digest* of December 1 and 15, 1971, National Archive of Australia 189/10/7, part 1. See also Siddiq Salik, *Witness to Surrender* (Karachi: Lancer, 1998; first 1977), an account by a PR officer of the Pakistani army.
49 In the sample used for Gerlach, "Echoes", very few mention Nazi radio propaganda. See also Christian Gerlach, "Indonesian narratives of survival in and after 1965 and their relation to societal persecution", *The Palgrave Handbook of Anti-Communist Persecutions*, eds. Christian Gerlach and Clemens Six (Cham: Palgrave Macmillan, 2020), 453.
50 See Gerlach, "Echoes".

100 to 125 refugees inside "and shouted, 'Here you come, Malaun' (*Malaun* is the slang for Hindus usually used by Muslims)."[51] Another account states: "We saw the vehicles carrying the Pak[istani] army to halt [sic!]. They had arrived just [with]in 10–15 minutes after our arrival [at the riverbank]. There was a roar from everywhere, 'Raise your hands, raise your hands!'"[52] These shouts could have been uttered either by the Pakistani military or by persons among the refugees, part of whom, as many said, surrendered, presented themselves to the military and stood in rows, hoping to be left unharmed. All of them were mowed down sometime later. Given the low number of Pakistani troops present, their shouts could also hardly have come from "everywhere". Two other accounts – although only one is from a witness of the scene described – mention in addition that Pakistani soldiers laughed after killing men and also a few protesting women while leaving other women alive.[53]

No other account mentions any audible emotional involvement of the Pakistani troops. Moreover, it seems that beatings were rarely meted out. No whips, sticks and truncheons were mentioned. More typical are statements that the soldiers pulled people, usually women or children, away from men and shot the latter from short range, and that they spoke little, if at all, to civilians. Khuku Rani Joardar recalled that "[t]hey did not say anything to the women and and children" while killing her husband, his brothers and her sister's husband.[54] Another description reads: "At that moment the army came [and] without any word opened fire on them [refugees at the bazaar]."[55] It should be added that there seems to have been little vandalism by the troops. However, the statements disagree upon how many houses (of Hindu families) were burned down, with some stating three and others an entire neighborhood.[56]

Taken together, this information regarding sounds implies that the Pakistani troops conducted the mass killing at Chuknagar in cold blood, behaving partially in accordance with the self-image of the Pakistani army conveyed in memoirs of

---

[51] Account by Mukundo Bihari Roy, *MM*, 114–115. Another example of soldiers shouting, but outside of the village, in order to call his father to them who was then shot is mentioned by Ershad Ali, as described in Tripathi, *Colonel*, 119.
[52] Account by Bukul Roy, *MM*, 113.
[53] Account by Shomoresh Mondol (a boy who was 12 years old in 1971), *MM*, 124; cf. account by A. B. M. Safiqul Islam, *MM*, 156.
[54] *MM*, 83.
[55] Account by Anil Krisno Roy, *MM*, 37.
[56] Account by Ashutosh Nandi (three houses), Arobindo Das ("many"), Shontosh Das ("some") and Shohorjan Bibi (the weaver's neighborhood), *MM*, 90, 154, 171, 174.

military officers: professional, well-disciplined and efficient.[57] This is part of their self-representation as an inherently superior Muslim elite that coolly and soberly fights even when being outnumbered or outmatched, a myth that seems to have been somehow paradoxically reinforced by Pakistan's failure to decisively win any of its wars.[58] Such a claim to professionalism has also been observed in other units committing mass murder, such as Nazi German mobile killing units,[59] although these engaged in a lot of shouting and cursing. From the sounds, it appears that the Pakistani troops at Chuknagar found themselves cool and behaved with the habitus of an elite, which was also meant to set them apart from the villagers, to whom they felt superior.

However, not everything supports this impression. To consider this, one must move partially beyond the history of sounds. To begin with, none of the witnesses reported hearing any orders among the military personnel. Hierarchical organization would probably be one of the characteristics that define the Pakistani army's self-image. A different piece of evidence that contradicts the self-representation of the army's cool, professional discipline concerns the rapes of women and girls in 1971 for which the Pakistani troops were notorious and which are also said to have taken place in Chuknagar, although only according to a few statements. One witness claimed to have actually seen rape taking place, another the abduction of several women when the troops left.[60]

Many witnesses said that the Pakistani soldiers largely shot Hindu men who were approximately between 15 and 60 years old. But since the killers did not herd the victims together and thousands ran away to try hiding in buildings, behind or on trees, and under water, the troops often shot from greater distances and at times with no clear vision of the target. This may explain why some said that the soldiers were shooting "haphazardly" or "indiscriminately".[61] As a result, they killed a considerable number of women and children, while many were left

---

57 See Salik, *Witness*; Niazi, *Betrayal*; Hakeem Arshad Qureshi, *The 1971 Indo-Pak War: A Soldier's Narrative* (Oxford et al.: Oxford University Press, 2002).
58 See. C. Christine Fair, *Fighting to the End: The Pakistan Army's Way of War* (Oxford et al.: Oxford University Press, 2014), esp. 8, 88, 99, 165. Stephen Cohen attributes this attitude in particular to what he calls the "American generation" of military personnel that dominated the Pakistani army around 1971: Stephen Cohen, *The Pakistan Army* (Oxford et al.: Oxford University Press, 4th ed. 2002), esp. 64, 69, 86, 90.
59 See Andrej Angrick, *Besatzungspolitik und Massenmord: Die Einsatzgruppe D in der Sowjetunion 1941–1943* (Hamburg: Hamburger Edition, 2003), 236.
60 Accounts by Mukundu Bihari Roy and Monoj Kanti Roy, *MM*, 116, 118. A recent study on rapes in this conflict in general is Mookherjee, *Spectral Wound*.
61 See acounts by Monoranjon Roy, Ruhidas Chandra Roy and Shuvash Chandra Tarafder, *MM*, 35, 51, 158.

wounded. The people included in the sample mentioned that 20 female relatives or acquaintances were killed, nearly 10 percent of the identified victims.[62] Sometimes the soldiers also shot while marching,[63] which must have compromised selective aiming.

The editor of the interviews estimated that 6,000 to 10,000 people were murdered in the Chuknagar massacre.[64] These figures have been challenged by a critic, given that most witnesses agreed that the number of perpetrators was only between 20 and 40, who had arrived on only up to four vehicles. This would mean, as she objected, that each soldier and officer would have killed 150 to 500 people within about five hours.[65] Was this possible, and could they have even carried so much ammunition? (Nobody mentions that troops were supplied from their trucks, or were supplying themselves, with additional ammunition.) Witness testimonies concerning the overall figure of people killed vary greatly and appear largely speculative. But several facts do indicate that people were killed in four-digit numbers. There is no doubt that Chuknagar was packed with thousands of refugees at the time. One Muslim man who worked with others to dump corpses into the river on May 21 stated that they disposed of 4,200 bodies, according to an incomplete count.[66] The 90 interviewees alone mentioned that 195 relatives and acquaintances known by name were killed (the 74 Hindus interviewed mentioned 193 of these victims; a few of these are double counts).[67] In addition, according to other accounts, soldiers said that they did not shoot women for lack of ammunition and that they spared people in the end, perhaps including men, because they ran out of bullets.[68]

In any case, while operationally the mass shooting in Chuknagar may appear efficient from the perspective of the Pakistani army, strategically it was in part counterproductive. From April to June 1971, the dominant strategy of the Pakis-

---

[62] My count based on *MM*. According to similar figures in Chowdhury, "Age", 8 percent of the identified victims at Chuknagar were women (5 of 62).

[63] For example, see account by Jitendro Mistree, *MM*, 164.

[64] Muntassir Mamoon, "Introduction", *MM*, 8.

[65] Bose, *Dead Reckoning*, 124–125 suggests a number of victims in the hundreds.

[66] Account by Ali Badsha, *MM*, 152. But this estimate can be questioned. According to Abul Bashar Mohammend Shafiqul Islam, 44 men worked removing the corpses, each removed 100 (which seems to be an assumption), and this is the basis of his estimate that 4,400 bodies were disposed of, not counting others washed away by the river, etc. Tripathi, *Colonel*, 122.

[67] My count based on *MM*. Chowdhury, "Age" once spoke of 62 identified victims at Chuknagar and at another point only of 37. Both figures are surprisingly low.

[68] Accounts by Kalidahi Mondol and Someer Biswas, *MM*, 52, 162. Ershad Ali, a witness also included in *MM* (54–55), mentions eight more Muslim deaths – among them five being children –, as described in Tripathi, *Colonel*, 119–120.

tani troops was to drive Hindus out of the province by arbitrary killings, sexual violence and looting in cities and countryside, prompting them to flee to India. In total, 7 to 9 million Hindus escaped to India within a few months.[69] Even at Chuknagar, the army squad did not want to kill all Hindus (otherwise, they would have needed to organize the massacre differently); instead, it wanted to spread terror. Yet, numerous Hindu survivors of the massacre in Chuknagar, who had been on their way to India, reconsidered and stayed in East Pakistan or deferred their flight because they were robbed of their possessions during the massacre, their relatives needed immediate medical attention or the loss of close relatives made them return home fatalistically, regardless of would happen to them.[70] Matching this 'failure', nobody within the Pakistani military seems to have ever taken responsibility for the massacre.[71]

However, many people who were not directly affected were possibly prompted to flee from other places after hearing the news about this mass murder, although I have no evidence to support this. After all, the carnage at Chuknagar was very much unlike what Wolfgang Sofsky described as the epitome of a massacre (without spelling out his sources and probably mainly expressing his phantasies): total destruction of the target population, their homes and their memory, without leaving survivors, very much like conceptions of genocide.[72] On the contrary, often perpetrators do not try to cover up a massacre; instead, they seek publicity and media coverage for it, which has been practiced for centuries.[73] The Chuknagar slaughter was contradictory in this light: never officially acknowledged, not accompanied by propaganda (or hardly even by words) and without leaving pictures, trophies and graves, it did by necessity produce so many survivors that it can hardly be understood as anything but an act of intimidation, terror, and, thus, communication. On the acoustic level, then, the medium of communication was the shots, which remained so vivid in civilians' memory.

---

69 See Gerlach, *Extremely Violent Societies*, 136–140.
70 Accounts by Kamola Roy, Monoranjon Roy, Nogor Biswas, Aswini Kumar Mondol, Ruhidas Chandra Roy, Kalidashi Mondol, Srimoti Anarotee Tarafdar, Krisnopodo Roy, Khuku Rani Joardar, Nirmul Kumar Roy, Swaramati Mondol, Komol Kanti Biswas, Bimol Mondol, Binoy Roy, Khokon Roy, Shomoresh Mondol, Saraswati Mondol, Aynamoti Golder, Sree Ashok Mollick, Mukundo Bihari Roy, Someer Biswas and Rajkumar Roy, *MM*, 27, 35–36, 44–45, 46–47, 51, 52, 53, 66–67, 83, 85, 86, 100, 105, 110, 119, 123–124, 126, 129–130, 138, 142–143, 163, 167.
71 Bose, *Dead Reckoning*, 125.
72 Wolfgang Sofsky, *Traktat über die Gewalt* (Frankfurt a.M.: Fischer, 1996), chapter "Das Massaker", 176–190, esp. 176–177. As a side note, what Sofsky describes resembles very much a long scene in Elem Klimovs film *Come and See* (1985), which is discussed in chapter 5 of this book.
73 See Christine Vogel, "Einleitung", *Bilder des Schreckens: Die mediale Inszenierung von Massakern seit dem 16. Jahrhundert* (Frankfurt a.M. and New York: Campus, 2006), 7–14, here 8.

On the Victims' Side

Civilians' most common reactions to the events involved crying, wailing and screaming. This mostly happened after the shooting when women, as well as men, were horrified and grief-stricken because of the violence and the loss of their relatives.[74] Women were also described as "howling" after the killings,[75] or such sounds were attributed to groups or crowds rather than individuals, including to wounded people. "We then lifted the dead bodies from the pond, the air was filled with screams, wails and screaming", Pushpo Rani Roy stated.[76] People cried, wailed and screamed during the massacre as well. Recalling how they fled by boat, Atiar Rahman described: "It was only the sound of howls that pierced our ears".[77] According to an earlier account by A. B. M. Shafiqul Islam concerning the events that took place at the market, "Repeated brush fire by the troops made the entire crowd quiet for a brief period. A few moments later, screaming of the victims created a terrible scene there."[78] During the massacre, many called for help.[79] Often, it was severely injured men who asked or, according to one statement, "shrieked" for water (a reference to the last rites in Hinduism before death) and died soon afterward.[80] Meena Gain, who was 11 in 1971, could not forget the last thing her father, who was hit in the head by a bullet, uttered to her mother, stating: "Whenever I recall that 'ma', that sad last cry of my father, fire runs through my blood."[81]

It is beyond the scope of this chapter to go into detail regarding the scholarship on the history of crying. Suffice it to say that weeping does not simply equal emotion, although emotions are often involved. Practices of weeping are not nec-

---

[74] About women: accounts by Purno Chandra Roy, Ershad Ali Morol, Bukul Dashi, Komola Jowardar, Mukundo Bihari Roy, Sree Ashok Mollick and Shuraf Chandra Tarafder, *MM*, 24, 54, 57, 82, 115, 138, 159. About men: accounts by Ershad Ali Morol, Krisnopodo Roy, Mukundo Bihari Roy, Bolai Goldar and Jogodish Das, *MM*, 55, 66, 143, 149, 169. For screaming and crying children, see the accounts by Bolai Krishna Kundu, Shomoresh Mondol and Aynamoti Golder, *MM*, 33, 123, 130.
[75] Account by Komol Kanti Biswas, *MM*, 100. For a man who "howled", see account by Shomoresh Mondol, *MM*, 123.
[76] *MM*, 141. See also the accounts by Shomoresh Mondol, S.M. Atiar Rahman, Monimohon Roy and Arobindo Das, *MM*, 123, 137, 148, 154.
[77] *MM*, 87. See also the accounts by Kamola Roy, Gopal Krisno Sarkar and Bimol Mondol, *MM*, 27, 102, 104.
[78] Quoted in Nandi, "Killing Fields".
[79] Accounts by Probodh Chandra Roy and Shorola Mondol, *MM*, 62, 160.
[80] Accounts by Md. Ansar Ali Sardar, Shomoresh Mondol, Monimohon Roy, Tulaiboti Boiragi and Shorola Mondol, *MM*, 70, 123 (quote), 148, 151, 161.
[81] *MM*, 127.

essarily natural but depend on culture, habits, era and even fashion, along with religious dogma, rites and an individual's age and social role. Tears are a way of communication, often enacted, highly ambiguous and multifunctional.[82] All of this makes weeping and crying an important topic of historical inquiry, although it is strongly under-researched. That said, some of the crying during and after the Chuknagar massacre was apparently automatic, involuntary, and indicative of strong emotional involvement: above all, stress, pain, fear and terror. In addition, much of the weeping at Chuknagar was collective, reconfirming family ties.[83]

A few survivors report that they were asked not to cry but to save themselves, or to stop crying for other reasons, although no restraint on religious grounds is mentioned.[84] One man was threatened with sticks by residents who told him not to cry because they were afraid that the army would come and start another shooting.[85] Another said regretfully: "One has to cry when one's father is dead. But the Almighty didn't grant us that time."[86] When the massacre was going on, children were crying or screaming out of fear, heat or hunger. Many adults felt that this endangered them because it could attract the attention of the shooters.[87] Some parents, trying to silence their children, threw them into a pond or the river or held them under water so that some drowned.[88] In this context, crying appeared as a

---

[82] See Tom Lutz, Crying: *The Natural and Cultural History of Tears* (New York and London: W.W. Norton, 1999); Thomas Dixon, *Weeping Britannia* (Oxford et al.: Oxford University Press, 2015); Anne Vincent-Buffault, *The History of Tears: Sensibility and Sentimentality in France* (Basingstoke and London: Macmillan, 1991); Kimberley Christine Patton and John Stratton Hawley, eds., *Holy Tears: Weeping in the Religious Imagination* (Princeton and Oxford: Princeton University Press, 2005).

[83] For a summary of influential anthropological studies that emphasize that death rituals, including collective crying, strengthen social ties in various cultures, see for example Peter Metcalf and Richard Huntington, *Celebrations of Death: The Anthropology of Mortuary Ritual* (New York et al.: Cambridge University Press 1991), 43–61.

[84] Accounts by Ershad Ali Morol, Komol Kanti Biswas and Shomoresh Mondol, *MM*, 54, 100, 124. Like other religions, Hinduist teachings discourage weeping and crying when a person dies, but crying is nonetheless customary then: Shirley Firth, *Dying, Death and Bereavement in a British Hindu Community* (Leuven: Peeters, 1997), 67–68, 143; Axel Michaels, *Der Hinduismus* (Munich: Beck, 1998), 153; but see John Stratton Hawley, "The Gopis' Tears" in Patton and Hawley, *Holy Tears*, 94–111.

[85] Account by Jogodish Das, *MM*, 169.

[86] Account by Rabindranath Boiragi, *MM*, 106. This part is marked in the text as literal quote.

[87] Accounts by Bolai Krishna Kundu, Md. Nazrul Islam Sarder, S.M. Atiar Rahman and Rajkumar Roy, *MM*, 33, 120, 136, 166.

[88] Accounts by Kali Dashi Roy and Pushpo Rani Royin, *MM*, 58, 141. Monoj Kanti Roys father recommended to gag his son before dying himself; see account by Monoj Kanti Roy, *MM*, 117. Similar acts of despair – infanticide of parents to silence their children in hiding, facing destruction – are known from the persecution of European Jews (see Gerlach, "Echoes").

dangerous sound to be avoided. Moreover, on a few occasions, people told others to remain silent so as to not infuriate the troops.[89] One survivor recalled that the troops themselves "asked everybody to make not a single sound" at the riverbank before lining people up and starting to shoot them.[90] Here silence symbolized subjugation and control.

Few talk about warning shouts at all: in one case each, these were shouts by a mother and a father to their family and in another case by people running away.[91] Some remember that "huge uproar" (which was not further specified) started among the crowd at the riverbank after the firing or possibly already before the firing.[92] This would mean that the troops did not maintain their control over sound (and order) for long. But there was also no kind of organized acoustic alarm among either the refugees or the locals.

These statements create an impression of passive victimhood and attempts at evasion. Virtually nobody seems to have opposed the troops by force. The only known exception consists of a Muslim man, seemingly an autonomy activist, who was shot dead by troops when holding a scissor in his hands, perhaps to confront them.[93] The only other challenges posed to the troops that the interviewees spoke of came from women who shouted at troops either in vain (sometimes falling to their knees and grabbing the legs of the soldiers) not to kill their relatives[94] or to shoot them too after they had killed their husbands or sons. According to the accounts, except for one instance, the troops refused to do so, in some cases saying that their bullets were reserved for men.[95]

Once again, one should also think about the absence of sounds that one could have expected. None of the statements contains anything about people praying and religious chants and songs, neither when they were facing death themselves nor when their relatives were dying or they were being confronted with the dead bodies of their loved ones. Many people cried, screamed and wailed loudly in both situations, as was said before, but apparently there were no audible rituals

---

[89] Accounts by Krisnopodo Roy and Komola Jowardar, *MM*, 66, 81.
[90] Account by Bijoy Kumat Roy, *MM*, 108.
[91] Accounts by Ershad Ali Morol, Bukul Roy and Shuvash Chandra Tarafder, *MM*, 54, 113, 158.
[92] Accounts by Nogor Biswas and Munkundo Bihari Roy, *MM*, 44, 142.
[93] Account by Ershad Ali Morol, *MM*, 54. Bose, *Dead Reckoning*, 118–119 mentions another incident (cf. ibid., 125).
[94] For example, accounts by Surjo Rishi Moni and Aynamoti Golder, *MM*, 76, 129.
[95] Accounts by Shorola Mondol, Kalidashi Mondol, Someer Biswas and Debola Bairagee, *MM*, 28, 52, 162, 172. In one place, several women were shot after such a confrontation: account by Shoromoresh Mondol (but he did not witness the scene himself), ibid., 124.

practiced that would have been common under normal circumstances[96] – very much unlike, say, in the case of Polish or Soviets Jews in the early 1940s when they were facing imminent death or when their relatives had been massacred. Why not? In the ensuing panic, when people ran away and tried to hide, there was no time for rituals and mourning – but what about afterward when the military squad had left and there was no immediate threat?

The scene was ghastly enough, but Hindus, who believe that dead bodies are threatening and impure,[97] must have felt a special horror when they had to step over, or on, corpses and literally wade through blood as they returned to the massacre site because the bodies were lying so densely.[98] And yet, many did search for their relatives, dead or alive. However, very few interviewees spoke of what can be identified as the performance of any death rituals, and if they were performed, these were usually silent ones and mentioned by people who were children in 1971. Some said that people poured a bit of water into the mouth of the dying or of all the dead people around, which is a common last rite of cleansing.[99] One man demanded water, shouting that he was dying.[100] Some fled to a Hindu temple to be saved by Bhagaban and waited there; the military eventually shot many men dead at this place.[101] More fortunate were some of the Hindus who fled to a mosque.[102] Floating the dead body of a loved one into the river can also be regarded by Hindus as a substitute for a proper funeral. Most of this was done by Muslims, and the rest by Hindu relatives.[103] A few interviewees were denied by – likely Muslim – residents permission to either take the dead body of a relative with them or give it proper treatment on the spot,[104] or the situation did not

---

[96] See Firth, *Dying*, 67–68, 77; Saifur Rashid, "Meaning and Rituals of Death: An Insight into Selected Ethnic and Religious Communities of Bangladesh", *Vietnam Social Sciences* 5, 193 (2019): 87–88; Michaels, *Hinduismus*, 149–150; Susan Thrane, "Hindu End of Life: Death, Dying, Suffering, and Karma", *Journal of Hospice and Palliative Nursing* 6, 12 (2010): 339.
[97] Michaels, *Hinduismus*, 149–153.
[98] Accounts by Probodh Chandra Roy, Mukundo Bihari Roy and Khokon Roy, *MM*, 62, 115, 119.
[99] Accounts by Chand Rani Das (11 years old in 1971) and Purnendu Gain (9 years old in 1971), *MM*, 131, 133. See also Michaels, *Hinduismus*, 149.
[100] Account by Shoromoresh Mondol (12 years old in 1971), *MM*, 123. People may also have asked for water because of severe loss of blood.
[101] Accounts by Shonjeet Gain and Purnendu Gain, *MM*, 111–112, 133.
[102] Account by Nitai Gain, *MM*, 74; another version of the same man's story is in Bose, *Dead Reckoning*, 119.
[103] Examples of the latter are in the accounts of Surjo Rishi Mondol and Chand Rani Das, *MM*, 76, 131.
[104] Accounts by Nogor Biswas and Komola Jowardar, *MM*, 44, 82.

allow it, and they still expressed regret about it after 29 years. One said: "We have a deep sorrow that we could not make a funeral for my father."[105]

The urge to flee must have been great, and people, especially women and minors, may have been too overwhelmed to perform rites if many relatives had been killed at once. Yet, the absence of chants, prayers and other rituals also indicates the social position of Hindus under the circumstances, their fear, subordination and subjugation in a hostile environment even after the troops had left. For loud noise is, in many situations, understood as a challenge and an attempt to dominate the public sphere.[106]

In contrast, some Muslims did report having (or were reported to have) started chanting, mostly in small groups, to demonstrate their loyalty to Pakistan and, thus, avoid becoming targets. Most of these chants were religious, which were uttered when military men demanded it as a marker of identification and on other occasions.[107] More rarely, people reported having shouted political slogans like "Pakistan Jindabad" (Long live Pakistan), either instead of religious chants or in addition.[108] Without knowing the troops, the expectation of these local Muslims, judging from their chanting, was that the operation was aimed at the Hindu minority rather than political opponents of the regime. However, their prayers did not seem to have any religious function in this situation; they were instead a marker of difference. Muslims too do not mention that they sang or prayed for the dead or the wounded after the killings. One man buried his father without proper burial cloth.[109]

Taken together, this information also suggests that there was no audible collective action by the Hindus present at Chuknagar. There are research studies which emphasize the partially organized character of the mass wave of refugees from East Pakistan at the time.[110] Judging from the level of sound, it was different

---

[105] Account by Khokon Roy, *MM*, 119. In the book, this part is marked as an original quote. See also Bokul Dashi, *MM*, 57.

[106] See, for instance, Wenzel, *Hören und Sehen*, 146, 153–154; Philip Schweighauser, *The Noises of American Literature, 1890–1985* (Gainesville: University of Florida Press, 2006), 40–41.

[107] Accounts by Anwar Ali Morol, Ashutosh Nandi, Sheikh Abul Kalam Mohiuddin, Md. Nazrul Islam Sarder, Dalil Uddin Sarker and Shohorjan Bibi, *MM*, 50, 91, 94, 120, 150, 173. See also Tripathi, *Colonel*, 121. One Hindu said that he survived like this even although first responding to soldiers that he was a Hindu: account by Monoj Kanti Roy, *MM*, 118.

[108] Accounts by Sheikh Abul Kalam Mohiuddin and Md. Nisar Ali Sardar, *MM*, 94, 96.

[109] Account by Ershad Ali Morol, *MM*, 55. According to Tripathi, *Colonel*, 119–120 the same man described the death of his father quite differently and said that he did find the necessary burial cloth.

[110] See Partha Mukherji, "The great exodus of 1971: I – Exodus", *Economic and Political Weekly* 9, 9 (March 2, 1974), 367–369.

at Chuknagar, as the crowd of refugees met there accidentally without showing any signs of organization and cohesion.[111]

The Inaudible Third

This section deals with the social environment in which the massacre took place. (Scholarship should emancipate itself from the undifferentiated concept of the 'bystander'.) This social environment did not *generate* the massacre but provided conditions under which it was materializing. According to the descriptions by witnesses and survivors, the role of local Muslim civilians in the massacre varied strongly, and the behavior of some of them was highly ambivalent. A number of them helped the troops – under duress, they claimed – to find residences of local Hindus who were subsequently killed.[112] One Hindu revealed having done this too.[113] Sometimes, Biharis are also mentioned in this context, but this is factually questionable. A group of Muslims dumped many of the victims' corpses in the river the day after the massacre; some under duress, but at least a few received a payment for it. There are conflicting statements regarding who told the men to dispose of the bodies, with some pointing to a local dignitary and others to the Pakistani military.[114] Smaller numbers of what appeared to be dead bodies of Hindus were also buried.[115] Locals who were apparently Muslims were looting the residences of local Hindus and rummaging through the clothes and possessions of those killed to steal their valuables.[116] One Hindu survivor also mentioned having

---

111 One account by Sardar Muhammad Noor Ali, *MM*, 48 describes organized help (lodging, food and escorts to the border) on the side of the local Awami League office.
112 Accounts by Mohammad Sher Ali Sardar (34 years old in 1971), Krisnopodo Roy and Md. Nazrul Islam Sarder in MM (12 years old in 1971), *MM* 43, 66, 120–121. The first and the third statements are by persons who helped the troops themselves. See also Bose, *Dead Reckoning*, 116.
113 Account by Arobindo Das, *MM*, 153 (17 years old in 1971).
114 Accounts by Ansar Ali Sardar, Afsar Ali Sarkar, Yakub Ali Sardar, Mohammad Sher Ali Sardar, Md. Ansar Ali Sardar, Shuvash Chandra Roy, Ashutosh Nandi, Sheikh Abul Kalam Mohiuddin, Md. Nisar Ali Sardar, Md. Nazrul Islam Sarder, Dalil Uddin Sarker and Ali Badsha, *MM*, 30, 38–39, 40, 42, 70, 79–80, 91, 95, 96–97, 121, 150, 152. See also Bose, *Dead Reckoning*, 121–122.
115 Accounts by Sheikh Abul Kalam Mohiuddin and Dalil Uddin Sarker, *MM*, 95, 150.
116 Accounts by Anwar Ali Morol, Kali Dashi Roy, Nitai Gain, Shonjeet Gain, Monoj Kanti Roy, Purnendu Gain, Bolai Goldar and Shohorjan Bibi, *MM*, 50, 58, 73, 112, 118, 134, 149, 174. Purnendu Gain (in *MM*, 132) assumes that local Muslims told people at the riverbank not to flee so that they could plunder the possessions after the military would have killed them (see also Bose, *Dead Reckoning*, 121). Numerous survivors state that they lost all their belongings in the massacre. A local Muslim ascribed the looting to the Pakistani troops: account by Sheikh Abul Kalam Mohiud-

done so.[117] One interviewee reported that locals took away all of the clothes, leaving the corpses naked.[118]

Hindu survivors also reported about mixed behavior of residents of Chuknagar and neighboring places toward them. Some denied help by either saying that offering assistance would endanger them, making derogatory remarks[119] or telling them to leave the local settlement.[120] But there are also examples of generous support and shelter provided by Muslims.[121] A few of them, despite refusing to take survivors in, did hand them food.[122] Medical doctors were mentioned favorably in the reports.[123] Medical help was also provided by lays, which included Muslims.[124]

It is especially worth noting here that the accounts contain virtually nothing about sounds of all this. No shouting by civilian Muslims is mentioned, no lowering of voices, no crying, no groaning under the burden of dead bodies to be disposed of, and no sounds of the pillage. As rich as the accounts are in terms of describing other noises, these are absent. All that is there are a few depictions of slogans signaling that people were Muslims and verbal exchanges without further specification of how they sounded.

However, it is unlikely that all of this action was silent. On that basis, there are three possibilities: such noises faded in the *memory* of the witnesses and survivors, they were left out in what they *said* in 2000, or those who *edited* the statements left them out. There is some indirect indication of the second scenario in survivors' accounts, such as in ominous statements like the following: "All our money and belongings were looted by some people."[125] Mikundo Bihari Roy, who was a young man in 1971 and a medical doctor by 2000, described how, after he returned to his village after the massacre, he was beaten up by several men one day after the massacre, stating: "Many of those who beat us that night are

---

din, *MM*, 94. Given their low number and lack of time, however, the soldiers could have only done a small part of the pillage.

117 See Bose, *Dead Reckoning*, 119.
118 Account by Komola Jowardar, *MM*, 82.
119 Account by Rajkumar Roy, *MM*, 167.
120 Account by Shuvash Chandra Roy, *MM*, 79.
121 Accounts by Krisnopodo Roy, Bolai Goldar (about the rescue of a baby) and Shuvash Vandra Tarafder, *MM*, 66–67, 149, 159.
122 Account by Horipodo Mondol, *MM*, 26.
123 Accounts by Nogor Biswas, Nitai Gain, Komola Jowardar (here about a Hindu doctor) and Binoy Roy, *MM*, 44, 75, 82, 110.
124 Accounts by Ansar Ali Sardar and Md. Ansar Ali Sardar, *MM*, 31, 71; see also Bose, *Dead Reckoning*, 120 (based on the report of survivor Shailendra Nath Joardar).
125 Account by Rashi Bala, *MM*, 77.

still alive but we do not want to mark them out or do not talk about them [sic!]."[126] As in this account, many, Hindus and Muslims alike, assign all guilt of having called in the troops to one local pro-Pakistani Muslim. Only a few Muslim witnesses (or helpers of the troops) named who did what. Hindu survivors mentioned no other name of a person involved except for that one person, and nobody revealed the name of any looter.

U.S. scholars Betsy Hartmann and James Boyce called the conditions in a Bangladeshi village where they did extensive fieldwork in the early 1970s "quiet violence", referring to the struggle for land and power and against poverty.[127] The accounts about the Chuknagar massacre – some of which, especially those by several Hindu women, were outspoken about how the event threw people into abject poverty for the rest of their lives, which also means that the looting affected them deeply[128] – reflect the silent violence of subjugation that, in all likelihood, prevented certain issues from being detailed. These things are sometimes mentioned, but not described. In particular, this applied to a public hearing like the one where the statements were collected. This raises considerable doubts about the methodology of the researchers involved in it.

Conversely, there are enough examples in the statements to conclude that by far not all Muslims in the village and the area behaved with hostility toward Hindus.[129] On May 20–21, 1971, such friendly demeanor had little influence, but if, as mentioned above, many Hindu survivors of the massacre returned home and stayed for the rest of Pakistani rule – despite harassment and persecution –, conditions must have existed that at least allowed for their survival. In other words: the social environment was fairly complex.

---

126 *MM*, 143.
127 Betsy Hartmann and James Boyce, *A Quiet Violence: View from a Bangladesh Village* (London: Zed, 1983).
128 These accounts appear in so far credible despite the fact that the interviewers did ask survivors whether they had received compensation and the respondents may have had expectations of obtaining financial gain through their narrative. See accounts by Nogor Biswas, Kalidashi Mondol, Surjo Rishi Moni, Komola Jowardar, Bukul Roy, Chand Rani Das and Pushpo Rani Roy, *MM*, 45, 52, 76, 82, 113, 131, 141.
129 This is compatible with an opinion poll among young male factory workers and peasants in East Pakistan in 1964 (a year of anti-Hindu riots) in which 30 percent said that Hindus did mostly harm, 8 percent that they did mostly good, and 62 percent that they did neither good nor harm. See Howard Schuman, "A Note on the Rapid Rise of Mass Bengali Nationalism in East Pakistan", *American Journal of Sociology* 28, 2 (1972): 290–298, here 295.

Conclusion

The large number of available accounts in the case of Chuknagar provides a rare opportunity to reconstruct different aspects of this mass killing in some detail. In this case, paying attention to sounds helps guide the inquiry in certain directions. This massacre was very loud, also in terms of human voice, which points to the fact of how much communication was involved. Attention to sounds reveals the cold, arrogant professionalism of the murderous troops involved, who committed a semi-organized massacre, creating panic instead of gathering their entire target group in one place. Some comparable massacres that claimed the lives of many villagers in East Pakistan were more tightly organized, but survivors also said that there was some degree of beating, kicking and shouting that took place in these incidents – often more than in Chuknagar.[130] By uncovering that although survivors cried and called for their loved ones, they did not perform any audible religious rites before and after their kin's death, the approach brings out their fear and subordination at the time, which interfered with their shock and grief. The same emerges when considering the lack of sounds conveyed that were made by locals who did not belong to the target group(s): subordination of Hindus, also when the statements were made in 2000. Thus, the level of sounds and speaking about sounds reveals social divisions – even decades and several regime changes later, when some education about 'genocide' had taken place.

However, the massacre at Chuknagar hardly works as the embodiment of a 'genocide' against Bangladeshis across-the-board, as propagated in Bangladesh and sometimes internationally, although it does demonstrate how ruthlessly Pakistani troops acted in what they regarded as their own country.

In 1971, Chuknagar was a village with a few thousand residents. It was a rural place, and most of the refugees who had gathered there on their way to India were villagers from other places, some of them being very poor. Many of those who survived remained rural dwellers in 2000, when the accounts were collected. Given this parochial, pastoral context and the fact that this was largely concerned with a massacre by the military from an Islamic state targeting the Hindu minority, the role that religion plays in these stories of death, murder, loss, survival and grief is remarkably insignificant. This point needs further exploration. In how far was this 'religious' violence? In the accounts, just one Hindu and one Muslim expressed regret that they could not perform proper rites for their close family members who were killed although many said in 2000 that they still feel the loss they suffered.

---

130 Bose, *Dead Reckoning*, 97–113.

Beyond the conflict in East Pakistan, research about sounds can help write a complex social history of persecuted groups, as this study shows. The analysis of auditive experiences, especially when multiple accounts are available, adds a new dimension to this effort and accentuates the social interaction involved. The following chapter sheds, with different methods, more light on the complexity of the processes that led to violence in East Pakistan, including multipolar violence.

4 Crowd Violence in East Pakistan/Bangladesh 1971–1972

Introduction

Some recent scholarship links violent persecutions in the 20th century to the rise of mass political participation.[1] This chapter substantiates this claim by exploring part of a country's history of crowd violence. Such acts constitute a specific form of participation in collective violence and shaping it. There are other forms such as forming local militias, small informal violent gangs or guerrilla groups, calls for violence through petitions or non-violent demonstrations and also acting through a state apparatus, meaning that functionaries contribute personal ideas and perceptions to the action of a bureaucracy in some persecution. Therefore, it seems to make sense to investigate specific qualities of participation in crowd violence. Subject to this inquiry is violence against humans by large groups of civilians, with no regard to other collectives of military or paramilitary groups, as large as they may have been.

My approach to this topic is informed by my interest in "extremely violent societies" that has already been outlined in the introduction. This means social formations in which, for some period, various population groups become victims of mass violence in which, alongside state organs, many members of several social groups participate for a variety of reasons.[2] Aside from the participatory character of violence, this is also about its multiple target groups and sometimes its multipolar character. Here, this means comparing the different degrees to which crowd violence was used by and against different groups and why.

The line between perpetrators and bystanders is especially blurred within violent crowds. I have questioned the usefulness of both, 'perpetrator' and 'bystander', as terms before and prefer to speak, more broadly defined, of "persecutors" rather

---

1 See Michael Mann, *The Dark Side of Democracy* (Cambridge et al.: Cambridge University Press, 2005); Christian Gerlach, "Extremely Violent Societies: An Alternative to the Concept of Genocide," in: *Journal of Genocide Research* 8, 4 (2006): 461–463.

This is the modified version of a chapter published before under the same title in: Frank Jacob, ed., *Genocide and Mass Violence in Asia* (Berlin and Boston: DeGruyter Oldenbourg, 2019), 15–39. A short version was presented at the conference, "On Collective Violence: Actions, Roles, Perceptions," Center for Conflict Studies, University of Marburg, 20 October 2016. I am grateful to the participants there and also Axel Paul, Benjamin Schwalb and Frank Jacob for their comments.

2 Siehe Christian Gerlach, *Extremely Violent Societies: Mass Violence in the Twentieth-Century World* (Cambridge et al.: Cambridge University Press, 2010), 1.

than 'perpetrators', to, among other things, avoid placing responsibility only on (often inferior) executors.[3] However, this does not solve the thorny problem of assigning responsibility concerning crowd violence.[4] Crowds are not one collective agent. Usually not all members of a crowd, and not even all of its armed members, hurt other people with their own hands. Nonetheless, these seemingly non-violent people in an armed crowd may encourage others, directly or indirectly, to commit physical attacks, intimidate people that become victimized and prevent the victims from escaping by physical or psychological means. Thus, it may be less interesting to assign a term like 'perpetrator' to people than to describe responsibilities, concluding from observations of a sufficient number of cases of crowd violence, as will be presented here. As spontaneously emerging collectives, crowds have especially little cohesion, which makes motives particularly difficult to identify even though people more or less volunteered to participate and institutional and longer-term factors such as subordination to orders and rules and group pressure were less intense.

Thus, this chapter addresses the following questions: In what situations, where and when was there crowd violence? And when was it relegated to the background, perhaps being replaced by other forms of collective violence? What groups used it against what other groups, and how did they interact? What were the discursive contexts of the violence and the intentions of the gatherings? What can be said (even if information is limited) about the relationship between individuals and the crowd? What was the relationship between the actors and the regime? And what pre-existing traditions of violence played a role?

East Pakistan/Bangladesh in 1971–1972 serves as a case study. This may be useful because of the multitude of victim groups, including many attacked by crowds, and because of the abundance of incidents. Conflicts in East Pakistan erupted in the wake of the first nationwide bourgeois-democratic elections in Pakistan. This chapter may lead to some insights into the relationship between mass participation in politics and mass violence in general. After some initial observations regarding traditions of political militancy in East Pakistan before 1971, I trace the occurrence of physical violence from among crowds through different phases from early 1971 to the spring of 1972.

---

3 See ibid., 4–5; Christian Gerlach, *The Extermination of the European Jews* (Cambridge et al.: Cambridge University Press, 2016), 15–16.

4 A collective volume on crowd violence is Axel Paul and Benjamin Schwalb, eds., *Gewaltmassen: Über Eigendynamik und Selbstorganisation kollektiver Gewalt* (Hamburg: Hamburger Edition, 2015), though only parts of that book address non-organized violence by large collectives. The chapters relevant here are by the editors (pp. 7–18, 383–408), Paul Dumouchel (pp. 103–123) and Ferdinand Sutterlüty (pp. 231–256).

Historical Context

At this point, a brief survey of events in East Pakistan in 1971 is at place. After partition in 1947–1948, the state of Pakistan emerged, consisting of two wings that were 1600 kilometers apart and differed widely culturally and economically. A little more than half of the population lived in largely rural East Pakistan (which became Bangladesh in December 1971), dominated by a peasant rice economy. Most inhabitants were Bengali-speaking Muslims. The most important minorities consisted of about 10 million Hindus and between one and two million Urdu-speaking former Muslim refugees from India, dubbed Biharis. The elites in the East that was economically stagnating and in the grip of deepening poverty protested, above all, the marginalization of the Bengali language and culture in the 1950s and economic discrimination in the 1960s. This led to demands for strong autonomy for the eastern part of the country that were championed by the Awami League, a political party under the chairman Mujibur Rahman. At the end of the 1960s, this movement merged with protests against the military dictatorship that ruled Pakistan since 1958. After the Awami League won the all-Pakistani elections in the end of 1970, open conflict erupted in March 1971. The military tried to crush the autonomy movement in a bloody crackdown, and, together with supportive local Muslim militias that included some Biharis as well as Bengali conservatives killed, arrested or expelled Awami League functionaries, students, pro-Bengali intellectuals and Hindus. In April, the army also started with massacres in villages, trying to defeat the emerging guerrilla movement with bases in India. Ten million people, mostly Hindus, fled to India, and even more people, largely Muslims, were displaced within East Pakistan. The army and their helpers also committed mass rapes. The number of killings reached hundreds of thousands. But mass violence of different kinds was also committed by civilians, including Bengalis who turned against Biharis and other non-Bengalis as well as Muslims persecuting Hindus, particularly in the countryside. Many instances of rape also occurred between neighbors and within families. In December 1971, Pakistani rule in Bengal was terminated by an Indian invasion along with Bangladeshi independence fighters. Afterward, attacks on Biharis and rapes continued, as did a famine that may have claimed more lives than direct violence, especially among returning refugees.

Given that few official Pakistani and Bangladeshi documents are available to scholars, this chapter is mainly based on observations and statements made by East Bengalis, Pakistani army personnel, foreign missionaries, journalists and diplomats. An additional problem is that accounts by Bangladeshis and Pakistanis are often bequeathed in publications where lines between facts and propaganda are blurred and that sometimes convey rumors, as do reports by foreign observers.[5] In a sense, my analysis is merely based on assertions about the occurrence of crowd violence. And yet, these sources are meaningful since it is characteristic how often and in which cases crowd violence was claimed to have taken place. In part of the cases, cross-checking allows for the verification of reports. Unclear language in the sources is another problem. As there is often no exhausting description or analysis of an event, only certain terms that were used, such as "mob" or "riot," indicate that it involved masses. By contrast, denominations like "gangs" or "goondas" point to small groups of actors. Unfortunately, most of the material is insufficient for in-depth micro-studies. In particular, one cannot say much about the identity of the people in those crowds – except that by far most were men – and who within a crowd turned violent. And at this point, little can be said about the important inner dynamics within those gatherings, although such knowledge would be highly desirable. This means that this chapter throws light on participatory violence and lethal social interaction, but – contrary to chapters 2 and 3 – regrettably not on an individual level, just on a group level. The social history of mass violence has limits in this case. But the material seems comprehensive and dense enough to identify significant patterns of group behavior, including the situations in which crowd violence came about.

Traditions of Political Militancy

Nationalist scholars from Bangladesh have spread the impression internationally that East Pakistan was peaceful and homogenous, except for Pakistani army violence.[6] Nothing could be further from historical reality. Bitter conflicts between social groups and between the sexes, the frequency of riots, aggressive practices of political struggle and repeated occurrences of mass violence in the quarter of a century before 1971 testify to the contrary.

Large parts of the agrarian population of East Pakistan (and thus the overall majority of inhabitants) suffered from lack of land, and land conflicts divided villages and families.[7] Comprehensive serious discrimination against women was

---

5 A critical evaluation of some of these rumors is in Sarmila Bose, *Dead Reckoning: Memories of the 1971 Bangladesh War* (London: Hurst, 2011).
6 One example is Rounaq Jahan, "Genocide in Bangladesh," in *Genocide in the Twentieth Century*, eds. Samuel Totten and William S. Parsons (New York/London: Garland, 1995), 371–402, esp. 384.
7 M. Ameerul Huq, ed. *Exploitation and the Rural Poor* (Comilla: Bangladesh Academy for Rural Development, 1976) describes the situation in 1974. Although disputes aggravated in and after 1971, they did not differ in principle from earlier years.

common before 1971, and domestic violence widespread.[8] Social antagonisms led to almost constant unrest. From 1958 to 1966, the number of officially registered riots reached approximately 5,000 annually, or 14 per day, and they were on the increase. This level was even surpassed by far from 1972 to 1974.[9] Among these almost everyday civil disturbances, some periods of mass violence stood out. Between 1946 and 1950 as well as in 1964–1965, many pogroms took place, victimizing mostly Hindus but also other groups such as the small Christian communities. Since 1946, at least four million Hindus fled East Bengal (and in the year of 1970 alone, 248,158 reached West Bengal in India), tens of thousands were murdered.[10] Politics in East Pakistan knew little regard for minorities.[11] Other waves of collective violence included the language riots of 1951, hunger riots and several cumulations of student unrest.[12]

All of these included violence committed out of crowds. From 1946 on, there were mutual collective assaults between Muslims and Hindus in the context of decolonization and partition also in East Bengal. By early 1948, this had forced 800,000 Muslims from India to flee to East Pakistan and one million Hindus in the opposite direction.[13] These conflicts reached their peak in 1950. Masses of angry Muslims torched Hindu houses or entire neighborhoods and/or looted them, especially if Hindus had refused to convert to Islam. Sometimes crowds ransacked all stores run by Hindus. Crowds also attacked steamboats, trains and busses in order to slaughter Hindus. Many Hindu girls and women were raped or abducted. As a result, the refugee wave to India rose.[14] In 1964–1965 there were similar pogroms. This time, Muslims among the work force of factories, including Biharis, were also incited to turn against Hindus and massacred them in some cases. Hundreds of thousands of Hindus lost their homes, more than 667,000 took refuge in

---

8 See Yasmin Saikia, *Women, War, and the Making of Bangladesh: Remembering 1971* (Durham, NC/London: Duke University Press, 2011).
9 Mohiuddin Alamgir, *Famine in South Asia* (Cambridge, MA: Oelgeschlager, Gunn & Hain, 1980), 139; Omar Noman, *Pakistan: A Political and Economic History Since 1947* (London/New York: Kegan Paul International, 1988), 32. I found no data for 1967 to 1971.
10 See A. Roy, *Genocide of Hindus and Buddhists in East Pakistan/Bangladesh* (Delhi: Kranti Prakashan, 1981), though this a very biased study; also Muhammad Ghulam Kabir, *Minority Politics in Bangladesh* (Delhi: Vikas, 1980). For 1970, see Marcus Franda, *Bangladesh: The First Decade* (New Delhi: South Asian Publishers, 1982), 103.
11 See Ghulam Kabir, *Minority Politics*.
12 Gerlach, *Extremely Violent Societies*, 131–132.
13 Willem van Schendel, *A History of Bangladesh* (Cambridge et al.: Cambridge University Press, 2009), 131–132.
14 Ghulam Kabir, *Minority Politics*, 108–112, 114, 120–121, 137–143.

India in 1964.[15] Unlike in 1950 and 1971, all political parties formed a committee that stopped the riots relatively quickly.[16] What followed in 1968–1969 were months of student unrest that was joined by violent protests of workers and peasants that claimed the lives of some local elites.[17]

Through this history of violence, certain patterns of assault against some groups emerged, as did patterns of response. Locally, events had repeated themselves in some places before 1971.[18] How to avoid fatalities was also known: as a meticulous study of a rural confrontation between over 10,000 Muslims and Hindus in 1954 demonstrates, there was no spontaneous fighting, but after deliberations among local leaders, and in the fighting, the many sickles, knives and spears were used only against arms and legs of the opponents.[19] However, past events could also precipitate serious political misjudgments, as the U.S. consul in Dacca concluded in a telegram in 1971:

> With benefit of hindsight it [is] now evident AL [Awami League] tragically miscalculated its position in its post-1 March confrontation with MLA [Martial Law Authority]. Mujib und AL believed they dealt from position of strength, based not only from overwhelming victory at polls which legitimized position vis-a-vis MLA, but also blind faith in "people power." Strongly held myth here is that masses in 1968–69 anti-Ayub agitation not only successfully confronted police and EPRs [East Pakistan Rifles], but also had the regular army cowed.[20]

Two widely used tactics of political struggle in East Pakistan deserve special mentioning. A *hartal* (general strike) was called relatively often, locally or regionally, and rigorously enforced, down to stopping car traffic.[21] For a *gherao*, a tactic introduced in the late 1960s, businesses, authorities or residences were surrounded by a crowd in a hostile posture in order to get concessions by those encircled before they were given back their freedom of movement. Both tactics took large, aggressive groups of people to the streets.

---

15 See Roy, *Genocide*, 10, 33, 38–51; for mass flights, see Franda, *Bangladesh*, 103.
16 Ghulam Kabir, *Minority Politics*, 74–75.
17 Van Schendel, *History*, 123; Kalim Siddiqi, *Conflict, Crisis and War in East Pakistan* (New York: Praeger, 1972), 121–131; David Loshak, *Pakistan Crisis* (New York et al.: McGraw Hill, 1971), 32–33.
18 Marian Olson, *Bangladesh: Tears and Laughter* (Willmar, MN: Willmar Assembly of God, 2002), 104–106 sketches the example of Gopalganj.
19 Beth Roy, *Some Trouble With Cows: Making Sense of Social Conflict* (Berkeley et al.: University of California Press, 1994), esp. 48–73, 81–85.
20 Telegram from about April 1971, quoted in Archer Blood, *The Cruel Birth of Bangladesh: Memoirs of an American Diplomat* (Dhaka: University Press, 2002), 210. Mohammed Ayub Khan was the military dictator in Pakistan in 1968–1969.
21 See for example Blood, *Birth*, 165.

General Elections and the Consequent Political Crisis, 1970–1971

The nationwide unrest of 1968–1969 forced the military government to change its frontman. The new leader of the junta, General Yahya Khan (1917–1980), promised general elections and actually organized them in November 1970. The Awami League won 75 percent of the votes in East Pakistan, which, through the majority voting system, made her claim 160 out of 162 seats from the East (the party did not run in the western part of the country) and, thus, the absolute majority in the Constitutional Assembly in Pakistan.[22] This was an outstanding political victory, but it did not mean that the East Bengalis sided united with one peaceful party. The turnout in East Pakistan was 57 percent of eligible voters, and during the election year, activists and supporters of the Awami League had attacked supporters of other parties also physically in order to intimidate them, and killed some of them.[23]

The leaders of the Awami League deduced from this election victory a claim to speak for, as it was called, the 75 million people in the East, and, as they took the election result support for their party's platform, also a hardly veiled claim to sovereignty for the East. The will of 75 million was not to be and could not be suppressed.[24] This argument also persuaded Henry Kissinger (1923–2023), the advisor for security affairs of the president of the USA, although Kissinger was not known as a friend of the founding of the state of Bangladesh.[25] The U.S. consul in Dacca called the Awami League's chairman Mujibur Rahman (1920–1975) by appearance and character a power-hungry man who derived his power from the masses.[26]

---

22 Gerlach, *Extremely Violent Societies*, 127.
23 See François Massa, *Bengale: Historie d'un conflit* (Paris: Éditions Alain Moreau, 1972), 141; Hakeem Arshad Qureshi, *The 1971 Indo-Pak War: A Soldier's Narrative* (Oxford et al.: Oxford University Press, 2002), 12; Siddiq Salik, *Witness to Surrender*, 3rd ed. (Karachi: Lancer, 1998), 5 and 15; Government of Pakistan, *White Paper on the Crisis in East Pakistan* (n.p. [Rawalpindi]: Government of Pakistan, August 5, 1971), 6–8. For the turnout, see L.F. Rushbrook Williams, *The East Pakistan Tragedy* (New York: Drake, 1972), 44.
24 See newspaper reports about speeches and interviews by Mujibur Rahman of 1, 21, 22 and 24 March 1971 in: *Bangla Desh Documents* (Delhi: Ministry of External Affairs n.y. [1971]), 189, 257, 261, 267; Peter Hess, *Bangladesh: Tragödie einer Staatsgründung* (Frauenfeld and Stuttgart: Huber, 1972), 57.
25 "[. . .] 75,000 Punjabi cannot govern 75 million Bengalis". Kissinger according to Minutes of Senior Review Group Meeting, July 30, 1971, in: *Foreign Relations of the United States, 1969–1976*, vol. XI (Washington: United States Government Printing Office, 2005), 301.
26 Blood, *Birth*, 47.

When Yahya Khan postponed the meeting of the Constitutional Assembly indefinitely on March 1, 1971 due to discord between the political parties, many Bengalis suspected that fraud was intended. According to pro-Bengali narratives, this triggered an unarmed movement of passive resistance, but in reality it was not peaceful.[27] Mujibur Rahman called the Bengalis to arm themselves and take on the struggle. After the movement had already suffered bloody losses, one could also sustain more of them.[28] Already on December 30, he had announced that "any attempt to delay or thwart [the realization of the] wishes of the people would be resisted to [the] bloody end."[29] During one of the biggest meetings involving him that was held on March 7, Mujibur Rahman spoke of peaceful non-cooperation but slogans called for the destruction of Pakistani troops.[30] After the military had shot at spontanous, sometimes violent, demonstrations, killing several demonstrators, Mujibur Rahman declared a *hartal* on March 2 that paralyzed public life, was modified on March 7 and then transformed into a parallel rule by the Awami League in East Pakistan including the control of media and financial institutions.[31]

This did not stop at rhetorics. Directly after Yahya Khan's indefinite postponement of the Constitutional Assembly meeting on March 1, masses of angry Bengalis took to the streets. Many were equipped with sharpened bamboo sticks and iron rods. For days, they smashed and looted stores and restaurants run by Biharis and Western Pakistanis, set several places ablaze and attacked opponents of East Pakistani autonomy as well as foreigners. Cars were torched and bricks thrown. Some groups, especially university students, tried to procure firearms, mostly by plundering arms stores. Some manufactured Molotov cocktails.[32] From March 2 onward,

---

27 Unarmed according to: Jahan, *Genocide*, 375. Bose, *Reckoning*, 18 and 24 argues the opposite way.
28 See an article by the *Hindustan Standard*, March 11, 1971, in: I. N. Tewary, *War of Independence in Bangla Desh: A Documentary Study* (New Delhi: Navachetna Prakashan, 1971), 118; Bose, *Reckoning*, 3; Mujibur Rahman's speech, 7 March 1971, in Rafiq ul Islam, *A Tale of Millions* (Dacca: Bangladesh Books International, 1981), 49; Mujibur Rahman's speech, 17 February 1971, according to *Pakistan Observer*, February 18, 1971 in *Bangla Desh Documents*, 165–166.
29 Telegram by U.S. Consul Blood, quoted in Blood, *Birth*, 131.
30 Blood, *Birth*, 173; see "Minority Group Obstructing Transfer of Power", in: *Dawn*, March 8, 1971, printed in: *Bangla Desh Documents*, 218–222, esp. 222.
31 "Mujib strongly condemns firing", in: *The People*, March 3, 1971, and "Mujib gives 10-point programme", in: *Dawn*, March 8, 1971, in: *Bangla Desh Documents*, 192 und 223; see also Blood, *Birth*, 157–158.
32 Bose, *Reckoning*, 23–26; Blood, *Birth*, 156–159; James und Marti Hefley, *Christ in Bangladesh* (New York et al.: Harper and Row, 1973), 13 und 15; Fazal Muqeem Khan, *Pakistan's Crisis in Leadership* (Islamabad et al.: National Book Foundation, 1973), 55–58; Rushbrook Williams, *East Pakistan Tragedy*, 53; "Wave of protests sweeps East Pakistan", in: *The Times*, March 3, 1971; Jahanara

violent clashes between demonstrators and the military took place, especially when civilians tried to storm public offices or blocked objects. According to the military, 172 persons died from March 2–4, though most in clashes between Bengali and non-Bengali civilians and as a result of police (not army) fire. Such incidents started on March 1.[33] The Awami League called these numbers grossly understated, and all victims were blamed on the military shooting at unarmed civilians.[34]

In several places, there were pogrom-like mass conflicts between Bengalis and Biharis that resulted in victims on both sides, but a higher number among the latter. The most lethal ones happened on March 3–4 in the port city of Chittagong, when Bengali demonstrators marched through a Bihari settlement in order to enforce the *hartal*, which was answered by shooting from Biharis. 200 people died on both sides, especially in neighborhoods inhabited by Bihari workers, sites that suggest that Bengalis were on the attack.[35] Other deadly clashes between Bengalis and Biharis in Chittagong followed shortly before March 25 when Biharis wanted to unload a ship of military goods quickly and Bengalis attempted to prevent that.[36] This time it was (at least according to Bengali sources) armed non-Bengali crowds who moved against Bengalis under the wrong assumption that the army would immediately come to their help. Many non-Bengalis were killed instead.[37] In several neighborhoods and suburbs of Khulna, crowds killed at least 57 non-Bengalis with improvised bombs, sickles and spears, mutilating them.[38] Angry crowds also appeared at highways and attacked, among others, cars that did not carry black flags

---

Imam, *Of Blood and Fire* (New Delhi: Sterling, 1989), 8–9, 27 (diary entries of March 1 and 16, 1971); *White Paper*, 29–30; Qutubuddin Aziz, *Blood and Tears* (Karachi: United Press of Pakistan, 1974), 21–22.

33 Salik, *Witness*, 48 und 56–57; A. M. A. Muhith, *Bangladesh: Emergence of a Nation* (Dacca: Bangladesh Books International, 1978), 202; *White Paper*, 30.

34 See for example Blood, *Birth*, 161.

35 Secretariat of the International Commission of Jurists, *The Events in East Pakistan, 1971: A Legal Study* (Geneva: International Commission of Jurists, 1972), http://nsm1.nsm.imp.edu/sanwar/Bangladesh%20Genocide.htm (last accessed January 8, 2008), chapter II a; *White Paper*, 31; account by Fazlul Rahman in *The Year That Was*, ed. Ishrat Firdousi (Dhaka: Bastu Prakashan, 1996), 345. A Bangladeshi author confirmed that this happened always in non-Bengali settlements though he claimed that there were only Bengali victims: ul Islam, *Tale*, 37–38. Aziz, *Blood*, 54–78 offers much higher victim numbers.

36 Letter by A. Majid from Zurich, in *International Herald Tribune*, August 9, 1971, printed in: *Bangladesh Genocide and World Press*, ed. Fazlul Quader Quaderi (Dacca: Begum Dilafroz Quaderi, 1972), 247.

37 Muhith, *Bangladesh*, 226–227.

38 *White Paper*, 31.

as demanded by the Awami League.[39] Trains were either stopped by crowds between stations or passengers encircled at stations and alleged or real opponents of political autonomy threatened. According to some sources, passengers of a local bus in Dacca were murdered by a crowd.[40] Violence from amidst crowds originated at several places from the attempt to enforce the general strike, which, in turn, was supposed to protest anti-democratic measures by the military junta, but also served as a vehicle for a creeping political takeover. Such violence built up incrementally.[41] However, it has to be added that witnesses attributed violence against non-Bengalis also often to small armed groups ("gangs"), rather than crowds.[42]

In the days after March 1, boycotts prevented army units in East Pakistan from the purchase of fresh food and crowds blocked unit movements, often without the military responding violently. The most bloody incident that did happen occurred in the town of Jodevpur on March 19 when there was shooting out of a crowd blocking a railway crossing at army troops which killed several people when returning the fire.[43]

All in all, there were many violent actions out of gatherings and demonstrations in several towns and cities from March 1–25, and not only during clashes with the army. Transitions between common practices of political struggle and mass violence were fluent. From about March 22 – three days before the army crackdown – mass assaults on Biharis began on a larger scale than in the weeks before. This can also be read from warnings of Bengali politicians which also indicate that the Awami League started to lose control of the events.[44] In one of the largest riots, 8,000 civilians, many of whom were armed, attacked residential neighborhoods in or around Saidpur on March 24–25.[45] The excitement and readiness for violence of those assembled sprung from their outrage because of political injustice and oppression, but often it was not directed against functionaries of the state but minorities that were considered alien, even though these were vaguely seen as linked with government and West Pakistani interests.

---

39 Jim McKinley, *Death to Life: Bangladesh as Experienced by a Missionary Family* (Louisville: Highview Baptist Church, n.y.), 9.
40 *White Paper*, 38; Aziz, *Blood*, 30.
41 In this point the *White Paper*, 29–39, appears realistic.
42 Aziz, *Blood*, 25–43.
43 Blood, *Birth*, 181–182; see details in Bose, *Reckoning*, 32–46.
44 See various articles in *Bangla Desh Documents*, 271–274.
45 *White Paper*, 39.

Crowd Violence in March/April 1971 and Its Suppression

After the army crackdown on March 25, the most common violence committed from within crowds in March and April 1971 consisted of massacres against Biharis.[46] Tens of thousands were killed. The most fatal incidents happened in Chittagong, Khulna, Jessore, Santahar (6,000 to 15,000 dead), in ten settlements in Mymensingh, where the crowds were armed with rifles, swords, spears and daggers (500 to 5,000 dead), and in Dinajpur.[47] Frequently this included the murder of women and children or the abduction of children.[48] In other places, only male adults were targeted. Such events may have been exaggerated in Pakistani propaganda or postwar pro-Pakistani studies (but see the partial confirmation by witnesses from the opposite side mentioned on the following pages). Nonetheless, such (pro-)Pakistani reports are significant in that they hold crowds, mostly called "mobs," responsible for attacks on non-Bengali civilians because they attest mass support to the political opponent, which undermines the idea that one should have kept a united state of Pakistan that is usually the basis of these publications. This lends such reports some credibility.

The slaughter of Jessore on March 30 and its results were observed by foreign journalists. Civilians armed with spears, rifles and other weapons hacked Pakistani soldiers and non-Bengali civilians to death.[49] A crowd of Bengalis was also about to lynch a U.S. missionary as an alleged "Punjabi" in a coastal area until a functionary of the Awami League clarified his identity.[50] The Pakistani authorities set up camps for about 25,000 Bihari widows and orphans.[51]

Pogroms against non-Bengalis have not only been described by Bihari survivors, Pakistani army officers, foreign media reporters and missionaries; they also

---

[46] Siehe Gerlach, *Extremely Violent Societies*, 148–151; Sumit Sen, "Stateless Refugees and the Right to Return: The Bihari Refugees of South Asia, part I", in: *International Journal of Refugee Law* 11, 4 (1999): 630–631. The strongly propagandistic book by Aziz, *Blood*, argues that there was violence from crowds (and not small armed groups) in many instances. Many of his data lack credibility in regard to timing, victim numbers and the arms allegedly used by attackers, but many of his descriptions also match depictions of the same case in other sources.

[47] See *White Paper*, 64–69; for Chittagong and Khulna, see: Aziz, *Blood*, 57–78, 82–93. For Santahar: Michael Hornsby, "Pakistan army intervention set off events which led to vengeance killings in East Pakistan", in: *The Times*, July 12, 1971. For Mymensingh: Blood, *Birth*, 277 (500 to 2.000 dead); *White Paper*, 69. For Dinajpur: Peter Hazelhurst, "Massacre of thousands of refugees by Bengalis alleged", in: *The Times*, April 6, 1971.

[48] For the latter point, see Saikia, *Women*, 84 (Saidpur).

[49] Nicholas Tomalin, "Mass slaughter of Punjabis in East Bengal", in: *The Times*, April 2, 1971.

[50] Hefley and Hefley, *Christ*, 20.

[51] Hess, *Bangladesh*, 145.

appear in collections of postwar Bengali memories, such as the mutual pogroms in Khulna which led to, at least, hundreds of fatalities.[52] A crowd's attack at the Kabuli building in Chittagong, where supporters of the Pakistani government had barricaded themselves (some of them armed) led to them being killed, to looting and the rape of women by the crowd.[53] In the town of Ishurdi, large groups of people hunted down scattered Pakistani soldiers and Biharis and killed them. Similar things happened in villages close to Lamonirhat near Rangpur.[54] Bengali student Najmul Ansar fled the Pakistani army from Dacca to Comilla, but once there, he was surrounded by a hostile crowd who alleged him to be a Bihari.[55] These reports show also how distrust grew on both sides, many people armed themselves, protective steps were taken, rumors circulated and finally hostile crowds from both sides attacked civilians, as happened in Chittagong.[56]

Military attacks could lead to bloody riots by Bengalis who accused Biharis of signaling to the Pakistani air force.[57] In Lalmonirhat (Rangpur district), the local Bengali pogrom against non-Bengalis took place after Major Ziaur Rahman's (1936–1981) radio speech in which he declared a state of Bangladesh on March 26. Local Bengalis succeeded in burning down a Bihari neighborhood, but they had severe losses and were afterwards attacked by non-Bengali prisoners freed by the military.[58]

Some sources say that functionaries of the Awami League were responsible for anti-Bihari pogroms. Even a Bangladeshi historian accused "Awami League volunteers" of a six-day riot against Biharis in Chittagong at the end of March 1971.[59] But there are a number of counter-examples, in which Awami League functionaries prevented or stopped riots and mass murder.[60] Already in March 1971, Mujibur Rahman had repeatedly warned of rioting against Biharis, albeit in ambivalent

---

52 Account by Mustafa Kamal in Firdousi, *Year*, 489; see also *White Paper*, 66.
53 A detailed description can be found in the account by Waliul Islam in Firdousi, *Year*, 17–24.
54 Accounts by Arief Razzaque and Golam Sarwar in Firdousi, *Year*, 330, 389–391.
55 Account by Najmul Ansar in Firdousi, *Year*, 406–407.
56 Account by Mohammad Ishaque in Firdousi, *Year*, 25–27; Yaqub Zainuddin's account in ibid., 513–514 portrays probably events in Chittagong as well.
57 Blood, *Birth*, 276–278 (Mymensingh, April 1971).
58 Account by Golam Sarwar in Firdousi, *Year*, 389.
59 Talukder Maniruzzaman, *The Bangladesh Revolution and Its Aftermath* (Dacca: Bangladesh Books International, 1980), 87. See *White Paper*, 31; Aziz, *Blood*, 16.
60 Blood, *Birth*, 275 (Faridpur); Peter Hazelhurst, "Hundreds of non-Bengalis slaughtered in Bangladesh", in: *The Times*, April 6, 1971 (Dinajpur); letter by the Central Committee of the Communist Party of East Pakistan,"On the situation in Bangla Desh", May 3, 1971, in: *Bangla Desh Documents*, 314 (Rangpur).

statements.[61] Accusations by the Pakistani justice authorities against Awami League functionaries concerning violence against non-Bengalis, West Pakistanis and "non-conformists" were mostly vague, and, above all, largely not explicitly related to directing violent crowds. Either this was rare, or the Pakistani authorities wanted to avoid the impression of mass support for such violent acts.[62] If the role of representatives of the leading political party was more conciliatory, this would mean that crowds, and individuals in these crowds, acted rather autonomously.

In several areas, crowds, defying death, but also with the intention to kill, also turned on troops identified as supporting (West) Pakistan (after March 25, 1971, other army units supported Bangladesh's independence). Before the army crackdown on March 25, popular action was directed against the supply and movements of all units, including those that consisted mainly of supposed Bengalis.[63] Afterward, this changed. Locally, this was organized by a "Liberation War Committee" headed by an Awami League member-elect of the National Assembly in Satkhira.[64] Allegedly, 8,000 people moved against the military base in Saidpur already on March 24.[65] On March 31, about 50 Bengali police officers, 100 students and 5,000 peasants attacked an army unit in Kushtia. Instead of a suicidal frontal attack, they surrounded the troops and shot at them with hundreds of previously captured rifles. Peasants hacked those soldiers to death who tried to drive away in panic. 134 military personnel died, 13 were captured.[66] On April 2, 5,000 people armed with sticks, bows and arrows, spears and firearms stopped an army platoon on the way from Rajshahi to Nababgunj and captured a tank.[67] In Jessore, peasants armed with hoes, truncheons and bamboo spears held a barack under siege in order to kill the soldiers located there.[68] A crowd hacked nine soldiers in Bogra to pieces on April 6, around the same time as armed groups moved against

---

61 See for example Blood, *Birth*, 162 and note 28 in this chapter.
62 "Charges against 16 more MNAs", in: *Pakistan Times*, August 18, 1971, Politisches Archiv des Auswärtigen Amtes Berlin (PA AA), B 37/629.
63 Salik, *Witness*, 56–57.
64 Suraiya Begum, "Introduction", in: *Rising from the Ashes: Women's Narratives of 1971*, eds. Shaheen Akhtar et al. (Dhaka: Ain O Salish Kendra and University Press, 2014; first in Bengali 2001), 105.
65 Massa, *Bengale*, 178.
66 "Pakistan. The Battle of Kushtia", in: *Time*, April 19, 1971, printed in: Quaderi, Bangladesh Genocide, 72–75. A unit of 300 men was annihilated in Pabna: Qureshi, *War*, 33.
67 Kalyan Chaudhuri, "Across the Border. The Masses Are Active", in: *Frontier*, May 1, 1971, printed in: *Media and the Liberation War of Bangladesh*, vol. 2, ed. Muntassir Mamoon (Dhaka: Centre for Bangladesh Studies, 2002), 109.
68 "Pakistan. Death of an Ideal", in: *Newsweek*, 12 April 1971, in Quaderi, *Bangladesh Genocide*, 50.

local Biharis. Similarly, in Ishurdi at the end of March, thousands of village residents took a stand against Pakistani troops, captured three soldiers and killed them later. Then Biharis were murdered and their property was looted.[69] In Mymensingh, pro-Bengali troops overpowered their circa 50 West Pakistani comrades, masses of civilians streaming into the base hacked those West Pakistanis to death who tried to flee, murdered their children and wives and kidnapped some of the women.[70] In the town of Feni, an armed crowd attacked a West Pakistani unit which had barricaded itself in a large building, holding Bengali soldiers prisoner. Many West Pakistanis, but also Bengali soldiers and many civilians died. South of the town, civilians held up a military column in fighting for several days.[71] West Pakistani soldiers and officers who lived outside closed quarters became easy prey to crowds who massacred them and often also their wives and children.[72] Some Pakistani military personnel moving around alone were also killed by armed groups or crowds between March 3 and 25.[73] Many of the sites of these actions indicate that the posture of these crowds was not necessarily defensive but that they pursued military units or men and/or confronted them at a favorable place for an attack. The passionate approach with no regard for one's own life, the low number of prisoners kept and the brutal ways of killing, all of this points to how strongly people in these crowds felt that their way of action was justified because it was for a just cause. It was widely held that Biharis and West Pakistanis deserved death, a view that was also adopted by some foreign missionaries. One of them wrote in late July 1971: "I became a Bengali . . . I revised my theology on the grounds that this business about loving your enemy needs rethinking. It was based originally on the supposition that the enemy is human."[74]

In turn, crowds of non-Bengalis turned against perceived opponents, especially in the wake of brutal army attacks like on March 27–28 in Dacca.[75] In some instances, the Pakistani military distributed arms among Biharis.[76] Large groups of Biharis acted in hostile ways against Bengalis trying to escape military vio-

---

69 Accounts by Arief Razzaque and Mazudur Rahman in Firdousi, *Year*, 330, 449–450, 453.
70 Bose, *Reckoning*, 83–84; Blood, *Birth*, 276.
71 McKinley, *Death*, 12–13.
72 For an example from Chittagong or Rangamati, see the account by Naseem Rahman in Firdousi, *Year*, 465; see also Gerlach, *Extremely Violent Societies*, 151.
73 Bose, *Reckoning*, 32–33.
74 Letter by U.S. missionary Goedert quoted in Hefley and Hefley, *Christ*, 50. See also Hess, *Bangladesh*, 148.
75 Hefley and Hefley, *Christ*, 18–19.
76 See Zaglul Haider, "Repatriation of the Biharis Stranded in Bangladesh: Diplomacy and Development", *Asian Profile* 31, 6 (2003): 631.

lence.[77] Violence by Bihari crowds occurred in particular where many Biharis lived, like in (or close to) certain towns and suburbs, and in railway settlements where they often formed the majority of residents.[78] As mentioned before, in Chittagong and its suburbs, there was mutual collective violence between Bihari and Bengali demonstrators. This resembled events in the Khalishpur neighborhood in Khulna and, to a degree, of the Mohammedpur area in Dacca.[79] A rare example of a lethal pogrom organized by Biharis on Bengalis late in 1971 is known for Chittagong.[80] But overall, it is striking that, although Biharis were accused both then and in the historiography of having committed atrocities, there is relatively little concrete evidence for Bihari *crowd* violence.

Even more than in the 1950s and 1960s (when also many Hindus were killed), factories and related settlements became the scene of brutal Bengali-Bihari infighting.[81] In many places, Biharis constituted a large portion of the management, but also of foremen, specialists and other workers. After March 25, it was often non-Bengalis, and especially superiors among them, who were slaughtered by Bengali workers who, at times, did not even spare their opponents' families.[82] When crowds of workers killed superiors (and when superiors killed workers), this also involved a class aspect, but workers were also pitted against workers. People acting out of crowds killed many Biharis and Western Pakistanis, military and civilians, as well as their families, at the Kaptai power station in the remote Chittagong Hill Tracts on March 25 and 26.[83] The most deadly of these incidents happened in two jute plants in Khulna around March 27, when both Bengalis and Biharis armed themselves and barricaded themselves in, the latter lost and many of them were killed, as well as some Bengalis.[84] Even before March 26, crowds

---

77 See Akhtar et al., *Rising*, 17–18, 154.
78 Secretariat of the International Commission of Jurists, *Events*, chapter IIb.
79 Account by Ferdousi Priyobashinee in *Tormenting Seventy One: An account of Pakistan army's atrocities during Bangladesh liberation war of 1971*, ed. Shariar Kabir (Dhaka: Nirmul Committee, 1999), n.p.; this was portrayed as one-sided violence in "Khulna's Days of Terror", in: *Bangladesh Observer*, 4 February 1972. For Mohammedpur, see Qurratul Ain Tahmina, "Zabunessa Begum: A Mother's Struggle for Her Family", in: Akhtar et al., *Rising*, 14–16.
80 Account by Abdul Gofran in Jahan, *Genocide*, 401–402 (events of November 10, 1971).
81 This is emphasized in Aziz, *Blood*.
82 Sen, "Refugees", 631; account by Naseem Rahman (steel workers' settlement near Chittagong) in Firdousi, *Year*, 466; account by Premankur Roy (brickworks near Phalpur close to Mymensingh) in ibid., 379. For the 1950s and 1960s, see Sen, "Refugees", 628; Richard Sisson and Leo Rose, *War and Secession: Pakistan, India, and the Creation of Bangladesh* (Berkeley et al.: University of California Press, 1990), 13; for attacks on Hindus, see Roy, *Genocide*, 40–41, 48.
83 Secretariat of the International Commission of Jurists, *Events*, chapter IIb.
84 Bose, *Reckoning*, 80–82; Shaheen Akhtar, "Ferdousi Priyobhashini: A Hidden Chapter", in: Akhtar, *Rising*, 144, 155.

apparently committed massacres targeting non-Bengalis in factories and factory settlements.[85] Long after the end of the war, on March 10, 1972, thousands of Biharis, including women and children, fell victim to another mass attack by Bengali civilians.[86]

After the Pakistani army had prevailed with brutal means and had all towns again under its control from about April 20, 1971, Bengali crowds no longer dared to turn openly against non-Bengalis (as it had still happened even in Dacca in the night from March 25 to 26[87]). In Dacca, army fire also stopped further vengeful pogroms of Biharis against Bengalis in late April, fueled by stories by refugees from the anti-Bihari pogrom in Mymensingh. Now the troops shot several Biharis,[88] after violent Muslim demonstrations that started from different points and converged at quarters with a population consisting mainly of Hindus and supporters of independence had still been permitted on April 13, which led to arson and murder.[89] It seems that the army moved, though reluctantly, against violent Biharis on a few other occasions after March 25. Some killers from their ranks received mild prison sentences.[90] Thereby the military stifled violent crowd action for the time being. Internationally, it wanted to show that it kept law and order, domestically the regime somewhat intensified its efforts to find Bengali allies after April 18 even among students and Awami League members, although without notable success.[91]

To be sure, violence in cities and suburbs continued on a high level, but for the most part as small operations by the army and the militias and "peace committees" supporting the regime who arrested or abducted individuals en masse, tortured and murdered them, abused women and robbed enemy property. Supporters of independence, in contrast, focused on tightly organized guerrilla attacks and bombings, refraining from violent mass demonstrations.[92]

In the countryside, the lack of Pakistani government control resulted in possibilities for crowd violence, especially when targeting Hindus. The historiography

---

85 Aziz, *Blood*, 44 und 47 (Narayanganj).
86 Bose, *Reckoning*, 159.
87 See Robert Payne, *Massacre* (New York: Macmillan, 1973), 22.
88 Blood, *Birth*, 277 mentions that the army shot seven Biharis on April 28; see also Imam, *Blood*, 68 und 70 (diary entries of April 23 and 25, 1971).
89 Ahmed Sharif et al., eds., *Genocide '71: An Account of the Killers and Collaborators* (Dhaka: Muktijuddha Chetana Bikash Kendra, 1988), 41–42.
90 Account by Yaqub Zainuddin in Firdousi, *Year*, 514.
91 Blood, Birth, p. 280; FRG Consulate General in Dacca, report, October 28, 1971, PA AA, B37/629.
92 A rare counterexample is mentioned in the account by Masudur Rahman in Firdousi, *Year*, 455 (date and place are unclear). A crowd demanded from three Mukhti Bahini to kill some alleged Pakistani collaborators. The guerrillas only beat and humiliated these prisoners.

blames violence there, too, usually on the Pakistani army in connection with local militias (*razakars*) and especially on Biharis. For villages, some responsibility is also attributed to Muslim neighbors or Muslims from the area, but the forms their action took are often unclear. One author spoke of "oppression,"[93] others of looting, assault and burning down of Hindu neighborhoods, sometimes apparently carried out by large collectives.[94] Between March 1 and 25, 1971, people among crowds in the countryside supposedly killed political leaders loyal to Pakistan and other persons dubbed as antisocial and burned their houses.[95] Given the high density of the rural population, large gatherings were not uncommon. But all in all, there is little information about crowd violence in rural areas. According to one report, in the large village of Sherpur, crowds of Muslim locals went on a pillage of houses by Hindus after being asked by Pakistani troops to do so in late April 1971. After an army massacre at a nearby river, a crowd of villagers from other places coerced relatives of those executed to leave the site because they were afraid of army reprisals if the dead bodies were taken.[96]

We also do not know much about crowd counter-violence by Hindus. Refugees who often moved in large groups – consisting of up to 300,000 people – tried to protect themselves against attacks by small groups, inter alia, by taking women and children in the middle and placing men on the sides. It is possible that some of these men were armed. In one case, a local peace committee forced refugees to pay a toll and disarmed them for this purpose. However, if a group of hundreds of thousands accepted such treatment, it was either not disposed toward violent behavior or its members did not feel to be in a position to use violence.[97]

A Restricted Return to Crowd Violence in Late 1971

When Indian troops attacked East Pakistan together with Bangladeshi independence fighters in December 1971, there was once again a power vacuum, chaotic scenes and persecution of civilians. But those who acted were often small groups

---

[93] Bose, *Reckoning*, 117.
[94] See Gerlach, *Extremely Violent Societies*, 160–161; Hefley and Hefley, *Christ*, 46; Peter Kann, "A Nation Divided", *Wall Street Journal*, July 23, 1971, printed in: *Bangla Desh Documents*, 422. A clear case from the area of Chittagong is in Jeannie Lockerbie, *On Duty in Bangladesh* (Grand Rapids: Zondervan, 1976), 121–122.
[95] Maniruzzaman, *Bangladesh Revolution*, 65.
[96] Suraiya Begum, "Binapani Saha: The Many Faces of 1971", in: Akhtar et al., *Rising*, 269, 271–272. This resembles events in Chuknagar some weeks later; see chapter 3 of this volume.
[97] Partha Mukherji, "The Great Migration of 1971. I – Exodus", *Economic and Political Weekly* 9, 9, March 2, 1974, 368.

of armed men who searched neighborhoods for Biharis and alleged collaborators of the Pakistani side, shot men, raped part of the women and plundered, especially at night.⁹⁸ However, the image of the 'collaborator' became also very important as target for Bangladeshi crowd action, as it is still today.⁹⁹ Several observers also reported crowd violence at the time in which Biharis were hunted down and their houses burned, but this was often weeks and months after the end of the war in early 1972 and even still in April.¹⁰⁰ Afterward, Biharis stayed in many places in their own camps or neighborhoods for protection. In the middle of December of 1971, a rather exceptional incident occurred in which armed independence fighters together with a crowd armed with sickles, spears, axes and firearms moved against non-Bengalis; some people were massacred by the crowd, whereas smaller groups later killed women and children who were held captive. The number of dead seems to have run at least into the hundreds. Indian troops liberated the survivors.¹⁰¹

One event appears symptomatic. An armed commando under leftist guerrilla leader Kader Siddiqi (b. 1948) presented four alleged collaborators, who were accused of having attacked Bengalis, looted and tried to abduct two women, in a sports stadium in Dacca on December 18, 1971, and tortured and bayoneted them to death for half an hour in front of the cheering crowd of 5,000. Foreign media representatives filmed and photographed the scene, which was later shown by some Western European TV stations.¹⁰² On a symbolic level, this can be interpreted in a way that the victorious guerrilla fighters who had risked their lives in the struggle for independence, which lent them some legitimacy, took the law into their own hands, acting on behalf of the people in a way that was perceived as just. Viewed from another angle, the onlookers left the reckoning to the armed fighters. Such a procedure reduced the active role of crowds in the violence to being supportive

---

98 For Dacca, see the accounts by Afsan Chowdhury, Humayun Kabir und Muneer-u-Zaman, Firdousi, *Year*, 343, 377 und 440; Olson, *Bangladesh*, 207; Julian Kerr, "Mukti Bahini settling old scores in Dacca", *The Times*, December 18, 1971. For other places, see Gerlach, *Extremely Violent Societies*, 152; also Sen, "Refugees", 633; Sami Mustafa, "Who Is Conducting a Genocide?", in: *Pakistan Forum*, 3, 4 (1973): 15–16.
99 See Nusrat Sabina Chowdhury, *Paradoxes of the Popular: Crowd Politics in Bangladesh* (Stanford: Stanford University Press, 2019), 129, 153–157.
100 Hefley and Hefley, *Christ*, 86; Ben Whitaker et al., *The Biharis in Bangladesh* (London: Minority Rights Group, n.y. [1977]), 9, 14 und 16 (Dacca and Khulna); Bose, *Reckoning*, 159–160 (Khulna, March 10, 1972); Peter Hazelhurst, "Hundreds of non-Bengalis slaughtered in Bangladesh", in: *The Times*, May 8, 1972 (Mirpur near Dacca).
101 See the account by Mohammad Jafar Al Khan in Firdousi, *Year*, 521–525.
102 See Hess, *Bangladesh*, 146 and photograph after 144; photographs in Aziz, *Blood*, ix–xii; Bose, *Reckoning*, 156–157; Gerlach, *Extremely Violent Societies*, 152.

onlookers. It is also characteristic that these atrocities of December 1971 are rarely collectively questioned in Bangladesh until today, whether in the historiography or in public memory, unlike by some, or even quite a few, murderers individually – including Kader Siddiqi, whose pangs of conscience led him, according to his own version, to adopt a traumatized baby orphaned by the war who is perhaps a child of Biharis.[103]

Beyond this single case and phase, in Bangladeshi public memory, Bengali people in violent crowds of 1971–1972 were not perpetrators, but victims and heroic resisters. Their violence is considered as legitimate as that by Biharis as illegitimate – just like it was viewed then. What prevails is still the "narrative of the enemy."[104] To my knowledge there was no prosecution of crowd violence in Bangladesh at all (probably not even against Biharis or Bengali supporters of the Pakistani government, because the cases about which I read of pertained to gang violence and more direct service to the Pakistani army); and, as mentioned, Pakistani prosecution of such cases up until December 1971 was extremely limited. Crowd violence was a crime that went unpunished, mostly due to a fundamental lack of a sense of guilt on all sides, resulting in the lack of will to prosecute and probably only secondarily because it was impossible to identify responsibility.

Conclusion

In East Pakistan/Bangladesh, massive, often deadly violence was committed in many cases out of crowds in 1971 and 1972. How many people were killed this way is hard to tell but the numbers probably ran into the tens of thousands. Such incidents accumulated in specific phases of contested rule with weakened government authority: in March and April 1971 and from December 1971 to April 1972. Between these periods, this happened only in the countryside where the Pakistani military, with just a few tens of thousands of troops, and the public administration exerted no full control.

Imaginations about irrational crowds are, to an extent, disclaimed by the evidence for East Pakistan. Crowds showed political consciousness, a pattern that is also said to be typical for today's crowds in Bangladesh (though they are easily influenced by rumors) and that seems to have emerged in the 1946 Hindu-Muslim

---

[103] See (also for Siddiqi's own interpretation of the execution) Saikia, *Women*, 238–239 und 257–258, note 33. General observations as mentioned are in part taken from Yasmin Saikia, "Insāniyat for peace: survivors' narrative of the 1971 war of Bangladesh", in: *Journal of Genocide Research* 13, 4 (2011): 481, 488–489.
[104] Saikia, "Insāniyat", 481.

riots.[105] The incidence of crowd violence was closely related to the overall political situation, mass mobilization and/or self-mobilization during intense political polarization. People responded to confrontations revolving around current questions of oligarchic power vs. democratic system and procedures, national unity of an Islamic state vs. regional popular sovereignty and West vs. East Pakistan concerning the distribution of resources. Both found their demands highly legitimate and near-sacred, which resulted in sharp confrontations and left little room for dialogue. In part, people connected these demands and rejections with negative collective prejudices about Bengalis, Pakistanis or Biharis, and since many tried to distinguish members of these groups by innate physical markers (i.e., skin complexion and body height), linking these to descent, I do not hesitate to call this a form of racism. Links were also made to other traditional social divisions and stereotypes which led to collective ascriptions such as that Hindus (and secular intellectuals) supported Bangladeshi autonomy/independence and Biharis the Pakistani government. Both sides found collective violence highly justified and tended to dehumanize the 'enemy'. The strong emotions that accompanied political conflicts were expressed in cruel ways of killing, mutilations, the murder of children and few criticisms of such action. However, as far as crowd violence is concerned, there were several, but fairly clear conflict lines instead of chaos.

Therefore, victims of this violence were mostly members of easily identifiable and located minority groups that were perceived as ethnically, religiously or culturally different. Non-Bengalis (so-called Biharis) and Hindus often lived in separate settlements, neighborhoods or houses. There were relatively weak ties between groups,[106] and ideas about the otherness of certain groups were widespread, having in part solidified during former conflicts. Non-Bengalis and West Pakistanis were recognized based on their broken Bengali, West Pakistanis by their fair skin color, male Hindus because they were not circumcized and female ones by their clothing and body painting. Interwoven with ethnoreligious difference was socioeconomic conflict: a majority of Bengalis still identified Biharis and Hindus with wealth and power although many of the latter groups had either lost their elite status before or their elites had left the country, and many members of these groups had been poor all along.

---

105 See Chowdhury, *Paradoxes*, 21; Janam Mukherjee, *Hungry Bengal: War, Famine, Riots, and the End of Empire 1939–1946*, Ph.D dissertation, University of Michigan, 2011, 315–350. But this may have already been the case in the Quit India protests of 1942, see Ram Sharan Vidyarthi, "The August Movement 1942", in S. K. Sharma, ed., Quit India Movement (Delhi: Mittal, 2009), 84–90.
106 See Imam Ali, *Hindu-Muslim Community in Bangladesh* (Delhi: Kanisha, 1992), 87–88, 198, 204–205.

Those who committed violence out of crowds, by contrast, belonged mostly to the majority.[107] First of all, for them (Bengalis, Muslims) it was easier to gather masses of people. Moreover, the majority of the population also derived legitimacy from their numbers. The will and demands of the majority played an important role in public discourse. In this context, to belong to a crowd reinforced the impression that one's actions were admissible, and violence was very much rationalized by presumedly fulfilling a collective will, which reached beyond the crowd in which one was situated. Many participants in mass gatherings acted with an unshakable feeling of entitlement. Accordingly, violence was often used in broad daylight and in public spaces. It was not by accident that violence came about when the course of action was contested after democratic elections. From this developed a particular idea of *Volksgewalt* (a German term that can both mean 'people's power' and 'violence by the people'). Tajuddin Ahmed (1925–1975), the Prime Minister of Bangladesh's government when it was not yet internationally recognized, said when he took office in a radio speech on April 11, 1971 that "Quislings ... will be destroyed by the people themselves."[108] Later, literary works from Bangladesh about the events in 1971 emphasized the same points, such as crowds' claim to sovereignty as well as the fact that they were violent (even to the point of killing undecided and uncommitted people who were no enemies).[109]

Mass gatherings and collective action also served to enforce unity or at least establish social delimitation and subordination – on the path to a national state. In the short run, such violence prompted millions to flee; in the longer run, it forced Biharis to barricade in refugeee camps and drove Hindus into an inferior social position. The political leadership played a considerable role in this process involving crowds. Accordingly, the Awami League used intimidation for their electoral victory in November 1970, and Muslim notables in the countryside forced many Hindus to convert to Islam under the threat of collective action (although most revoked their Islamification in 1972).[110]

Though not much can be said about the internal mechanisms of the crowds, violence likely added some cohesion to them as well. This is supported by the infrequency of information, according to which not only individuals[111] but also

---

107 This is so although the majority of those killed in the conflicts of 1971 by all kinds of violence were Bengalis.
108 Printed in *Bangla Desh Documents*, 282–286, here 285.
109 Chowdhury, *Paradoxes*, 11–14.
110 For the latter point Gerlach, *Extremely Violent Societies*, 146.
111 See for the example of a Bengali neighbor who saved a Bihari girl from a crowd that was about to rape it, from the perspective of one of the girl's abductors, in Yasmin Saikia, "Beyond

groups within crowds in East Pakistan opposed violence.[112] Earlier violent mass gatherings tended to solidify collective identity and trained according behavior, which was the intention of some of the instigators and organizers of these shows of force.[113] But again, whatever the degrees of intentionality of the various actors, it is likely that the violence, much more than consolidating *this* specific collective (the crowd), sent out political messages to broader audiences, restructuring social and geographical spaces and visibly occupying the public sphere. Personal greed resulting in direct plunder played a secondary role in urban areas, but was important in the countryside.[114]

Minorities mobilized violent crowds only if they felt supported or tolerated by the political regime. This was especially the case for the Biharis until the Pakistani army moved against such mass attacks. Afterward, Biharis could still denounce adversaries and form militias or informal gangs for violence. Usually it was more the defense of a united Pakistan than of Islam as such that was used as justification for this, in close connection with the defense of their own group as well as its status.

Violence committed out of crowds was a kind of political participation. It was also open to the lower strata of society, as great numbers of peasants and workers are reported to have taken part in many events. But this was not necessarily about weapons of the weak but rather about the exertion of power. Strictly speaking, these were often not peaceful demonstrations. Many participants were armed, which points to much readiness for violence from the start. On the one hand, heavy and automatic weapons were not carried, which meant that the crowds' preparations were clearly inferior to the weaponry of army troops; on the other hand, the arms at hand had great lethal potential such as knives, axes, sickles, spears, sharpened bamboo sticks, iron rods, hunting rifles, shot guns, self-made bombs and Molotov cocktails. Through these weapons, the violence was rooted in the everyday (and the means were common and easy at hand) and in tradition. In

---

the Archive of Silence: Narratives of the 1971 Liberation War of Bangladesh", in: *History Workshop Journal* 58, 2004: 285; another example is in the account by Golam Sarwar, in: Firdousi, *Year*, 390.

112 See the account by Yaqub Zainuddin in Firdousi, *Year*, 516. Zainuddin relates that he and other Biharis continued to stab Hindu women and children despite objections expressed by other Biharis, abusing the latter in Urdu as "enemies of our nation". Tahmina, "Zabunessa", 17–19 is also about varying behavior of a Bihari crowd in which some wanted to kill Bengalis, others wanted save them, and some of the rescuers nonetheless looted Bengalis' property.

113 This is suggested by the microstudy of Roy, *Cows*, concerning events in 1954.

114 Mukherjee, *Hungry Bengal*, 21–22, 321, 335–342 found looting of great importance also in the city of Calcutta in 1946, also as a result of a brutalization through famine, which, however, had little impact in urban Bangladesh in late 1971 and early 1972.

many cases, men were experienced in their use and production, also from past civil strife.

It would appear that the subject matter of this chapter belongs in the context of a long tradition of political militancy involving masses in East Bengal that stretches to the present. Instead of being restricted to a transitional period to democracy,[115] this specific regional tradition has lasted and evolved over many decades and different political systems: late colonialism, West Pakistani dominance, independent Bangladesh, military dictatorships and formal democracy. Under the conditions of 1971, some restraints that normally limited such militancy ceased to apply and forces of non-violence were often subdued. The next chapter analyzes non-violence as a result of social interaction in a different context.

---

115 This is the context within which Mann, *Dark Side*, places participatory violence.

5 Narratives of Suffering: Soviet Movies About World War II

This chapter considers mass violence to be a participatory process and points to a rarely acknowledged Soviet line of remembrance of World War II: the war as a tragedy, a line which came about through the efforts of many committed individuals.[1] Thus, I try to employ an understanding of mass violence as social interaction to cultural history in order to explore the construction of memory of mass violence and challenge conventional views about state-controlled remembrance. Specifically, this chapter deals with the construction of the memory of the German-Soviet war (1941–1945) in Soviet fictional movies,[2] which supposedly took place under tight control by the state and the Communist Party of the Soviet Union (CPSU). Thus, I try to shed light on the relations between official and private remembrance. Memory, in this view, is the outcome of complex social relations instead of being easily determined by a state. In a way, this chapter explores the agency of social forces in the construction of non-violence and peace-building.

From the Second World War the Soviet Union emerged victorious and as a world power. However, in absolute numbers, the USSR also suffered immense war losses (although the specific figures are contested). Therefore, this chapter traces what narratives played which role in Soviet films and in particular in how far were these stories of victory, heroism, suffering and victimization. In contrast to a large portion of the literature, I argue that the tragic element, which emphasized suffering and pain, was always strong and became increasingly influential. To do this, several themes and elements of the plots are examined, among them the war situation in which the plots were placed and who among the characters dies and who survives. In the war, many sorts of people were victimized; hence, it is important to explore how the experience of people who met an especially painful fate was represented (who, it is often said, were near absent in Soviet war memory), such as Jews, war-disabled people and famine victims. For insights into the impact that the war had on social relations, as per these movies, I describe how the sensitive issue of sexual infidelity and faithfulness was dealt with. There

---

[1] I gladly acknowledge my gratitude to Moritz Feichtinger, Andrej Kotljarchuk, Julia Richers, Gregor Thum and Magdolna Zsivnovszki for sharing information and insights on the topic of this chapter with me. I am also grateful to all students who took a class "Sowjetische Erinnerungskultur: Filme über den Zweiten Weltkrieg" with me at the University of Bern, especially to Julian Flückiger and Michael Schmocker.
[2] For my sample of 25 films, see the filmography.

Open Access. © 2024 the author(s), published by De Gruyter. This work is licensed under the Creative Commons Attribution-NonCommercial-NoDerivatives 4.0 International License.
https://doi.org/10.1515/9783111568737-005

is also the question of the analysis that the films offered for those who caused Soviet suffering: how are the Germans depicted in these films?

While the aspects mentioned so far refer to the memory of violence imposed on Soviet people externally, Soviet troops and civilians also exerted violence in World War II. Next to military combat, this was primarily about killing or letting German prisoners die, mass rape, and Soviet terror against Soviet citizens. This raises the question, do memories of this appear in Soviet war films, and how does this fit with the overall narratives? Finally, how can it be explained that the tragic narrative became so prominent in Soviet fictional war movies, and what does that say about the public memory of World War II in the Soviet Union in general? I ask these questions against the background of the fact that films made in any country can be called ideological;[3] my objective, rather, is to find specific ideological elements.

In the scholarship on the Soviet memory of World War II, which concentrates on monuments and commemoration festivities, films have not played a big role.[4] As for artistic works, researchers have sometimes taken novels, poems and paintings into account, but movies have primarily been examined by film historians and only at times by general historians of Eastern Europe. My work builds on the studies by several film historians, such as Denise Youngblood, Neya Zorkaya and Jeremy Hicks, who pointed to some of the tendencies that I emphasize here. Methodologically, this chapter deviates from many film historians in several ways. My analysis pursues themes, constellations and narratives diachronically whereas the existing works often distinguish between different phases which, as they argue, should be kept apart. In fact, some studies proceed film by film. Moreover, I confront Eastern Europeanists' assertions about Soviet official memory with films. This chapter also differs from many existing studies by comparing films' themes, constellations and scenes with their literary model.[5]

Movies appear to me as a significant subject of research for two reasons: their vulnerability to censorship and their impact. In the USSR, films were part of state-produced memory construction. They were made in state-owned studios by

---

[3] See Detlef Kannapin, "Avantgarde, Agonie und Anpassung: Die ideologischen Grundlagen des sowjetischen Kinos nach 1945" in Lars Karl, ed., *Leinwand zwischen Tauwetter und Frost: Der osteuropäische Spiel- und Dokumentarfilm im Kalten Krieg* (Berlin: Metropol, 2007), 21–23.

[4] For exceptional statements, see Lev Gudkov, "Die Fesseln des Sieges: Russlands Identität aus der Erinnerung an den Krieg", *Osteuropa* 55, 4–6 (2005): 63; Beate Fieseler and Jörg Ganzenmüller, "Einführung" in: idem., eds., *Kriegsbilder: Mediale Repräsentationen des 'Grossen Vaterländischen Krieges'* (Fulda: Fuldaer Verlagsanstalt, 2010), 9.

[5] This course is also taken in Olga Gershenson, *The Phantom Holocaust: Soviet Cinema and Jewish Catastrophe* (New Brunswick et al.: Rutgers University Press, 2013).

state-paid directors, actors and cameramen, shown in state-owned cinemas and advertised and discussed in state-controlled newspapers and journals. Compared to novels, films were even easier to control for officials given the large funding they required and their complex production and distribution processes. Film censorship was actually tightened after World War II and again after the Brezhnev takeover.[6] Moreover, movies reached far more people than novels, poems and museums. For example, *Young Guard* (1948), shown in two parts, sold 42.4 million tickets with its first part and 36.7 million with its second part, *Story of a Real Man* (1948) sold 34.4 million tickets, *Ballad of a Soldier* (1959), although it was not considered a box office hit, sold 30.1 million, *Cranes Are Flying* (1957) 28.3 million, *Fate of a Man* (1959) 39,25 million, *Clear Skies* (1961) 41.3 million, the two parts of *The Living and the Dead* (1964) sold over 40 million tickets each, *Hot Snow* (1972) 22.7 million, *They Fought for Their Motherland* (1975) 40.6 million, *Come and See* (1985) 28.9 million, *Ivan's Childhood* (1962) 16.7 million and *Ascension* (1977) sold 10.7 million tickets. By contrast, *The Mirror* attracted only three million viewers.[7] In addition, many films were later repeatedly shown on TV. The wide outreach of most of these films cannot be disputed.

The State of Research: Victory, Heroes and Sufferings

According to the dominant interpretation, the memory of the Second World War was of great political importance for the Soviet rulers. Thus, it has been argued that it was distorted by political propaganda[8] and censorship. This is, at least im-

---

6 Beate Fieseler, "Keine Leidensbilder: Der Invalide des 'Grossen Vaterländischen Krieges' in sowjetischen Spielfilmen", Fieseler and Ganzenmüller, *Kriegsbilder*, 81; according to Denise Youngblood, *Russian War Films: On the Cinema Front, 1914–2005* (Lawrence: University Press of Kansas, 2007), 56 censorship was loosened during the war. For Brezhnev, see Lars Karl, "Von Helden und Menschen: Der Zweite Weltkrieg im sowjetischen Spielfilm (1941–1965)", *Osteuropa* 52, 1 (2002): 82.
7 Beate Fieseler, "Der Kriegsinvalide in ausgewählten sowjetischen Spielfilmen der Kriegs- und Nachkriegszeit (1944 bis 1964)", Bernhard Chiari et al., eds., *Krieg und Militär im Film des 20. Jahrhunderts* (Munich: Oldenbourg, 2003), 206, 215; Christine Engel et al., eds., *Geschichte des sowjetischen und russischen Films* (Stuttgart and Weimar: Metzler, 1999), 128, 139, 187; Youngblood, *Russian War Films*, 93, 124, 129, 136, 184, 197 and 277 note 5. For the GDR film *I Was Nineteen* (1968), a figure of 2.5 million cinema viewers indicates a large impact too (Holger Südkamp, "Ich war neunzehn: Zur filmischen und politischen Bedeutung von Konrad Wolfs DEFA-Film", *Europäische Geschichtsdarstellungen – Diskussionspapiere* 2, 3 (2005): 12, docserv.uni-duesseldorf.de/servlets/DerivateServlet/Derivate-6991 (retrieved November 22, 2013).
8 Martin Hoffmann, "Der Zweite Weltkrieg in der offiziellen sowjetischen Erinnerungskultur", Helmut Berding, ed., *Krieg und Erinnerung* (Göttingen: Vandenhoeck & Ruprecht, 2000), 129–143.

plicitly, based on the concept of totalitarianism which assumes that socialist rulers control the masses by force and manipulation. Although not all academic proponents of totalitarianism theory categorize the Soviet Union after Stalin's death as totalitarian, some scholars on Soviet war memory have explicitly done so.[9] "State and Party monopolized the history of the war and made the victory one of the main sources of legitimation of their rule" after 1964 under Brezhnev.[10] A view popular among Eastern Europeanists holds that there was official silence on World War II in its aftermath under Stalin and a "victory narrative",[11] or narratives of victory and heroism, prevailed under Brezhnev.[12] "Only triumphalist, heroic narratives were available in public".[13] Overall, "sufferings and privation, death and destruction were purged from the public memory of the war in favor of a mere cult of heroes", as the dominant historiographical narrative has it.[14] For decades, as has been argued, there was no "representation of grief, pain and guilt" in Soviet movies.[15] Generally speaking, traumatic memories were "almost entirely lost", or, in another version, the traumatic losses of life were not worked through in the USSR.[16] This has culminated in a film historian's essentialist charges that Russians only have the capacity for melancholy but do not mourn, as Europeans do and is considered normal.[17] The cult of the veterans, annual com-

---

9 Sabine Arnold, *Stalingrad im sowjetischen Gedächtnis: Kriegserinnerung und Geschichtsbild im totalitären Staat* (Bochum: Projekt, 1998), esp. 18–19. Lev Gudkov, "The fetters of history: How the war provides Russia with its identity", www.eurozine.com/articles/2005-05-03-gudkov.en.html (retrieved November 23, 2013) even applies this to post-Soviet Russia – not to mention many diatribes by scholars in the recent anti-Russian campaigns.
10 Christian Ganzer and Alena Pašković, "'Heldentum, Tragik, Tapferkeit': Das Museum der Verteidigung der Brester Festung", *Osteuropa* 60, 12 (201): 94; similarly Gudkov, "Fetters", 5; Arnold, *Stalingrad*, 393.
11 Bernd Bonwetsch, "Der 'Grosse Vaterländische Krieg': Vom öffentlichen Schweigen unter Stalin zum Heldenkult unter Breshnew", Babette Quinkert, ed., *"Wir sind die Herren dieses Landes": Ursachen, Verlauf und Folgen des deutschen Überfalls auf die Sowjetunion* (Hamburg: VSA, 2002), 178–181.
12 Hoffmann, "Weltkrieg", 131; Nina Tumarkin, *The Living and the Dead: The Rise and Fall of the Cult of World War II in Russia* (New York, Basic Books, 1994), 110, 126–127, 135–145; Arnold, *Stalingrad*, 22–23.
13 Tatiana Zhurzhenko, "Heroes into victims: The Second World War in post-Soviet memory politics", www.eurozine.com/articles/2012-10-31-zhurzhenko-en.html (retrieved November 21, 2013), 4.
14 Bonwetsch, "'*Grosse Vaterländische Krieg*'", 168.
15 Fieseler, "Keine Leidensbilder", 81.
16 Catherine Merridale, *Nights of Stone: Death and Memory in Russia* (London: Granta, 2000), 201, 304 (quote).
17 See Evgenia Bezborodova, *Die Rolle des Imaginären in sowjetischen Kriegsfilmen*, Ph.D dissertation, Ludwig-Maximilians-Universität München, 2018, 256–295.

memorative anniversaries and monuments in particular fostered the heroic narrative.[18]

While narratives of victory and heroism are certainly known to everybody who visited or visits the area of the former Soviet Union, many of these statements seem excessive. If one follows some of these views, only literary works were, as it is often phrased, "more open", "more sincere" and "closer to reality", depicting less heroic truths about the everyday in the war.[19] According to one version, the image of the "heroic defender" contrasted with the individual experience of "personal tragedy".[20] Another author leaves it undecided whether private memory was marginalized and silenced or processed and manipulated.[21]

Scholars have offered varying periodizations of Soviet war memory. Among them, the view is widespread that there was some openness in 1945–1946, the cult of victorious Stalin prevailed from 1946 to 1953, de-Stalinization between 1953 and 1964 and a "bombastic" remembrance practiced in the so-called stagnation period from 1964 to 1987, which again emphasized victory above all.[22] Some conceded that in a few films during the thaw period, but only then, the war memories were presented "as history of destruction and grief",[23] and Neia Zorkaia argues that this was preceded by similar tendencies during the war, in 1941–1945, when "tears, suffering, fear and humiliation" were depicted on Soviet film screens.[24] Another analyst found that a shift "from triumph to trauma" occurred only after the end of socialism.[25] Before 1991, in these views, "narratives of suffering [were] secondary to heroic narratives", and "Soviet commemorative culture required

---

18 Guido Hausmann, "Die unfriedliche Zeit: Politischer Totenkult im 20. Jahrhundert", Manfred Hettling and Jörg Echternkamp, eds., *Gefallenengedenken im globalen Vergleich* (Munich: Oldenbourg, 2013), 427–435.
19 Bonwetsch, "Grosse Vaterländische Krieg", 174, 182; near-identical Bernd Bonwetsch, "'Ich habe an einem völlig anderen Krieg teilgenommen': Die Erinnerung an den Grossen Vaterländischen Krieg in der Sowjetunion", Berding et al., *Krieg*, 159; Fieseler, "Keine Leidensbilder", 80; Tumarkin, *Living*, 111.
20 Hoffmann, "Weltkrieg", 140.
21 Gudkov, "Fesseln", 6, 9.
22 Bonwetsch, "Grosse Vaterländische Krieg", 169–172, 178–181.
23 Peter Jahn, "Patriotismus, Stalinismuskritik und Hollywood: Der 'Grosse Vaterländische Krieg' in russischen TV-Serien der Gegenwart", Fieseler and Ganzenmüller, *Kriegsbilder*, 128.
24 Neja Zorkaja, "Kino in Zeiten des Krieges: Visualisierungen von 1941 bis 1945", *Osteuropa* 55, 4/6 (2005): 328–334 (quote 328).
25 Zhurzhenko, "Heroes", 2; for the merely deductive rationale ibid., 5.

martyrs rather than victims".[26] After 1991, some observe a pluralization of narratives in Russian films about World War II.[27]

Many students of the Soviet remembrance of World War II have written on the assumption that there were two types of remembrance, individual memory based on private experience and official, state-directed memory. Without much elaboration, they usually acknowledge that there was some middle ground. Some think of them as intertwined rather than disconnected, with individual memory and private desires also influencing official remembrance and propaganda.[28] In particular, this argument has been made for literary works.[29] Although Sabine Arnold, unlike me, thought that it was primarily official memory that influenced private memory, I accept a term mentioned by her, "public memory"[30] for what I explore because the films analyzed here were state-produced and in the public arena, but not official, since they reflected the artistic work of individuals.

My sample includes 25 films[31] made between 1943 and 2010. This study is focused on the Soviet period; just one film covered here was made after 1987. Further, I largely exclude movies produced during the war, and all films included in my sample were shown in Soviet cinemas. The films were selected because they are well-known, often also internationally, having won several accolades. This means that my selection neglects works that critics and historians have considered to possess lower artistic value. The narratives of the latter may well have differed from those discussed in this chapter, but, again, most films I cover did reach large audiences, and one could easily add a dozen more that convey stories and imageries similar to those that I have written about.

Narratives of Suffering and Tragedy

Deep sadness can be felt in many Soviet war films. Pain, loss and grief are not marginal but constitutive aspects of them. Moreover, almost all of these films, even the ones produced during the war, show dead or dying Soviet people. In *Hot*

---

26 Ibid., 3.
27 Isabelle de Keghel, "Glaube, Schuld und Erlösung: Religion im neuen russischen Kriegsfilm", *Osteuropa* 59, 1 (2009): 97–108; Zhurzhenko, "Heroes", 2.
28 Hoffmann, "Weltkrieg", 132, 139.
29 Ilja Kukulin, "Schmerzregulierung: Zur Traumaverarbeitung in der sowjetischen Kriegsliteratur", *Osteuropa* 55, 4–6 (2005): 236.
30 Arnold, *Stalingrad*, 19, cf. 174–175.
31 One of the motion pictures included is a documentary (*Ordinary Fascism*), one a fictional movie from the GDR (*I Was Nineteen*), and one Soviet fictional film is entirely set in the postwar period (*Today There Will Be No Leave*).

Snow (1972), for example, a young Soviet officer searches despairingly for the surviving members of his unit, a general climbs over Soviet corpses, and those still alive receive medals from him with gloomy faces. These films often dwell on Soviet citizens suffering under collective and individual German atrocities (as those of the wartime period did[32]). At least from the late 1950s onward, the strong tragic element and downplaying of heroism in these films was not lost on contemporary Western European film critics.[33]

Film historians have identified a turn to tragedy primarily based on four movies that came out between 1957 and 1962.[34] Three of them show how the life of the protagonist is destroyed. The viewer watches them suffer one blow after another. Importantly, the individual tragedy is not depicted as a sacrifice instrumental to the common good of the people, and the disaster is not remedied by a comforting meaning.[35] In *Cranes Are Flying* (1957), a young woman loses her parents and her fiancé to whom she is temporarily unfaithful. In *Ivan's Childhood* (1962) a boy of about twelve years, tormented by nightmares and memories related to the murder of his mother and sister at the hands of the Germans, is active as a Soviet agent behind the German lines until he is brutally executed. In *Fate of a Man* (1959), a Soviet soldier gets captured by the Germans, deported, starved, tortured and used as a forced laborer. He manages to escape, but his entire family is killed by the Germans, leaving him mentally broken. This character, who is also the narrator of the film, calls his war experience "bitter", emphasizes his "sufferings" and asks, "Why has life played such pranks on me?" Only the young protagonist in *Ballad of a Soldier* (1959) avoids suffering major losses of family or friends, but he himself, depicted as the ultimate altruist, does not survive (which the viewers are already told at the beginning of the film). Furthermore, his love from a brief furlough from the front remains unfulfilled, and his last meeting with his mother, planned to be several days long, shrinks to a few minutes and is framed as a dramatic farewell, suggesting that they will not be seeing each other again. It is symbolically significant that the protagonists in *Cranes Are Flying* and

---

[32] Dmitri Shlapentokh and Vladimir Shlapentokh, *Soviet Cinematography 1918–1991: Ideological Conflict and Social Reality* (New York: Aldine de Gruyter, 1993), 118; Youngblood, *Russian War Films*, 57–81.
[33] See Oksana Bulgakowa and Dietmar Hochmuth, eds., *Der Krieg gegen die Sowjetunion im Spiegel von 36 Filmen: Eine Dokumentation* (Berlin: Freunde der Deutschen Kinemathek e.V., n.y. [1992]), 69–70, 85, 96, 120. The reviews collected there refer to *Cranes Are Flying*, *Fate of a Man*, *Ivan's Childhood* and *Ascension*.
[34] Shlapentokh and Shlapentokh, *Soviet Cinematography*, 211–232; Karl, "Von Helden", 76–81; Engel et al., *Geschichte*, 118–128; Youngblood, *Russian War Films*, 118–127.
[35] Shlapentokh and Shlapentokh, *Soviet Cinematography*, 136 make this argument for *Cranes Are Flying*.

Fate of a Man also spoil their farewell from their loved ones or miss to meet them. This happens even twice in *Clear Skies* (1961), once in a haunting scene showing hundreds of women on a railway station platform screaming because the train with their husbands or partners does not stop as expected.

Such storylines were typical for many Soviet movies about the war but also controversial. The makers of *Fate of a Man*, for example, were urged to cut down on the scenes set in camps and asked to not exhibit the "sufferings of an innocent" so extensively.[36] But the producers resisted, and this choice was confirmed by the reason why cultural policy-makers nominated the film as the official Soviet contribution to the International Moscow Film Festival: to show the brutal character of imperialism by depicting the suffering and struggle in the Great Patriotic War and demonstrating the Soviet support for peace.[37] A script writer wanted the boy in *Ivan's Childhood* to survive, but director Andrei Tarkovsky rejected this idea because he wished the "painful life phase" of the protagonist to end with death ("nothing follows afterwards"), without any "acts of heroism".[38] The film *Come and See* (1985) was a point of culmination of this film poetics, as, by optical and acoustical means, it places the viewer in the position of a victim of various types of atrocities, including an overwhelming scene toward the end of the film where villagers are burned alive in a wooden church. This has been called "the most powerful antiwar film in Soviet cinema".[39]

Soviet war films carried this potent tragic element at all times. As film experts have shown, this is, first of all, true for many movies made during World War II,[40] certainly including *The Unvanquished* (1945), which shows as part of its story the murder of the local Jews, dramatically set in the middle of the film. As in that scene, the tragic element can also be found in the motion picture *Young Guard* (1948), especially in its use of music. Shostakovich's elegiac cello tune evokes seriousness from the start, and the film ends with the execution of most of the heroes and a mourning ceremony organized by the Communist Party. Young Oleg Koshevoi is driven to become the fanatical leader of the resisting youth in town by secretly watching a German mass execution, which provokes him at first to exclaim to his mother in desperation: "How can we live on after this?!" Even in

---

36 Quoted in Bulgakowa and Hochmuth, *Krieg*, 85.
37 Lars Karl, "Zwischen politischem Ritual und kulturellem Dialog: Die Moskauer Internationalen Filmfestspiele im Kalten Krieg 1959–1971", Karl, *Leinwand*, 284.
38 Quotes from Bulgakowa and Hochmuth, *Krieg*, 94–95.
39 Youngblood, *Russian War Films*, 197.
40 Peter Kenez, *Cinema and Soviet Society, 1917–1953* (Cambridge: Cambridge University Press, 1992), 192, 196–199; Fieseler, "Keine Leidensbilder", 78; Karl, "Von Helden", 71; Engel et al., *Geschichte*, 87–95.

The Fall of Berlin (1950), Soviets, especially women, suffer, although this film is primarily about victory.[41] *Story of a Real Man* (1948) is less serious in its treatment of its topic, despite all the suffering that the protagonist Meresiev goes through and the depression he falls into after having both his legs amputated due to injuries. But Meresiev, a self-made hero seemingly without family and friends, becoming a fighter pilot once again with the help of protheses, is too schematic a character to be the subject of a tragedy. Still, suffering and tragedy were not principally absent even in late Stalinism (1945–1955). As noted, the tragic narrative became very strong during the thaw period (1956–1964), and, as will be seen in the following, it was lost neither in the Brezhnev era (1964–1982) nor afterward. The move "from triumph to trauma" came long before the breakdown of socialism.[42]

The transition from late Stalinism to the Khrushchev period visible in the films *Immortal Garrison* (1956) and *Leningrad Symphony* (1956–1957) is noteworthy. *Immortal Garrison* starts with dramatic martial music and a dedication to the heroes of the Brest Fortress who fought under siege for four weeks (another real episode of the war). The protagonists in the film talk a lot about willpower and communism, but the battle scenes are in fact rather short, all the main characters die except for one (their death is often shown on screen), the Germans are depicted as mowing down surrendering women and children, people are shown crying and many end up dying of exhaustion and excruciating thirst.[43] Their weakness is exhibited extensively.[44] The film's subtitle reads "A Heroic Tragedy", which, linguistically speaking, emphasizes tragedy over heroism while combining both.

Leningrad Symphony deals with the staging of Shostakovich's Symphony No. 7 in Leningrad, which he dedicated to his home-town during the brutal German siege in 1942. Stressing the moral and cultural superiority of the Soviets over the attackers, the film dwells on German artillery fire and partisan fighting more than on hunger and cold although the latter, in reality, claimed many more victims. Tragedy strikes twice dramatically but shortly in the film when a woman who had starved to death is discovered and a soldier finds the house of his friends that was erased by a German bomb attack; the latter is similar to scenes in *Cranes Are Flying* (1957) and *Fate of a Man* (1959). The climax is particularly significant. From the concert, one mostly hears the fourth bombastic and militant set of Shostakovich's symphony, but it is underlaid with pictures of a partisan

---

41 Kenez, *Cinema*, 232–235.
42 This is in contrast to Zhurzhenko, "Heroes", 2, 5.
43 See also Josephine Woll, *Real Images: Soviet Cinema and the Thaw* (London and New York: I.B. Tauris, 2000), 71–72.
44 This is especially the case after 1:04:30.

horsecart convoy with provisions reaching the city. What could have been triumphal is not because the partisans suffered heavy losses and their leader, beloved to the concert's female organizer, is brought back dead. The Leningraders receive the convoy like a funeral procession, weeping and taking their caps of. Finally, the sad message reaches her in the concert hall. Thus, in this transitional period, narratives of tragedy and victory were brought together.

The very situations in which these movies' stories are set have tragic narratives written all over them, and filmmakers would obsessively return to them. Two of the films depict the epic but hopeless defense of the Brest fortress in which (allegedly) no defender survived: *Immortal Garrison* (1956) and *Fortress Brest* (2010). This topic still seems to have much appeal, given that the latter was made quite recently and was a critical and commercial success in Russia.[45] Like *The Living and the Dead* (1964), these films deal with the Soviet defeats of 1941. Of those set in 1942, two show, instead of victory, events during the disastrous retreats of July 1942, among them *They Fought for Their Motherland* (1975). Even the plot of the lyrical romance *Ballad of a Soldier* (1959) takes place exactly during the days leading up to July 28, 1942 – the day Stalin gave the harsh no-step-back order no. 227, although that order is not mentioned in the film. Two films in the sample depict the battle of Stalingrad but emphasize times when the Soviets were on the defense (*Nobody Is Born a Soldier* in 1969 and *Hot Snow* in 1972). Thus, for all their monumentality, the narrative of suffering was principally kept during the Brezhnev period.

Two other films, *Leningrad Symphony* (1956–1957) and *Clear Skies* (1961), show the siege of Leningrad that appeared heroic but resulted in immense losses of life. *Clear Skies* also touches upon the unheroic issue of captivity, which is central in *Fate of a Man* (1959). Other films show defeat or retreat in partisan warfare (*Ascension* in 1977 and *Come and See* in 1985) or death in underground struggle (*Ivan's Childhood* in 1962 and *The Young Guard* in 1948). And two pictures depict the precarious situation during evacuation, which is not a particularly heroic topic either (*Cranes Are Flying* in 1957 and *The Mirror* in 1974).[46]

A few films do show general situations of victory, which, however, is usually ruined by the last-minute battle death of main characters or their loved ones like the son of Andrei Sokolov in *Fate of a Man* or Djengiz in *Ich war neunzehn* (1968),

---

[45] *Fortress Brest* is assessed as a model of a Russian program of war education in Francesca Mazzali, *The Kremlin's Propaganda for Patriotic Education and Russian War Movies (2000–2010)*, Ph.D. dissertation, Charles University, Prague, 2016, 93, 196–206, 221.

[46] For evacuation as an unheroic topic and rare in Soviet war films, see also Olga Gershenson, "The Missing Links of Holocaust Cinema: Evacuation in Soviet Films", *Post Script* 32, 2 (2013): 53–62.

which is based on a true-life story.[47] In *Fate of a Man*, Sokolov looks at the celebrating troops with a stoney face out of grief. In *Ivan's Childhood*, officer Bondarev, shortly after victory, discovers that the Germans executed the child agent Ivan when searching files in a Berlin government building.[48] The film ends with the chilling sounds of Ivan being dragged to his execution, contrasted with his happy childhood memories. Both scenes do not indicate triumph. In *Cranes Are Flying* (1957), the film ends when Veronika gets to know that her fiancé Boris fell in battle long ago from his comrade, which turns a homecoming-cum-victory celebration into a sad scene. Boris' father then takes her by the arm and leads her into the crowd, for she still has Boris' family and another, as the camera move suggests – the Soviet people.

The motif of loss at the last minute is even present in the super-Stalinist war fairy tale *The Fall of Berlin* (1950) during the storming of the Reichstag building, where, however, Stalin's genius manages to overshadow any tragedy. However, in general, victory is not the main element in these films, and the last-minute death is often shown because without death and loss, *any* film about this war would have appeared unrealistic in the USSR, even to the makers of the cineastic absurdity that was *The Fall of Berlin*.

How do the main protagonists in these films fare personally? Very many of them die, on or off screen,[49] like the young heroes in *Young Guard* (1948). Further, the loss of main characters' loved ones is omnipresent. A few examples shall suffice. Sometimes, there is only one survivor to tell the story. In *Ivan's Childhood* (1962), it is Galtsev who survives, while Ivan, Cholin and Katasonov fall in battle or are murdered by the Germans. In *Immortal Garrison* (1956), only Baturin remains alive. *Fortress Brest* (2010) depicts real historical characters and tells the audience that all perished but invents a young boy who manages to sneak out (in contradiction to the above, they also let us know in writing that Major Gavrilov returned from a German POW camp at the end of the war). Flyora in *Come and See* (1985) loses his mother and little sisters in a German massacre. Similar to *Hot Snow* (1972), the four main characters in *They Fought for Their Motherland* (1975) do survive for the moment (although in one case, it is not clear), but viewers are told that from their entire regiment, only 26 men are still alive. And probably not for very long, as even though the regiment is replenished because it kept its banner through all the battles, it is going to be sent to a new place – the battle of Stalingrad that is about to begin, where losses were high, as every viewer knows.

---

47 Südkamp, "Ich", 8.
48 Tumarkin, *Living*, 112.
49 See also Woll, *Real Images*, 81.

In *Ascension* (1977), four out of the prison's five cell inmates are hanged by the Germans and their local helpers. The fifth, Rybak, survives as a German auxiliary policeman, who starts this job by helping hang his former partisan comrade Sotnikov. Also remains the nihilist pro-German prosecutor Portnov, who, significantly, tells Sotnikov during his interrogation that nobody will ever hear of his refusal to cooperate because the German side will spread false stories about him. Nevertheless, Sotnikov becomes a role model for a little boy who watches the execution. The film was based on a novella written by Vasil Bykau, who, in his writings, often lets his main, affirmatively portrayed character be killed after not having achieved anything in military terms; and the few who survive are tormented by their memories.[50] The way *Ballad of a Soldier* (1959) is narrated is symptomatic: viewers are told at the beginning of the film that the main character will not survive the war. In his case, three women mourn him for a long time afterward, but two of these women do not know about the third, and she does not know them.

In connection with the stories of suffering that Soviet war movies told it is striking how often and how strongly Christian symbols are used throughout all phases of the Soviet depiction of World War II, including late Stalinism.[51] The most obvious example in my sample is *Ascension* (1977) which likens the main character Sotnikov to Christ not only in the title but in much of the film, mostly through the use of imagery. This was not the first time that a parallel between German executions and Golgatha and crucifixion was constructed in a Soviet war film.[52] *Come and See* (1985) is an apocalyptic film[53] the title of which is borrowed from the Gospel according to John. In *Fate of a Man* (1959), the Germans herd Soviet prisoners of war in a damaged church. A prisoner needs to defecate but cannot do so in a church due to his Christian convictions; mocked by his fellow Soviet prisoners, he tries to get out and is shot by the Germans, which leaves his fellow POWs shocked and ashamed. *Ivan's Childhood* (1962), like other films by Tarkovsky, is replete with Christian symbols (for example, an askew cross), and Ivan and Galtsev meet and stay in a half-destroyed chapel. Sergei Bondarchuk inserted an ironic scene in *They Fought for Their Motherland* (1975) where, as a battle becomes life-threatening, the character (played by the director himself) starts to pray, mumbling that, after all, this is allowed as he is not a member of the Communist Party, but stops because praying will not make a good impression on his

---

50 See Wassil Bykau, *Romane und Novellen* (Cologne: Pahl-Rugenstein, 1985, 2 volumes).
51 For the wartime period, see Engel, *Geschichte*, 94–95; Youngblood, *Russian War Films*, 62. For the time after 1991, see de Keghel, "Glaube".
52 For *Zoia* of 1944, see Tumarkin, *Living*, 77.
53 Bulgakowa and Hochmuth, *Krieg*, 127–132.

comrades in arms. Generally, the emphasis on Christian symbols was part of the wartime mobilization of Russian nationalism and was used in the films to underline the Russian character as well as the unity of the Soviet people during the conflict. Russophiles became quite strong in 1970s and 1980s Soviet cinema, also beyond war stories.[54] In war movies, Christian symbols are often used to depict the sacrifice of the innocent.

Like Christian motifs, the contrast drawn between life in the prewar period and during wartime is to evoke the feeling that war is an unnatural state[55] (rather than being celebrated as an opportunity to show bravery or communist superiority). The most glaring example of this is the contrast between the glistening, dreamlike prewar family scenes and the gloomy war imagery in *Ivan's Childhood*. The films about the Brest Fortress, which was attacked on the early morning of the first day of the German invasion, begin with the wonderful summer day and private happiness on the eve of that event (*Immortal Garrison* of 1956 and *Fortress Brest* of 2010). Several films show Soviet citizens receiving the news that the war has started – sometimes by listening to Prime Minister Molotov's radio announcement – on a sunny, optimistic Sunday morning (for instance, *Cranes Are Flying*, 1957[56]). *Young Guard* (1948) and *Clear Skies* (1961) set some initial happy moments into wartime before tragedy strikes. It should be added that such scenes implicitly downplay the tragedy and gravity of Soviet mass persecution before 1941.

The motif of the child soldier also conveys strong messages of a world in a terrible condition. The most famous example is *Ivan's Childhood*, in which the twelve year-old boy appears as a mentally disturbed child who suffers from ghastly nightmares and daydreams and feels a fanatical and fearless urge to act against the enemy. Compared to the novella *Ivan* by Vladimir Bogomolov, which the film is based on, the film focuses even stronger on the theme of lost childhood by changing the title and introducing intensity to the narrative by adding Ivan's dreams, nightmares and memories of his happy life with his family that was murdered.[57] Like many other movies covered here, this film was meticulously researched and portrayed the boy as a victim, the troops' affection for him and the boy's agency, which was typical of many actual Soviet child soldiers.[58] Later So-

---

54 Shlapentokh and Shlapentokh, *Soviet Cinematography*, 141–143, 167, 208.
55 This unnatural state is also expressed by depictions of nature, on which I cannot elaborate here.
56 See Woll, *Real Images*, 79–80.
57 See Wladimir Bogomolow, *Leuchtspur über den Strom* (Berlin [East]: Kultur und Fortschritt, 1960). The Russian title of the book was *Ivan*.
58 See Olga Kucherenko, *Little Soldiers: How Soviet Children Went to War, 1941–1945* (Oxford et al: Oxford University Press, 2011), 151–192.

viet/Russian movies continued to depict Soviet suffering through the eyes of minors and used them as examples of suffering, but they tended to treat the very existence of child soldiers less and less critically (*Come and See* in 1985 and *Fortress Brest* in 2010[59]). However, the fact that child soldiers fought on the Soviet side was not hidden in Soviet films.

The artistic doctrine of Socialist Realism was only applied in the early films.[60] Defining artworks as being 'socialist in content, realist in style', socialist realist pieces were to show tough but victorious struggles of progressive social forces. In their most dogmatic versions, such pieces would make clear that the Communist Party led this struggle correctly. However, this was only the case in a few films included in this sample, such as *Young Guard* (1948) and *The Fall of Berlin* (1950), to some extent also in *Immortal Garrison* (1956) and, interestingly, in the post-socialist Russian-Belarusian co-production *Fortress Brest* (2010). But especially the latter two hardly pictured the Communist Party leading a *successful* struggle. In this context, it is notable that, according to Peter Kenez, few of the Soviet war films made until 1945 had a communist as the main character.[61] While most of the movies covered here had positive lead characters, these were increasingly individualized, their fate was sad rather than uplifting, and/or their behavior was flawed rather than model-like. There are some more films in my sample where main characters – always men – are marked as communists (like in *They Fought for Their Motherland* (1975)), but they often fail in their struggle, and sometimes they do so more or less alone like in *Cranes Are Flying* (1957) and *Ascension* (1977). In the plots of *Clear Skies* (1961), *The Living and the Dead* (1964) and *One Isn't Born a Soldier* (1967) the CPSU, as part of Stalinist repression, discriminates against lead males who are communists, who, nevertheless, prevail in the end and strike military success.

Yet, the main characters are usually not winners. In movies such as *Cranes Are Flying* and *Ivan's Childhood*, the protagonists do not fire any shots at the Germans. If heroism is at all central to these films,[62] then it would have to be another sort of heroism than the one associated with military success – one of endurance and preservation of one's humanity. The word "human being" (chelovek) appears prominently in several films. In two cases, it is used in the titles of the films, although this gets lost in the English translation. Translated literally, the titles should read *Story of a Real Human Being* (1948) and *Fate of a Human Being* (1959),

---

59 For literary depictions, see Kucherenko, *Little Soldiers*, 249.
60 See also Kannapin, "Avantgarde", 28.
61 Kenez, *Cinema*, 201.
62 Youngblood, *Russian War Films*, 119, 125 denies any.

and in the latter film, a traitor is simply called a "bad human being".⁶³ In *The Unvanquished* (1945), Ukrainian worker Taras pays his respect to his friend Dr. Fishman when watching him being taken to the mass execution of the Jews; Fishman stops and responds: "Thank you, human". And in *Clear Skies* (1961), Astakhov, a victim of Soviet persecution, says that the Communist Party had not taught him that vigilance meant universal suspiciousness, insisting that he is "a human being" seeking the truth. (The very next moment, he receives the message: "Stalin is dead"). Disappointing from a Marxist point of view, this insistence on humanity is closely related to the individualizing stories that most of these films tell.

Most of them were *not* monumental, deindividualized and full of grim determination like the sort of Soviet memory that many scholars describe.⁶⁴ They usually did not celebrate victory. Often, they showed martyrs only in a certain sense: some protagonists are passive victims of German violence, and among those who are involved in active struggle, many are unsuccessful, although some are explicitly called heroes in films such as *Ballad of a Soldier* and *They Fought for Their Motherland*. Neither do they want to die for the cause, nor is their sacrifice shown as being uplifting, resulting in collective harmony. Soviet narratives of heroism and suffering could be closely connected,⁶⁵ but many of these films did not propagate the kind of self-sacrificial heroism that war monuments celebrate internationally by honoring heroes who saved the day through their self-sacrificial deeds in seemingly hopeless military situations.⁶⁶ The films discussed here did not present "the war [. . .][as] one of the best pages of our [Soviet] history".⁶⁷ Additionally, these movies went beyond the common practice of soldiers pitying themselves after the war⁶⁸ and internationally familiar narratives of the failed reintegration of former soldiers into civilian life.

---

63 Only in *Story of a Real Human*, human is used in a heroic sense, for a real human, according to the film, is a Soviet human (who can successfully fly fighter planes with two leg protheses). But this hero too has to go through half a film of suffering and endurance.
64 Tumarkin, *Living*, 124–157.
65 See Tumarkin, *Living*, 133–135, 145–146; Arnold, *Stalingrad*; Mazzali, *Kremlin's Programme*, 19.
66 One example is the depiction of World War I heroes in the U.S. Soldiers and Sailors Memorial at Pittsburgh, Pennsylvania (I refer to the state of the exhibition in 2006).- Gudkov, "Fesseln", 67 asserts that all public Soviet war narratives, including films, were only variations on the theme of "heroic self-sacrifice".
67 This is in contradiction to the cited statement by Aleksander Shpagin, "The Religion of War", *Iskusstvo kino* 5 (May 2005), 57, quoted after Youngblood, *Russian War Films*, 131.
68 For example, see Nadire Mater, ed., *Voices from the Front: Turkish Soldiers on the War with the Kurdish Guerrillas* (New York and Basingstoke: Palgrave Macmillan, 2005).

The Depiction of Jews and Their Persecution

Another stereotype among researchers, which serves to emphasize the purportedly uniform character of Soviet war memory, is that Jews were absent from it because Soviet memory politics allowed only for one victim group, the Soviet people.[69] Although this has been disproven, such assertions are widespread.[70] Soviet citizens, it has been argued, could learn "that the German occupiers had persecuted the Jewish population specifically" only from the works of two novelists or one poet due to censorship.[71] This has also been considered true for fictional films, except for the time till 1945. "Jews, their religion, and their culture were nonexistent in Soviet movies (as well as theatre and literature) in the four decades prior to perestroika. [. . .] It is impossible to name a single positive character in pre-Glasnost Soviet movies who can be identified as a Jew".[72] A recent itemization of Soviet fictional movies representing Jews lists no more than three from 1946 to 1981.[73]

Again, works of some scholars and my material suggest something else, and in addition, there were many Soviet documentaries on the Nazi persecution of Jews.[74] Jews do appear in at least eight of the films analyzed for this chapter,[75] usually as positive figures (some as fighters), and in characteristic ways. This is not so surprising in the case of films made by directors with a Jewish background. Mark Donskoi's *The Unvanquished* (1945) shows the persecution of Jews (and other groups) in a Ukrainian town through a side character, the physician Fishman. In a long scene, Jews are being marched off to a ravine to be shot by Germans with machine pistols and revolvers, which is underscored with tragical

---

[69] Zhurzhenko, "Heroes", 3–4; for official commemorative events: Merridale, *Nights*, 292.
[70] See Karel Berkhoff, "'Total Annihilation of the Jewish Population': The Holocaust in the Soviet Media, 1941–1945", *Kritika* 10,11 (2009): 61–105, who also sums up and corrects the earlier literature on the topic.
[71] Bonwetsch, "Grosse Vaterländische Krieg", 182 (quote); nearly identical Bonwetsch, "Ich", 159; see Tumarkin, *Living*, 114–124.
[72] Shlapentokh and Shlapentokh, *Soviet Cinematography*, 223; only slightly more guarded is Engel et al., *Geschichte*, 95.
[73] Valérie Pozner and Natacha Laurent, eds., *Kinojudaica: les représentations des Juifs dans le cinéma de Russie et d'Union soviétique des années 1910 aux années 1980* (Paris: Nouveau monde, 2012), 501–503.
[74] See Jeremy Hicks, *First Films of the Holocaust: Soviet Cinema and the Genocide of the Jews* (Pittsburgh: University of Pittsburgh Press, 2012); Gershenson, *Phantom Holocaust*; Pozner and Laurent, *Kinojudaica*, 509–556.
[75] In addition to the films discussed below, there were side characters recognizable as Jewish also in *Wait for Me* (1943) and *Hot Snow* (1972). See Gershenson, *Phantom Holocaust*, 42, 176, 188.

music (41:00–44:40). This scene, climax of this movie, was in fact filmed at the Babyi Yar gorge in Kiev, the original place of the German massacre of more than 33,000 Jews in late September 1941.[76] The literary source the film is based on describes the Jews being marching off but refrains from describing the massacre in detail, unlike the film.[77] A few passing references to the Germans persecuting Jews in particular appeared in other wartime Soviet fictional films.[78] In Mikhail Romm's documentary *Ordinary Fascism* (1965), the specific persecution and murder of Jews constitute a substantial portion. Jews are, though not always, mentioned in the comment or visible as Jews (Jewish stars appearing on the screen and the commentator speaking of ghettos).[79] Notably, their murder is portrayed as one of the first steps toward a larger (supposed) German scheme for annihilating the Slavs.

Jews also appear in the works of non-Jewish filmmakers. In *Ascension* (1977), the little girl named Basya, a supporting character, is recognizable – although this is not said explicitly – as a Jewess by her fate and appearance (and played by a Jewish actress). In the film, the audience learns that she was hiding for months, possibly from extermination. It is clear that she has been abused by pro-German policemen, and by the end, she is hanged with the rest. If the protagonist represents Christ, she appears as a saint-like figure. In *Come and See* (1985), a German anti-Jewish leaflet is cited, and there is a short scene where a Jewish man receives special torment by Germans and their Soviet helpers during the orgy of violence where almost the entire population of a village is massacred.

In *Fortress Brest* (2010), there are two Jewish figures, both of whom are political commissars. One of them is Weinstein, who first denies the danger of a German invasion, wrongly so, but later becomes a brave leader in the defensive battle in which he is killed. Before the invasion, he, at a rehearsal, aptly shows to soldiers how to perform a Russian folk dance, and even during the battle, he tries to cheer up his comrades with some folklore dancing steps, indicating that he is well-integrated. The second man, Fomin, a lead character in the film, is a serious, hardened hero who commands part of the troops. Having been overwhelmed and

---

[76] Jeremy Hicks, "Confronting the Holocaust: Mark Donskoi's *The Unvanquished*", *Studies in Russian and Soviet Cinema* 3, 1 (2009): 33–51; Hicks, *First Films*, 134–156; Gershenson, *Phantom Holocaust*, 40–48; Olga Gershenson, "*Les Insoumis* (1945) ou comment un roman soviétique et devenue un film juif", Pozner and Laurent, *Kindojudaica*, 341–364; Zorkaja, "Kino", 334.
[77] Boris Gorbatov, *Die Unbeugsamen* (Stockholm: Neuer Verlag, 1944), 85–88.
[78] Hicks, *First Films*, 87–88, 97.
[79] See also Gershenson, *Phantom Holocaust*, 63–66. The assertion that there is no verbal mentioning of Jews in the film (Bulgakowa and Hochmuth, *Krieg*, 161) is incorrect, cf. chapters 6 and 13 of *Ordinary Fascism*.

run out of ammunition, he is captured along with a few others. When a German officer declares that "commissars, [communist] party functionaries and Jews are being punished", he steps forward, proudly stating "I am a commissar, communist and Jew", and is shot as a result. (This is based on a real person who was famous in the postwar narrative about the fortress.[80])

Even more impressive is the depiction of the fate of the Jews in *Fate of a Man* (1959). When a crowd of Soviet prisoners of war is being held in a damaged church shortly after being captured by the Germans, a Jewish physician-soldier is shown walking around and selflessly helping the wounded.[81] He appears as a Good Samaritan and is shot the next morning when the Germans begin searching for commissars and Jews. Still more important is a ghastly scene exactly in the middle of the film when a train with Soviet POWs arrives at a German camp, illogically in the same train that carries other people, including many (Western European) Jews marked by yellow stars, among them many women and children. While playing loud music, the Germans announce through loudspeakers that Jews have to walk through one gate, Soviet POWs through another and all others through a third gate. The film depicts children being torn away from the Jews. Hundreds of Jews – unlike people of other categories –, are made to follow a sign that reads "Bath – Disinfection" and walk calmly and silently in several columns toward a building with a huge and menacing, strongly smoking furnace, which is obviously a crematorium with a gas chamber. Shortly afterward, the voice of the narrator, who is the lead character, says that the Soviet POWs were sent on as "probably Hitler's ovens were not sufficient for everybody". Nonetheless, unnoticed by historians as it seems, the film optically presents the murder of the Jews as yardstick for German murders and human suffering, almost creating an equivalence between the fate of Soviet POWs with that of the Jews, but not quite, to emphasize the victimhood of the Soviet prisoners. Otherwise, the movie closely follows its literary template, a novella by Mikhail Sholokhov. The scene just described, however, was original to the film.[82]

On a different note, some historical agents in the films included in my sample who were Jewish in real life were fictionalized and 'Russified' in war films, such as conductor Karl Eliasberg in *Leningrad Symphony* (1957) and commissar Jefim Fomin in *Immortal Garrison* (1956).

---

80 See Amir Weiner, *Making Sense of War: The Second World War and the Fate of the Bolshevik Revolution* (Princeton and Oxford: Princeton University Press, 2001), 218.
81 In the book from which the film was adapted, this doctor is not Jewish: see Michail Scholochow, *Ein Menschenschicksal* (Frankfurt a.M.: Büchergilde, 2009 [1957], 58–59.
82 *Fate of a Man*, minutes 43–47; see Scholochow, *Menschenschicksal*, esp. 68.

Depictions of Jews and their persecution were not infrequent in Soviet films about World War II and are found in every time period of film-making. Some characters recognizable as Jewish were lead characters, some supporting cast. In some films, Jews appeared passive, in others active and resolved. Both could be stereotypical: they were represented either as passive civilians, especially in the case of women, children and elderly men, or as active political commissars, physicians or artists. That the representation of Jews in these films is usually positive is unsurprising, given that suffering is such a point of emphasis in them. In some cases, they are even idealized and likened to figures of Christian mythology. Jews are also depicted as patriotic and well-integrated into Soviet society (through music and friendship), although in two films they are betrayed or mistreated by Soviet compatriots siding with the Germans (*Ascension* and *Come and See*). Often, Jews appear as victims but never as the only victims. This reinforced the image of the entire Soviet people as having been under the threat of annihilation, but fictional films, which had to individualize people unlike commemorative speeches dealing with collectives, also showed them as members of particular groups, with others being communists, farmers, POWs, or Russians. In these films, Soviet and Jewish victimhood could coexist.

Infidelity and Faithfulness

The image of the impeccable, heroic and ultimately victorious defender of the homeland would be matched by steady relationships between male and female protagonists in film stories. This would also have fitted with the rigorous and repressive sexual morality of the Stalin era. Moreover, the idea that their wives or girlfriends are not faithful while they are in battle is an old fear among warriors. Konstantin Simonov's famous 1941 poem, *Wait for Me*, addressed this issue, saying that she shall wait, also when there is no message from him and others say he is dead, because only her waiting will make him survive and return.[83] Many soldiers are said to have known this poem by heart. So popular was it that it was converted into a 90-minute feature film, *Wait For Me* (1943), which ends with the husband finally returning to his wife who has waited for all this time (and worked in a factory).

However, in the films covered here, sexual infidelity is not uncommon, prominently mentioned, usually committed by women, and the filmmakers often do not condemn it. The best-known example is Veronika in *Cranes Are Flying* (1957),

---

[83] Konstantin Simonow, *Wie lang vergessene Träume* (Berlin [East]: Volk und Welt, 1975), 58–61.

who does not wait for the return of her fiancé Boris who volunteered for the front. Veronika gets involved with Boris' treacherous cousin Mark, whom she goes on to marry. Nobody is shown to be blameless in the film; but Veronika leaves Mark when it turns out that he is a corrupt coward, she is still accepted as part of Boris' family and then waits for Boris's return until she gets the confirmation of his death at a victory celebration for returning troops in Moscow. Sasha in *Clear Skies* (1961) promises to marry her innocent young friend after the war but does not keep this promise, although he continues to love her. Her sister also does not wait for the return of her boyfriend as she marries an older man instead, who is a nasty coward. Sasha falls in love with famous pilot Alexei and has a child with him although they do not marry. She sticks by Alexei when he is declared dead by the authorities as well as after his return from captivity, when he is being suspected as an enemy of the people and becomes a bitter drunkyard. In *Djamila* (1969), the titular character does not wait for her brutal young husband to return from the front and flees with the half-disabled young war veteran and farmworker Danijar. Their relationship is portrayed as a romantic and sympathetic love story.

By contrast, in *They Fought for Their Motherland* (1975), Nikolai tells a comrade that his wife left him for another man on the first day of the war, at which the other soldier curses her and all women as unreliable. Such contempt for the infidelity of women is also seen in side casts in *Ballad of a Soldier* (1959) and *Wait for Me* (1943).

The films also show examples of faithfulness, including *Ballad of a Soldier* (1959), where three women – his mother, his travel acquaintance Zhura and his former neighbor's girl – are still mourning or waiting for the late Alexei after the war. Needless to add, these examples carry deep sadness. However, infidelity was also prominently depicted in its many complications, not for accusatory purposes but to indicate that the war had also upset private lives and profoundly disturbed and damaged society. Here, unfaithfulness evoked tragedy more than treachery, reinforcing the basic narrative of suffering by that of women.

The Presence of War Disabled and the Absence of Hunger

A sense of tragedy could also be felt in cinematic representations of the war-disabled, who existed in millions as a result of World War II. However, as some recent publications have argued, disability was a problem that was only shown in Soviet films as a hardship that had to be overcome and that characters could cope with. Pictures of crippled beggars, alcoholics or criminals were purportedly not shown.[84] Such euphemistic tendencies in depicting the disabled did exist, for example in the portrayal of Alexei Meresiev in *Story of a Real Man* (1948), who manages to become a fighter pilot again although both of his legs had been amputated (based on a real story; the actual Meresiev later became a member of the Supreme Soviet). However, some of these statements need qualification.

War-related disability surfaced in several of the movies discussed here. In *Ballad of a Soldier* (1959), a veteran with an amputated leg initially decides to never see his wife because he feels useless, but he is later persuaded of the contrary. In *Djamila* (1969), Djamila mocks Danijar who is not very strong and limps after a leg injury at the front but later falls in love with him. A manager of a collective farm in *They Fought For Their Motherland* (1975) wears an artificial leg. More significantly, one of the three main characters, Nikolai, returns to his unit even though he is deaf and constantly quivers after having been shell-shocked in a German attack. The second main character, Nekrasov, complains that he suffers from what he calls trench disease, which involves nightmares of being buried or trapped in a deep hole, but the others laugh at him for this. The third, Sergintsev (who is played by director Sergey Bondarchuk), is shown loudly moaning and complaining when being stitched together by doctors in a seven-minute-long scene. This film, sometimes presented as a typical bombastic war epic of the Brezhnev era[85] that was the most expensive production on the occasion of the 30th anniversary of the 1945 victory, actually is very clear about conveying that even war survivors suffered lasting damages.[86]

This is also true for *Fate of a Man* (1959), also based on a book by Mikhail Sholokhov, in which the protagonist is left with a broken heart mentally and physically.[87] He worries that he will die in sleep next to his adopted little son. In other Soviet war movies, male or female veterans, whether disabled or not, are often depicted as hardened people left with few friends and sometimes living without a life partner.[88] Thus, it is incorrect that "no film explores the psychological consequences – for example destroyed partnerships" – due to disability.[89] Somewhat veiled, a few films did tell moviegoers that the physical or psychologi-

---

[84] Fieseler, "Kriegsinvalide", especially 217–218.
[85] Engel et al., *Geschichte*, 194.
[86] Down to details true to the literary template: Michail Scholochow, *Sie kämpften für die Heimat* (Berlin [East]: Kultur und Fortschritt, 1960); for a similar movie from 1961, see Woll, *Real Images*, 121.
[87] See Woll, *Real Images*, 90.
[88] Neya Zorkaya, *The Illustrated History of the Soviet Cinema* (New York: Hippocrene, 1989), 200, 205, 253–254.
[89] Fieseler, "Kriegsinvalide", 218.

cal life of a veteran was not easy, which many probably knew anyway from personal observation. War-disabled and veterans might have been considered victors but were at times also depicted as victims.

Hunger was common during the Soviet war against Germany, as millions starved to death, including Soviet POWs in German captivity, people in Leningrad, soldiers at the front, and civilians in evacuation, during the German occupation or elsewhere. But very little of this made it to postwar cinema. In my sample, there are no depictions of starving soldiers at the front. Almost the same goes for scenes of people in evacuation areas. For instance, the characters in *Cranes Are Flying* (1957) seem to have enough to eat. In *The Mirror* (1974), the mother at least tries to sell jewelry to pay for food.[90] But the hunger of straying pilot Alexei Mareyev in the novel *Story of a Real Man*[91] is omitted in its film adaptation.

The partisans and the refugees under their protection in *Ascension* (1977) and *Come and See* (1985) do suffer from hunger, which sets in motion risky missions to procure food. Depictions of POWs mention starvation: in *Clear Skies* (1961) very briefly and purely verbally, in *Fate of a Man* (1959) in repeated references, showing the meticulous sharing of one bread in equal parts by a crowd of prisoners and their weakness during forced labor. However, this is in contrast with the physical appearance of lead actor and director Sergey Bondarchuk, who is a sturdy giant. In *Nobody Is Born a Soldier* (1967), Soviet troops liberate a Soviet POW camp, and the narrator begins describing gruesome scenes of starvation, but the picture is blurred so that one cannot see anything. Later, survivors are shown in a cellar but they are almost invisible under their blankets.

In two films set during the Leningrad siege (during which at least 600,000 civilians died of famine and cold[92] and a fraction of the victims died of shelling and bombing), starvation does not play a major role. *Clear Skies* (1961) lets the two lead characters have their days of initial romance in late November 1941, among happy, well-fed onlookers, when, in reality, thousands perished of hunger and cold each day. *Leningrad Symphony* (1956–1957) focuses on artists' struggles for public morale against fascism and on military battle but does refer to hunger in two scenes, one involving documentary street-life images and the other showing a soldier visiting a private apartment and discovering a child in bed with its mother, who turns out to be dead.[93] Like in *Clear Skies*, long, twisted stove pipes

---

90 For another example of deprivation in a movie on evacuation, see Zorkaya, *Illustrated History*, 288–89.
91 Boris Polewoi, *Der wahre Mensch* (Berlin [East] and Weimar, 1975), 36–42.
92 Jörg Ganzenmüller, *Das belagerte Leningrad 1941–1944* (Paderborn et al.: Schöningh, 2005), 239–240.
93 See also Youngblood, *Russian War Films*, 135.

crisscrossing the rooms point to the pervasive cold, as do people who still wear sweaters, shawls or coats in summer.

The only film in my sample that portrays hunger intensely is *Day Stars* (1968). It dwells on women in besieged Leningrad walking agonizingly slowly through snowy streets, exhausted, tottering and sinking to the ground. In passing, it shows the lead character, a nurse, stealing bites of food while feeding wounded soldiers in an open-air hospital (in wintertime). But this film is an exception in regard to its detailed description of hunger.[94] *Immortal Garrison* of 1956 at least portrays deadly thirst. Hunger was typically not visualized in these films. In particular, none of these films presents any emaciated body, let alone something like cannibalism. Hunger was either downplayed in these motion pictures or cut out because it seemed to fundamentally undermine the legitimacy of a state that could not provide for the survival of its citizens. Starvation – humiliating, demoralizing and divisive as it is – also seems to have been a form of suffering that was not even being admitted in many tragic narratives.[95]

The Flip Side of Soviet Suffering: Demonized Germans

In order to magnify Soviet suffering, their enemies were portrayed as beasts just as they were in the reports of the Extraordinary Commissions investigating German atrocities in the Soviet Union in 1944–1946. The famous film director Alexander Dovzhenko explained this connection to a cameraman in 1942.[96] In *Ivan's Childhood* (1962) the Germans appear as sadists (indirectly also in *Today There Will Be No Leave* in 1959), in *Fate of a Man* (1959) and *Fortress Brest* (2010) many of them do; in *Ascension* (1977) they are portrayed as disinterested, ruthless colonialists. *Come and See* (1985) shows two types of Germans: sadists who deny their deeds and sadists who aggressively rationalize their exterminatory actions. The apocalyptic images in the film require an "animal" as opposite force.[97] In 1980, screenwriter Ales Adamovich still seemed to defend his earlier dehumanization of Germans.[98] *The Living and the Dead* (1964) shows Germans as robot-like mowing down Soviet soldiers who have already surrendered. In *They Fought for Their*

---

94 For another exception of 1944, see Youngblood, *Russian War Films*, 71.
95 Zhurzhenko, "Heroes", 4. I do not agree with the argument by Ganzer and Paškovič, "'Heldentum'", 92 that starvation was not shown because Soviet citizens were not allowed to appear as passive victims.
96 Hicks, *First Films*, 113.
97 "Komm und sieh: Interview mit Regisseur Elem Klimow", leaflet, Berlin [West], n.d. 1, 3.
98 Ales Adamowitsch, "Chatyn berichtet über sich selbst", *Kunst und Literatur* 28 (1980): 454.

Motherland (1975), German troops are being mocked for their arrogance,[99] but the Soviet soldiers also call them beasts, as do Soviet female civilians in *Come and See*. In some movies like *Cranes Are Flying* (1957) no Germans appear, but they are indirectly present through the tragedies that they cause. Typical is a dialogue between the child soldier Ivan and lieutenant Galtsev in *Ivan's Childhood*: finding a print of Dürer's painting of the four horsemen of the apocalypse in a book, Ivan asks whether these are Germans, to which Galtsev responds that this is only a piece of art, but Ivan replies: "No. I know them."

Films made in the late Stalin period after 1945 showed a slightly less demonizing and more differentiated picture. In particular, a range of behaviors is shown in the depiction of German soldiers and officers in *The Young Guard* (1948). Although Germans execute resisters *en masse*, deport people for forced labor, loot and torture, their everyday life during the occupation beyond atrocities is also depicted, in which some German soldiers are trying to behave correctly in some scenes, and one, who courts Ljubov Shevtsova, a member of the underground organization, is shown to be witty. Upon her arrest, he slaps her, but they exchange sarcastic remarks; he may not be not humane, but he is human. Importantly, Oleg Koshevoi, the leader of the resistance group, who is going to be executed, tells one of his Soviet pro-German henchmen: "It is not you who are terrible; what is terrible is what spurs fascism." Such a politically correct analysis from a Marxist-Leninist perspective, although a bit unrealistic in this situation, is almost non-existent in post-Stalinist films. Even *The Fall of Berlin* (1950), while showing German atrocities, differentiates (though in a highly schematic way), dwells on Hitler and other leading Nazis and backers, such as industrialists, and shows a Nazi atrocity on Germans, the flooding of the Berlin subway. Traces of such a more complex portrayal can still be found in *Immortal Garrison* (1956): Germans shoot surrendering women and children, but one of those whom the Soviets captured turns out to be a Social Democratic worker. Also, a German general declares the Soviet commander of the Brest fortress Baturin to his troops as being worthy of a war medal; and when Baturin is carried out of the fortress unconscious and half dead, German officers – unrealistically –salute him as a great enemy. Such differentiation, connected with a bit of erosion of the good-evil dichotomy, reappeared on Russian screens in the 2000s.[100]

Although some of the earlier films at least depict some contradictory behavior by Germans, hardly any film offers any explanation for their motives, espe-

---

[99] Arrogance that was also ascribed to the Germans in many Soviet films made during World War II.
[100] Isabelle de Keghel, "Ungewöhnliche Perspektiven: Der Zweite Weltkrieg in neuen russländischen Filmen", *Osteuropa* 55, 4–6 (2005): 337–346, esp. 342–343.

cially not in the way of an analysis of German aims and policies. This is consistent with the notion that beasts cannot be explained. Of course, the Germans were not devils but humans, and any inquiry into their actions might put their demonization into question. It is worth emphasizing that the demonization and dehumanization of Germans had not only been ordered by Stalin, or any leaders, but originated in part from Soviet troops and civilians themselves, being magnified in a 1942 hate campaign by some of the same artists who would later be involved in the making of the films discussed in this chapter, such as Konstantin Simonov and Ilya Ehrenburg, combined with the rejection of the idea of dwelling on the psychology of Germans.[101]

The GDR movie *I Was Nineteen* (1968), directed by a German-born Soviet Army veteran who was a GDR citizen, shows the difference glaringly. Aimed at East German audiences, the film, set during the Soviet conquest of Berlin, presents different types of Germans (based on their dialects, they also represent different regional parts of Germany and social groups) and lets several of them talk about their thoughts and motives. They include a subservient Nazi town mayor, a refugee girl, an airy-fairy intellectual, several liberated antifascists, a bureaucratic officer, two child soldiers, a concentration camp murderer, a fanatical high-ranking SS officer, a hesitant German general and a witty Berlin worker who, in a last-minute shoot-out between SS and Soviets, takes the side of the latter even though he knows that he will go into Soviet captivity. These varieties exemplify different options for German postwar political life. Although East Germany was a Soviet ally, I know nothing of that sort in any Soviet movie. For Soviet filmmakers, the background of the Germans did not really matter as it would have in a Marxist analysis.

Ordinary Fascism (1965), a feature-length documentary, would have offered room for a differentiated analysis, but this opportunity was lost. Instead, director Mikhail Romm argued that most Germans had given up their individuality and become "masses" through unconditional obedience to Hitler, on whom the film dwells extensively. Romm explains with help of a simple manipulation thesis that Germans had become cruel barbarians who had "stopped thinking". These ideas drew greatly from totalitarianism theory,[102] and whether Romm also alluded to conditions under Stalin's rule or not,[103] it is clear that his film did little to differentiate Germans (except for mentioning a few brave anti-fascists and those who "started thinking again" in the last phase of the war) and revising their dehuman-

---

101 See Kucherenko, *Little Soldiers*, 134–138; for the campaign, see also Tumarkin, *Living*, 74–75; Merridale, *Night*, 282–283.
102 For these reasons, *Ordinary Fascism* resembles very much the later FRG documentary "Hitler – a career" (1977), directed by Joachim Fest and Christian Herrendoerfer.
103 This point is discussed in Bulgakowa and Hochmuth, *Krieg*, 156–167.

ization. In 1965, Romm stated that a fascist was "a being that is the contrary of the term 'human'".[104]

Memories of Soviet Violence and Stalinism

If violence by Soviet troops or partisans appears in my selection of war movies, it is usually because Germans brought it upon themselves. What is shown, implied or narrated for the most part is that German combatants who surrendered or were captured are being shot out of hatred or revenge for their atrocities. In several movies, there are disagreements among Soviet troops regarding this point. *I Was Nineteen* (1968) shows how Soviet troops find what is most likely a hidden SS man from the nearby, just liberated Sachsenhausen concentration camp and shoot him after an argument in which one Soviet soldier almost shoots another who demands that this German should not be killed instantly. In *The Living and the Dead* (1964), Sintsov criticizes a soldier who has shot a German prisoner for being a coward, acting against Soviet interests (for the German could have been asked about militarily relevant information), but also for being wrong in principle when shooting prisoners. In the follow-up to this film, *Nobody Is Born a Soldier* (1967), there is talk suggesting that Soviet troops have killed surrendering Germans in Stalingrad in understandable rage after they discovered German atrocities. Even in the über-Stalinist *The Fall of Berlin* (1950), popular steelworker-soldier-super hero Alexei Ivanov prevents a comrade from killing a German soldier by capturing him instead. Despite all the torment he has endured, Andrei Sokolov in *Fate of a Man* (1959) is careful to only knock out German officers without killing them when he flees.

In other cases, German troops do not fare so well. *Story of a Real Man* (1948) shows a place in the forest where Soviet partisans destroyed a German convoy and tied a dead German officer to a tree along with a menacing sign. Notably, the latter image is not in the source novel.[105] Partisans in *Come and See* (1985) brutally massacre German SS men and their local helpers after these have annihilated the population of a Belarusian village. For the guerrilla, it was a problem to keep prisoners; nevertheless, murdering them was morally problematic. Director Elem Klimov signalled symbolically that the Soviets must still try to remain humane through the boy Flyora who shoots at images of Hitler but stops when he sees a

---

[104] Interview with *Komsomolskaia Prawda*, April 6, 1965, quoted in Bulgakowa and Hochmuth, *Krieg*, 157.
[105] Polewoi, *Der wahre Mensch*, 35–36.

picture of Hitler as a baby. This scene was the reason behind the authorities preventing the making of the film at first in 1977.[106] Still, the message is, as usual, that Soviet troops should refrain from falling to the inhumanity imposed on them by the Germans. They are not killers for any autochthonous reasons. It was very disturbing for Russian audiences and led to protests to see Soviet NKVD officers massacre not unsympathetic German POWs unprovoked and in cold blood in a 2005 Russian motion picture.[107]

The other sort of violence by Soviet citizens against unarmed people shown on screen was the killing of individuals who cooperated with the Germans, taking away their property and sometimes verbal abuse. Such action by partisans against village elders is shown in *Ascension* (1977) and *Come and See* (1985). In *The Young Guard* (1948), young communists overpower and hang a 'collaborator' after a mock trial. Partisans also shoot 'collaborators' for their participation in atrocities with the Germans in *Come and See*. In *Fate of a Man* (1959), Andrei Sokolov chokes a Soviet soldier who threatens to reveal to German guards that a co-prisoner of war is a communist. This is the only of these scenes where the perpetrator indicates that he feels this is ghastly, albeit necessary. Usually, such acts of violence are depicted as being directed against people who undoubtedly deserved it. While such scenes admitted that there had been differences between Soviet people in the war, they carried the doctrinal view that anybody siding with the Germans was an unworthy traitor who deserved no sympathy whatsoever. These were no accounts of civil war, but of just punishment meted out to perfectly illegitimate enemies.

Soviet soldiers committed mass rapes in Germany, Poland, other countries of Eastern Europe and Manchuria, but sexual violence by Soviet soldiers or men surfaces only a few times in these films and usually in passing through veiled references. In *They Fought For Their Motherland* (1975), Lopachin, a supposedly positive character (played by the very popular actor Vasili Shukshin, who was also a writer and film director), is a womanizer who sexually harasses Soviet women, who are able to fend him off. A similar scene is seen *en passant* in *Leningrad Symphony* (1956–1957). A nameless German refugee girl living in a suburb of Berlin in the GDR film *I Was Nineteen* (1968), directed by former Soviet army soldier Konrad Wolf, seeks the protection of the 19-year-old German-born Soviet town commandant because, as she says, "[sleeping] with one is better than with all of them".[108] Already in *Ballad of a Soldier* (1959), a young girl named Zhura is shocked, starts to scream

---
106 See leaflet "Komm und sieh", 1–2.
107 Christine Engel, "60 Jahre danach: Neue Sichtweisen auf den 'Grossen Vaterländischen Krieg' im Film *Polumgla*", Fieseler and Ganzenmüller, *Kriegsbilder*, 96–110; for other recent films Youngblood, *Russian War Films*, 219–230.
108 For a similar scene in a 1961 Soviet movie, see Woll, *Real Images*, 122.

and tries to jump from a rolling train after she illegally enters a freight car and finds herself alone in it with a young soldier, Aljosha, who fortunately has no bad intentions. Mark in *Cranes Are Flying* (1957) pursues Veronika, the fiancé of his cousin, kisses her against her will and probably rapes her;[109] despite this, she marries him afterward. Clumsy lieutenant Galtsev in *Ivan's Childhood* (1962) has a young nurse sent back to the rear not only because he thinks that war is unwomanly but also to protect her from an officer pursuing her. In the hinterland, the homecoming soldier Sadiq in *Djamila* (1969) unsuccessfully tries to kill his wife who has fled with her lover.

Films made later, such as *Come and See* (1985) and *Fortress Brest* (2010), blame German occupiers for brutal acts of rape and graphically show the half-dead or dead victims. In *Ascension* (1977), the perpetrators who sexually abuse a girl of perhaps twelve years (which is only mentioned and not shown) are Belarusian auxiliary police who serve the Germans. Generally, sexual violence itself is not shown on screen in the Soviet films covered here, and sexual abuse by Soviet soldiers is marginalized, although its depiction is not a total taboo. Obviously, this was a controversial topic and did not match the self-image of Soviet society where illegitimate violence was generally projected or blamed on the German invaders.

This also resonates with the way how Stalinist terror appears in these films. Mostly it is a marginal aspect. In *Fortress Brest* (2010), Major Gavrilov initially complains about a lack of vigilance because of the dominant turn against so-called panic-mongering, and later, Fomin rationalizes an attempted breakthrough from the siege by carefully avoiding the impression that this could appear as a retreat. The narrator of the film criticizes the post-1945 repression against Gavrilov. The strongest reference to the terror in *The Mirror* (1974) is not connected to the war; the mother suddenly panics because she is not sure if she deleted a certain word from a text that she typed and is to be published that could appear counter-revolutionary. This film also presents images from the Cultural Revolution in China as a menace, indirectly accusing Stalinism. *Tomorrow There Was War* (1987), set in 1940, depicts intrigues and political pressure at a Soviet high school during which one student is driven to suicide.

The two strongest indictments of the terror are in *Clear Skies* (1961) and *Nobody Is Born a Soldier* (1967), both pointing to discrimination, persecution and mistrust against Red Army officers who had been captured by the Germans or

---

109 As in ibid., 74.

temporarily been unintentionally on the other side of the front.[110] Substantial censorship defused the message: in *Clear Skies*, any reference to pilot Astakhov having been in a Soviet punitive camp was cut, as were the scenes of brutal interrogation during the Soviet terror in *Day Stars* (1968).[111] Likewise, in *The Living and the Dead* (1964), the scene from the original book involving the menacing screening of Sintsov by the Soviet military intelligence after he breaks eastward through the front line is missing[112] (despite the film being more than three hours long), and the anti-Soviet panic in Moscow in October 1941 during the German approach has also been virtually erased. However, the viewer learns that General Serpilin, a positive main character, had been in the Gulag before the war like many innocently persecuted officers.

Generally, Soviet terror was rarely mentioned in these films, but if it was, it appeared either disconnected from the war or Stalin was blamed for having crippled Soviet fighting power through senseless terror. What these movies did not argue was that Stalinism had brutalized Soviet society, led to violent inner conflict or contributed to illegitimate violence against enemies in the war. If anything, the protagonists were victims of Soviet terror and persecution, not its agents. This was consistent with the general sense of victimization in these films.

Non-state Agents Shaping Film Narratives About Violence

How could all this possibly be the case? After all, state control and censorship did exist, World War II was a vital ideological issue for the governing Communist Party of the Soviet Union after 1945, and the cinema did influence the masses. If narratives of suffering, pain and tragedy entered Soviet film in contradiction to doctrines governing history construction, it was because directors of different generations, screenwriters, novelists, actors and music composers were using their moral authority, often based on personal traumatic war experiences, to get their views accepted against considerable resistance.

Most of the films were based on literary works by prose writers, some of whom had enough prestige that film directors could invoke their names to gain respect for their projects. Alexander Fadeev, the author of *The Young Guard*, was a founding father of the doctrine of Socialist Realism and a member of the party's

---

110 This topic was already shown in a Soviet film and screened in 1944: Engel et al., *Geschichte*, 92–93.
111 Ibid., 141.
112 See Konstantin Simonow, *Die Lebenden und die Toten* (Berlin [East]: Kultur und Fortschritt, 1975 [1960]).

Central Committee and the state's Supreme Soviet.[113] Mikhail Sholokhov, the author of *Fate of a Man* and *They Fought for Their Motherland*, was one of the few writers to win both the Stalin Prize and the Nobel Prize for Literature. Mark Donskoi, Sergei Gerasimov and Mikhail Romm had their own standing as experienced and decidedly communist film directors, while Shostakovich was respected as a composer. In January 1943, Romm wrote to Stalin, demanding war films to be more realistic and of better quality, which seemingly triggered the CPSU to take steps in the recommended direction.[114]

Konstantin Simonov, author of the novels *The Living and the Dead* and *Nobody Is Born a Soldier*, as well as the screenwriter for *Wait For Me* and *Immortal Garrison* (he starred in another war movie himself), had experienced dangerous situations as a front correspondent, like Sholokhov, Boris Polevoi and others. Sometimes dubbed a conservative, Simonov defended Donskoi's film *The Unvanquished* in 1945 on the grounds that it was important to preserve the memory of the German atrocities, also of those against Jews.[115] Authors such as Vladimir Bogomolov and Vasil Bykau, after whose works *Ivan's Childhood* and *Ascension*, respectively, were made, had been front fighters. Bykau allowed the story to spread that he had escaped death so closely that his name was inscribed on a mass grave.[116] Not only did this give such men authority in the debates; it also fueled their passions to forward their interpretation of the 'truth' about the war. The same went for a woman like Olga Berggolts, who was a poet and survivor of the Leningrad siege and author of the text that was later adopted into *Day Stars*.[117]

This was also true for Ales Adamovich, who wrote the script for *Come and See* (1985). A former partisan in Belarus, he wrote about the German occupation and guerrilla war all his life. In *Come and See*, the population of a village is crammed into a wooden church and then burned alive; Adamovich's own family was in a crowd that was forced into a barn similarly, but the Germans called off the massacre at the last minute.[118] In the late 1960s, Adamovich, along with two other novelists, did something no historian did by collecting the accounts of nearly 300 survivors of German mass shootings and village burnings for a book

---

113 Michail Ryklin et al., "Deutscher auf Abruf: Vom *Schwarzbuch* zur *Jungen Garde*", *Osteuropa* 55, 4–6 (2005): 171.
114 Carola Tischler, "Der Krieg als Komödie: Die Wiederkehr der sowjetischen Filmgroteske während des Zweiten Weltkrieges", Fieseler and Ganzenmüller, *Kriegsbilder*, 69.
115 Gershenson, "Insoumis", 351–352; for Polevoi and Simonov opposing the pompous design of the Stalingrad memorial, see Arnold, *Stalingrad*, 273–276; for Simonov and Gerasimov supporting Alexei German's banned film *Roadblock* in 1971, see Bulgakowa and Hochmuth, *Krieg*, 108–111.
116 Bykau, *Romane*, vol. II, back cover.
117 See Olga Bergholz, *Tagessterne* (Berlin [East]: Kultur und Fortschritt, 1963).
118 Adamowitsch, "Chatyn", 460–461.

that is almost unbearable to read because of its cruel descriptions.[119] Which other novelist has tried to describe the feelings of a fetus in the womb at the moment it dies because the mother is being shot?[120] With Daniil Granin, he also gathered painful testimonies of survivors of the siege of Leningrad.[121] By the mid-1980s, he developed, in discussions with Bykau, the idea of a "super-literature" that should be able to effectively counter the threat of atomic war during another peak of the nuclear arms race.[122] The burnt villages in Belarus in World War II appeared to him like a "Hiroshima [done] by conventional means", a menacing example.[123] All this influenced his work, resulting in a strong emotional impact on the viewer of *Come and See*.

Many of these artists were driven by their own experiences. *I Was Nineteen* was Konrad Wolf's attempt to process his memories of the battle of Berlin; Elem Klimov had seen Stalingrad burn when he was being evacuated from the city as a boy in 1942; and Andrei Tarkovsky had suffered during evacuation in the war and was then the same age as his young protagonist Ivan who, as Tarkovsky said, symbolized the "situation of my generation".[124] Sergei Bondarchuk had fought at the front and then starred in *Young Guard* in 1948, as well as later in his own movies.[125] For *Young Guard*, director Sergei Gerasimov, who had developed a semi-documentarian style of acting, let Bondarchuk and the other young actors live for some time in the real families of the executed young communists whose fate they would have to enact.[126] Some elderly lay actors in *Come and See* (1985) had themselves survived the German destruction of Belarusian villages; it was similar with lead actors in Donskoi's 1944 film *Rainbow*.[127] All of this made the efforts such contributors put into these films especially persuasive and lent them special authority. This seemed to be of particular value because somewhat shallow concepts of desirable authenticity prevailed in the Soviet Union, according to which no technically ahistoric details were permitted, such as those concerning

---

119 Ales Adamovich et al., *Out of the Fire* (Moscow: Progress, 1980).
120 Ales Adamowitsch, *Henkersknechte* (Berlin [East] and Weimar: Aufbau, 1982), 266–267.
121 Ales Adamowitsch and Daniil Granin, *Das Blockadebuch* (Berlin: Volk und Welt, vol. I 1987, vol. II 1984).
122 Ales Adamowitsch, "Über das neue Denken und das adäquate Wort", *Kunst und Literatur* 35 (1987): 707–712.
123 See G. Belaja, "Ales Adamowitsch über Kriegsprosa", *Kunst und Literatur* 30 (1982).
124 Bulgakowa and Hochmuth, *Krieg*, 94 (quote), 132.
125 Engel et al., *Geschichte*, 114; Shlapentokh and Shlapentokh, *Soviet Cinematography* 221.
126 Bulgakowa and Hochmuth, *Krieg*, 64; Engel et al., *Geschichte*, 102.
127 See Zorkaya, *Illustrated History*, 188.

uniforms and types of weapons.[128] Consequently, these artists could make the claim to speak as the authoritative voice of the people's suffering.

Filmmakers, like other political and social actors, also wished to make their own contribution to important commemoration dates with their films. Klimov and Adamovich intended to contribute to the celebration of the 40th anniversary of the Soviet victory in 1985 and Konrad Wolf to the 50th anniversary of the October Revolution in 1967.[129] Bondarchuk celebrated 30 years of Soviet victory with *They Fought for Their Motherland* (1975), Jegiasarov brought out *Hot Snow* 30 years after the battle of Stalingrad, and in *Ordinary Fascism* (1965) Romm showed street scenes of the celebrations of the 20th anniversary of the victory. Apparently, some films also became politically influential in turn: *Fate of a Man* (1959) was meant to contribute to the ongoing historical rehabilitation of former Soviet POWs in German hands, and *Immortal Garrison* in 1956 and a non-fiction book by Sergei Smirnov in 1964 more or less coincided with the two waves of the recognition, mostly posthumous, of Soviet defenders of the Brest Fortress.[130]

There were heated debates about many films sampled here. One of the problems was that censorship, too, was not a matter of one state or party authority but multi layered and decentralized, involving various groups of participants. Director Grigori Nikulin remembered later that his film *Don't Forget, Kaspar!* (1964) was forbidden to enter cinemas after 13 different panels, committees and authorities had reviewed it.[131] This could also result in contradictory stories: the anti-Stalinist movie *Clear Skies* (1961) was distorted by cuts, but part of the message remained recognizable, and it was submitted as an official Soviet contribution to the International Moscow Film Festival.[132] These conflicts were harsh, and although the films covered here were usually not dissident, but conveyed tolerated lines of memory construction, some of those involved moved on to become anti-communist activists in the late 1980s, most notably the writers Adamovich and Bykau.

It should be added that controversy and censorship sometimes led to a deradicalization of the films planned or produced as shown, but, somewhat counterintui-

---

[128] For similar tendencies in museums and visitors insisting on these concepts of authenticity, see Anne Hasselmann, *Wie der Krieg ins Museum kam: Akteure der Erinnerung in Moskau, Minsk und Tscheljabinsk, 1941–1956* (Bielefeld: Transcript, 2022).
[129] Leaflet "Komm und sieh", 2; Südkamp, "Ich", 3.
[130] Information taken from plates in the film *Fortress Brest*.
[131] Interview, July 25, 1991 in Bulgakowa and Hochmuth, *Krieg*, 99–103. On the mechanisms of Soviet film censorship, see Gershenson, *Phantom Holocaust*, 8–11.
[132] Karl, "Zwischen", 285.

tively, in several cases cited above, the films became more radical or drastic than their literary source even though more people were involved in their making.[133]

Conclusion

This chapter has shown that elements of tragedy, pain, suffering and victimization were very influential in Soviet films about World War II. Often, these elements were not combined with a triumphal narrative. Only in part did this different line of war memory reflect the will of the CPSU party leadership. This remembrance was public; movies served the role of a bridge between private experiences and official war memories. Fictional films contributed, like literary prose, to a continuous soul-searching among Soviet citizens about the war, its impact and meaning, not unlike the *Vergangenheitsbewältigung* (coming to terms with the past) in West Germany that is sometimes praised, though in a very different context. Similar was also the inability to *bewältigen* (overcome or master) anything. Soviet films could address war trauma but, of course, not heal it.[134] And, so, the efforts went on.

This is not to say that the tragic narrative was the only kind that was told, as stories of victory and heroism continued to exist. Writers such as Sergei Smirnov and Konstantin Simonov showed or advocated for heroic stories on Soviet TV.[135] Even Andrei Tarkovsky co-directed a heroic thriller about the risky but victimless postwar recovery of ammunition from a town center called *Today There Will Be No Leave* (1959), which was released just three years before *Ivan's Childhood*. Multiple lines of remembrance co-existed. This pluralistic memory allowed for the construction of a past common suffering of *the* Soviet people (and for many historians, this was the only narrative) side by side with regional versions of the war's history (like a special Belarusian or Ukrainian narrative[136]). The pluralistic character of memory also explains why, to a degree, narratives of particular group experiences such as representations of the German persecution of Jews could appear. To be sure, all of this did not develop in total harmony, as there were heated debates over differing views.

---

133 This refers to scenes discussed above in *The Unvanquished, Story of a Real Man, Fate of a Man* and *Ivan's Childhood*, notably all of them from the first half of the time period under inquiry.
134 For Soviet literary works addressing traumata, see Kukulin, "Schmerzregulierung".
135 Engel et al., *Geschichte*, 159–160.
136 For the latter, see Weiner, *Making Sense*, 298–363.

On a general scholarly level, these findings show once more how inadequate the state-focused totalitarianism theory is. Many students of historical memory have simply overlooked the quite obvious tragic narratives due to their preconceptions. Films had to be a central element of Soviet government manipulation, so what could be expected from them? Film historians were somewhat less prone to such interpretations. In reality, there was no total control over the content of Soviet movies and no total streamlining of memory production. Contrary to general deductions about collectivist mindlessness, individuals had quite a bit of leeway in the Soviet system to popularize their views, although they needed to overcome resistance, including censorship, as Denise Youngblood has argued with some reservations.[137] One book states, "The Soviet Union did not mourn her fallen of the Second World War":[138] the nonsense in the second half of this statement corresponds with the invention of a monolith called "the Soviet Union" in the first half, based on the totalitarianism concept. Soviet war memory was not monolithic but constructed by real people, different groups of actors and with some degree of disagreement.[139] For this volume, this is an important example of the fact that not only violence is generated by social actors but also anti-violence (in this case, anti-war messages).

For historians, this chapter questions periodizations offered in previous research. First of all, memories of suffering were not completely absent in Soviet war movies at any point. A social history perspective, as opposed to a state-centered analysis, helps explain these continuities. Changes were gradual. I suggest that a turn to giving less prominence to Soviet suffering, but no total disappearance, can be located in 1948, not 1946, and lasted until 1955. After putting much emphasis on the tragic sides of the war during the thaw after 1956, many films in the Brezhnev era (1964–1982) were also far from fading out tragedy. The impression that the publicly constructed memory of the war in the Brezhnev period was not uniform, not merely bombastic, and not only reflecting conservative dogmatism is also confirmed on an aesthetic level. Most of the films discussed in this chapter employ conventional artistic means, but five can be considered

---

[137] "Through these films, it is evident that autonomous action *was* possible in late Soviet society, even from those working within the system" (Denise Youngblood, "*Ivan's Childhood* (USSR, 1962) and *Come and See* (1985): Post-Stalinist Cinema and the Myth of World War II" in John Whiteclay Chambers II and David Culbert, eds., *World War II, Films, and History* (New York and Oxford: Oxford University Press, 1996), 95; emphasis in the original). But Youngblood limited this statement to post-Stalin times (unlike me), and she called war films "a counter-analysis to official history" (ibid.), whereas I emphasize that they were part of state-produced memory construction.
[138] Arnold, *Stalingrad*, back cover.
[139] This is a point also made by Hasselmann, *Wie*.

avant-garde. Two of these are from the Khrushchev period – *Cranes Are Flying* (1957) and *Ivan's Childhood* (1962) – and three from the Brezhnev era – *Day Stars* (1968), *Djamila* (1969) and *The Mirror* (1974).[140] *Day Stars* and *The Mirror* create mazes from the personal memories of artists (Olga Berggolts and Andrei Tarkovsky) that are not easily accessible to audiences, presenting their dreamlike, surrealistic scenes in a confusing, associative order. *Djamila*, with its dramatic cuts and occasional use of psychedelic colors in a largely black-and-white film, also takes the perspective of an artist, the fictional narrator, in this narrative of a young boy who will later become a painter and remember the story.

The strengthening of the narrative of suffering and grief around 1960 was not only a Soviet thing. In a striking parallel to developments in the USSR, narratives of suffering and victimization became hegemonic in Israel with the Eichmann trial in 1961. Like in the USSR, the Israeli remembrance of the Nazi persecution of Jews is said to have previously been dominated by stories of heroism and, if not victory, at least armed struggle. The voices of survivors were not new in Israel around 1961, but they had been less influential before; in fact, the prosecution, which designed the trial like a history lesson, selected witnesses against Eichmann based on their already recorded and sometimes already published memories. One criterion was how tragic they were, although few witnesses had ever seen Eichmann before the trial. It served to popularize their memories and narrative.[141] Oriented toward past victimization, both Israeli and Soviet society became caught up in a backward-looking habitus though anti-war messages were less influential in Israel.

Moreover, on the level of films about mass violence in World War II, the tragic turn and an increasing emphasis on senseless sacrifice could also be observed in other Western and Eastern European countries at the same time. To keep this analysis short, it would suffice to point to films like *Night and Fog* (France, 1955), *Canal* (Poland, 1957), *Eroica* (Poland, 1958), *Stars* (GDR/Bulgaria, 1959), *The Bridge* (FRG, 1959) and *Kapò* (Italy, 1960). These parallels exemplify that

---

140 Youngblood, *Russian War Films*, 141, 147–150 makes a similar argument though without mentioning any of the three last mentioned movies.
141 Hanna Yablonka, The State of Israel vs. Adolf Eichmann (New York: Schocken, 2004), 89–99, 218–235. This turn toward tragedy also explains in part the intensely hostile reactions to Hannah Arendt's book, *Eichmann in Jerusalem* (Hannah Arendt, *Eichmann in Jerusalem: A Report on the Banality of Evil* (New York: Viking, 1965, revised ed.). On the one hand, Arendt tried to explain "evil" precisely when others tried to mystify the Nazis because they wanted to construct a narrative of infinite suffering. On the other hand, Arendt's interpretations had grave deficiencies. Among others, she made the counterproductive effort to use the metaphysical concept of "evil" for rationally accounting for violence, using a brash tone when others demanded a solemn, commemorative one.

perspectives of global history may generate some insights that narrow national histories do not offer.[142] I presume that one of the reasons for this development toward narratives of victimization in these anti-war movies was the second peak of the nuclear peril in the Cold War with the introduction of massive nuclear bomber forces and long-range missiles,[143] as embodied by Alain Resnais' film *Hiroshima mon amour* (1959). This issue would deserve further research.

Thinking about mass violence as social interaction helps, in this case, recover the traces of the construction of the memory of mass violence as a social process and the outcome of negotiations, rather than remembrance being merely subject to centrally directed state manipulation. Through films, private memory became part of the public one instead of simply being suppressed. Personal experiences drove many people involved in filmmaking and lent them authority. However, although few absolute taboos existed, there were limits to public memory in the Soviet Union. This included everything that could not be blamed on the enemy. How hunger was represented in these films and how it could not appear are symptomatic. Within limits, even violence and injustice by the Soviet state did surface, as did violence by Soviet citizens if it struck illegitimate enemies (i.e., Germans and their Soviet helpers). What was not shown or mentioned (until the 2000s[144]) was supposedly illegitimate violence exerted by loyal Soviet citizens, as it would have contradicted the self-images of Soviet society.

Besides, there was another limitation: Soviet victimization and tragedy required, by tendency, absolute evil on the other side (see the following chapter). As the Soviet representation of Germans, in the films and much of the historiography, was subordinate to constructing images of Soviet history and society, there was no explanation of German action and no genuine interest in such an explanation either.

Nonetheless, the war films discussed here took an anti-war stance by emphasizing tragedy and suffering. One could argue that they aimed at non-violence, which is also the result of social interaction, and this chapter has described how non-violence was produced on the basis of personal experiences and individual and collective initiatives, mostly after the war. In contrast, the next chapter examines how indirect and direct violence against non-combatants was also produced collectively during World War II, in the Soviet Union and many other countries.

---

142 This is even more so as *Night and Fog* can also be seen as an instrument to denouncing the French war in Algeria. For this insight I am grateful to Richard Derderian.
143 I owe insights about the role of the nuclear threat in thought around 1960 in part to contributions by Peter Krause at the conference "Eichmann nach Jerusalem" at the University of Vienna, Austria, on March 24, 2013.
144 See Jahn, "Patriotismus", 118–119, 129.

Filmography

Wait For Me, 1943, director: Aleksander Stolper, script: Konstantin Simonov.
The Unvanquished, 1945, director: Mark Donskoi.
The Young Guard, 1948 (1964 director's cut), director: Sergej Gerasimov, music: Dmitri Shostakovich.
Story of a Real Man, 1948, director: Aleksander Stolper.
The Fall of Berlin, 1950, director: Mikhail Chiaureli, music: Dmitri Shostakovich.
Immortal Garrison: A Heroic Tragedy, 1956, directors: Zachar Agranenko with Eduard Tisse; script: Konstantin Simonov.
Leningrad Symphony, 1956–1957, director: Zachar Agranenko.
Cranes Are Flying, 1957, director: Mikhail Kalatosov.
Ballad of a Soldier, 1959, director: Grigori Chukhrai.
Fate of a Man, 1959, director: Sergei Bondarchuk.
Today There Will Be No Leave, 1959, directors: Aleksander Gordon and Andrei Tarkovsky.
Clear Skies, 1961, director: Grigori Chukhrai.
Ivan's Childhood, 1962, director: Andrei Tarkovsky.
The Living and the Dead, 1964, director: Aleksander Stolper.
Ordinary Fascism, 1965, director: Mikhail Romm.
Nobody Is Born a Soldier, 1967, director: Aleksander Stolper.
Day Stars, 1968, director: Igor Talankin.
I Was Nineteen, 1968, director: Konrad Wolf.
Djamilja, 1969, director: Irina Poplavskaia, script: Djengiz Aitmatov.
Hot Snow, 1972, director: Gavriil Jegiasarov, script: Yury Bondarev, music: Alfred Schnittke.
The Mirror, 1975, director: Andrei Tarkovsky.
They Fought for Their Motherland, 1975, director: Sergei Bondarchuk.
Ascension, 1977, director: Larisa Shepitko, music: Alfred Schnittke.
Come and See, 1985, director: Elem Klimov, script: Ales Adamovich, music: Alfred Schnittke.
Tomorrow There Was War, 1987, director: Yuri Kara, script: Boris Vasiliev.
Fortress Brest, 2010, director: Aleksander Kott.

Part II: **Conditions of Violence**

6 Famines and Imperialism: For a Different History of World War II

I hold the following. World War II was not a fight between good and evil, and good has not won. It was an imperialist war from all sides, a war for economic zones of influence, spheres for capital investment, resources and strategic territories. And virtually all powers committed mass violence against non-combatants, often in connection with the scramble for resources, their redistribution and resource denial to some, that is, by creating conditions of violence. The Allies killed at least ten million non-combatants. The violence also had to do with the fact that it was a racist war from all sides due to imperialism. By maintaining that this was a fight between good and evil, the dominant historiography is a continuation of the war with other means, and because of its Eurocentrism and systematic construction of non-combatant victims of different importance and value, which includes ignoring or marginalizing certain large victim groups (especially those with a darker skin tone), the mainstream historiography itself is racist.

A reminder of the war's dimensions might be useful here. There were more refugees in World War II than soldiers. At about 140 million at least, the number of refugees, including domestic refugees and evacuees, surpassed that of the 100–120 million in the military (out of which about 30 million died and 35 million were taken prisoner).[1] The majority of the refugees were from China.[2] Approxi-

---

[1] For the number of soldiers, see Richard Overy, *Blood and Ruins: The Great Imperial War, 1931–1945* (London: Allan Lane, 2021), ix, 377, 381–382. The estimate of the number of POWs is from S. P. MacKenzie, "The treatment of prisoners of war in World War II", *Journal of Modern History* 66 (1994), 487.

[2] For the number of Chinese refugees, see Diana Lary, *The Chinese People at War: Human Suffering and Social Transformation, 1937–1945* (Cambridge and New York: Cambridge University Press, 2010), 175–176; Rana Mitter, *China's War with Japan, 1937–1945* (London et al.: Penguin, 2013), 6, 117–118; Overy, *Blood*, 833; Lizzie Collingham, *The Taste of War: World War II and the Battle for Food* (New York: Penguin, 2012), 250; R. Keith Schoppa, *In a Sea of Bitterness: Refugees during the Sino-Japanese War* (Cambridge and London: Harvard University Press, 2011).- For refugees from other countries, see Rebecca Manley, "The Perils of Displacement: The Soviet Evacuee between Refugee and Deportee", *Contemporary European History* 16, 4 (2007): 495 (USSR); Overy, *Blood*, 829–832 (German, Japanese and Italien refugees 1945–1946 from lost territories, foreign countries and colonies); Robert Lilly, *Taken by Force: Rape and American GIs in Europe during World War II* (Basingstoke and New York: Palgrave Macmillan, 2007), 45 (Britain); Srinath Raghavan, *India's War* (New York: Basic Books, 2016), 265–270 and Christopher Bayly and Tim Harper, *Forgotten Armies: The Fall of British Asia, 1941–1945* (Cambridge: Belknap, 2005), 167 (at least one million refugees from Indian cities between December 1941 and April 1942 plus 600,000 from British-Burma); Janam Mukherjee, *Hungry Bengal: War, Famine, Riots, and the End of Empire*

mately 70 million people (including civilians) died,³ and half of them were Asians. Displacement and the misery it entailed belonged to the core experiences of the war; the total number of displaced was considerably higher than 140 million and included POWs, camp inmates, resettlers and those deported to forced labor, internment or death.

Three percent of the world's population died and nearly ten percent may have been displaced – but occupation was an even more common experience, with about 800 million affected from 1937 to 1947, constituting more than one-third of humanity.⁴ Together with nearly 600 million living in colonies that were not occupied by another power, the majority of mankind lived for some time under foreign rule in the 1940s.⁵ To continuously reside in one's own independent state was atypical. Existence under foreign domination, too, brought misery and deprivation. A lot of the violence in that war was indirect. These facts underscore

---

1939–1946, Ph.D dissertation, University of Michigan, 2011, 63–64, 118. Among other people, ten million French fleeing the advance of German troops in 1940, about that many Germans relocated for protection from aerial warfare and eight million Japanese under similar circumstances need to be added. Overy, *Blood*, 679. For expulsions of 18 million ethnic German and Japanese civilians in 1944–1947, see below. For example, the number of 140 million does not include the refugees from partition in South Asia.

3 Daniel Hedinger, *Die Achse: Berlin – Tokio – Rom 1919–1946* (Munich: Beck, 2021), speaks of 30 million war dead in Asia (but omits, for example, Allied-occupied Iran). Insecurity concerning the worldwide estimate is primarily about Soviet War losses (mostly given as between 20 and 27 million) and those of China that were between 14 million and 35 million, with Chinese president Xi Jinping presenting figures at the upper end. Mitter, *China's War*, 6; John Dower, *War Without Mercy: Race and Power in the Pacific War* (New York: Pantheon, 1986), 296; Collingham, *Taste*, 257; Overy, *Blood*, 784; Evan Mawdsley, "World War II: A Global Perspective", Simo Laakkonen et al., eds., *The Long Shadows: A Global Environmental History of the Second World War* (Corvallis: Oregon State University Press, 2017), 38; Xi Jinping, "Remember the Past and Our Martyrs, Cherish Peace, and Build a New Future", September 3, 2015, Xi Jinping, *The Governance of China*, vol. II (Beijing: Foreign Language Press, 2017), 485. In a global perspective, population losses in occupied areas and among POWs should be added.

4 More than 300 million non-Japanese came under Japanese rule; Hedinger speaks of 350 to 500 million: Hedinger, *Achse*, 354. The number of 160 million that Overy, *Blood*, 785 gives is far too low; 160 million was about the size of the Chinese population under Japanese rule. See Collingham, *Taste*, 250. 250 million non-Germans came under German rule: Christian Gerlach, *The Extermination of the European Jews* (Cambridge et al.: Cambridge University Press, 2016), 194. Add to this Allied-occupied Germany, Japan and Korea, the British occupied areas in West Asia (Lebanon, Syria, Iraq and large parts of Iran) and Africa, the Soviet ones in Eastern European countries that the Germans had not occupied (like Romania), the Italian ones in Africa, U.S. occupations in the Pacific, Romanian, Finnish, Thai occupations, etc.

5 According to Laakkonen et al., World War II "engulfed" 1.7 billion people (out of a world population of 2.3 billion). Simo Laakkonen et al., "The Long Shadows", Laakkonen et al., *The Long Shadows*, 7.

why a social history of the war and the violence is needed and why the concept of conditions of violence may be useful here.

Thus, I try to substantiate the initial claims by outlining some basic tendencies in the existing historiography, most importantly its omissions, and scrutinizing the kind of mass violence that the Allies committed against non-combatants, as well as their rationales at the time. The centerpiece of this chapter consists of a survey of World War II famines. Famine is not just an arbitrary issue in this context. As Lizzie Collingham argued, 20 million people died from hunger and related diseases in World War II and "the Allied powers made their own substantial contribution to wartime hunger, malnutrition and starvation", as did Axis countries.[6] My own account lists more famines than Collingham's did, as hunger crises occurred in almost all regions of the world, especially in occupied countries or colonies. The genesis and causes of these famines show how deadly conditions of violence were created, for whom, and why – as a contribution to the history of World War II as well as to exemplify how conditions of violence come about in general and what they lead to.

Shocking as my general argument may appear to some, the facts it rests on are not entirely novel. This chapter is based on published research, and I draw from many studies of a general character, national histories as well as specialized historical analyses, including those about colonies during the war. This is also to say, substantial parts of scholarship cannot be addressed as racist. In addition to published studies, I also refer sporadically to survivor and witness accounts.

In constructing my argument, I can build on efforts by other authors, such as Martin Thomas' concept of World War II as a "resource war",[7] although I attempt to draw global consequences from it. Aimé Césaire's dictum that what the "Christian bourgeois" "cannot forgive Hitler" for is not "the crime against man as such, it is the crime against the white man",[8] remains another valuable point of reference. However, it should be used as a point of departure for a broader insight: 'Christian bourgeois' condemn imperialism within Europe but not against non-whites, at least not if this was (and is) imperialism by liberal powers. Although attempts to conceptualize World War II as an imperialist war do exist and are very important, such as those by Ernest Mandel and Richard Overy, they have

---

6 Collingham, *Taste*, 1, 12 (quote).
7 Martin Thomas, "Resource War, Civil War, Rights War: Factoring Empire into French North Africa's Second World War", *War in History* 18, 2 (2011): 225–248.
8 Aimé Césaire, *Discourse on Colonialism* (New York: Monthly Review Press, 1972), 14.

been qualified, conditional and partial.⁹ My impression is that such an understanding of World War II should be consistent, but this is still missing.¹⁰

All of this means that I attempt to combine global and social history, a formidable task, and bring more of the 'world' into World War II history. In the context of noting that the history of the world wars "has largely not been written as global history", Heike Liebau et al. have already called for a "global social history".¹¹

I start with a survey of the existing historiography and draw some conclusions, followed by a brief analysis of Allied violence. Afterwards, I present an account of World War II famines as well as the imperialist redistribution and denial of resources and de facto unpaid labor at their core, and then I try to relate this to Allied justifications for their violence, before I offer a conclusion.

This chapter concentrates primarily on mass violence committed by the Allies, much of which is understudied and underacknowledged. By doing so, I do not say or mean to say that the Axis was 'good'. Given that in the past, I have published four monographs and dozens of articles and book chapters on Axis violence, I do not need to cover it here in detail once again to 'prove' that I am critical of it.

The Existing Historiography

The historiography of World War II is often normative, Manichean, Eurocentric and racist.¹² According to the dominant narrative of World War II, it was fought between two alliances, the Axis and the Allies, who were fundamentally different.

---

9 See Ernest Mandel, *Der Zweite Weltkrieg* (Frankfurt am Main: ISP, 1991), 10–15, 43–44 and recently Overy, *Blood*, who speaks of an "imperial war".
10 By saying that this was an imperialist war from all sides, I also argue that the Soviet Union was imperialist. As the Soviet Union was a socialist state, this is in contradiction to Marxist teachings. The fact that the Soviet Union was an imperialist power in World War II is evident, in political terms, from its many annexations in the war's course (including territories that had never been Soviet or part of the Russian empire, such as Carpatho-Ruthenia and northern East Prussia) and the creation of a strategic glacis, and, in economic terms, from the control the Soviet Union gained of natural resources (such as East German and Czechoslovak Uranium), industrial capital (later organized in the Council of Mutual Economic Assistance, although this was not merely a Soviet creation) and human resources (for instance, foreign physicists needed for developing nuclear arms). All of this served the cause of world communism but also, more specifically, to secure and stabilize socialism in the USSR.
11 Heike Liebau et al., "Introduction", Heike Liebau et al., eds., *The World in World Wars: Experiences, Perceptions and Perspectives from Africa and Asia* (Leiden and Boston: Brill, 2010), 1, 19, 23. See also Andrew Buchanan, "Globalizing the Second World War", *Past & Present* 258 (2023): 246–281.
12 For a brief discussion of my own previous work on mass violence in World War II and beyond, see chapter 1 of this volume.

The Allies defended themselves against the Axis aggressors and their imperial ambitions.[13] They won because of their superior political system(s), moral superiority, economic supremacy and better organization.[14] Unlike the Allies, Axis politicians were deeply racist and, thus, committed many crimes, killing millions, purportedly senselessly. As one German scholar succinctly summarized this view, "The Second World War was [. . .] an imperialist war for the redivision of the world but from the beginning with qualitatively opposite aims: the fascist powers were positioned against enlightenment, democracy and human dignity, which were defended by their adversaries."[15]

As a result of this depiction, and to draw political 'lessons' from the war, which all sorts of people claim to do all the time,[16] World War II histories concentrate, aside from military history, on political history, with an emphasis on the history of political ideas. Usually, World War II is characterized as a victory of liberalism (and sometimes, socialism) over fascism, although this epistemic imperialism is not always and everywhere successful.[17] Meanwhile, the social history of the war is underdeveloped, in contrast to that of World War I, and not accidentally so. With this approach, scholars studiously avoid the topic of the methods and social costs, i.e. the human costs, of Allied warfare. All of this is being done with the claim to represent universal and humanistic values.

In light of this claim and the fact that approximately half of the war's victims died in Asia, the geography in the war's historiography is strange. Usually it deals with Europe and, in addition, the USA and Japan, although the rhetoric of global dimensions has become common in the titles of publications.[18] In Martin Gilbert's

---

[13] Overy, *Blood*, x; Akira Iriye, *The Origins of the Second World War in Asia and the Pacific* (Abingdon and New York: Routledge, 2013), first published in 1987.

[14] For example, see Richard Overy, *Why the Allies Won* (New York and London: W.W. Norton, 1996).

[15] "Der Zweite Weltkrieg war seinem Charakter nach zunächst ein imperialistischer Krieg um die Neuaufteilung der Welt, doch von Anfang mit qualitativ gegensätzlichen Zielen: Die faschistischen Mächte standen gegen Aufklärung, Demokratie und Menschenwürde, ihre Gegner verteidigten diese." Mario Kessler, "Postkolonialismus und Internationalismus", Susan Neiman and Michael Wildt, eds., *Historiker streiten* (Berlin: Propyläen, 2023), 155–170, 169.

[16] My Google search for "World War II 'lessons'" on April 2, 2024 led to 69.4 million hits.

[17] For this and competing narratives of national liberation in Southeast Asia, see Diana Wong, "Memory Suppression and Memory Production: The Japanese Occupation of Singapore", T. Fujitani et al. (eds.), *Perilous Memories: Asia-Pacific War(s)* (Durham and London: University of North Carolina Press, 2003), 218–238.

[18] Symptomatic is Gerhard Weinberg, "Total War: The Global Dimensions of Conflict", Roger Chickering et al., eds., *A World at Total War: Global Conflict and the Politics of Destruction, 1937–1945* (Cambridge: Cambridge University Press, 2005), 19–31, and that volume overall. As a side note, the German historiography is even more Eurocentric. As one example, Rolf-Dieter

atlas of the conflict, according to my count, 160 maps depict Europe; 34 Asia, the Pacific and Australia; five Africa; one Latin America; and 32 are either global in character or deal with at least two continents – often in relation to naval warfare, reflecting British interests.[19] Overviews of the war by Martin Gilbert and Gerhard Weinberg have been criticized for omitting Subsaharan Africa.[20] Scholars' lack of attention to Africa was, it has been argued, "due in part to the imperial powers' explicit efforts to downplay and obscure the extent to which they relied on their African subjects to fight and win the war".[21] The omission of Africa indicates a disregard for the colonies in general. As Srinath Raghavan stated, "the story of India's war is only dimly remembered",[22] and Sugata Bose and Ayesha Jalal called the Bengal famine "one of the most catastrophic, though least publicized, holocausts of the Second World War".[23] "Analyses of the social economic and political impact" of the war on India are also often "relegated to the footnotes in the history of modern India", while nationalist and interreligious struggles, military measures and mobilization are central.[24]

More elaborate surveys add a bit of Asian, African and global history as a result of the humanities being under pressure in the age of 'globalization'.[25] Out of the 50 chapters in a recent book on World War II by Antony Beevor, 32 deal with Europe, ten with Asia and the Pacific, four-and-a-half with Africa (mostly, North Africa) and the Atlantic, and three-and-a-half deal with the United Nations or the global framework.[26] However, the main revision was the addition of China, which had been neglected until the 2000s, and taking China into account could in turn

---

Müller, *Der Zweite Weltkrieg* (Darmstadt: Wissenschaftliche Buchgesellschaft, 2015), overwhelmingly treats Axis and Allies in Europe with the exception of bits on their fight in North Africa and a dozen pages that cover Japan and the Pacific (110–120, 151–153).

19 Martin Gilbert, *The Routledge Atlas of the Second World War* (London and New York: Routledge, 2008). For the neglect of Latin America in mainstream surveys of the war, see Buchanan, "Globalizing", 254–255.

20 Judith Byfield, "Preface", Judith Byfield et al., eds., *Africa and World War II* (New York: Cambridge University Press, 2015), xviii.

21 Timothy Parsons, "The Military Experiences of Ordinary Africans in World War II", Byfield et al., *Africa*, 3.

22 Raghavan, *India's War*, 2.

23 Quoted in Indivar Kamtekar, "A Different War Dance: State and Class in India 1939–1945", *Past & Present* 176 (2002): 2. See also Buchanan, "Globalizing", 257.

24 Mukherjee, *Hungry Bengal*, 216.

25 For the general trend, see Sebastian Conrad, "Erinnerung im globalen Zeitalter", *Merkur* 75, 867 (2021): 5–17.

26 Antony Beevor, *Der Zweite Weltkrieg* (Munich: Bertelsmann, 2014).

spark more interest for the British empire in Asia during the war.[27] But the claim to see "World War II as a global whole" has sometimes been exhausted with this addition of China.[28] At times, one wonders whether what Euro-Americans describe as World War II would not be more appropriately called White War II.

One of the most influential early postwar depictions of World War II was Winston Churchill's multi-volume account. Even though Britain had sucked resources and labor out of India virtually without wartime payment, which caused the death of at least three million Indians especially in the Bengal famine, and recruited two million soldiers from British-India who were deployed to all war theatres, Churchill wrote: "No great portion of the world population was so effectively protected from the horrors and perils of the World War as were the peoples of Hindustan. They were carried through the struggle on the shoulders of our small island."[29] In 1953, he received the Nobel Prize for Literature for this work. By July 1943 (during the Bengal famine), he had already made the baselessly assertion that Britain had "suffered a greater drop in the standard of living than India", rejecting aid deliveries.[30] World War II historiography has changed in recent decades, but it has not cut off its roots.

Most studies on the war condemn illiberal imperialism but include little to no discussion of liberal imperialism.[31] Few see parallels between, for example, British and Japanese imperialism and the collapse of both empires in and after World War II.[32] In the same vein, nationalism in Allied countries is played down or glossed over.

Some recent, broader studies have compared Axis countries, or countries occupied by the Axis, with each other and discussed the entanglements between them. With their assertion that the Axis was profoundly unlike the Allies, their lack of theoretical reflection of the comparative approach, their emphasis on po-

---

27 Mawdsley, "World War II", 38–39. However, Thomas Zeiler, *Annihilation: A Global Military History of World War II* (New York and Oxford: Oxford University Press, 2011) mentions China only on 30 of 418 pages of text, according to the index, not much more (relatively speaking) than the 51 out of 920 pages in Gerhard Weinberg, *A World at Arms: A Global History of World War II* (Cambridge et al.: Cambridge University Press, 1994).
28 Evan Mawdsley, *World War II: A New History* (Cambridge et al.: Cambridge University Press, 2009), 5 and in general.
29 Winston Churchill, *The Second World War, vol. IV: The Hinge of Fate* (London et al.: Cassell, 1951), 181. Also quoted in Madusree Mukerjee, *Churchill's Secret War: The British Empire and the Ravaging of India during World War II* (New York: Basic Books, 2010), ix.
30 Quoted ibid., 141.
31 Overy, *Blood*, xi, 597, 601–602 but see 607.
32 But see Aaron William Moore, *Bombing the City: Civilian Accounts of the Air War in Britain and Japan, 1939–1945* (Cambridge et al.: Cambridge University Press, 2018), 6–11.

litical history (and mostly elite politics and political ideas) and their disinterest in social history they worked to consolidate the warped mainstream narrative.[33]

Several works with more of a social history outlook do make comparisons across the alliance systems and have found striking similarities by examining populations' experience of aerial warfare, the treatment of children fathered by occupation forces or famines.[34] When comparing U.S. and Japanese warfare, John Dower already found many parallels between them, although with fewer elements of social history, concluding, inter alia, "[a]part from the genocide of the Jews, racism remains one of the great neglected subjects of World War Two".[35]

According to the mainstream narrative, World War II was a war between good and evil where, splendidly, the good emerged victorious. "[O]ften it gets boiled down to simplistic retellings of the massive forces battling; good and evil, Axis and Allies." This is also true for general historical studies of the war, which usually concentrate on a few fronts.[36] The vast majority of studies carry the good vs. bad narrative explicitly or implicitly. The national histories and school lessons in the USA, Britain, Russia/the Soviet Union and China also say so, with the USA and Britain dominating the world market in history books. The image of the "good war" has been systematically constructed and cultivated by a huge entertainment industry during and after the conflict.[37] On top of films, documentaries

---

[33] See Aviel Roshwald, *Occupied: European and Asian Resonses to Axis Conquest, 1937–1945* (Cambridge: Cambridge University Press, 2023); Hedinger, *Achse*. Hedinger subsumes Japan under the concept of fascism.

[34] See Moore, *Bombing*; Florian Armingeon, *Organisationen von Besatzungskindern des Zweiten Weltkrieges im Vergleich*, Master's thesis, University of Bern, 2023; less explicit about parallels that are nonetheless obvious from their work are Sugata Bose, "Starvation amidst Plenty: The Making of Famine in Bengal, Honan and Tonkin, 1942–45", *Modern Asian Studies* 24, 4 (1990): 699–727; Lance Brennan et al., "War and Famine around the Indian Ocean during the Second World War", *Ethics of the Global South* 18 (2017): 5–70.

[35] Dower, *War* (quote 4).

[36] The insights and quote are from Chris Murray, "Introduction: Forgotten fronts", Chris Murray, ed., *Unknown Conflicts of the Second World War: Forgotten Fronts* (London and New York: Routledge, 2019), 1.

[37] For the USA, see Philip Beidler, *The Good War's Greatest Hits: World War II and American Remembering* (Athens and London: University of Georgia Press, 1998) and Sebastian Haak, *The Making of* The Good War*: Hollywood, das Pentagon und die amerikanische Deutung des Zweiten Weltkriegs 1945–1962* (Paderborn: Schöningh, 2013); for the People's Republic of China, see Rana Mitter, *China's Good War: How World War II Is Shaping a New Nationalism* (Cambridge and London: Belknap, 2020) and Lu Xun, "Wartime collaborations in rural North China", Murray, *Unknown Conflicts*, 171. See also Moore, *Bombing the City*, 203.

and novels, this is also being done in the world of computer games.[38] In 2015, China's president Xi Jinping called World War II "a decisive battle between justice and evil, between light and darkness, and between progress and reaction", and there is no reason to believe that he has changed his mind since.[39] Strong notions of good and evil were even inherited and not only a matter of states and propaganda but also shared in the populace. This becomes visible in the everyday postwar experience of ostracization that children fathered by soldiers from various occupying powers have been going through. Many of these children internalized this Manichean view.[40]

Some, however, have questioned this Manichean perspective by pointing to the fact that, for example, the Soviet Union, the brutal dictatorship in the Dominican Republic and South Africa were among the Allies, devaluing "the Allies' stock phrases praising freedom and international solidarity".[41] As Mark Mazower added, Jan Smuts, one of the forefathers of apartheid in South Africa and the man who drafted the preamble of the UN charter, said in late 1940, as Prime Minister of racist South Africa, that the Allied fight against Nazism was one of "civilization", "progress" and "enlightenment" against "racial domination",[42] and Chris Murray pointed to the "ugly truth of brutality displayed by participants on all sides".[43] However, occasionally there is ambiguity in statements of this kind, such as in Thomas Zeiler's assessment that this was a "war of annihilation" from both sides but there was "no moral equivalence" between Axis and Allies: "No doubt the Allies crossed moral thresholds – Dresden, Hiroshima, taking human war trophies on Pacific islands, shooting German and Italian prisoners, and a host of Soviet atrocities – but they did so to speed an end of the war."[44] Essentially, in this justification of mass killing – and he was not alone in doing so – there was good violence and bad, de-

---

38 See remarks by Chris Kempshall in Adam Chapman and Chris Kempshall, "Battlefield 1: Can The Great War Be a Great Game?", *The Ontological Geek*, 16 February 2017, ontologicalgeek.com/battlefield-1-can-the-great-war-be-a-great-game/ (accessed August 16, 2023) (I am grateful to Dario Gomes Caliandro for pointing me to this); Murray, "Introduction", 1.
39 Xi, "Remember", 484.
40 I take this from Armingeon, *Organisationen*.
41 Eric Paul Roorda, "The Dominican Republic: The Axis, the Allies, and the Trujillo Dictatorship", Thomas Leonard and John Bratzel, eds., *Latin America during World War II* (Lanham et al.: Rowman and Littlefield, 2007), 89–90, making the point about the Dominican Republic.
42 Mark Mazower, *No Enchanted Palace: The End of Empire and the Ideological Origins of the United Nations* (Princeton and Oxford: Princeton University Press, 2009), 28–65, quotes 57.
43 Murray, "Introduction", 1.
44 Zeiler, *War*, 2. Zeiler goes on by saying that the Soviets "sought to annihilate whole populations as the purpose of the war itself" in the end of the conflict, namely Germans (ibid.). It is hard to see more than fiction in this statement.

pending on the purpose they served. (One also wonders whether the Axis did *not* want to "speed an end of the war" and how exactly "taking human war trophies" sped up the end of the war.)

One notable part of the narrative is the demonization of the Axis, which is built on war propaganda covered in another section of this chapter. For example, Ernest Mandel called German crimes "monstrous".[45] Films about the war made in the People's Republic of China frequently speak of "Japanese devils".[46] There was even self-demonization: despite of their elaborate postwar re-education in Chinese detention as a way to have them face their personal responsibility, or because of it, some Japanese who had committed murders argued that they had become demons.[47]

Criticism of the good-against-evil narrative, if it occurred at all, has often been within limits, immanent and could, thus, be coopted into the mainstream. Although the Trotskyist Ernest Mandel called World War II an imperialist war from all sides and argued that Germany was not principally different from other imperialist powers, he insisted that many just wars were fought in it – a just Soviet "war of self-defense", an anti-imperialist war by the Chinese people, an anti-imperialist war by Asian peoples against colonialists and national liberation wars by occupied European countries (by which he, of course, meant only those occupied by the Axis).[48] Others also maintained the good-against-evil narrative even if they were incriminating Allied colonialism, Richard Overy by finding a "moral inversion" in Axis states but not saying the same about the Allies.[49] An observer as thoughtful as Charlotte Wiedemann stated: "Hundreds of thousands of Black Americans also fought for our freedom without being free themselves."[50] This raises some questions: did they actually fight to liberate the enemy, and who is 'we' here? Although Michael Adams came up with a sarcastic title for his book *The Best War Ever*, he mainly referred to the brutal battles and nervous break-

---

45 Mandel, *Der Zweite Weltkrieg*, 35.
46 Timothy Tsu et al., "The Second World War in postwar Chinese and Japanese film", King-fai Tam et al., eds., *Chinese and Japanese Films on the Second World War* (London and New York: Routledge, 2015), 5.
47 Accounts by Ken Yuasa and Shozo Tominaga, Haroku Taya Cook and Theodore Cook, eds., *Japan at War: An Oral History* (New York: New Press, 1992), 43, 147, 463–467.
48 Mandel, *Der Zweite Weltkrieg*, 10–15, 26, 43–44, quote 43.
49 See Overy, *Blood*, quote 598; the volume Rheinisches JournalistInnenbüro, *"Unsere Opfer zählen nicht": Die Dritte Welt im Zweiten Weltkrieg* (Berlin and Hamburg: Assoziation A, 2005), esp. 13–24.
50 "Für unsere Freiheit kämpften, ohne selbst frei zu sein, gleichfalls Hunderttausende Schwarze Amerikaner." Charlotte Wiedemann, *Den Schmerz der anderen begreifen: Holocaust und Weltgedächtnis* (Berlin: Propyläen, 2022), 18.

downs among U.S. troops, U.S. propaganda and censorship, the discrimination of African American soldiers and venereal diseases, demonstrating that he had little interest in anybody other than the 'Americans'.[51]

Few have taken the step to fully deny the Manichean image. Aaron William Moore, who found many strong parallels between the experiences of the British and Japanese population in aerial attacks, criticized the customary "simple categorization of Japan and Britain into 'good' and 'evil' powers", stating in the end: "The Second World War was never a 'good war'".[52] He did so as a consequence of a study of social, rather than political, history.

However timid and limited, studies that take more of a global perspective are greatly appreciated, so are comparative studies and is overcoming the Manichean world view. Other positive signs can be found in the scholarly recognitions of World War II as a conglomerate of multiple and manifold conflicts. Aside from the struggle between two coalitions of states, it included several bilateral interstate wars and occupations and was "a mosaic of overlapping conflicts, civil wars, and revolutions".[53] Other such views included the one that "the conflict needs to be redefined as a number of different kinds of war" and another, according to which there were many "different [. . .] wartime conflicts": interstate war, civil wars and "civilian wars" of resistance.[54] This has important implications, especially as an acknowledgment of how deeply and in which complicated ways civilians were affected or involved, as well as regarding the causes of the war. For example, Yugoslavia was a "fractured society with deep class, religious and ethnic divisions".[55] I agree with Ernest Mandel that World War II should be viewed as a "union of activities of a broad spectrum of nations, social classes and strata, political parties and smaller coteries (financial, industrial, military and political) across the whole world".[56]

These changes would imply a turn toward a social history outlook. "Those whose gaze is fixed more squarely on the war itself", Martin Thomas bemoaned, overlook "trade disruption" and "food shortages" (although he did not quantify

---

51 Michael Adams, *The Best War Ever: America and World War II* (Baltimore and London: Johns Hopkins University Press, 1994).
52 Moore, *Bombing*, 16, 214.
53 Murray, "Introduction", 2, citing Antony Beevor.
54 Overy, *Blood*, x-xi, 690.
55 Murray, "Introduction", 5.
56 Mandel, *Der Zweite Weltkrieg*, 33 ("Verbindung von Aktionen eines breiten Spektrums von Nationen, gesellschaftlichen Klassen und Schichten, politischen Parteien und engeren Cliquen (finanziellen, industriellen, militärischen und politischen) über die ganze Welt"). Mandel's study bore many contradictions, but its chapter on the direct causes of the war is indeed global (ibid., 20–32).

how many historians did so).⁵⁷ Historians of Africa noted relatively early what has been called colonial reform or the second colonial occupation, exploitation and the "coercion of African manpower for labour or military purposes" by colonial – such as British –officials, though concentrating on the military recruitment, front experience and the political impact of returned veterans on decolonization movements.⁵⁸ Richard Overy's recent study is important because it has more infusions of social history than some of his previous works, but the fact remains that in his study's section on female (and male) labor, the population of the colonies does not appear.⁵⁹ The relationship between interstate war and conflicts within societies is not always clear; therefore, more remains to be done.

This wider understanding of what war is feeds into reflections about the duration of the war. With struggles between ethnicities and social classes, for and against communism, for and against monarchies and for and against feudalism intermeshed and many conflicts beyond the war against Germany and Japan enduring, it is no wonder that much of the violence did not stop in 1945 and expulsions, selective starvation, mass revenge, purification urges and civil wars did not end.⁶⁰ This implies that World War II had no clear dates marking its beginning and end.⁶¹

Some specialists of World War I now prefer to date this global conflict from 1911 or 1912 to 1923 (called the "Greater War").⁶² World wars are not defined, and their periodization becomes quite arbitrary as a result. Given that the Chinese-Japanese front, one of the two major fronts of World War II, was established in July 1937, I, for the purposes of this chapter, set the beginning of the war at that point (as do others⁶³), rather than the Eurocentric version of September 1939 (thus, I side with Stalin against Churchill, Hermann Göring and Adolf Hitler⁶⁴).

---

57 Thomas, "Resource War", 228.
58 Ashley Jackson, *Botswana 1939–1945: An African Country at War* (Oxford: Clarendon, 1999), 4–7.
59 Overy, *Blood*, 416–430. The same can be said about Mandel's chapters about war economies and logistic; see Mandel, *Der Zweite Weltkrieg*, 46–53, 71–76.
60 See Keith Lowe, *Der wilde Kontinent: Europa in den Jahren der Anarchie 1943–1950* (Stuttgart: Klett Cotta, 2014), esp. 444.
61 Hedinger, *Achse*, 72–73 makes the same point.
62 See Robert Gerwarth and Erez Manela, *Empires at War, 1911–1923* (Oxford: Oxford University Press, 2014), esp. 16, and *The Greater War* book series (general editor: Robert Gerwarth).
63 Mawdsley, "World War II", 38.
64 Stalin stated that the second "imperialist war" had started in 1937 (obviously with the Japanese attack on China), Churchill propagated September 1939 as the beginning, and Göring declared that the world war had begun in December 1941. For Stalin, see Tobias Privitelli, *Irredentism, Expansion and the Liberation of the European Proletariat: Stalin's Considerations on how to Bring Communism to the Western Neighbors of the Soviet Union, 1920–1941*, Ph.D dissertation, University of Bern, 2008, 252–253, 276; for Churchill, see Winston Churchill, *The Second*

One could also have it begin in 1935 with the Italian attack on Ethiopia, in 1936 with the soon-internationalized Spanish Civil War, or in the early 1930s because of the Sino-Japanese conflict and the Japanese conquest of Manchuria.[65] Some would perhaps see the end of the war in 1949 (the Chinese revolution, Indonesia's independence and the foundation of two German states). In this chapter, I assume that the end was in 1947, when several large famines ended, although slowly.

In addition to all of this, the mainstream historiography has steep hierarchies between the war's victims, despite claims to universalism in memory. These hierarchies are reflected in the amount of attention paid to different groups in scholarship and public, but they have also been made quite explicit through certain historical constructs.[66] Germans annihilated six million Jews and three million Soviet POWs, but while there are innumerable books in English exclusively about the murder of the Jews (thousands at least), there is not a single one in English exclusively about the destruction of Soviet prisoners of war.[67] This shows how 'universal' and 'humanist' such scholarship is. Although many of its proponents insist on empathy for the victims, the circle of persons for which empathy is reserved is strictly limited. Jews have more importance than others in the literature; within that group, Western European Jews are given more importance than those from Eastern Europe and bourgeois, highly educated city Jews more than lower-class small-town Jews. This is not all there is to hierarchies: white lives count more than dark, literates more than illiterates and Western Europeans more than Eastern Europeans in general. For example, there are many more publications about the forced labor of British, U.S. and Australian POWs in Japanese hands than that of Southeast Asians in Japanese hands (although the Asian's death figures and death rates were higher).[68] To be sure, these

---

World War: The Gathering Storm (New York: Houghton Mifflin, 1948); for Göring and Hitler, see Christian Gerlach, "The Wannsee Conference, the Fate of German Jews, and Hitler's Decision in Principle to Exterminate All European Jews", *Journal of Modern History* 70, 4 (1998): 784–785. The 1939 version is still in Mandel, *Der Zweite Weltkrieg*, 26 and Weinberg, "Total War".

65 Overy, *Blood*, x pleads for the latter version. Buchanan, "Globalizing", 254 sees an "extended series of regional wars" from 1931–1953 and a "central paroxysm" from December 1941 to September 1945.

66 Dirk Moses, *The Problems of Genocide: Permanent Security and the Language of Transgression* (Cambridge et al.: Cambridge University Press, 2021), 17 points to consequences of the concept of "genocide" in this context.

67 For an example of evolving local knowledge and (non-)memory about the fate of Soviet POWs in Germany, see Wiedemann, *Den Schmerz*, 95–115.

68 See Paul Kratoska, "Introduction", Paul Kratoska, ed., *Asian Labor in the Wartime Japanese Empire* (Armonk and London: M. E. Sharpe, 2005), xvi. Kratoska's observation is still accurate. For the death figures and rates of the Southeast Asians employed, see Nakahara Michiko, "Malayan Labor on the Thailand-Burma Railway", Kratoska, *Asian Labor*, 252; see also Neil MacPherson, "Death Railway Movements", n.d., http://www.mansell.com/pow_resources/camplists/death_rr/movements_1.html.

practices have developed over time (they seem to have intensified in and after the 1980s), were multicausal, and they do not apply everywhere because of national differences in memory and scholarship. Still, assigning a higher value to the loss of life of certain groups of people than to others based on distinctions of race, ethnicity or skin color is racist.

One construct that postulates victims of different value is the thesis of the singularity of the murder of the Jews. Michael Rothberg, among others, has concluded that the uniqueness thesis "potentially creates a hierarchy of suffering", that its advocates de-historicize the extermination of the Jews, reject "all attempts to compare or analogize the Holocaust" and call all doubts about its uniqueness a "relativization" that ought to be condemned.[69] This is not only about maintaining that these were persecutions of a different *kind* but also about believing that they were of a different *value*.[70] Advocates of the singularity thesis find it particularly "problematic" if comparisons are made or parallels are drawn to the suffering of Jews, especially if this is for "upgrading a victimization experience";[71] an "uplift

---

[69] Michael Rothberg, *Multidirectional Memory: Remembering the Holocaust in the Age of Decolonization* (Stanford: Stanford University Press, 2009), 7, 9; see also Jean-Michel Chaumont, *La concurrence des victimes* (Paris: Éditions la Découverte, 1997), esp. 125. The singularity or uniqueness thesis is based on the nonsensical interpretation of the crime having been irrational and, thus, non-instrumental, unlike any other, and also more total than any other mass murder (although comparable proportions, about 80 percent of the Tutsi in Rwanda 1994 and of the Armenians within the reach of the Ottoman authorities in 1915–1918, were killed in other cases).

Those who call the murder of the Jews 'Holocaust' (i.e., burnt sacrifice) indicate by doing so that they take part in systematic mystification. The term obscures the event (most Jewish victims did not die through fire, and burning the dead was common in large parts of the world in World War II, instead of being specific for the fate of Jews), it explains nothing and gives that annihilation a quasi-sacral aura, which is irreconcilable with an effort at scholarly analysis. Against this backdrop, it is characteristic that 'Holocaust' has become the most widely used term for the murder of the Jews in scholarship and public opinion. Helen Fein conceded as much in 1975 as to say that "some" scholars found the annihilation of the Jews "non-explicable" and a "mystifying or transcendent event" and was harshly criticized for it. Quoted in Moses, *Problems*, 442.

[70] This becomes obvious one way or another. Dan Diner assures readers that he rejects to "qualify [different] suffering as ethically different and, thus, disparage [some of it]", only to add immediately that the "Holocaust" is more significant than other mass murders because only it causes a "cognitive horror" and was a "rupture of civilization". Dan Diner, "Über kognitives Entsetzen", in Saul Friedländer et al., *"Ein Verbrechen ohne Namen": Anmerkungen zum neuen Streit über den Holocaust* (Munich: Beck, 2022), 79 ("das jeweils erlittene Leid als ethisch verschieden zu qualifizieren und damit herabzusetzen"; "kognitive Entsetzen"; "Zivilisationsbruchs").

[71] Monique Eckmann and Gottfried Kössler, "Polarisierungen verweigern: Spanungsfelder in der pädagogischen Auseinandersetzung mit dem Antisemitismus", in Matthias Böckmann et al., eds., *Jenseits von Mbembe: Geschichte, Erinnerung, Solidarität* (Berlin: Metropol, 2022), 125–140, 137 ("zum Aufwerten einer Opfererfahrung").

comparison", according to this view, is "always [. . .] a derision of the victims of the Shoah".[72] This means that proponents of this thesis want to keep other experiences of victimization and mass murder in a lower rank. By always insisting on the singularity of the 'Holocaust', that it should be talked about more than any other mass crime and that those who died in the 'Holocaust' are in another league of victimhood and by insisting that this one – large – victim group must be put at the center of mass violence in World War II – or even World War II as a whole or history as a whole[73] – they are constantly devaluing and demoting all other victim groups.[74] This, too, is racist, but it is just one example.

Mass Violence by the Allies

Many cases of Allied mass violence are well known, others are much less familiar. This mass violence was committed by Soviets as well as British, Chinese, U.S. Americans, French, Belgians, Poles, Czechoslovaks, Yugoslavs and citizens of other Allied countries.

One part of World War II Allied violence directed against enemy civilians consisted of the British and U.S. fire bombings of German and Japanese cities, which killed at least one million people, including the U.S. nuclear attacks on Hiroshima and Nagasaki.[75] These attacks were not only fueled by ruthless propaganda but

---

[72] Erik Petry, "Die erkenntnistheoretische falsche Frage: Was ist Antisemitismus?" in Böckmann et al., *Jenseits*, 107–116, 116 ("immer ist es aber eine Verhöhnung der Opfer der Shoah durch einen Erhebungsvergleich").
[73] It is such a tendency that Achille Mbembe criticizes in statements made by Alain Finkielkraut. See Achille Mbembe, *Ausgang aus langer Nacht: Versuch über ein entkolonialisiertes Afrika* (Frankfurt a.M.: Suhrkamp, 2016), 202–203.
[74] See also Chaumont, *Concurrence*, 9–10, 52.
[75] For accounts of survivors of these bombings in general, see Siegfried Schaarschmidt, ed., *Schrei nach Frieden: Japanische Zeugnisse gegen den Krieg* (Düsseldorf and Vienna: Econ, 1984), 15–57; Erhard Klöss, ed., *Der Luftkrieg über Deutschland 1939–1945* (Munich: dtv, 1964), 60–122 and medical reports 122–172. For Hiroshima and Nagasaki, see accounts in *Kinder von Hiroshima* (Frankfurt a.M.: Röderberg, 1981 (fourth edition)); Hermann Vinke, ed., *Als die erste Atombombe fiel. . . : Kinder aus Hiroshima berichten* (Ravensburg: Otto Maier, 1982); *Pika-don über Japan* (Cologne: Maximilian, 1955); Schaarschmidt, *Schrei*, 187–264; Tatsuichiro Akizuki, *Nagasaki 1945* (London et al.: Quartet, 1981); Shuntaro Hida, *Der Tag, an dem Hiroshima verschwand: Erinnerungen eines japanischen Militärarztes* (Bremen: Donat, 1986); Michihiko Hachiya, *Hiroshima Diary* (Chapel Hill: University of North Carolina Press, 1985 (10th ed.)); Paul Takashi Nagai, *Die Glocken von Nagasaki* (Luzern: Schweizer Volk-Buchgemeinde, 1955 (fourth ed.)); Toyofumi Ogura, *Letters from the End of the World* (Tokio et.al.: Kodamsha International, 2001); Narihiko Ito et.al., eds., *Seit jenem Tag: Hiroshima und Nagasaki in der japanischen Literatur* (Frankfurt a.M.: Fischer,

also by mass sentiments. British and U.S. air forces also killed tens of thousands of civilians in France, Italy, Romania, Hungary and China.[76] In a December 1945 survey for *Fortune* magazine, 22.7 percent of U.S. residents regretted that the USA had not dropped more Atomic bombs on Japan.[77]

Enemy population was also targeted in the mass death of prisoners of war, which was mainly caused by starvation, exhaustion and cold due to undersupply and hard labor. This did not concern all groups of prisoners. While the treatment of European POWs in U.S., British and French hands did not lead to elevated mortality, between 0.5 million and 1.5 million prisoners in Soviet hands died, which in absolute numbers were mainly Germans and Japanese, but those with the highest mortality rates were Italians and Romanians.[78] Many Japanese also appear to have died in British captivity in 1945.[79]

Moreover, Soviet troops killed an unknown but very high number of German (and probably also Italian) troops who surrendered to them (though their number was lower than that of Soviet troops killed upon surrender by the Germans). Troops from the USA and Britain often either did the same to Japanese soldiers and sailors or refused to rescue those who were shipwrecked due to unrestrained submarine warfare. Often, these were hate crimes, committed out of conviction, initiated by individual soldiers or middle to high ranking officers and, in the U.S. case, based on popular racism against the Japanese.[80] U.S. troops also extracted gold teeth from the mouths of Japanese soldiers they had killed.[81] They killed many tens of thousands of civilians on the Japanese island of Okinawa.[82] The attitude prevail-

---

1984), 14–33; Helmut Erlinghagen, *Hiroshima und wir* (Frankfurt a.M.: Fischer, 1982), 13–22, 31–48; P.T. Siemes, "The Atomic Bomb on Hiroshima: An Eye-Witness Account", *The Irish Monthly* 74, 873 (1946): 93–104 and 74, 874 (1946): 148–154.

76 See Overy, *Blood*, 673–674, 678, 791–793; Rolf-Dieter Müller, *Der Bombenkrieg 1939–1945* (Berlin: Christoph Links, 2004), 8; Moore, *Bombing*, 13; Studs Terkel, *"The Good War": An Oral History of World War II* (New York: Pantheon, 1984). A formidable study of the effects of nuclear bombing is Susan Southard, *Nagasaki: Life After Nuclear War* (New York: Viking, 2015).

77 Dower, *War*, 54.

78 Overy, *Blood*, 777, 780; Gerlach, *Extermination*, 235–238.

79 Accounts by Masatsugu Ogawa and Shogo Iitoyo in Cook and Cook, *Japan*, 276, 414–415; account by Maskatsu Nomura in Schaarschmidt, *Schrei*, 80.

80 Overy, *Blood*, 773–774; Christian Gerlach and Nicolas Werth, "State Violence – Violent Societies", in Michael Geyer and Sheila Fitzpatrick, eds., *Beyond Totalitarianism: Stalinism and Nazism Compared* (Cambridge et al.: Cambridge University Press, 2009), 167; Adams, *The Best War*, 61, 111–112; Jonathan Glover, *Humanity: A Moral History of the Twentieth Century* (London: Pimlico, 2001), 175–176.

81 Dower, *War*, 63–68; account by E.B. Sledge in Terkel, *"Good War"*, 62.

82 Dower, *War*, 218; Cook and Cook, *Japan*, 367; see survivor accounts in Schaarschmidt, *Schrei*, 121–182.

ing in the U.S. military toward the Japanese was much less friendly than toward Germans or Italians. Commenting on the reasons for the fact that postwar U.S. military courts had only three German military officers executed compared to about 1,000 Japanese ones, Telford Taylor, U.S. chief prosecutor during the Nuremberg Trials of War Criminals, later suggested: "I suppose it was race."[83]

In addition, there were collective expulsions of 18 million German and Japanese civilians from Eastern Europe, China and Korea in 1944–1947. Germans were expelled from Poland, Czechoslovakia, the USSR, Yugoslavia and other countries. In addition, hundreds of thousands of Hungarians were expelled from Czechoslovakia and Romania. An estimated half a million Germans and at least 200,000 Japanese died in the process due to massacres, killings and deprivation.[84] The UN Relief and Rehabilitation Administration (UNRRA) excluded the over 3.5 million children of ethnic Germans who were expelled from Eastern Europe from their aid.[85] Soviet authorities deported more than 200,000 individuals from Eastern Europe shortly after the war for forced labor in the Soviet Union. Most of these men and women were (ethnic) Germans. Over 20 percent of them died before repatriation in this scheme of "reparation through [providing] labor force".[86]

There are only vague estimates regarding the number of women raped by Soviet troops in Germany, Poland, Hungary, Manchuria and elsewhere; by U.S., British and French soldiers in Germany and elsewhere; and by U.S. troops in Japan. This would have hardly been less than one million.[87] Not all women and

---

83 Terkel, *"Good War"*, 461. For racial discrimination of African Americans, Hispanics and Italian Americans in the U.S. military, see ibid., 146–185.
84 Richard Bessel, "Unnatural deaths", Richard Overy, ed., *The Oxford Illustrated History of World War II* (Oxford: Oxford University Press, 2015), 336; Cook and Cook, *Japan*, 403; Collingham, *Taste*, 62.
85 Katherine Rossy, "The UN search for stolen and hidden Polish children (1944–47)", in Murray, *Unknown Conflicts*, 226.
86 See Pavel Poljan, "Westarbeiter: Reparation durch Arbeitskraft: Deutsche Häftlinge in der UdSSR", Dittmar Dahlmann and Gerhard Hirschfeld, eds., *Lager, Zwangsarbeiter, Vertreibung und Deportation: Dimensionen der Massenverbrechen in der Sowjetunion und in Deutschland 1933 bis 1945* (Essen: Klartext, 1999), 337–367.
87 Overy, *Blood*, 809–810, 814; see also Mark Edele, *Stalinism at War: The Soviet Union in World War II* (London et al.: Bloomsbury, 2021), 167; Lilly, *Taken*, 12, 30–31; Miriam Gebhardt, "Eine Frage des Schweigens? Forschungsthesen zur Vergewaltigung deutscher Frauen nach Kriegsende," Barbara Stelzl-Marx and Slike Satjukow, eds., *Besatzungskinder: Die Nachkommen alliierter Soldaten in Österreich und Deutschland* (Vienna et al.: Böhlau, 2015), 68–69. For Manchuria, see accounts by Teruko Nishioka and Matsuko Fukomoto and for Okinawa, Japan, Sumi Tonouchi, in Schaarschmidt, *Schrei*, 90, 109, 159.
Many analysts have rationalized the Soviet mass rapes with Soviet soldiers' bitterness about the earlier German atrocities, but this hardly explains the rapes in Poland and Manchuria.

girls survived these assaults. British military in India also sexually exploited women in labor camps and established at least one brothel.[88] Rape and individually shooting prisoners or enemy soldiers who had surrendered were participatory practices of violence.

However, much Allied violence was also directed against their own citizens or colonial subjects. The citizens were particularly targeted in the USSR and China.

In the Soviet camp system called Gulag, the number of prisoners reached a high level during World War II and 974,000 inmates died in these camps, usually as a result of starvation, cold and hard labor.[89] Many of them were social outsiders, petty criminals or violators of work discipline and, in increasing numbers, women and ethnic minorities. This is not counting the many civilians who died under famine conditions during the war, particularly in 1942–1943.

'Preventive' or 'punitive' mass resettlement of entire ethnicities from western areas of the USSR during World War II affected Poles in 1939–1941, Germans in 1941–1942, and Chechens, Ingush, Karachays, Kalmycks and Crimean Tatars in 1943–1944. About three million people of these minorities were deported from their homelands and more than half a million died from hunger, exhaustion and cold during transport or due to inadequate shelter.[90] It is often said that these forced resettlers, the Gulag inmates and foreign POWs just suffered from hunger like the rest of the Soviet population did, but this is evidently not true when one looks at the death rates.

---

[88] Mukerjee, *Churchill's Secret War*, 158, 184.

[89] Overy, *Blood*, 785; Edele, *Stalinism*, 126–128 suggests somewhat lower figures. See also Donald Filtzer, "Starvation Mortality in Soviet Home-Front Industrial Regions during World War II", in Wendy Goldman and Donald Filtzer, eds., *Hunger and War: Food Provisioning in the Soviet Union during World War II* (Bloomington and Indianapolis: Indiana University Press, 2015), 330, 307 note 52.

[90] Ethnic minorities and foreign groups were also deported and interned in other Allied countries. U.S. authorities deported and interned close to 150,000 citizens and residents of Japanese extraction 1942–1945, though they were held under better conditions with no elevated mortality. French governments of the Third and Fourth Republics 1938–1940 and 1944–1946 incarcerated more people in internment camps than Vichy France did in 1940–1944, especially foreign (mostly Spanish) citizens, nomads (above all, Roma), communists, Jews and persons affiliated to the Vichy regime. See Denis Peschanski, *La France des camps: L'internement 1938–1946* (Paris: Gallimard, 2002), esp. 475.- For Soviet policies, see the remarks by Nicolas Werth in Gerlach and Werth, "State Violence", 158–161; Edele, *Stalinism*, 62–64, 171; Jan Gross, *Revolution from Abroad: The Soviet Conquest of Poland's Western Ukraine and Western Belorussia* (Princeton: Princeton University Press, 1988); Michael Schwartz, "Ethnische "Säuberung" als Kriegsfolge", in Rolf-Dieter Müller, ed., *Das Deutsche Reich und der Zweite Weltkrieg*, vol. 10/2: *Der Zusammenbruch des Deutschen Reiches 1945 und die Folgen des Zweiten Weltkrieges*, sub-volume 2: *Die Auflösung der Wehrmacht und die Auswirkungen des Krieges* (Munich: Deutsche Verlags-Anstalt, 2008), 573.

The Chinese government acted with similar recklessness but in different ways. The most striking case was the Yellow River flood of 1938, where Chinese troops destroyed a dyke to induce intentional flooding to block an offensive by Japanese troops. Although no Japanese were killed in this and the fall of Wuhan to the Japanese was only briefly delayed, 70,000 sq. kilometers were submerged, between 400,000 and 900,000 Chinese died, and the flooding caused three to nine million domestic refugees.[91] The worst among many other manifestations of Chinese scorched-earth policy was when the Guomindang state's military burned down the city of Changsha and killed 20,000 Chinese in November 1938. It acted similarly in Guilin in the fall of 1944.[92] Chinese airplanes strafed the International Settlement in Shanghai on August 14, 1941, killing over one thousand people, mostly Chinese.[93] Guomindang-led Nationalist China used terror and torture against its citizens in punitive camps and elsewhere.[94] But the Chinese military also treated its own recruits with utter contempt. It is estimated that 1.4 million of them – often mobilized by force – died in the army due to diseases, hunger and mistreatment before even reaching their front units.[95] This ruthlessness against its own people during the war (in combination with corruption) caused a fundamental loss of confidence in the population for the Guomindang regime and contributed heavily to the latter's defeat in the Civil War of 1945–1949. For example, parts of the areas of the Yellow River flood became communist strongholds before 1945 and remained under their control from 1946 to 1949.[96]

In suppressing a major anti-colonial and anti-war movement in British-India, British colonial authorities arrested 25,000 Indians until 1941 and another 60,000 in the months from August 1942 and killed at least a thousand. To crush the 1942 Quit India movement, British colonialists bombed crowds of Indians from airplanes at least five times, using incendiary bombs and machine guns, not to dwell on mis-

---

91 Diana Lary, "Drowned Earth: The Strategic Breaching of the Yellow River Dyke, 1938", *War in History* 8, 2 (2001): 191–207; Kathryn Jean Edgerton-Tarpley, "From 'Nourish the People' to 'Sacrifice for the Nation': Changing Responses to Disaster in Late Imperial and Modern China", *Journal of Asian Studies* 73, 2 (2014): 448, 457–458; Micah Muscolino, "Violence Against People and the Land: The Environment and Refugee Migration from China's Henan Province, 1938–1945", *Environment and History* 17 (2011): 295; Mitter, *China's War*, 161.
92 Lary, *Chinese People*, 46, 49, 62–64, 153; Mitter, *China's War*, 204; Schoppa, *Sea*, 239–260.
93 Mitter, *China's War*, 94.
94 Mitter, *China's War*, 283–289.
95 Overy, *Blood*, 383.
96 Bose, "Starvation", 726; Lary, "Drowned Earth", 204.

treatments and pillaging.[97] These were the actions of a 'democratic' power intended to suppress an anti-colonial uprising in a colony, in the name of which colonial officers alone had declared war in Germany. Quit India, in which millions participated, was in part also an anti-war movement, by far the biggest worldwide during the war; against this backdrop, it is remarkable that a British author wrote: "Pacifism in the democracies did not suffer direct persecution".[98] British and U.S. troops in Burma and Australian troops in Japanese-occupied East Timor (a Portuguese colony) exploited colonial subjects for all sorts of services, including fighting, but were quick to kill locals if they were suspected of cooperating with the Japanese.[99] Based on the racism among the British, Australian, French and sometimes U.S. troops, similar things happened in the western Pacific.[100]

Along with the many famines under Allied rule, the number of victims of Allied policies and activities surpassed ten million people, and probably so by far. There were famines in China (in Henan and other provinces) and British-India; in the British colonies of Nigeria, Kenya, Tanganyika and others; in Allied-occupied Iran (a neutral country), Germany, Japan and Austria; in French-Algeria and French-Tunisia and in the Belgian colonies of contemporary Burundi and Rwanda. These famines were caused by conditions of violence created by the ruthless exploitation of these countries, including colonial forced labor programs in Africa and the Pacific. The next section will examine this in more detail.

This brief survey allows for several conclusions to be drawn. These were not marginal or freak events. Hiroshima, the Gulag, the Bengal famine and the Yellow River flood were defining parts of Allied behavior. And one who kills ten million non-combatants cannot be considered 'good' except for what would be a very peculiar meaning of the word.

But there is more to the Allied record of conduct. Axis countries primarily killed enemy populations (and if these were non-combatants, usually in occupied countries). But most victims of Allied action against non-combatants were *not*

---

[97] Francis Hutchins, *India's Revolution: Gandhi and the Quit India Movement* (Cambridge: Harvard University Press, 1973), 230–232; S.K. Sharma, ed., *Quit India Movement* (New Delhi: Mittal, 2009), esp. 91, 97; Mukerjee, *Churchill's Secret War*, 20, 85; Mukherjee, *Hungry Bengal*, 104.
[98] Overy, *Blood*, 649. See ibid., 645–660 on pacifism (which for Overy is mostly Christian pacifism).
[99] Michele Turner, *Telling: East Timor: Personal Memories, 1942–1992* (Kensington: New South Wales University Press, 2003), 6, 26–32; account by Henry Hatfield, Terkel, *"Good War"*, 376.
[100] Lamont Lindstrom and Geoffrey White, "War Stories", in Geoffrey White and Lamont Lindstrom, eds., *The Pacific Theatre; Island Representations of World War II* (Honolulu: University of Hawaii Press, 1989), 8–13; see account by Masatsugu Ogawa in Cook and Cook, *Japan*, 273.

from the enemy side. The majority were actually their own citizens or colonial subjects: in the Gulag and ethnic resettlements, among Chinese peasants and recruits, and in Bengal and Burundi. Given these facts, the Allied phrases about their fight for freedom, democracy, anti-racism and freedom from want do not only sound hollow, they were a brutal mockery that continues until today.

The celebrated economist John Kenneth Galbraith once said about the USA in World War II: "Never in the history of human conflict has there been so much talk of sacrifice and so little sacrifice."[101] Worse, there was a great deal of sacrifice on the Allied side, but why was so much of it made by people with dark skin or by rural dwellers and ethnic minorities that the ruling classes of their own countries regarded as inferior?[102]

The Allied war effort was inherently racist. Regarding that, it was similar to the Axis. However, one should not stop at a denunciatory statement. The point is, why was all this racism there? The answer is, of course, complex; in this chapter, I would like to point to certain racist *practices* and explain why so many people killed by the Allies died of a lack of resources, and hunger in particular. One part of the explanation lies in conditions of violence constituted by labor relations, value extraction and resource distribution in combination with disenfranchisement, restrictions of movement and convenient racial hierarchies during the war, as I will show in the next section.

As a side note, to assert that Soviet policies and actions were not racist would be ridiculous. The whole Soviet population suffered terribly from the war, that is, from the invasion by Germany and other Axis countries, from fighting, exhaustion and the lack of resources, but disproportionate suffering was meted out against certain groups that were apparently deemed worthy only of especially scarce resources and died in great numbers due to their lack: Gulag inmates, foreign prisoners of war and ethnic minorities; and the latter two were ethnically defined.[103] And so were the foreign women targeted in mass rapes, the prisoners who were not taken, and populations expulsed. This violent factual racism was directed against both foreigners and compatriots, and while some of it was built into a system with a complex division of labor (in the Gulag and POW camps), other parts were the product of popular racism and individual action *en masse*

---

101 Galbraith's account in Terkel, *"Good War"*, 323.
102 For peasants, see also Collingham, *Taste*, 263.
103 Another example of disproportionate suffering is the fact that the German siege of Leningrad killed between 600,000 and 1,000,000 civilians, one-fifth to one-third of the initial population, whereas most of the prison inmates starved to death. Jörg Ganzenmüller, *Das belagerte Leningrad 1941–1944* (Paderborn et al.: Schöningh, 2005, 238–239, 279–280, 293.

(rapes, taking no prisoners or killing them before they reached the camps). This, too, requires an explanation.

Conditions of Violence: Why Were There So Many Famines in World War II?

Hunger was a part of many people's experiences of World War II. People noted their loss of weight in their diaries. They turned to substitute foods and new cooking recipes. Mothers desperately tried to pull their children through. In some families, there were squabbles about food, theft and denial of help to outsiders in need were regular occurrences. People turned to black market activities or to other illegal action as a remedy, gleaned fields after harvest and commuted to relatives or friends in the countryside. It was also a time of food phantasies and digestive problems – which could become fatal. Around 1945, clothes would hang loosely from many people's meagre bodies. People lacked everything: calories, fat and diverse micronutrients.[104]

The war was a time of scarcity of almost every good, especially consumer goods outside the military. In general, food production decreased because of a lack of inputs such as fertilizer, machinery, fuel, draught animals, and in particular human workforce, in combination with a lack of economic production incentives, new regulations and disrupted economic relations.[105] However, it was not only food availability decline and governmental mismanagement that caused hunger. Factors such as the exploitation of colonies, colonial subjects and occupied areas; official and private looting; mass detention of people regarded as undesirable; political and other hierarchies in rationing systems, and exclusion thereof; food denial for certain groups; sieges and naval blockades; the redistribution of resources; inflationary processes; hoarding and speculation; and struggles related to land ownership all contributed to mass suffering which had, thus, political, military, economic and social aspects. Often this led to famine, in several cases in connection with drought.[106]

---

[104] This section draws substantially from an earlier book chapter of mine: Christian Gerlach, "Hunger in den besetzten Gebieten im Zweiten Weltkrieg – deutsch und global", Haus der Geschichte Baden-Württembergs, ed., *Hunger: Zur Geschichte einer existenziellen Bedrohung* (Ubstadt-Weiher: Verlag Regionalkultur, 2019), 151–164.
[105] See, for example, Brennan et al., "War", 61–64.
[106] Many of these aspects are also noted in ibid., 5–70.

The magnitude and reach of the famines become clear in Table 6.1.[107]

---

[107] For Spain, see Miguel Ángel del Arco Blanco and Peter Anderson, "Introduction: Famine, not hunger?", Miguel Ángel del Arco Blanco and Peter Anderson, eds., *Franco's Famine: Malnutrition, Disease and Starvation in Post-Civil War Spain* (London et al.: Bloomsbury, 2022), 5–6, 10. For Greece, see Violetta Hionidou, *Famine and Death in Occupied Greece, 1941–1944* (Cambridge et al.: Cambridge University Press, 2006), esp. 2, 158. For Poland, see Mariusz Jastrząb, "Rationierungspolitik in Polen zwischen 1945 und 1953", Matthias Middell and Felix Wemheuer, eds., *Hunger, Ernährung und Rationierungssysteme unter dem Staatssozialismus (1917–2006)* (Frankfurt am Main et al.: Peter Lang, 2011), 183–211 and own estimates. For the Soviet Union in 1942–1943 (or, broader, in 1941–1945), see Filtzer, "Starvation Mortality", 265–338, esp. 269–270, 275, 279; Nicholas Ganson, *The Soviet Famine of 1946–47 in Global and Historical Perspective* (New York and Basingstoke: Palgrave Macmillan, 2009), 6. For Leningrad, see Ganzenmüller, *Das belagerte Leningrad*, esp. 238–239. For foreign POWs in the Soviet Union, see note 78 of this chapter. For Cyprus, see E.M.H. Lloyd, *Food and Inflation in the Middle East 1940–1945* (Stanford: Stanford University Press, 1956), 189, 328, 356 (Lloyd does not say that there was a famine, but British military spending in Cyprus was high, the island had a disastrous harvest in 1941 and the infant mortality rose to 50 percent above peacetime levels in 1942). For the Netherlands, see Henri van der Zee, *The Hunger Winter: Occupied Holland 1944–5* (London: Jill Norman & Hobhouse, 1982); Nicki Hart, "Famine Maternal Nutrition and Infant Mortality: A Re-Examination of the Dutch Hunger Winter", *Population Studies*, 47, 1 (1993): 27–46. For Germany, see Alexander Häusser and Gordon Maugg, *Hungerwinter: Deutschlands humanitäre Katastrophe 1946/47* (Berlin: List, 2009); estimate based on data in James Bacque, *Crimes and Mercies: The Fate of German Civilians under Allied Occupation, 1944–1950* (Toronto: Little, Brown & Co, 1997), 123, 128, 211 (despite its tendentious character). For Austria, see Hildegard Hemetsberger-Koller, "Unternehmen Bergius "Nahrung aus Holz": Prestigeprojekt der Hungerjahre 1945/46", *Zeitgeschichte* 26, 2 (1999): 108. For the Soviet Union in 1946–1947, see: Ganson, *Soviet Famine*; Donald Filtzer, "Die Auswirkungen der sowjetischen Hungersnot im Jahr 1947 auf die Industriearbeiter", Middell and Wemheuer, *Hunger*, 59–85.

For Burma, see Christopher Bayly and Tim Harper, *Forgotten Armies*, 167, 182–183, 186–187. For Travancore, the Madras and Bombay areas, Cochin and Orissa, see Mark Tauger, "The Indian Famine Crises of World War II", *British Scholar* 1, 2 (2009): 188–192; Raghavan, *India's War*, 353–355; Benjamin Siegel, *Hungry Nation: Food, Famine and the Making of Modern India* (Cambridge et al.: Cambridge University Press, 2018), 28 note 22; Henry Knight, *Food Administration in India 1939–1947* (Stanford: Stanford University Press, 1954), 114, 201–202. For Bengal, see Mohiuddin Alamgir, *Famine in South Asia* (Cambridge: Oelgeschlager, Gunn and Hain, 1980), 77–92; Mukerjee, *Churchill's Secret War*, 267–272; Collingham, *Taste*, 1, 142. For China in general, see Anthony Garnaut, "A Quantitative Description of the Henan Famine of 1942", *Modern Asian Studies* 47, 6 (2013): 2007–2045, esp. 2032–2036, 2042, who shows convincingly that famine deaths in Henan province can hardly have surpassed one million, but also that there were very many additional deaths in Shanxi, Hebei, Shandong and Zhejiang provinces (largely under Japanese rule) and Hubei province (under Guomindang rule). For Shandong, see also Lary, *Chinese People*, 129. For Henan, see Garnaut, "Quantitative Description"; Bose, "Starvation"; Lary, *Chinese People*, 124–126. For Hongkong, see Rheinisches JournalistInnenbüro, *"Unsere Opfer"*, 238. For East Timor, see James Dunn, *Timor: A People Betrayed* (Gladesville et al.: Jacaranda Press, 1983), 22–26; Turner, *Telling*, iv; Douglas Kammen, *Three Centuries of Conflict in East Timor* (New Brunswick and London: Rutgers University Press, 2015), 110. For Iran, see Mohammad Gholi Majd, *Iran under Allied Occupation in World War*

II (Lanham et al.: University Press of America, 2016), esp. 527–562, 689; Mohammad Gholi Majd, "The Three Famines and the Makings of a Malthusian Catastrophe in Iran (1869–1944)", *Quarterly Journal of the Iranian Islamic Period History* 12, 27 (2021): 80, 97–100 (Gholi Majd's calculations, which are entirely based on demographic data and projections, appear inflated); Lloyd, *Food*, 157–169; Stephen McFarland, "Anatomy of an Iranian Political Crowd: The Tehran Bread Riot of December 1942", *International Journal of Middle East Studies* 17, 1 (1985): 51–65. For Iraqi Kurdistan, see W.G. Elphinston, "The Kurdish Question", *International Affairs* 22, 1 (1946): 99; David McDowell, *A Modern History of the Kurds* (London et al.: I.B. Tauris, 2021, fourth edition), 294. For Singapore, see note 307 in this chapter. For Yemen, see Mary Fletcher, "Famine in Arabia, 1943–1947", https://www.britishempire.co.uk/article/faminearabia/htm (last accessed August 31, 2023); Lloyd, *Food*, 20, 65, 353. For various of the Caroline islands, see Lin Poyer, "Micronesian Experiences of the War in the Pacific", White and Lindstrom, *Pacific Theatre*, 85–86; Suzanne Falgout, "From Passive Pawns to Political Strategists: Wartime Lessons for the People of Pohnpei", White and Lindstrom, *Pacific Theatre*, 287–288; Collingham, *Taste*, 298–299. For Vietnam, see Geoffrey Gunn, *Rice Wars in Colonial Vietnam: The Great Famine and The Viet Minh Road to Power* (Lanham et al.: Rowman and Littlefield, 2014); Bùi Minh Dũng, "Japan's Role in the Vietnamese Starvation of 1944–1945", *Modern Asian Studies* 29, 3 (1995): 573–618; Gregg Huff, "The Great Second World War Vietnam and Java Famines", *Modern Asian Studies* 54, 2 (2020): 621; David Marr, *Vietnam 1945: The Quest for Power* (Berkeley et al.: University of California Press, 1995), 104–105. For Hunan in 1944–1945 and 1946, see Overy, *Blood*, 866; see also Dower, *War*, 295. For the Philippines, see Collingham, *Taste*, 303; Ricardo Jose, "The Rice Shortage and Countermeasures during the Occupation", Setsuho Ikehata and Ricardo Troba Jose, eds., *The Philippines under Japan: Occupation Policy and Reaction* (Manila: Ateneo de Manila Press, 1999), 213. For Java, see Pierre van der Eng, *Food Supply in Java During War and Decolonization, 1940–1950* (no place, 2008), http://mpra.ub.unibe.uni-muenchen.de/8852/ (last accessed November 20, 2014), esp. 38; Huff, "Great", 622; Stein Tønnesson, *The Vietnamese Revolution of 1945: Roosevelt, Ho Chi Minh and de Gaulle in a World at War* (London: Sage and PRIO, 1991), 293. For Nauru (473 of 800 Nauruans whom the Japanese deported to Truk died there), see Lamont Lindstrom and Geoffrey White, *Island Encounters: Black and White Memories of the Pacific War* (Washington and London: Smithsonian Institution Press, 1990), 57; Nancy Pollock, "Nauruans during World War II", White and Lindstrom, *Pacific Theatre*, 91–107 (she offers different figures and mentions also hunger deaths by Nauruans on Nauru itself); Rheinisches JournalistInnenbüro, *"Unsere Opfer"*, 384–387. For Palau, see Karen Nero, "Time of Famine, Time of Transformation: Hell in the Pacific, Palau", White and Lindstrom, *Pacific Theatre*, 120, 122, 127, 130. For Japan, see Collingham, *Taste*, 467; for the decline in the consumption of staples, see Takafusa Nakamura, "The Age of Turbulence: 1937–54", Takafusa Nakamura and Kônôsuke Odaka, eds., *The Economic History of Japan: 1600–1990, vol. 3: Economic History of Japan 1914–1955: A Dual Structure* (Oxford et al.: Oxford University Press, 2003), 71. For India in 1946, see Knight, *Food Administration*, 148, 190, 248–262. For Indonesia in 1946–1948, see below in this chapter.

For Cape Verde in 1940–1943, see Malyn Newitt, "The Portuguese African Colonies during the Second World War" in Byfield et al., *Africa*, 233–235; Gervase Clarence-Smith, "The Impact of the Spanish Civil War and the Second World War on Portuguese and Spanish Africa", *Journal of African History* 26, 4 (1985): 319; Cormac O'Grada, *Famine: A Short History* (Princeton and Oxford: Princeton University Press, 2009), 22; Collingham, *Taste*, 124. For Nigeria, see Michael Watts, *Silent*

Table 6.1: Famines in World War II, 1941–1947.

Country	Colonial power or occupier	Time	Number of victims (estimates)
Europe			
Spain		1941–1942	200,000
Greece	Germany, Italy, Bulgaria	1941–1944	300,000
Poland	Germany (1939–1945)	1941–1947	
Jews starved in			
Ghettos and camps	Germany	1940–1944	300,000
Soviet Union	Germany	1941–1944	
Leningrad	German siege	1941–1943	>600,000
Soviet POWs	Germany	1941–1944	2.5 million
Soviet Union		1942–1943	1.5 million

Violence: Food, Famine and Peasantry in Northern Nigeria (Berkeley et al.: University of California Press, 1987), 326–336. For Niger, see Boureima Alpha Gado, *Une histoire des famines au Sahel* (Paris: L'Harmattan, 1993), 184. For Burundi, see Gaëtan Feltz and Jean-Étienne Bidou, "La famine Manori au Burundi 1943–1944", *Revue française d'histoire d'outre-mer* 81, 304 (1994): 265–304; Christian Thibon, *Histoire démographique du Burundi* (Paris: Karthala, 2004), 83–122. For Rwanda, see Dantès Singiza, *La famine Ruzagayura (Rwanda, 1943–1944)* (Tervuren: Musée royale de l'Afrique centrale, 2011), esp. 92–97, http://www.africamuseum.be/museum/research/publications/rmca/online/famineruzagayura_singa.pdf (last accessed April 25, 2018); Collingham, *Taste*, 124. For Algeria, see Jacques Cantier, *L'Algérie sous le régime de Vichy* (Paris: Odile Jacob, 2002), 111, 173, 179; Thomas, "Resource War", 240, 248; Mohamed Khenouf and Michael Brett, "Algerian Nationalism and the Allied Military Strategy and Propaganda during the Second World War", David Killingray and Richard Rathbone, eds., *Africa and the Second World War* (Basingstoke and London: Macmillan, 1986), 261, 272–273; Alistair Horne, *A Savage War of Peace: Algeria, 1954–1962* (New York: Macmillan, 1977), 24, 41. For Tanganyika, see Nicholas Westcott, "The Impact of the Second World War on Tanganyika, 1939–49", Killingray and Rathbone, *Africa*, 145–148; Gregory Maddox, "Food Disruption and Agricultural Policy in Tanganyika", Laakkonen et al., *Long Shadows*, 239–240, 244; Ashley Jackson, *The British Empire and the Second World War* (London and New York: Continuum, 2006), 206. For South Africa (Limpopo province), see Louis Grundlingh, "The Military, Race and Resistance: The Conundrums of Recruiting Black South African Men during the Second World War", Byfield et al., *Africa*, 87. For Kenya, see Ian Spencer, "Settler Dominance, Agricultural Production and the Second World War in Kenya", *Journal of African History* 21, 4 (1980): 505–508; Jackson, *British Empire*, 199. For Botswana, see Jackson, *Botswana*, 156, 183–186. For Tunisia, see Latifa Hénia, "Les grandes sécheresses en Tunisie au cours de la dernière période séculaire", Paul Arnoult and Micheline Hotyat, eds., *Eau et environnement: Tunisie et milieux méditerranéens* (Lyon: ENS, 2003), 25–36, http://books.openedition.org/enseditions/863?lang=fr (last accessed April 25, 2018). For Cape Verde in 1946–1948, see O'Grada, *Famine*, 22.

Table 6.1 (continued)

Country	Colonial power or occupier	Time	Number of victims (estimates)
Foreign POWs in Soviet hands	Soviet Union	1942–1946	0.5–1.5 million
Cyprus	Britain	1942	
Netherlands	Germany	1944–1945	22,000
Germany	Soviet Union, Britain, France, USA	1945–1947	1 million?
Austria	same	1945–1947	
Spain		1946	
Soviet Union		1946–1947	1–1.5 million
Asia and Oceania			
Burma	Britain	1941–1942	80,000
India	Britain	1941–1944	
Travancore	Britain	1941–1943	
Cochin	Britain	1942–1943	
Madras area	Britain	1942–1943	
Bombay area	Britain	1942–1943	
Orissa	Britain	1942–1943	
Bengal	Britain	1942–1943	3 million
China	parts occ. by Japan	1940–1944	>3 million
Shandong	Japan	1940–1944	>100,000
Henan		1942–1943	1 million
Hunan		1944–1945	2–3 million?
Hongkong	Japan	1944–1945	
East Timor	Japan	1942–1943	40–60,000 (10–15% of population)
Iran	Britain, Soviet Union, USA	1942–1943	up to 3 million (?)
Singapore	Japan	1942–1945	40,000
Iraq (Kurdistan)	Britain	1943	
Yemen	Britain	1943–1944	>10,000 (1.5% of population)
Caroline islands	Japan	1943–1945	

Table 6.1 (continued)

Country	Colonial power or occupier	Time	Number of victims (estimates)
Tonkin (Vietnam)	Vichy France, Japan	1944–1945	0.7–2 million
Philippines	Japan	1944–1945	400,000
Java	Japan	1944–1945	2.4 million
Nauru	Japan	1944–1945	>473 (12% of population)
Palau	Japan	1944–1945	>5,000
Japan	USA	1945–1946	>100,000
China (Hunan)		1946	4 million?
India (southern)	Britain	1946	
Indonesia	Netherlands et al.	1946–1948	
Africa			
Cape Verde	Portugal	1940–1943	25,000 (16% of population)
Algeria	Vichy/Gaullist France	1941–1945	>120,000
South Africa (northern Transvaal)		1941–1943	
Tanganyika (Central Province)	Britain	1941–1943	
Kenya (Central province)	Britain	1942–1943	
Nigeria (northern)	Britain	1942–1943	
Burundi	Belgium	1943–1944	up to 160,000 (8% of population)
Rwanda	Belgium	1943–1944	36,000–300,000
Niger	France	1943–1944	
Botswana	Britain	1944–1945	
Tunisia	France	1945–1947	
Cape Verde	Portugal	1946–1948	30,000 (18% of population)

Many conclusions can be drawn from this table, which lists famines that claimed the lives of somewhere between 15 million and 27 million people.[108] The fundamental observation is that almost all these cases occurred in occupied countries or colonies where many disenfranchised people died. Famines did not only take place near the frontlines, and the fact that some happened very far away from any fighting, for example in Cape Verde, Burundi or Botswana, points to the near global, deadly imperialist grip on resources. Hunger was an everyday reality in large parts of the world. Most people perished in Asia, but those in Europe, Africa and Oceania were also gravely affected, relative to their population sizes. The colonial and occupation powers, which were responsible for the well-being and certainly for the survival of these populations, included, in terms of their alliance status, Axis, Allies and a neutral power (Portugal). All major Allied powers were involved. In terms of political system, the countries that had the responsibility included bourgeois democracies, fascist regimes, authoritarian one-party states and a state ruled by communists. In terms of socioeconomic system, they included capitalist and socialist states. No system was immune to acting this way, and there was no principal difference between the Axis and the Allies or between fascism and liberal imperialism.

Where famine struck the citizens of an independent, unoccupied state, parts of the population were either treated similarly to colonial subjects (like rural dwellers in the unoccupied parts of China) or 'enemized' (i.e., declared to be enemies), partially in combination with ethnic discrimination (in the unoccupied, annexed or reconquered parts of the Soviet Union).

Table 6.1 does not cover all instances of famine during World War II as a result of problems of definition, insufficient documentation, my lack of knowledge of non-European languages and, probably, my ignorance. Collingham spoke of another famine in northern Burma (contemporary Myanmar) in 1945, when the front cut the region off from the surpluses in the south of the country,[109] and, using a very doubtful reference, one in Guangdong province caused by the Chinese army that purportedly killed 1.5 million in 1944–1945.[110] Out of 220,000 Japanese civilians living in Manchuria in 1945, 67,000 reportedly starved to

---

108 It is notoriously difficult to determine how many people die in a famine. Among the reasons are many officially unregistered deaths (with no medically certified cause of death), the unwillingness or inability of authorities to count famine deaths or the reinterpretation of their cause of death, the impossibility to distinguish between death from hunger, from related and from unrelated diseases and the widespread mobility of the population. See David Grigg, *The World Food Problem* (Oxford and New York: Basil Blackwell, 1986), 5–30.
109 Collingham, *Taste*, 237.
110 Collingham, *Taste*, 256.

death.¹¹¹ Famine, especially in mountainous areas where the landless and poor lacked grain and some ate grass for long periods, was reported from three parts of Kurdistan: in British-occupied Iraq, Turkey and British-occupied French-Syria.¹¹² Hunger and malnutrition were also raging in Thailand in 1943.¹¹³ Although scholars do not think that there was a wartime famine in British-Palestine, food rations were down to 1356 to 1550 calories per adult, and many Arab families, along with some Jewish ones, could not pay the necessary food expenses, as a result of which many Arab children were malnourished.¹¹⁴ Likewise, food shortages were reported from British-Ceylon (contemporary Sri Lanka), but no famine.¹¹⁵

This continues in the African countries. In parts of Mozambique, such as Quelimane province, famine seems to have occurred because the Portuguese colonialists enforced an expansion of cotton production, replacing food crops.¹¹⁶ Many people went hungry in French Somaliland (Djibouti) in 1941–1942 as a consequence of a British naval blockade that prevented imports from French-Madagascar. Locals suffered from starvation, scurvy and also political terror.¹¹⁷ Scholars disagree about whether to call a similar situation in the Gaullist French colony of Réunion 1942–1944 a famine.¹¹⁸ Jackson argued that "crisis" (famine) was prevented in British-Mauritius by some food imports in 1943 but mentions a high mortality level in

---

111 Collingham, *Taste*, 62; see survivor accounts in Schaarschmidt, *Schrei*; 86–115.
112 For the area of Mardin, Turkey, see Jordi Tejel, "The Kurds and World War II: Some Considerations for a Social History Perspective", *Kulturní Studia* 21 (2), 2023: 11–13; Ramazan Aras, *The Wall: The Making and Unmaking of the Turkish-Syrian Border* (Cham: Palgrave Macmillan, 2020), 70–71. For Iraqi Kurdistan, see Elphinston, "The Kurdish Question", 99; McDowell, *A Modern History*, 294. For the area of Afrin, Syrian Kurdistan, see Katharina Lange, "Peripheral Experiences: Everyday Life in Kurd Dagh (Northern Syria) During the Allied Occupation in the Second World War", Liebau et al., *World*, 417–418, and for Syria more generally, Elizabeth Thompson, "The Climax and Crisis of the Colonial Welfare State in Syria and Lebanon during World War II", Steven Heydemann, ed., *War, Institutions and Social Change in the Middle East* (Berkeley et al.: University of California Press, 2000), 74 and 96 note 26.
113 Rheinisches JournalistInnenbüro, *"Unsere Opfer"*, 246.
114 Sherene Seikaly, "A Nutritional Economy: The Calorie, Development and War in Mandate Palestine", Mark Crowley and Sandra Trudgen Dawson, eds., *Home Fronts: Britain and the Empire at War, 1939–1945* (Rochester: Boydell, 2017), 47, 52, 54.
115 Ashley Jackson, "Ceylon's Home Front during the Second World War", Crowley and Trudgen Dawson, *Home Fronts*, 111–129; for a greatly decreasing rice supply, see Jackson, *British Empire*, 323.
116 Clarence-Smith, "Impact", 321–322; Leroy Vail and Landeg White, *Capitalism and Colonialism in Mozambique: A Study of Quelimane District* (London: Heineman, 1980), 295–299; Byfield, "Producing", 38.
117 Oliver Coates, "The Indian Ocean", Murray, *Unknown Conflicts*, 80, 87.
118 Coates, "The Indian Ocean", 81 speaks of a greatly elevated mortality rate, especially for infants, but Hervé Le Joubioux, "L'île de la Réunion dans le Seconde Guerre mondiale", *Revue historique des armées* 263 (2011): 8, 13 note 47 offers much different figures.

1942, partially caused by malaria.[119] Edward Lloyd admitted that "famine conditions" prevailed in British-Somalia in early 1944.[120] Further, David Killingray and Richard Rathbone noted cases of "acute food shortage" in many parts of British Africa, including South Rhodesia (contemporary Zimbabwe), and famine in parts of British-Uganda in 1944.[121] British-Tanganyika (contemporary Tanzania) experienced "food shortage" or "famine" again in 1946.[122] In Egypt, which contributed many workers and great amounts of grain, sugar, oil and shipping space to Britain's war effort, most analyses found no graver situation than wartime shortages.[123] With a bit of exaggeration, one could wonder exactly which part of the British empire was *not* affected by famine, except for the British Isles.

However, hunger-induced mortality even increased markedly in Western European industrial countries under German occupation, such as France, the Netherlands and Belgium in 1940–1944, along with unoccupied, fascist Italy in 1941–1943.[124] All of this just underscores how widespread the phenomenon was and how important it is to pay attention to it.

Some examples must suffice to illustrate the complex imperialist character of these hunger crises.

German administrations and forces tried to systematically extract foodstuffs and other resources from occupied countries in Europe. Together with worker exploitation, different forms of occupation tributes, food blockades and disrupted agricultural input and other trade, this affected approximately 200 million people, bringing misery to many and causing outright famines in Greece 1941–1944, parts of the German- occupied Soviet territories in 1941–1943 and the Netherlands in 1944–1945. This exploitative occupation forced people in droves into illegalized economic activities and made many farmers and consumers subject to repression. On top of undersupply by providing insufficient food rations which hit interned people hard (including millions of forced workers), the Germans also tried to exclude some population groups largely or entirely from food supply and killed them through hunger, among them Soviet POWs (but no other POWs), disabled people and concentration camp inmates. The murder of large parts of European

---

119 Jackson, *War*, 167, 170.
120 Lloyd, *Food*, 58.
121 Killingray and Rathbone, "Introduction", 79.
122 Westcott, "Impact", 149.
123 See Lloyd, *Food and Inflation*; Collingham, *Taste*, 131. But Rheinisches JournalistInnenbüro, *"Unsere Opfer"*, 190 mention what they call hunger revolts. For the contributions, see Emad Ahmed Helal, "Egypt's Overlooked Contribution to World War II", Liebau et al., *World*, 231–238; Robert Vitalis and Steven Heydemann, "War, Keynesianism, and Colonialism", Heydemann, *War*, 131.
124 See Gerlach, *Extermination*, 216. See also Collingham, *Taste*, 171–172.

Jewry that came under German assault was fueled in part by the weighty argument of Jews as 'useless eaters', especially if they were assessed to be unfit for work, and food policy contributed to the great acceleration of the mass murders of Soviet and Polish Jews in 1941–1942. This culminated when one-third of all the murdered Jews were killed within only four months, from July to October 1942.[125] Thus, their mass annihilation should not be left out of a history of World War II or separated from it but was an intrinsic part of it, a part of imperialist warfare built on the denial of resources to certain population groups.

Under Japanese occupation, attrition left the population of the Dutch East Indies (then emerging Indonesia) miserable in 1944–1945. Reduced production of goods, disturbed transportation networks, initial exports of goods, Japanese financing of the occupation through the printing press and their misguided attempt to reorganize and steer the food economy (including a ban on inter-regency trade), but to a lesser extent direct requisitions by the relatively small occupation force, led to strong inflation, smuggling and black marketeering. People were dressed in rags, while cases of dysentery doubled each year. A large part of the hundreds of thousands of forced laborers outside the colony, as well as many forced workers who remained within Java, perished from privation. Due to a lack of labor force, cattle, transportation capacity and economic incentives, the harvested area and per capita calory supply decreased drastically, especially in 1944–1946, as did production, particularly rice production in Central Java in 1944. In 1945, many poor rural dwellers of Java succumbed to hunger, with the best estimate suggesting 2.4 million deaths.[126] Unlike many urban dwellers, the rural population was not protected by rations.[127]

The modus operandi of the small Japanese occupation forces in Vietnam, who were in cooperation with France's colonial authorities, was similar. Producing alcohol out of rice (while the production of industrial crops instead of rice

---

125 Gerlach, *Extermination*, 100, 215–260.
126 See Huff, "Great", 627, 634–637, 640–643; van der Eng, *Food*, 20–24, 30, 38; Pierre van der Eng, "Regulation and Control: Explaining the Reduction of Food Production in Java, 1940–6", Paul Kratoska, ed., *Food Supplies and the Japanese Occupation in South-East Asia* (Basingstoke: Macmillan, 1998), 191–194; William Frederick, *Visions and Heat: The Making of the Indonesian Revolution* (Athens: Ohio University Press, 1989), 127 note 134; Benedict Anderson, *Java in a Time of Revolution: Occupation and Resistance, 1944–1946* (Ithaca and London: Cornell University Press, 1972), 11–13; Shigeru Sato, *War, Nationalism and Peasants: Java and the Japanese Occupation 1942–1945* (Armonk and London: M. E. Sharpe, 1984), emphasizing bad Japanese adminstration; Ethan Mark, *Japan's Occupation of Java in the Second World War* (London: Bloomsbury, 2018), 263–270; Kratoska, *Asian Labor*, 129–234; "The Problem of Rice: Stenographic Notes on the Fourth Session of the Sanyo Kaigi, January 8, 2605, 10:00 A.M.", *Indonesia* 2 (October 1966): 86, 100–101.
127 Van der Eng, *Food*, 9, 33, 35.

had a lesser impact), forced procurement of rice and Japanese rice removal from Vietnam, a sizable French land tax, temporarily banning the storage of rice, high occupation tributes and money creation by the printing press, interrupted transportation lines due to Allied attacks and a lack of relief efforts (with interprovincial rice trade suspended for some time) contributed to inflation and hunger, which may have killed between one and two million inhabitants.[128]

The case of Algeria shows an almost seamless exploitation and starvation across political systems. Under Vichy France, it had to deliver a substantial part of its agricultural products to the colonial power and imports of foodstuffs, mineral oil and raw materials dropped steeply, both of which contributed to inflation. Workers' remittances from France also decreased. Very bad harvests in 1940 and 1942 (including that of fruit) left the Muslim population hungry, while the outbreak of typhus resulted in many victims. Mortality due to hunger and disease from 1939 to 1942 almost doubled for the Muslim population and increased by about 50 percent for the European settlers. The famine continued under the Gaullist regime in 1943–1945, when the colony still received few imports, and contributed to motivating the anticolonial uprising in Sétif, which started with a Muslim nationalist demonstration on victory day (May 8, 1945).[129] Several comparative studies have also shown striking similarities between famines in a number of Axis and Allied-occupied areas, colonies or similar regions.[130]

The Allied war economy reached for British-Tanganyika's sisal, rubber, pyrethrum, food and other materials, but Britain did not deem Africans worth much in return, cutting imports to the colony by half until 1942–1943 and deferring payments to it in part so that Tanganyika accumulated a substantial balance of payments surplus. A large percentage of adult men was brought to plantations, farms and mines owned by Europeans. Thus, rural families lacked manpower while relief measures were limited after drought hit in 1942 and 1943.[131] Locals called this "Europe's famine".[132] The situation was similar in neighboring British-Kenya, where European settlers, promising to deliver products to the state (at high pri-

---

[128] See Geoffrey Gunn, "The Great Vietnamese Famine of 1944–45 Revisited", *Asia-Pacific Journal*, no date [2011], japanfocus.org/-geoffrey-gunn/3483/article.htlm (accessed November 20, 2014); Huff, "Great", 630–633, 644–646; Tønnesson, *Vietnamese Revolution*, 294–295; Marr, *Vietnam 1945*, 31 note 53, 33, 98, 100, 126–127.
[129] Cantier, *L'Algérie*, 11, 173, 179; Thomas, "Resource War", 232, 240, 248; Christine Levisse-Touzé, *L'Afrique du nord dans la guerre 1939–1945* (Paris: Albin Michel, 1998), 139; Khenouf and Brett, "Algerian Nationalism", 261, 272–273; Jean-Louis Planche, *Sétif 1945: Histoire d'un massacre annoncé* (Paris: Perrin, 2006), esp. 49–52, 72–73, 99–100, 105.
[130] Brennan et al., "War"; Bose, "Starvation"; Collingham, *Taste*.
[131] Maddox, "Food Disruption", 231–249; Westcott, "Impact", 145–148; Jackson, *British Empire*, 206.
[132] Collingham, *Taste*, 136.

ces), became very influential. Many Africans were conscripted to work on their farms and, as a result, were missing from home to plant emergency foods when cold and drought struck in 1942–1943. Because Africans were offered only low procurement prices for their products, including grain, many had planted relatively little, on top of which European farmers had bought much of it as they received higher prices from British authorities than Africans, and there were livestock requisitions as well. This brought about a famine in rural areas in Central Province in 1943, and the settlers had to send many African workers temporarily home to take care of their families. Civil labor conscription was reinstalled in response to settlers' demands in June 1943.[133]

In Iran, the impact of economic exploitation was even more indirect and complex. British and Soviet troops occupied Iran in August 1941, violating the country's neutrality, and were later joined by some U.S. forces. Over 75,000 Allied soldiers were stationed in Iran, and the USSR alone used 85,000 tons of Iranian grain. The British, who controlled Iran's foreign trade, employed 75,000 Iranians, paying them wages without adjusting for inflation, for, among other things, building north-south road connections.[134] The Allies took control of Iran's railways, using much of their capacity as well as half of all trucks. This practice, while facilitating the delivery of five million tons of lend-lease goods from the USA to the Soviet Union (making Iran the second most important delivery corridor), left few means of transportation to ship grain to needy areas within the country.[135] This means that the Allies had high expenditures in Iran from using labor and means of transportation but hardly provided any goods or hard currency payments in return, paying for workers and services in rial provided by the National Bank, which caused inflation that left poor wage earners at risk and gave businesspeople incentives to hoard grain and other goods.[136] In 1942, Allied military expenditure explained almost all of the increase in the circulation of banknotes.[137] According to a U.S. diplomat, Allied monthly expenditure was 300 million rials for the British occupants, 100 million for the Soviet oc-

---

[133] See Spencer, "Settler Dominance", 504–511; John Lonsdale, "The Depression and the Second World War in the Transformation of Kenya", Killingray and Rathbone, *Africa*, 122–123; Jackson, *British Empire*, 199; Brennan et al., "War", 10–18.
[134] McFarland, "Anatomy", 52, 55, 57; Lloyd, *Food*, 162.
[135] Gholi Majd, *Iran*, 1; McFarland, "Anatomy", 52.
[136] Lloyd, *Food*, 157–169, 179–193, 196–197, 209
[137] Lloyd, *Food*, 162–163.

cupants and 15 million for the U.S. occupants.¹³⁸ Iranian grain production sank to low levels in 1940–1942, especially in 1941.¹³⁹

All of this led to famine in various provinces amid rampant inflation and low actual food rations (for urban dwellers).¹⁴⁰ In this context, up to 400,000 Iranians died from typhus in 1942–1943, after the British rejected or ignored Iranian pleas for one million doses of vaccine.¹⁴¹ A high estimate of the number of famine deaths in Iran put it at up to three million. British, Soviet and U.S. representatives and the Iranian public all knew about the famine.¹⁴² Collingham, who did not mention the famine in Iran, praised instead Britain's "Middle East Supply Centre" (inter alia, in charge of Iran) as a "success", "preventing food shortages from sparking off civil unrest" and "cushioning the indigenous population from the impact of the war".¹⁴³ In reality, the British, using delaying tactics, sent many words to Iran instead of goods.¹⁴⁴

An estimated three million people died in the Bengal famine of 1943–1944. Starvation deaths peaked in 1943 and those due to starvation-related diseases in 1944.¹⁴⁵ The case illustrates how colonial exploitation, merciless war measures, the impact of weather, political and administrative incompetence on different levels, reckless profiteering in a class society and ethnoreligious factionalism interacted. Like elsewhere, it also stands for a combination of state dirigisme and market mechanisms. Years of wartime colonial exploitation had driven inflation up and real wages down, especially those of rural workers. Defence measures made high demands on labor and buildings. Besides, many refugees were streaming in.¹⁴⁶ The colonial authorities had encouraged jute cultivation, which reduced rice growing to an extent.¹⁴⁷ When Japanese troops conquered most of Burma in 1942, the British, apprehensive of the Japanese army moving into Bengal, adopted a so-called denial policy, which meant concentrating rice stocks in defensible pla-

---

138 Gholi Majd, *Iran*, 294, citing a telegram by Dreyfus, October 12, 1942. Although Soviet troops used Iranian resources and sent 50,000 tons of agricultural goods from Iran to the USSR and were first viewed by Iranians as "exploiters and savages", they consequently acquired a reputation as disciplined and benevolent. Ibid., 432 (quote), 434, 446.
139 Lloyd, *Food*, 356.
140 Gholi Majd, *Iran*, 283, 460, 468, 527–562.
141 See Gholi Majd, *Iran*, 145, 535, 563–577.
142 See in extenso Gholi Majd, *Iran*.
143 Collingham, *Taste*, 123, 131; see the comment by Gholi Majd, *Iran*, 3.
144 See Gholi Majd, *Iran*.
145 Amartya Sen, *Poverty and Famines* (Oxford: Clarendon, 1981), 55; Mukherjee, *Hungry Bengal*, 280.
146 Sen, *Poverty*, 75; Knight, *Food Administration*, 72.
147 Mukerjee, *Churchill's Secret War*, 107.

ces and confiscating or destroying all ships and boats in their reach; consequently, 19,471 boats were removed, 26,675 destroyed and about 20,000 not found. This interrupted transportation that was vital to life in Bengal, a river delta region, it stripped many fishermen of their income and the population of significant amounts of protein.[148] The usual rice imports from Burma (normally constituting six percent of the demand) were cut off by the Japanese advance.[149] Moreover, some harvests in 1942 turned out bad.[150] After the food trade had first been deregulated in 1942, aiding industrialists' hoarding, the grain trade between Indian provinces was banned. The British government rejected providing food imports to India and in particular shipping space to transport relief goods there as a waste, and, for the most part, it also prevented or delayed U.S., Australian and Canadian aid shipments, because "[t]he thing was to win the war".[151] In early 1943, British shipping space in the Indian Ocean had been reduced by 60 percent and moved to the Atlantic, which seemed more important.[152] Not much was done in terms of relief. In August 1943, "an order was passed barring any private organization from feeding more than 50 people in Calcutta".[153] Hope alias Linlithgow, the British viceroy, was well aware of how many people died.[154]

Those who were pushed into the abyss in this situation were largely certain groups of the Bengali rural poor: the families of fishermen, transportation workers, paddy huskers, agricultural laborers and craftsmen, as well as small peasants whose income had dropped greatly.[155] Hoarding and speculation by wealthy farmers and traders added much to their misery by driving up food prices.[156] Notoriously, there were record numbers of land sales because wealthy ruralites took advantage of peasants in distress.[157] The preferential and subsidized supply of over one million workers in Calcutta pulled grain out from the countryside in the interests of greedy industrialists, such as those from the armament and textile

---

[148] Mukherjee, *Hungry Bengal*, 82–93; Brennan et al., "War", 43; Mukerjee, *Churchill's Secret War*, 64–66; Knight, *Food Administration*, 75.
[149] Knight, *Food Administration*, 26, 43.
[150] There are three major harvesting seasons in Bengal.
[151] Mukherjee, *Hungry Bengal*, 79, 214; Mukerjee, *Churchill's Secret War*, 199 (quote); Sen, *Poverty*, 77. Once Churchill also argued that Greeks (formerly starved by him) were more deserving of food aid than Indians: Mukherjee, *Hungry Bengal*, 195.
[152] Collingham, *Taste*, 125, 151; Mukerjee, *Churchill's Secret War*, 110.
[153] Mukherjee, *Hungry Bengal*, 189.
[154] Ibid., 213.
[155] Sen, *Poverty*, 63–73.
[156] Sen, *Poverty*, 76.
[157] Mukherjee, *Hungry Bengal*, 263, 279.

sector, both British and Indian.[158] What was most strongly publicized at the time was the death and suffering of hunger refugees streaming into Calcutta, but the bulk of the mass death happened in the villages.[159] The local press denounced the reckless behavior of the colonialists.

However, in Henan, it was the Chinese nationalist government that behaved like an occupation army in their own country. It lived off the land, heavy taxes and grain levies served to supply between 300,000 and a million Chinese soldiers in the province, grain and oxen requisitioning continued during the disaster and forced labor of civilians for the troops contributed to the calamity. Moreover, relief was little and late.[160] During the famine, the Chinese government asked Washington for arms, not food.[161] The rural population lost out in a conflict over resource appropriation.[162] The earlier artificial flood had greatly damaged agriculture, followed by drought and heat in 1941–1942, lessening grain production substantially, especially the summer crop of 1942, which was important for local consumption. The same was true in neighboring provinces. Grain stocks were low; consequently, famine set in in 1942–1943.[163] The Chinese regime did not favor inter-provincial grain trade, and the front cut off some potential grain delivery routes and also stripped Henan of its eastern markets for soybeans and cotton to earn cash.[164] At that time, millions affected by the Yellow River flood who still lived as refugees in several provinces including Henan were particularly vulnerable.[165] Others fled now, sold their land, or they sold their relatives, particularly girls, into servitude or prostitution.[166] Millions perished. The communists, by contrast, though not free of blame, behaved in a less exploitative manner toward the peasants.[167] Many locals started to support the Japanese as the lesser threat, hoping for their conquest of Henan. Locals disarmed about 50,000 Chinese troops in 1944 and slaughtered about 10,000 of them, and they repaired some roads that the Chinese army had destroyed to

---

158 Sen, *Poverty*, 56, 77; Mukherjee, *Hungry Bengal*, 8, 13, 46, 143, 162 note 192, 175, 190.

159 See Mukherjee, *Hungry Bengal*, 195–199; Mukerjee, *Churchill's Secret War*, 151–167 with gruesome details.

160 Collingham, *Taste*, 254; Edgerton-Tarpley, "From 'Nourish the People'", 459; Edgerton-Tarpley, "Between", 111–113; Lary, *Chinese People*, 124–126; Garnaut, "Quantitative Description", 2023–2026; Bose, "Starvation", 719.

161 Bose, "Starvation", 720.

162 Micah Muscolino, "Conceptualizing Wartime Flood and Famine in China", Laakkonen et al., *Long Shadows*, 105–107.

163 Garnaut, "Quantitative Description", 2012–2032, 2035 note 48; Muscolino, "Violence", 300.

164 Garnaut, "Quantitative Description", 2023, 2026–2027, 2044.

165 Muscolino, "Violence", 300, 302.

166 Lary, *Chinese People*, 125; Edgerton-Tarpley, "Between", 106.

167 Collingham, *Taste*, 257–260.

block the Japanese advance.[168] Soon after, the area became a communist stronghold.[169] It has to be added that demographic figures indicate that the famine also struck neighboring provinces such as Hubei, Shanxi, Hebei and Shandong hard, with the latter three largely being under Japanese control.[170]

The famines that occurred in different parts of the world shortly after 1945 were in connection with imperialism and under conditions similar to the preceding war years. Contemporaries, also in the United Nations, spoke of a world food crisis until 1948,[171] in which food was distributed very unevenly. Allied-occupied Germany and Austria were not only starved of food (Germany through the foreign annexation of important staple food surplus areas and both countries through the lack of food imports) but also starved of industrial assets and income by occupation powers creating and enforcing new borders, dismantling and removing some of the machinery (according to plans to systematically reduce German industrial production) and restricting German foreign trade by denying it many licenses for importing industrial raw material necessary for production.[172] Among the causes of the Soviet famine of 1946–1947 were sizable grain exports to secure the newly won Soviet zone of influence (Poland and Czechoslovakia), the halting of U.S. controlled UNRRA deliveries to the USSR in 1947 and the disruption caused by the introduction of a new economic system in Soviet-annexed territories, i.e., the collectivization of agriculture (Moldavia, Western Ukraine), against the backdrop of war-related impoverishment, mass homelessness and a drought.[173] Meanwhile, many people in

---

168 Collingham, *Taste*, 257; Mitter, *China's War*, 325–326; Garnaut, "Quantitative Description", 2008.
169 Edgerton-Tarpley, "Between", 113; Bose, "Starvation", 726.
170 See Garnaut, "Quantitative Description", 2042.
171 See Charles Coe, *Food for now or coffins for later; the meaning of the world food crisis* (New York: Farm Research, 1946); "Mitteilungen über die Welternährungswirtschaft der Verwaltung für Ernährung, Landwirtschaft und Forsten des Vereinigten Wirtschaftsgebietes, Abt. VI Planung und Statistik", no. 2, 15 August 1949, German Federal Archive, B 116/1856. In this document, the West German authorities complained (incorrectly) that grain "rice deficit countries" of Asia had imported grain after 1945 "and thus aggravated the lack of bread in Europe".
172 A classical account of West Germany's economic situation is Werner Abelshauser, *Wirtschaftsgeschichte der Bundesrepublik Deutschland* (Frankfurt a. M.: Suhrkamp, 1980). The situation in the Soviet zone of occupation in Germany was not much different.
173 Ganson also cites too high state procurement quotas to favor industrial workers as a reason, but half of the deaths occurred among urban dwellers in a country where urbanites were far less than half of the population. This relativizes Ellman's argument that those who died were primarily those without entitlements, unprotected by the Soviet state. See Ganson, *Soviet Famine*, 95–105, 114; I. M. Volkov, "The Drought and Famine 1946–47", *Russian Studies in History* 31, 2 (1992): 31–60, esp. 45–46; Michael Ellman, "The 1947 Soviet famine and the entitlement approach to famine", *Cambridge Journal of Economics* 24 (2000): 603–630, esp. 606, 612–613, 621.

Spain, and political prisoners in particular, were starving in part because of the country's international isolation, or self-isolation, its policy of autarky and the subsequent lack of agricultural inputs.[174]

The British War Cabinet did not permit the colonial Government of India to apply for UNRRA support for the starving colony. Instead, it donated US$ 30 million of India's wartime earnings to UNRRA, making India the sixth largest donor of that organization.[175] Deliveries to Europe again became the priority after the official end of the war, and countries like India and Vietnam received little or nothing, through UNRRA or otherwise.[176] In anticipation of this, the Deputy Governor of the Dutch East Indies, Charles van der Plas, who was residing in Australia, wrote the following on March 17, 1945, during the devastating famine in Java and five months before the Japanese surrender:

> Absolute world shortage of food, textiles should indeed make us refrain from any promises. We can say, however, that, from the day of liberation on, all goods the country so amply produces shall be properly distributed [. . .].
>
> I have instructed our people, since there is no hope that the United Nations will be able to cope with the terrible food and textile shortage in the Netherlands East Indies, especially Java, to refrain from any promises and to begin preparing the people for the idea the Japanese destructiveness will be the cause of hardships even after liberation.[177]

This attitude was not only irresponsible, it was murderous. On the same day, van der Plas told Dutch collaborators that a part of the Indonesian elite were enemies (but also that the colony needed to be treated with caution so as to not lose it).[178]

The case of Indonesia during its war of decolonization (1945–1949) is illustrative of the immediate postwar period in several ways. Partly as a result of very

---

[174] See del Arco Blanco and Anderson, "Introduction", 5–6; Miguel Ángel del Arco Blanco, "The famine that 'never' existed: Causes of the Spanish famine", in del Arco Blanco and Anderson, *Franco's Famine*, 19–35.

[175] Mukerjee, *Churchill's Secret War*, 208.

[176] Knight, *Food Administration*, 257–262; Benjamin Zachariah, "The Creativity of Destruction: Wartime Imaginings of Development and Social Policy, c. 1942–1946", Liebau et al., *World*, 574–577; for the famine in Vietnam, see David Marr, *Vietnam: State, War, and Revolution (1945–1946)* (Berkeley et al.: University of California Press, 2013), 327; by contrast, for UNRRA deliveries to Greece, see Michael Palairet, *The Four Ends of the Greek Hyperinflation of 1941–1946* (Copenhagen: Museum Tusculanum Press, 2000), 72; Charles Shrader, *The Withered Vine: Logistics and the Communist Insurgency in Greece, 1945–1949* (Westport and London: Praeger, 1999), 48.

[177] National Archive of Australia, 403/2/1/1, 23, Netherlands East Indies Government, Brisbane, van der Plas to Stokes, Australian Department of External Affairs, 17 March 1945 (copy).

[178] See William Frederick, "The Man Who Knew Too Much: Ch.O. van der Plas and the Future of Indonesia, 1927–1950", Hans Antlöv and Stein Tønnesson, eds., *Imperial Policies and Southeast Asian Nationalism 1930–1957* (Richmond: Curzon Press, 1995), 53.

small food imports, acute food crises were reported in 1946–1948 from various parts of Java, often with high mortality,[179] and from several other Indonesian islands, both under Dutch and Republican control.[180] In Surabaya, the death rate rose to 91.9 per thousand in late 1946, a level not even found in any rural area on Java during the 1944–1945 famine. From Surabaya and Semarang, horrendous death rates of 3 to 6 percent per month were reported in early 1947, and food rations (for those who received a ration at all) were at only 600 to 900 calories.[181] In November 1945, an Australian observer commented on calculations about a rice deficit in the six months to come: "I feel that it is very likely that Java faces a famine which may easily mean death through starvation to at least 1 million persons". According to his report, Indonesian leaders did not see the situation as so grave but anticipated "very difficult times" for coastal towns.[182]

Both sides in the Indonesian war of independence (1945–1949) used food as a weapon. The Dutch blocked the supply of food, and of industrial products such as textiles, to Madura in 1946 and to Republican territories in 1948–1949 and, for instance, did not supply food to people who refused to cooperate with their administration in Yogyakarta in 1949, which was the great majority – in this case, in an area under Dutch control. This policy is likely to have caused deaths.[183] An ob-

---

[179] Frederick, *Visions*, 280 (Surabaya area, late 1946, under Dutch control); van der Eng, *Food*, 45 (Priangan, West Java, 1946), 54–55 (Surabaya, Semarang and Jakarta), 59 (Mojokerto and elsewhere in East Java), 62–63 (various areas of Java, 1946–1949); Shigeru Sato, "Economic life in villages and towns", in Peter Post et al., eds., *The Encyclopedia of Indonesia in the Pacific War* (Leiden and Boston: Brill, 2010), 277 (Sukabumi, early 1946); Anthony Reid, *The Indonesian National Revolution 1945–1950* (Westport: Greenwood, 1974), 126 (Yogyakarta, 1947–48, under Republican control); George McTurnan Kahin, *Nationalism and Revolution in Indonesia* (Ithaca: Cornell University Press, 2003 [first 1952]), 396 (Yogyakarta, 1948); Frances Gouda with Thijs Brocades Zaalberg, *American Visions of the Netherlands East Indies/Indonesia: US Foreign Policy and Indonesian Nationalism, 1920–1949* (Amsterdam: Amsterdam University Press, 2002), 33 (Delanggu region, Central Java, rural area under Republican control).
[180] NAA 402/4/1/1, part 1, 210, handwritten note, 29 October 1946 (East Borneo, under Dutch control); ibid., 215, "Extract from Far Eastern Intelligence and Information Report No. 74" up and until 13 October 1946 (Madura, under Republican control); NAA 404/1/1/1, part 1, 63, "[Radio] Djogjakarta", 18 September 1946 (Borneo and Celebes, under Dutch control); ibid., 64, "[Radio] Djogjakarta", 23 September 1946 (handwritten note) (Moluccas and South Celebes, under Dutch control); ibid., 79, "Radio Makassar", 14 August 1946 (Flores, under Republican control); van der Eng, *Food*, 45 (parts of Sumatra, 1946), 59 (Madura, 1947, and North Sumatra, 1948).
[181] Frederick, *Visions*, 280; van der Eng, *Food*, 54–55.
[182] NAA 404/1/1/1, part 1, 158, memo W. Macmahon Bell to Dr. Burton, 26 November 1945, containing a report by J.E. Isaac, "The Food Situation in Java". For warnings by Dutch and British officials since late 1945, see van der Eng, *Food*, 44.
[183] For Yogyakarta, see Kahin, *Nationalism*, 396–397 and in general 250–252. For Madura, see NAA 402/4/1/1, part 1, 215, "Extract from Far Eastern Intelligence and Information Report", no. 74,

server linked the communist uprising in Madiun against Republican rule in late 1948 with a steep rise of food prices in an area with a food deficit even at normal times, exacerbated by the Dutch blockade, one million refugees in the region and rural-urban tensions.[184] The Republic practiced food embargos against cities under Dutch control and local food boycotts against Europeans, forcing the Dutch to bring in food especially in 1945–1947.[185] Those who suffered in particular from high prices on the black markets were Indonesian and ethnic Chinese urbanites without Dutch employment, who were not entitled to receive Dutch rations. Organized smuggling to these cities, or trade across the fronts on licenses, became a source of making great profits and amassing wealth, although individual peasant women also carried food there.[186]

Like in Indonesia (and Henan, as mentioned before), mass hunger inspired populations under foreign rule in many countries such as Greece and colonies such as Vietnam and India to organize anti-colonial and in many instances communist political mobilization, as they often refused to stay passive victims.[187] A

---

13 October 1946. In general, see Kahin, *Nationalism*, 250–252; van der Eng, *Food*, 56–57, 59–60. In 1947, Dutch authorities painted their occupation of Madura as necessitated by a humanitarian emergency, unconvincing to U.S. and Australian observers: Gouda, *American Visions*, 208–209.

184 George McT. Kahin, "The Crisis and Its Aftermath", *Far Eastern Survey* 17, 22 (17 November 1948): 262; see also Ann Swift, *The Road to Madiun: The Indonesian Communist Uprising of 1948* (Ithaca: Cornell University, 1989), 41, 79–80.

185 Van der Eng, *Food*, 48, 53, 56; Frederick, Visions, 280; NAA 404/1/1/1, part 1, 139, "Statement of N.E.I. Government on Food Position in Java [. . .]", 25 April 1946 and ibid., 146, W.A.M. Doll, Currency Adviser, "Financial Situation of Java" (travel report, January 1946).

186 See Robert Cribb, *Gangsters and Revolutionaries: The Jakarta People's Militia and the Indonesian Revolution 1945–1949* (Sydney: Allen and Unwin, 1991), 42, 77–78, 82; John Smail, *Bandung in the Early Revolution 1945–1946: A Study in the Social History of the Indonesian Revolution* (Singapore: Equinox, 2009 [first 1964]), 155; Tuong Vu, "Of rice and revolution: The politics of provisioning and state-society relations on Java, 1945–49", *South-East Asia Research* 11 (3), 2003: 253–254; van der Eng, *Food*, 41–43. For peasant women, see T. B. Simatupang, *Report from Banaran: Experiences During the People's War* (Ithaca: Cornell University, 1972), 63.

187 For Henan, see note 96 in this chapter. For Vietnam, see Gunn, *Rice Wars*, 4, 229, 268; Tønnesson, *Vietnamese Revolution*, 294, 335–336, 342, 348–349; Marr, *Vietnam 1945*, 207–209, 375, 393, 402–425, 550; Marr, *Vietnam*, 320–321; Gunn, *Rice Wars*, 4, 229, 237, 268; Huff, "Great", 651–653. For Greece, see Mark Mazower, *Inside Hitlers Greece* (New Haven and London: Yale University Press, 2001), 108–114, 124–125; Hionidou, *Famine*, 96; Violetta Hionidou, "Relief and Politics in Occupied Greece, 1941–4", *Journal of Contemporary History* 48 (2013): 773–774. For Bengal, see Siegel, *Hungry Nation*, 21–49; Joanna Simonow, "Der Hungertod in Bildern: Fotografie in der öffentlichen Debatte um Hungerhilfe in Bengalen 1943", *Zeithistorische Forschungen* 18 (2021): 346–362. For the acquiescing political language of the nationalists in Indonesia, see Tuong, "Of rice", especially 256–259; see also Cribb, *Gangsters*, 26, 28; Sato, *War*, 144–148.

graphic expression of this was found in the numerous political graffiti all over these countries, often including the countryside.[188]

Famines: Inflation and Labor Extraction

However, it is important to understand that the famines in World War II were not only, and not necessarily, caused by a lack of food and the extraction of food. Two other aspects were crucial: the redistribution and exploitation of labor as well as the extraction of resources generally, which led to inflation. Above all, the tributes of the colonies and occupied areas were paid in labor, not food.

Forced labor was an important element in this. The coercion indicated the will to strip countries from resources without pay as well as a strong will to exploit the workforce. All colonial powers in Africa stepped up labor conscription during World War II, including Italy (and Germany), Vichy France, Gaullist France, Britain, Belgium, Portugal and Spain.[189] As David Killingray stated long ago, "conscription of non-combatant labour occurred in every British African territory".[190] Contrary to the pompous promises made by Gaullist France (which may have been a "Free" France for whites), forced labor in French West Africa and Madagascar continued because European settlers demanded so, it was not officially abolished until 1946, and the last workers were released in 1950. There were many 'desertions'.[191] Numerous Guineans responded to forced labor for the railways, for road construction, on plantations and for colonial officials (which affected 20,000 in 1943) by fleeing to Liberia and Senegal.[192] The Australian colonial administration recruited forced

---

[188] For Greece, see Mazower, *Inside*, 91–92, 113, 116, 278; for northern Vietnam, see Marr, *Vietnam 1945*, 207; John Kleinen, *Facing the Future, Reviving the Past: A Study of Social Change in a Northern Vietnamese village* (Singapore: ISEAS, 1999), 76; for Indonesia, see Gouda, *American Visions*, 48, 55.

[189] David Killingray and Richard Rathbone, "Introduction", in Killingray and Rathbone, *Africa*, 15. They assert, contrary to facts, that Britain "acted more carefully". See also David Killingray, "Labour Mobilisation in British Colonial Africa for the War Effort, 1939–1946", Killingray and Rathbone, *Africa*, 70, 78; Clarence-Smith, "Impact", 309–326; for Belgium, see Singiza, *Famine*, 37–44.

[190] Killingray, "Labour Mobilisation", 78. See also Jackson, *British Empire*, 45.

[191] Ruth Ginio, *French Colonialism Unmasked: The Vichy Years in French West Africa* (Lincoln and London: University of Nebraska Press, 2006), 77; Coates, "The Indian Ocean", 80; Babacar Fall, *Le travail forcé en Afrique occidentale française (1900–1945)* (Paris: Karthala, 1993), 271, 276–277; Catherine Bogosian Ash, "Free to Coerce: Forced Labour during and after the Vichy Years in French West Africa", Byfield et al., *Africa*, 126.

[192] Elizabeth Schmidt, "Popular Resistance and Anticolonial Mobilization: The War Effort in French Guinea", Byfield et al., *Africa*, 451.

labor in New Guinea (contemporary Papua New Guinea), where the Allies employed a total of 49,500 people, who had to work 54 hours per week.[193] In the famine year of 1943, 400,000–500,000 people were forced to do work on dykes in Henan province, China, where some died from exhaustion and hunger.[194]

Much of the forced labor was done for private entrepreneurs who aspired to become war profiteers and were, in many cases, successful at that. 84,500 Africans were conscripted in British-Tanganyika for work on private estates, especially Sisal plantations, where food rations were low and conditions miserable. Many estate workers "grew thin" and fell ill.[195] Forced labor increased in British-Kenya in 1941–1942, often to serve European settlers.[196] Much of this also occurred in the British colonies of South Rhodesia (contemporary Zimbabwe), North Rhodesia (Zambia), Tanganyika (Tanzania) and Nigeria, where European estate holders tried to raise their profits.[197] In Vichy-French West Africa, forced labor was reduced for public works but hardly for private (European) employers. The majority of absentee employment in April 1941 was for private employers. In the French colony of Madagascar too, there was an increase in coerced labor.[198] In Portuguese and Spanish Africa, forced labor was also increased because entrepreneurs wanted cheap labor in the wartime boom and the state needed to generate foreign exchange.[199]

Colonial subjects were often also recruited to the military by force, for example in British-Mauritius.[200] "Quotas and round-ups, it would seem, occurred in all parts of Africa" for this purpose.[201] There were manhunts for this in southern British-

---

193 Rheinisches JournalistInnenbüro, "Unsere Opfer", 321; Lamont Lindstrom, "Working Encounters: Oral Histories of World War II Labor Corps from Tanna, Vanuatu", White and Lindstrom, *Pacific Theatre*, 398–400.
194 Kathryn Edgerton-Tarpley, "Between War and Water: Farmer, City, and State in China's Yellow River Flood of 1938–1947", *Agricultural History* 90, 1 (2016): 112–113.
195 Killingray, "Labour Mobilisation", 86; Westcott, "Impact", 147 (quote). For British Subsaharan Africa more generally, see Jackson, *British Empire*, 45.
196 Spencer, "Settler Dominance", 504–505.
197 Alfred Tembo, *The Impact of the Second World War on Northern Rhodesia (Zambia), 1939–1953*, Ph.D dissertation, Bloemfontein: University of the Free State, 2015, 18–20, 206–213.
198 Ginio, *French Colonialism*, 76–89, esp. 78–79; Fall, *Travail forcé*, 249; Eric Jennings, *Vichy sous les tropiques: La Révolution nationale à Madagascar, en Guadeloupe, en Indochine 1940–1944* (Paris: Bernard Grasset, 2004), 100–105; Rheinisches JournalistInnenbüro, *"Unsere Opfer"*, 104. For Upper Volta (today's Burkina Faso), see Brigitte Reinwald, "Zwischen Imperium und Nation: Westafrikanische Veteranen der französischen Armee am Beispiel des spätkolonialen Obervolta", Gerhard Höpp and Brigitte Reinwald, eds., *Fremdeinsätze: Afrikaner und Asiaten in europäischen Kriegen, 1914–1945* (Berlin: Das Arabische Buch, 2000), 237.
199 Clarence-Smith, "Impact", 310.
200 Jackson, *War*, 83.
201 See Jackson, *Botswana*, 12 and for some qualifications, 31–56.

Tanganyika (Tanzania) and in Basutoland (contemporary Lesotho), and some men escaped to toil as mine workers to avoid military conscription.[202] British recruitment often worked through local chiefs, which permitted the colonialists to state that they used no coercion.[203] During the famine in Central Province, British-Tanganyika, military recruitment was suspended from February to April 1943.[204] In all of British-Africa, over half a million male African soldiers were recruited for the military, with a preference for men from what the British perceived as "martial races".[205] The same applied to colonial India, where the British recruited over two million men, technically as volunteers, especially from rural lower classes and preferably from Punjab and the Northwestern Frontier Province and among Muslims, peaking in 1942.[206] The about 15,000 men that Britain recruited in North Rhodesia (contemporary Zambia) for the military "served in Kenya, Somaliland, Madagascar, Ceylon, Burma, Palestine and India"; it was similar with those from contemporary Malawi.[207] Of course, sovereign states also conscripted military personnel by force, like the Guomindang army in Henan, China, in the famine year of 1943, where some who were trying to escape were shot.[208]

However, forced labor did not only increase in countries under control of the Allies and the Axis. Forced labor impositions in neutral Portugal's colonies of Mozambique and Angola were stepped up dramatically, although less so in Portuguese-Guinea (contemporary Guinea Bissau). The conditions of such labor were especially tragic in São Tomé.[209] As an official measure to combat famine, 1,700 Cape Verdeans were shipped to São Tomé and Príncipe to toil on cocoa plantations, which lacked workers.[210]

Elsewhere, workers were not recruited by force; nevertheless, their work in the interest of the Allies (or Axis, in other cases) meant the extraction of resources from the country and an increase in the food demand by non-self suppliers, as it was in occupied Iran, where 70,000 workers and an additional 100,000 oil work-

---

202 Killingray, "Labour Mobilisation", 77, 79.
203 Overy, *Blood*, 390.
204 Killingray, "Labour Mobilisation", 79.
205 Disu Oleyemisi Abayomi and Raheem Oluwafunminiyi, "Fighting for Britain: Examining British Recruitment Strategies in Nigeria", Murray, *Unknown Conflicts*, 12–18; Tembo, *Impact*, 70–72; Overy, *Blood*, 389.
206 Kamtekar, "Different War Dance", 193–194; Raghavan, *India's War*, 65, 74.
207 Tembo, *Impact*, 3–4; for Malawi, see Timothy Lovering, "Military Service, Nationalism and Race: The Experience of Malawians in the Second World War", Liebau et al., World, 111.
208 Edgerton-Tarpley, "Between", 111.
209 Clarence-Smith, "Impact", 320–323.
210 Newitt, "Portuguese African Colonies", 234; Clarence-Smith, "Impact", 319.

ers received a special food supply in 1941–1942.[211] In Pacific island colonies, Allied forces (Australians, U.S. and British) used locals under various forms of employment between forced and voluntary wage labor.[212]

The link to famine was that the absence of many adult men led to a situation where not enough labor was available on farms when crops failed (usually because of drought), which, in turn, led to hunger among the residue families. In British-Kenya's Central Province, 40 percent of adult males were employed outside their province in the famine year of 1943, not counting those in military service.[213] In British-Tanganyika, the African work force employed by Europeans grew from 240,000 to 340,000 during the war, and in the famine year of 1943, it was estimated that 45 percent of the men were absent from their homes.[214] Elsewhere, similar rates of absence of about 30 percent of men in the countryside, including in North Rhodesia (contemporary Zambia) and parts of Bechuanaland (Botswana), led to reduced food production. Meanwhile, the population of towns, and especially mining areas, increased, and so did the demand by non-self suppliers of food.[215] In French New Caledonia and British Fiji, the U.S. military employed five percent of the total population each (a dimension similar to the British in Tanganyika).[216] Usually, it was not the forced workers who suffered from famine, but those in northern Nigeria (inter alia, toiling in tin mines) were in fact afflicted with lack of food, bad housing conditions and lack of medical treatment, which led to high death rates among them in 1943. However, the rural population was more strongly affected.[217]

One can assume that similar mechanisms as the ones that Ulrich Herbert has pinpointed for the German forced labor program in World War II prevented those who organized this forced labor, profiteered from it or witnessed it among the power-holding population from the understanding that this was criminal.[218]

---

211 Gholi Majd, *Iran*, 85.
212 Lindstrom and White, "War Stories", 32; Robert Franco, "Samoan Representations of World War II and Military Work: The Emergence of International Movement Networks", White and Lindstrom, *Pacific Theatre*, 382, 384.
213 Spencer, "Settler Dominance", 512; see also Brennan et al. "War", 11, 16.
214 Westcott, "Impact", 147; see also Brennan et al., "War", 20–21.
215 Tembo, *Impact*, 77–78, 203–204; Brian Mokopakgosi III., "The Impact of the Second World War: the Case of Kareneng in the then Bechuanaland Protectorate, 1939–1950", Killingray and Rathbone, *Africa*, 160, 167.
216 Lindstrom and White, "War Stories", 32.
217 Rheinisches JournalistInnenbüro, *"Unsere Opfer"*, 139; Carolyn Brown, "African Labor in the Making of World War II", Byfield et al., *Africa*, 44; Buchanan, "Globalizing", 263–264 estimates that 10,000 of the tin miners died.
218 See Ulrich Herbert, "Arbeiterschaft im 'Dritten Reich': Zwischenbilanz und offene Fragen", *Geschichte und Gesellschaft* 15, 1989: 352.

In a similar vein, Lizzie Collingham spoke of the "quiet and unobtrusive nature of death" in World War II famines.[219] Creating conditions of violence or abetting them allowed people to pretend that there was no violence.

While discussing the famines in Greece, Bengal, Henan and Tonkin, Richard Overy stated that "the food deficit was artificially created by military seizures, the greed of middlemen and incompetence or indifference of authorities".[220] This list is important but incomplete. Overy himself pointed in addition to market distortion, rising food demand, the large-scale movement of people and the dispossession of some, the role of naval sieges and the denial of shipping space for food deliveries, making the following more comprehensive argument: "Famine was the ultimate consequence of wartime disruption in both Europe and Asia."[221] Not only was the food trade disrupted, but, most importantly, so were general economies. As Richard Bessel aptly summarized, those who died from World War II famines were "victims not just of the misguided, incompetent, or willful policies of regimes concerned more with fighting a war than with safeguarding the welfare of civilians, they were also victims of economic conditions created by the war, in particular inflation [. . .] leading to soaring grain prices that put basic foodstuffs beyond the reach of vulnerable social groups" and the impact of other "economic imbalances".[222] One needs to add, these economic conditions and imbalances were made not by 'the war', but by people, and those who suffered were especially disenfranchised due to the color of their skin, their legal status or their geographic location (such as rural dwellers).

Thus, food was not even the most important item the extraction (or blockade) of which led to famine. The main issue was the drain of all sorts of resources, including monetary tributes, goods and services, which caused shortages and inflation. There have been some incomplete attempts to quantify these. For instance, both Germany and Britain "relied on substantial contributions from [. . .] imperial or occupied territories" – according to one estimate, Reichsmark 115 billion for the former and £3.4 billion for the latter for unpaid goods from the colonies.[223] On the German side, this included the use of different techniques, such as occupied countries' official payments for occupation costs, currency manipulations, bloated clear-

---

219 Collingham, *Taste*, 1.
220 Overy, *Blood*, 416.
221 Overy, *Blood*, 414–416, quote 414; Richard Overy, "Frontline II: Civilians at War", in Overy, *Oxford Illustrated History*, 306.
222 Bessel, "Unnatural Deaths", 338.
223 Overy, *Blood*, 400. At the rate of 1941, £3.4 billion were the equivalent of about RM 40 billion, based on figures in Bank für Internationalen Zahlungsausgleich, Zwölfter Jahresbericht, 1. April 1941 bis 31. März 1942, 28 and 36.

ing accounts, requisitions, individual plunder, Germans buying cheaply on black markets in occupied countries in an unequal exchange and appropriating part of the property of foreign Jews.[224]

Similar things applied to other colonizers and occupants. Take the example of British-India, where industrial and agricultural production rose only slightly during the war, except for a few sectors like the railroads even though they were forced to give 10 percent of their material (tracks, locomotives and railroad cars) to other parts of the British Empire.[225] Britain let the colony pay officially for half of her expenses in India and deferred payments for the other half, and goods for £1.3 billion, to a period after the war through a "forced loan". India's sterling balances saw their greatest growth in 1943 and 1944.[226] Distorting what had happened, Churchill spoke in cabinet of "the monstrous idea that we should spend millions about millions in the defence of India, then be told to clear out, and on top of it all we owe India vast sums incurred on her behalf" and was assisted in 1944 by John Maynard Keynes, who proposed to repudiate Britain's debt to India.[227] Britain had exploited Indians greatly, but one should keep in mind that others benefitted from India as well: the USA emerged as India's biggest trade partner during World War II.[228] This profiteering may explain in part the U.S. government's reluctance to mitigate the Bengal famine.[229] The Bengal famine and "Argentina's sudden wealth" were both the interconnected result of a warped "world market" during the global conflict, as Ernest Mandel argued.[230]

Research on colonial Africa has done much to illuminate the mechanisms involved. It demonstrated, as Ashley Jackson summarized, a "tightening of the colonial grip on African economies" and an intensification of the "imperial extraction of resources".[231] "Europe's war-time relation with Africa is essentially one of increased economic exploitation", concluded David Killingray and David Rathbone, stating that trade was reduced and redirected, some manpower was lost, goods and financial gifts were sent to the colonial powers and consumer goods lacking because production for local consumption did not rise and shipping space for outside

---

[224] See Götz Aly, *Hitlers Beneficiaries: Plunder, Racial War and the Nazi Welfare State* (New York: Metropolitan Books, 2006).
[225] Kamtekar, "A Different War Dance", 195; Raghavan, *India's War*, 326–329, 332–334, 338.
[226] Kamtekar, "A Different War Dance", 197–198 (quote 197); Raghavan, *India's War*, 339; Overy, *Blood*, 913; Mukerjee, *Churchill's Secret War*, 45.
[227] Raghavan, *India's War*, 340–341 (quote 340).
[228] Raghavan, *India's War*, 219–220.
[229] See M. S. Venkataramani, *Bengal Famine of 1943: The American Response* (Delhi et al.: Vikas, 1973); Mukherjee, *Hungry Bengal*, 287.
[230] Mandel, *Der Zweite Weltkrieg*, 76.
[231] Jackson, *Botswana*, 8, 9.

deliveries was denied.[232] Referencing Tom Stoppard's dictum that "war is capitalism with the gloves off", Nicholas Westcott stated that in World War II "Tanganyika experienced colonialism with the gloves off".[233] In July 1939, before Britain even entered the war, British colonialists developed secret plans to restrict imports to Nigeria and commercial exports to extract resources from that colony.[234] In British Africa, the colonial governments became monopoly purchasers of agricultural products, paying farmers less than world market prices.[235] The District Commissioner in Maun, British-Bechuanaland (Botswana), outlined the results in May 1945 thus: "The African is being drained of his wealth at an alarming rate and the country is becoming poorer."[236] From October 1940 to October 1941, French North Africa shipped over one-quarter of their fruit, vegetables and grain to France, along with large amounts of phosphate ore.[237] Imperialists in the Second World War claimed the 'right' to appropriate all resources of the world for themselves.

Inflation was the result. In British-India, banknote circulation rose sevenfold from 1938/1939 to 1945 (while real GDP increased just by 10.6 percent), and the steepest inflation occurred in early 1943, precisely when the famine in Bengal and some other regions built up.[238] Even the price of *rationed* food rose by 300 percent, as compared to 18 percent in Britain.[239] Increased British spending in India and cash availability, primarily in cities, worked in such a way that food was sucked out of rural areas into cities.[240] In British Northern Rhodesia (contemporary Zambia), there were two separate cost of living indices within one territory: the one for Europeans showed an increase of 36 percent and the one for Africans showed 90 percent.[241] Worse, from 1941 to 1945, the price index in the Japanese-occupied Dutch East Indies (Indonesia) rose 66-fold, and, as elsewhere, farmers were offered next to no consumer goods in exchange for agricultural products.[242] Edward Lloyd, a leading British food administrator before and during the war, in hindsight regarded inflation as key to the danger of famine and identified the fact as decisive that colonies and occupied countries were affected by heavy Allied expenditure

---

232 Killingray and Rathbone, "Introduction", 8–9, quote 9.
233 Westcott, "Impact", 143.
234 Abayomi and Oluwafuminiyi, "Fighting", 9–10.
235 Tembo, *Impact*, 4.
236 Jackson, *Botswana*, 123.
237 Levisse-Touzé, *L'Afrique*, 139.
238 Raghavan, *India's War*, 326, 347; Knight, *Food*, 61. Different data but with the same tendency are in Kamtekar, "A Different War Dance", 198 note 41.
239 Kamtekar, "A Different War Dance", 201.
240 Mukerjee, *Churchill's Secret War*, 46.
241 Tembo, *Impact*, 155.
242 Huff, "Great", 642–643.

without a matching influx of goods, and indeed facing the extraction of goods.[243] In the parts of China under Guomindang control, money circulation was fabi 1.4 billion in 1937 and 462.3 billion in 1945. Although hyperinflation seems to have hit Henan only in 1943–1944, food prices rose beyond reach for the poor already during the famine in 1942–1943.[244] In Greece, hyperinflation occurred in no less than four phases in 1941–1946, after which inflation was by no means over.[245] Japan did not extract huge amounts of goods from Southeast Asia, but it did extract a great amount of labor, often paying nothing or with scrip. Except for Thailand and French-Indochina, inflation in Japan's zone of influence in Southeast Asia rose much higher than the increase in currency supply, and three countries suffered from hyperinflation – Burma, Malaya and, late in the war, the Philippines.[246]

These are just examples. To my knowledge, there was not a single occupied country or colony where there was no substantial inflation during World War II. Those who suffered most from it and from shortages in Asia and Africa were in the final effect rural, and not urban, dwellers. The former were not protected by (even meager) food rations or political agency, were disenfranchised and marginalized. These included landless workers and those who became dependent on food purchases when their crops failed, as well as rural refugees starving to death on city streets as strangers.[247] Building on Sugata Bose, Anthony Garnaut spoke of "similar agrarian systems and a wartime political economy that conspired to deprive landless labourers of their customary food entitlements".[248]

The literature reports no wartime famines from Latin America but its citizens suffered from inflation and shortages of goods and transportation because their countries delivered relevant materials to the USA at fixed, unfavorable prices. All governments had joined the economic warfare against the Axis, although most refrained from sending troops and six South American countries did not declare war on Axis countries before 1945.[249] A notable case is Bolivia, which lost at least US$670 million in tin exports to the USA at artificially low prices (not counting other

---

[243] Lloyd, *Food*, 179–193, 196–197, 209. Lloyd's main point of reference was occupied Iran.
[244] Overy, *Blood*, 401; Bose, "Starvation", 714, 718.
[245] Palairet, *Four Ends*, (for 1946–1951, see 95).
[246] See Gregg Huff and Shinobu Majima, "Financing Japan's World War II Occupation of Southeast Asia", *Journal of Economic History* 73, 4 (2013): 937–977, esp. 938, 953–954.
[247] For example, see Huff, "Great", 639–641 on Vietnam and Indonesia; Kamtekar, "A Different War Dance", 218, on Bengal. This is contrary to the statement in Jackson, *Botswana*, 11.
[248] Garnaut, "Quantitative Description", 2011.
[249] See the contributions in Thomas Leonard and John Bratzel, eds., *Latin American during World War II* (Lanham et al.: Rowman and Littlefield, 2007), esp. 10, 44.

resources), which contributed to inflation.[250] Wherever they were capable and found it necessary, the Allies occupied countries to exploit them, as it was with British and U.S. troops being deployed to Congo, violating the neutrality that Belgian colonial authorities had declared, helping to take out copper, tin and uranium.[251]

Given the hectic economic activity and growth in some sectors of the economy and the rise of public demand for all sorts of resources, Amartya Sen has called the Bengal famine a "boom famine", and Sugata Bose has extended this judgment to the famines in northern Vietnam and Henan (China).[252] This points to the great role of states in victimizing primarily rural dwellers and great socioeconomic imbalances.

In the final analysis, what imperialist powers extracted from colonies and occupied countries can be expressed as labor value. (But it can also be conceptualized as energy flows enforced from constantly enlarged rear areas of the war[253]).

Economic warfare is a weapon of choice of dominant, established powers. During World War II, Germany and Japan were targeted this way, but to overcome the strains and difficulties this created and in consonance with their ambitions, these two countries also practiced economic warfare against the population of large territories that they conquered precisely to appropriate their resources. In other words, they tried to deflect Allied economic warfare at the cost of dozens of millions, who were condemned to misery through resource denial, as a result of which millions perished, including many little children. With unmistakable clarity, Hermann Göring said in reference to the German-occupied territories in a radio speech on 4 October 1942: "If people go hungry, certainly not in Germany!"[254] Secret service surveillance reports show that many Germans wanted Soviet prisoners of war to starve to death or die otherwise to make food available for Germans.[255] They thought so as a matter of course.

One example is particularly telling. As corrupt as Iran's members of parliament and other political elites were, at one point they balked at the idea of allowing the British larger expenses within Iran (actually to be financed by the Iranian government). The minister of the USA in Tehran, Louis Dreyfus, commented

---

250 See Jürgen Lieser, *"Unser Reichtum hat immer unsere Armut hervorgebracht": Zur Geschichte und Gegenwart wirtschaftlicher Abhängigkeit und politischer Unterdrückung in Bolivien* (Bonn and Trier: Informationsstelle Lateinamerika and Bolivienhilfe, 1982, second edition), 203–204, 236.
251 See Overy, *Blood*, 110, and Byfield, "Producing", 33–34.
252 Sen, *Poverty*, 75; Bose, "Starvation", 703.
253 For energy flows, see Muscolino, "Conceptualizing", 97–115, esp. 110.
254 "Wenn gehungert wird, in Deutschland auf keinen Fall!" The speech is in Götz Aly, ed., *Volkes Stimme: Skepsis und Führervertrauen im Nationalsozialismus* (Frankfurt a.M.: Fischer, 2006), 149–194, quote 155.
255 See Gerlach, *Extermination*, 234.

on October 24, 1942: "Deputies fail to understand Iran's basic monetary questions or to comprehend the urgent and overriding nature of [the] Allied problem in Iran. They are so obsessed with the dangers of inflation and starvation that they cannot see conditions in [a] realistic or practical light."[256] In plain words, Allies came first, whites mattered, and having all Iranians survive was impractical – how could anybody not understand this? Already in April 1942, Maurice Peterson, assistant undersecretary in the British Foreign Ministry, had commented on Iran by stating that Britian had "no desire to bully the Iranians, but sometimes it is useful to have a bit of bullying in the air".[257] Blackmailed by the British, who denied food deliveries to Iran and generally used "these situations [of food scarcity] as a lever to obtain their desires", Iran's parliament gave in on November 19, 1942 in exchange for nothing more than a vague Allied declaration of intent that, although feeding Iranians was the responsibility of the Iranian state, the Allies would do everything possible to help (which, for the most part, remained empty words).[258] As a result, Iranians starved to death in droves, just as the members of parliament had apprehended. It was foreseeable, and it was foreseen, not only in this case. Besides, it could be foreseen all the more in this case since the British-Russian occupation of Iran in the First World War had already led to famine and disease, which claimed up to *nine* million lives.[259]

Despite it all, it is important to realize that World War II had an "only limited environmental impact".[260] By no means was imperialism almighty. In most cases, the imperialist powers were unable to increase the *production* of 'natural resources' through mining, agriculture and forestry (some examples of this would be the German-occupied Soviet territories and British-India, as well as the wartime story of rubber[261]). Their power to mobilize nature turned out to be limited, putting the concept of 'anthropocene' into question. It was precisely because they were incapable of taking possession of the entire planet ecologically that imperi-

---

[256] Quoted in Gholi Majd, *Iran*, 300. This document puts a big question mark behind Gholi Majd's interpretation according to which Dreyfus was a positive exception among imperialist politicians in occupied Iran.
[257] Quoted in Gholi Majd, *Iran*, 103.
[258] See Gholi Majd, *Iran*, 293, 389 (the quote is from a Dreyfus report of 24 February 1943). The Allies hardly delivered any food but the British sold some gold in Iran in 1943–1944, which in substance meant that they paid for some of the Iranian services they had received. See also Lloyd, *Food*, 164–165, 211–212.
[259] See Gholi Majd, "Three Famines", 93–97 with a high-end estimate.
[260] Mawdsley, "World War II", 42. In my view, this statement is corroborated by the entire volume of Laakkonen et al., *Long Shadows* devoted to the environmental history of the war.
[261] For the latter see William G. Clarence-Smith, *The Battle for Rubber in the Second World War: Cooperation and Resistance*, working paper (London: School of Oriental and African Studies, 2009).

alist powers turned to fiercer, murderous exploitation of humans and the exclusion of some groups from consumption through resource denial.

Generally, World War II famines had complex mechanisms and were based on a drain of all kinds of resources. Although this is also true for British-Bengal and the German-occupied Soviet territories, a different sort of calculation is striking: Bengal imported 296,000 tons of grain in 1941 but exported 185,000 tons in 1942, a difference of about 480,000 tons or the consumption of 2.4 million people at 200 kilograms per capita and year, and about three million died in the famine (and British-India exported 360,000 tons of grain from April 1, 1942 to March 31, 1943, in comparison to imports of over one million tons before the war, the difference equalizing the consumption of seven million people; but the British army's demand of 450,000 tons in 1943 explains the difference only in part).[262] As for the Germans, they extracted 2.1 million tons of grain annually from the occupied Soviet territories in 1941–1944, sufficient to feed 10.5 million people, and killed or let die 7–9 million people.[263] Thus, the direct extraction of food did matter, of course.

Racism was an integral part of the structures and practices during the war. The utilitarian justifications of violence, including 'sacrifices', were racist if the lives of *some* should be sacrificed for higher values; this is obvious if one sees *who* was sacrificed. In German-occupied Europe, official food rations differed widely on a hierarchy based on the construct of race and ethnicity, but also a country's degree of industrialization and its alliance status with Germany. Those with lower rations were also exposed to greater insecurity and less dignity, since they had to turn to illegalized economic activities.[264] According to Lizzie Collingham, "even in the more benign sphere of the Allies, race was still a deciding factor in determining who was well fed, who went hungry and who starved".[265] White settlers in British-Kenya in 1941–1942 received about double the price for their corn than what African farmers were paid.[266] In the British colony of Northern Rhodesia (contemporary Zambia), butter rations were only for white people. Moreover, officials distinguished between

---

[262] For data and some considerations, see Knight, *Food*, 19, 48, 74, 76, 229, 249, and Mukerjee, *Churchill's Secret War*, 67, 130. See also Raghavan, *India's War*, 338; Brennan et al., "War", 44. Mukherjee, *Hungry Bengal*, 77 talks of exports of 232,000 tons of grain from January to April 1942. However, according to Sen, *Poverty*, 60–61, 200,000 tons of grain were imported to Bengal in the following year of 1943.
[263] For food procurement, see Rolf-Dieter Müller, ed., *Die deutsche Wirtschaftspolitik in den besetzten sowjetischen Gebieten: Der Abschlussbericht des Wirtschaftsstabes Ost und Aufzeichnungen eines Angehörigen des Wirtschaftskommandos Kiew* (Boppard: Harald Boldt, 1991), 98.
[264] See already Boris Shub, *Starvation over Europe (Made in Germany)* (n.p. [New York]: Institute of Jewish Affairs, 1943); Gerlach, *Extermination*, 215–260.
[265] Collingham, *Taste*, 263.
[266] Judith Byfield, "Producing for the War", Byfield et al., *Africa*, 36–37.

two different cost of living indices, one for Europeans and one for Africans, and the latter rose much steeper than the former in 1939–1946. Further, among returning military veterans in British African colonies, whites received land whereas Africans did not.[267] The racist rationing system was similar to Dakar, Senegal, under the rule of Vichy France, where under circumstances of food scarcity, bread was for whites only. It was the same in Vietnam under French rule since December 1944.[268] In the British-occupied parts of Iran, Polish refugees – who in Euro-American accounts are often depicted as deprived – received in 1942 much more food per capita than famished Iranians.[269] In the British military, whites received higher food rations than colonial subjects.[270] African British colonial soldiers in conquered Ethiopia in 1941 "angrily noted that Italian POWs lived better than they did",[271] and in neighboring Eritrea, another former Italian colony, anti-Jewish racial laws were abolished under the British but anti-African ones were not.[272] Regardless, during World War II, marriages between Africans and Europeans were still banned in British-Kenya,[273] and the "racist use of the term 'monkey' to describe Africans appears to have been a universal complaint" of Malawians (colonial subjects from British-Nyasaland) who reported about their service in the British military during World War II.[274]

Famines: Other Factors in Conditions of Violence

Ruthless economic warfare killed millions, but not only colonial rulers or foreign occupiers bore the responsibility for this. Economic warfare was also about blockades and sieges, which came from all sides.[275] In this context, Churchill was already known in France for his World War I policies as "the famisher".[276] The German

---

267 See Tembo, *Impact*, 147, 155, 234.
268 Ginio, *French Colonialism*, 62; Gunn, *Rice Wars*, 240.
269 Gholi Majd, *Iran*, 223.
270 Overy, *Blood*, 398.
271 Parsons, "Military Experiences", 7. African American and Mexican workers on U.S. farms made the same experience in comparison with German POWs working there: Buchanan, "Globalizing", 263.
272 Giulia Barrea, "Wrestling with Race at the Eve of Human Rights: The British Management of the Color Line in Post-Fascist Eritrea", Byfield et al. *Africa*, 259–275.
273 Bethwell Ogot, "Mau Mau and Nationhood: The untold story", in: E.S. Atieno Odhiambo and John Lonsdale, eds., *Mau Mau & Nationhood: Arms, Authority & Narration* (Oxford et al.: Ohio University Press 2003), 27.
274 Lovering, "Military Service", 116.
275 O'Grada, *Famine*, 229.
276 Mukherjee, *Hungry Bengal*, 33.

siege of Leningrad is the most obvious example in the context of World War II, during which 600,000 to one million of the three million Soviet inhabitants died due to cold and hunger (whereas comparatively few died of bombardments).[277] Germany occupied areas that normally produced a large part of Soviet food and other goods, a loss that greatly contributed to famine on the Soviet side in 1942–1943, and Japan conquered areas that produced much of Chinese food, causing a similar effect in unoccupied China.[278] Allied operations also cut off economic relations. Since August 1940, a British naval blockade interrupted overseas imports to continental Europe via the Atlantic and the Mediterranean.[279] There was also an Allied blockade against Axis transports in the Indian Ocean.[280] With this, they also prevented food deliveries to Axis-occupied countries deliberately and systematically. This is why historians have accused Britain of bearing part of the responsibility for the Greek famine (which was also caused by Italian and German resource and labor extraction and occupation costs, the Bulgarian annexation of Greece's north, local hoarding and speculation).[281] Likewise, Gopal Haridas, a physician who had treated many cases of beriberi in children in Singapore during the Japanese occupation, many of which died, explained in 1947 the wartime "shortage of essential foodstuffs" there in part by "the stranglehold exerted by the Allies on Japanese communications".[282] This is to say, many people died of interlocking, competing regimes of resource extraction and denial. Here, the word "regime" means an order created by not only states, but also myriad individuals.

The Allies even largely prevented food aid deliveries out of their countries to Jews and other camp prisoners in Axis countries until 1944 – except for sending many millions of parcels to Allied prisoners of war in Axis hands.[283] With its naval blockades, Britain also contributed to one of the deadliest famines of the war in relative terms in the Portuguese colony of Cape Verde.[284] The famines or famine-

---

277 Ganzenmüller, *Das belagerte Leningrad*, esp. 238–239.
278 For China, see Collingham, *Taste*, 250.
279 Collingham, *Taste*, 66.
280 For its efficiency, see the figures in Henri Labrousse, *L'Océan Indien dans le Seconde Guerre Mondiale* (Paris: Economica, 2007), 75–78, 81–88.
281 See Hagen Fleischer, *Im Kreuzschatten der Mächte: Griechenland 1941–1944* (Frankfurt a.M. et al.: Peter Lang, 1986), 116, 122, 125; Overy, "Front Line II", 305.
282 G.[opal] Haridas, "Infantile Beri-beri in Singapore in the Latter Part of the Japanese Occupation", *Archives of Disease in Childhood* 22, 1947: 26.
283 See Jan Láníček and Jan Lambertz, eds., *More Than Parcels: Wartime Aid for Jews in Nazi-Era Camps and Ghettos* (Detroit: Wayne State University Press, 2022).
284 Collingham, *Taste*, 124. The Portuguese responded with small corn deliveries from their colony of Angola, a ban on sugar cultivation (for rum production) and with shipping laborers to other colonies: Clarence-Smith, "Impact", 319.

like situations in Vichy French colonies at or in the Indian Ocean (French Somaliland, Réunion) and, to an extent, in French-Algeria, as well as the famines in the Japanese colonies in the West Pacific were due to U.S., British and Australian attacks by sea, submarine warfare and air. These actions aimed to prevent any transportation activity and, in the Pacific, starve the Japanese troops.[285] In part, they succeeded, also because of the surprising fact that some Japanese would rather starve than rob Micronesians, who called them "walking 'stick men'" (which was unlike Japanese actions in Thailand).[286] U.S. sea mining, bombing and submarine warfare against shipping and the railways also played a major role in the lack of transport from south to north in French Indochina, which helped cause the Tonkin famine that probably killed more than one million people – and the U.S. military was aware of their impact.[287] It was not by accident that the U.S. bombing campaign against Japan in 1944–1945 was called "Operation Starvation".[288]

Lizzie Collingham defended the U.S. use of atomic bombs against Japan in August 1945 with the amazing argument that this allegedly saved many Japanese from famine, disregarding the fact that, as she herself mentioned in another part of her book, 100,000 Japanese starved to death in Tokyo alone from August to November 1945 under U.S. occupation. Similar conditions also prevailed in other parts of Japan.[289] It is perhaps indicative of the magnitude of the problem of hunger that Nagasaki Medical College, the precursor of Nagasaki University, was inoperative for one month after the nuclear explosion in August 1945 (many professors and students were absent from the city, survived and started to work again on an outside campus), whereas in Tokyo, the university was closed down for two months in late 1945 because of the famine.[290]

Portuguese East Timor (contemporary Timor Leste) is a case of yet another type of imposed famine. After Australian troops violated Portuguese neutrality first, it was occupied by Japanese troops in 1942. The Australians continued fighting there until December 1942, after which they left small commandos behind, harassing the Japanese with the help of local aides. The Japanese troops, who also

---

285 For the Pacific, see, for example, Nero, "Time", 120–127; Lin Poyer, "Micronesian Experiences of the War in the Pacific", White and Lindstrom, *Pacific Theatre*, 85–86. For French Somaliland, Réunion and Algeria, see the literature mentioned in notes 117, 118 and 129 in this chapter.
286 For example, see Suzanne Falgout, "Lessons from Wartime Pohnpei", Geoffrey White, ed., *Remembering the Pacific War* (Honolulu: University of Hawaii, 1991), 126; for Thailand, see account by Kihei Matsuhara, Schaarschmidt, *Schrei*, 74.
287 See Huff, "Great", 646–649; see also Tønnesson, *Vietnamese Revolution*, 294 and 303 note 113.
288 O'Grada, *Famine*, 230.
289 Collingham, *Taste*, 313–316, 467; see also Hedinger, Achse, 379.
290 For Tokyo, see account by Akira Miuri, Terkel, *"Good War"*, 206. For Nagasaki, see "Nagasaki University", https://en.wikipedia.org/wiki/Nagasaki_University (last accessed August 31, 2023).

found local allies, reacted by destroying many villages, food stores and trees needed for food production, preventing one planting season, and with arrests, torture, rape and executions. All of this forced the rural population into the bush, where many died of hunger and disease. Estimates about deaths range from 40,000 to 60,000 victims, including ethnic Chinese whom the Japanese herded in camps and some East Timorese who died from Australian aerial attacks. The Australian press celebrated the fact that their troops forced Japan to keep a full division on the island that could not be used elsewhere, but some troops felt upon their retreat that they had betrayed the East Timorese "and brought nothing but misery to these poor people".[291] This case shows that the prime responsibility was with the Japanese, but the Australians were involved, as were locals in a fratricidal conflict, all co-producing conditions of violence.

More generally, conditions creating deadly famines were not only imposed by foreign rulers. In part, it was compatriots who created such conditions in social struggles for rapid redistribution. Surplus farmers and traders, including black marketeers, benefitted from the scarcity in African colonies. In the shadow of rich white settlers, some wealthy Kenyan peasants also made good business in the time of the famine, as in other parts of Eastern Africa under British colonialism.[292] It was the same for some African farmers and traders in British-Bechuanaland (contemporary Botswana) at a time when shops became the main source of food for many.[293] In Mauritius, where there were at least food problems, owners of sugar plantations and black marketeers became richer.[294] Widespread atomization and lack of solidarity are captured in the name that people in Niger, then a French colony, gave the famine of 1942: "withdraw and separate from the wife".[295]

In a pioneering article, Indivar Kamtekar has painted a more comprehensive picture of social developments in British-India during the war. Aside from regional disparities ("Punjab prospered, Bengal suffered"), he argued that the British penetration into the Indian economy was not even that strong; that the war with its public demand orders, the colonial pricing system, hoarding and high profit rates gave a boost to Indian industrialists and other businessmen; that surplus farmers managed to get rid of their debts; that the situation for Indian civil servants was

---

[291] See Turner, *Telling*, iv, 1–6 and the accounts by Lance Bomford, John Keneally and Paulo Quintao in the same volume, 11, 18 (quote), 23–24; Dunn, *Timor*, 22–26; Kammen, *Three Centuries*, 110.
[292] See Spencer, "Settler Dominance", 497–514; Collingham, *Taste*, 132–138.
[293] Mokopakgosi III., "Impact", 170–172.
[294] Ashley Jackson, *War and Empire in Mauritius and the Indian Ocean* (Basingstoke: Palgrave, 2001), 161, 163–168.
[295] Thurston Clarke, *The Last Caravan* (New York: Putnam, 1978), 167.

ambiguous with more jobs available but dropping real income; that urban workers saw a steep decline of their real wages; and that agricultural workers suffered greatly from skyrocketing food prices. 1943 was simultaneously the year of the famine, the lowest real wages and the highest profits.[296] During the Bengal famine, the journalist Vasudha Chakravarty summed up the complexity of the situation thus: "Who is the enemy of the people? [. . .] Is it the foreigner? Is it the nature? [. . .] The imperialist, the fascist, the profiteer, the corrupt official – or all together?"[297]

Hoarders and corrupt officials were also accused by the leftist press (and British propagandists) of causing suffering to the people in Allied-occupied, famine-stricken Iran.[298] The dozens of millions of domestic refugees in China were ruthlessly cheated on by merchants and exploited as cheap labor by entrepreneurs.[299] Because of the bad tenancy conditions, tenants in Henan had only one-third of the prewar amount of grain available to their families in 1942, and the starving landless laborers were even worse off.[300] The situation was similar in the Tonkin famine of 1944–1945, where haunting episodes of the abandoned poor were reported especially about the half of the population that was landless.[301] In Greece, stricken by famine and hyperinflation, surplus farmers and some traders benefitted, and private owners accumulated more than seven tons of gold 1941–1946 and another five tons in the five hungry years that followed.[302] When the Greek government fled into exile in April 1941, it took the country's existing gold reserves with it, and the "banknote printing plates as well".[303]

Social mechanisms as described in the previous three paragraphs could also work the other way, for example in networks of kin and mine workers sending remittances to family members in Northern Rhodesia (contemporary Zambia).[304] Domestic mass migration into cities marked another kind of attempt to escape

---

[296] Kamtekar, "Different War Dance", 201–212, quote 216; see also Raghavan, *India's War*, 330.
[297] Quoted in Siegel, *Hungry Nation*, 25.
[298] Gholi Majd, *Iran*, 284–285, 434–435.
[299] See Schoppa, *In a Sea*.
[300] Garnaut, "Quantitative Description", 2029–2030.
[301] See Ngô Viñh Long, *Before the Revolution: The Vietnamese Peasants under the French* (New York: Columbia University Press, 1991 [first 1973]), 22, 24, 219–276; Gunn, *Rice Wars*, 273; Motoo Furuta, "A Survey of Village Conditions during the 1945 Famine in Vietnam", Kratoska, *Food Supplies*, 231, 233.
[302] Palairet, *Four Ends*, 104; Hionidou, *Famine*, 223–234. Palairet argues against the widespread narrative that ruthless greed by businessowners caused misery for the masses in wartime Greece but many facts mentioned by him do not quite support his interpretation (see Palairet, *Four Ends*, 48, 76, 84).
[303] Palairet, *Four Ends*, 25.
[304] See Tembo, *Impact*, 77–78.

the threatening conditions in the countryside and also indicated social mobility, whether in India or many areas of Southeast Asia.[305] However, migrating to cities was by no means a safeguard against starving to death, as could be seen in the streets of Calcutta and on the roads to it.

The case of Singapore illustrates how the socially conflictual character of hunger crises can lead to their denial. Public memory and most scholars agree that there was no wartime famine in Singapore.[306] In fact, this is incorrect. According to available contemporary statistics, the city experienced an excess mortality of over 60,000 if one compares the years of 1942–1945 with prewar levels. A large part of these additional deaths, which primarily hit in 1942, 1944 and 1945, were from beriberi and dysentery, which can be linked to malnutrition, and another large portion of the deaths were caused by pneumonia and tuberculosis, which can be indirectly linked to malnutrition. The number of children who died due to beriberi kept rising.[307] If one takes into consideration that Singapore's population had increased through refugees arriving in late 1941 and early 1942 by about one-third (approximately 250,000 people[308]), to reach about 900,000 to one million, the adjusted excess mortality was between 40,000 and 50,000, or 4–5

---

[305] For India, see Raghavan, *India's War*, 459; for various Asian countries, see Gregg Huff and Gillian Huff, "Urban growth and change in 1940s Southeast Asia", *Economic History Review* 68, 2 (2015): 522–547.

[306] For example, see Wong Hong Suen, *Wartime Kitchen: Food and Eating in Singapore 1942–1950* (Singapore: Editions Didier Millet and National Museum of Singapore, 2009), 78, 89; Paul Kratoska, *The Japanese Occupation of Malaya and Singapore: A Social and Economic History* (Singapore: NUS Press, 2018, second edition), 250; Huff and Huff, "Urban growth", 536; Gregg Huff and Gillian Huff, "The Second World War Japanese Occupation of Singapore", *Journal of Southeast Asian Studies* 51, 1–2 (2020): 250, 253; Lucius Nicholls, "The State of Nutrition in Singapore before, during and after the Japanese Occupation", Supplement to the *British Medical Journal*, March 6, 1948: 37. Mary Turnbull wrote: "Many people were dying of malnutrition", though without using the word famine. C. M. Turnbull, *A History of Modern Singapore* (Singapore: NUS Press, 2016), 219.

[307] See data in Kratoska, *Japanese Occupation*, 280 (other frequently recorded causes of death were "[i]infantile convulsions", "[f]ever" and malaria); beriberi and dysentery combined caused c. 21,000 excess deaths. See also data in Shimizu Hiroshi and Hirakawa Hitoshi, *Japan and Singapore in the World Economy: Japan's Advance into Singapore 1870–1965* (London: Routledge, 1999), 129; Huff and Huff, "The Second World War Japanese Occupation", 264, 267; Haridas, "Infantile Beri-beri", 23–33. Lucius Nicholls argued that the excess mortality was more than 71,000, including 51,000 excess deaths of males. Nicholls, "State", 38–39.

[308] Huff and Huff, "The Second World War Japanese Occupation": 250; Takuma Melber, *Zwischen Kollaboration und Widerstand: Die japanische Besatzung in Malaya und Singapur (1942–1945)* (Frankfurt a.M. and New York: Campus, 2017), 331–332, note 168; Gregg Huff and Shinobu Majima, eds., *World War II Singapore: The Chosabu Reports on Syonan* (Singapore: NUS Press, 2018), 135–138; Huff and Huff, "Urban growth", 546.

percent of the population.³⁰⁹ In view of the most frequent causes of death, this indicates a famine, in combination with bad housing conditions to which the frequent fatalities from respiratory diseases point. Thus, it appears reasonable to assume that the excess deaths were of the city's poor and the refugees who had not found proper shelter. This means that they point to conflict within the population between classes, between ethnicities, and between locals and refugees amidst inflation, profiteering in shady business and frantic black-marketeering in a city where virtually all cats and dogs were eaten.³¹⁰ These conflicts may well be part of the story of why the history of the occupation period has a reputation among Singaporeans, and Singaporean politicians in particular, of being divisive and detrimental to nation-building, which has led to tendencies to keep silent about it.³¹¹ However, such social conflicts were not unique to Singapore.

Finally, it is no wonder that most of the famines occurred in 1942–1943 and 1945. The year 1942, when the war was on the razor's edge, was also a year with an intensified imperialist grip on the reachable resources and a globalization of economic warfare. The "world market [...] changed dramatically" in 1942, and eastern Africa, for instance, became a strategic supply base for the British war effort and the Indian Ocean area strongly contested.³¹² I have made a similar argument for German-occupied Europa.³¹³ In 1945, many social groups were worn down by the long deprivation and new populations came under occupation.

In conclusion, wartime destruction played a lesser role than one might think in these famines, and the same is true for the direct requisition or plunder of food in famine-affected areas. Much more important were economic disruption through sieges and lack of means of transportation, new borders and administrative restrictions to the flow of food, but also other goods. Usually, food production decreased due to a lack of inputs, particularly labor and, in some cases, also draught animals and farmyard manure, fertilizer, machinery and fuel, all of which were in high mil-

---

309 Apparently, these losses do not include the Japanese massacres of 1942. Singapore's population losses place it among the more seriously affected countries in World War II.
310 For social developments in Singapore, see Huff and Majima, *World War II Singapore*, 129–154; Kratoska, *Japanese Occupation*, 161–210; for "mushroom millionaires", see Huff and Huff, "Urban growth", 539, and for cats and dogs ibid., 534. See also Huff and Huff, "The Second World War Japanese Occupation", 267 for differences in infant mortality rates between the main ethnic groups in Singapore and 266–267 pointing to particularly harsh conditions for refugees of Indian extraction.
311 One account of the politics of memory is Hamzah Muzaini and Brenda Yeoh, *Contested Memoryscapes: The Politics of Second World War Commemoration in Singapore* (London and New York: Routledge, 2016).
312 See Lonsdale, "Depression", 120–121; Westcott, "Impact", 146 (quote).
313 See Gerlach, *Extermination*, 9–10.

itary demand. This shattered national economies into small local pieces.[314] Economic imbalances were great, meaning that some regions and economic sectors boomed, contributing to urbanization in Asia and Africa,[315] while others were in a deep crisis, small-scale agriculture being among them. Since peasants received few goods in exchange for their products, had to sell at artificially low prices and lost traditional markets, they produced fewer surpluses and sold products on the black market. On top they were burdened by enforced labor conscription of different kinds and, sometimes, impositions to grow industrial crops. The enforced restructuring of economic links led to a scarcity of consumer goods and inflation, and authorities' attempts to regulate the food economy often added to the problems and did not protect rural dwellers anyway, such as through food rationing. Racist hierarchies dominated the distribution of food, and political hierarchies disadvantaged certain groups in internment. Those on the lower ends were given low priority. Illiberal and liberal imperialists alike, old and new imperialists, exploited colonial and occupied areas ruthlessly on four continents, including Europe. Yet, the conditions of violence they imposed also strengthened anticolonial and communist movements to the point that many were successful in the mid-to-late 1940s. These also responded to intra-societal conflicts between urbanites and ruralites and a desolidarization through which some tried to make fortunes on the back of others.

The kind of exploitation that prevailed in a country determined where hunger was concentrated. Since large parts of Europe were quite urbanized, it was primarily urbanites who went hungry.[316] In other parts of the world, above all, rural dwellers were the most exploited and affected, especially landless laborers and tenants who were unprotected by entitlements through rationing, insurance and property, along with being considered politically irrelevant and cannon fodder at best, often illiterate, and scorned.

Those who created these conditions of violence included politicians and strategists, commanders, officers and troops (benefitting, confiscating and sometimes looting on their own), administrators, political and paramilitary organizations, industrialists, merchants, black marketeers, wealthy farmers and a host of other groups in complex interaction.

---

314 For disturbances of domestic transportation, see, for example, Aiko Kurasawa, "Transportation and Rice Distribution in South-East Asia during the Second World War", Kratoska, *Food Supplies*, 44–48; Marr, *Vietnam 1945*, 31, 100; Gunn, "Great Vietnamese Famine"; Mazower, *Inside*, 46–48.
315 For World War II urbanization in Asia, see note 305 in this chapter; Mukherjee, *Hungry Bengal*, 323.
316 In the semi-urbanized countries Greece and the Soviet Union, the famines affected in part urban and rural populations. See Hionnidou, *Famine*; Filtzer, "Starvation Mortality"; Ganson, *Soviet Famine*, 95–105, 114.

Notably, this chapter's focus on famines means to concentrate on medium-term effects of imperialism during the war but not on imperialists' long-term war aims such as the lasting control, and exploitation, of foreign economies in India, Africa, Latin America or Eastern Europe and their effects long after 1945.

Rationales of Allied Mass Violence

In August 1947, when the so-called Nuremberg Code against involuntary human experiments was issued by a U.S. military tribunal, the U.S. military just conducted arguably what was the biggest human experiment in history, which was on the medical effects of the atomic bomb attacks on survivors of Hiroshima and Nagasaki, while Japanese publications on the issue were forbidden, including medical ones, to suppress the Japanese narrative.[317] In October 1946, Fritz Sauckel was hanged in Nuremberg for having organized Germany's forced labor deportation program, but in World War II, all colonial powers had expanded their forced labor programs in Africa, including, as shown, Britain, "Free" France and Belgium on the Allied side. The Atlantic Charter of August 1941, soon adopted by all Allied governments, promised "freedom [. . .] from want", and yet at least five million people died in wartime famines in Allied countries and colonies.[318]

As far as rationales for violence are concerned, Nazis, Young Turks and Hutu power advocates are easy targets, but why not, for once, inquire into justifications of mass violence that were widely successful? To reflect on rationales behind mass violence can deepen our understanding of the process that war is. In this process, justifications are not only explanations, but can become causes of action. Moreover, justifications are often quite revealing about the ideas of those who use them.

The basic justification for the Allies' war was that they defended themselves against Axis aggression. That the Germans and Japanese were aggressors was the main point of indictment in the postwar Nuremberg and Tokyo trials.[319] This is also standard fare in almost any war propaganda (from any ever) and the foundation for the claim to a just war.[320]

---

[317] Monica Braw, *The Atomic Bomb Suppressed: American Censorship in Occupied Japan* (Armonk and London: M.E. Sharpe, 1991).
[318] "Atlantic Charter", August 14, 1941, https://avalon.law.yale.edu/wwii/atlantic.asp (last accessed August 21, 2023).
[319] Overy, *Blood*, 609.
[320] See Anne Morelli, *Die Prinzipien der Kriegspropaganda* (Springe: zu Klampen, 2021, third edition; French 2004). This is also true for wars fought by Muslims. See Souleymane Bachir Diagne, "On philosophy in Islam and on the question of a 'West African Islam'", Souleymane Bachir Di-

Hand in hand with the trope of aggression went the claim that the Axis sought expansion, whereas the Allies did not. The latter point was enshrined in the Atlantic Charter signed by U.S. President Franklin D. Roosevelt and British Prime Minister Winston Churchill on August 14, 1941, adopted by all Allied countries by early 1942, which stated in its first clause that "their countries seek no aggrandizement, territorial or other".[321]

This was also a lie, like so many things in the Atlantic Charter (including the proclamation of all peoples' right to self-determination), which the United Nations regard to this day as one of their foundational documents.[322] In World War II, virtually all main Allied powers annexed territory. The Soviet Union acquired areas of nine different countries: Finland, Estonia, Latvia, Lithuania, Germany, Poland, Czechoslovakia, Romania and Japan, not to count Tuva.[323] The USA acquired colonies in the western Pacific such as the Marshall Islands, the Caroline Islands and Palau from Japan (and with them, millions of square kilometers of territorial waters), some of which are still under U.S. rule, like the Northern Mariana Islands. China acquired Taiwan from Japan.[324] Moreover, Britain took over Libya, Italian-Somaliland and Eritrea as colonies from Italy; Poland annexed large parts of eastern Germany; Yugoslavia acquired parts of Istria from Italy; and Greece took Corfu and the Dodecanese from Italy, although this fell far short of Greek elites' plans for expansion.[325] These facts do not keep historians from calling Britain, the Soviet Union and the USA a "satisfied power" or a "status quo power",[326] thereby denying, obscuring or concealing their imperialist character.[327] And the same historians do little to examine these countries' policies in their already existing colonies.

---

agne and Jean-Loup Amselle, *In Search of Africa(s): Universalism and Decolonial Thought* (Cambridge and Medford: Polity, 2020), 85.
321 See the text of the Atlantic Charter, https://avalon.law.yale.edu/wwii/atlantic.asp (last accessed August 21, 2023).
322 "Preparatory Years: UN Charter History", https://www.un.org/en/about-us/history-of-the-un/preparatory-years (last accessed August 21, 2023).
323 For the state of Tuva, which repeatedly asked for joining the USSR in 1939–1944, see Timeo Antognini, *Geschichte der Tuwinischen Volksrepublik*, Master's thesis, University of Bern, 2022, 54.
324 For the conquest of Japanese-annexed Taiwan as a Chinese war aim, see Mitter, *China's Good War*, 45.
325 Fleischer, *Kreuzschatten*, 269.
326 Mawdsley, *World War II*, 15, 19, 21. Overy, *Blood*, is similar; see inter alia 597, 601–602, although he does say more about the colonies.
327 Some, as Hannah Arendt, who began to do so in 1945, went so far as to justify Euro-American imperialism by making a distinction between good "imperialism" and bad "conquest". Moses, *Problems*, 407–409.

The Atlantic Charter proves that not only the Axis but also the Allies wanted a new world order.[328] The flowery humanitarian language – also used at the 1943 UN Conference on Food and Agriculture in Hot Springs[329] – and "universalizing language of freedom and rights" could also be understood as "a veil masking the consolidation of a great power directorate that was not as different from the Axis powers".[330] The Charter, among its "principles [. . .] for a better future of the world", also listed that all states enjoy "access, on equal terms, to the trade and raw materials of the world" and "all men to traverse the high seas and oceans without hindrance",[331] but, in reality, established naval blockades, the denial of resources and a net of economic 'sanctions' before and after World War II, all of which are relevant to this chapter.

One main Allied propaganda line that emerged was "that the Allies were saving civilization and humanity from the barbarity" of the Axis.[332] Upon Britain's declaration of war against Germany, British Prime Minister Neville Chamberlain said in a radio address on 3 September 1939 that Britain was fighting "evil things".[333] On the same day in another radio speech, Victor Hope, alias Linlithgow, the British colonial viceroy of India, announced his deliberation that India declare war on Germany (no Indian had been involved in the decision), saying, "India will make her contribution on the side of human freedom as against the rule of force".[334] In 1940, when Indian Congress politician Jawarlahal Nehru

---

328 Overy, *Blood*, 134 (about the Tripartite Pact in 1940); for Japan's ambitions, see Iriye, *Origins*, 156; account by Shigeo Hatanaka, Cook and Cook, *Japan*, 66; see also Tony Palomo, "Island in Agony: The War in Guam", White, *Remembering*, 135. The Joint Declaration of the Greater East Asia Conference in Tokyo, November 6, 1943, https://en.wikisource.org/wiki/Joint_Declaration_of_the_Greater_East_Asia_Conference, made similar promises like the Atlantic Charter plus that of anti-racism.
329 The records of the Hot Springs Conference are at the FAO Archive, Record Group 3. Axis observers accused the USA, Britain (with Canada) and the Soviet Union that they wanted to construct a new international grain economy that would hold particularly Europe in dependence, "a formidable weapon against all the other peoples", as an Italian report put it. See Italian foreign office, D.A.T. – III, "Appunto per l'Excellenza Acerbo: Conferenza Alimentare di Hot Springs", June 11, 1943, FAO archive, Record Group 1, N 370. Similar arguments were then made in the German press and, from a neutral country, in Ernst Laur, "Die Beschlüsse der Internationalen Lebensmittel- und Agrarkonferenz der Vereinigten Nationen in Hot Springs (U.S.A.)", in Ernst Laur, *Beiträge zum Ausbau der schweizerischen Wirtschaft* (Brugg: Verlag des Schweizerischen Bauernsekretariats, 1943), 74–83, 77–78,80.
330 Mazower, No Enchanted Palace, 7, 10.
331 "Atlantic Charter", August 14, 1941, https://avalon.law.yale.edu/wwii/atlantic.asp (last accessed August 21, 2023).
332 Overy, *Blood*, 605.
333 Quoted in Overy, *Blood*, 604.
334 Quoted in Raghavan, *India's War*, 1.

pointed out in his speeches that India had been coerced into the war "in the name of freedom and self-determination and democracy", he was arrested.[335]

Britain did not stand alone. In 1942, U.S. President Roosevelt said that the war against the Axis was to "cleanse the world of ancient evils". According to his statement in January 1942, there could be no "compromise between good and evil".[336] Guomindang China's wartime narrative was that China fought for the righteous cause of uncompromised sovereignty.[337] During his visit of Calcutta in 1942, Jiang Jieshi (Chiang Kai-shek) said: "The present struggle is one between Freedom and Slavery, between Light and Darkness, between Good and Evil, between Resistance and Aggression".[338] So, he was disappointed about a meeting with Gandhi on that trip, concluding that the Indians only cared about themselves and that non-violence was an illusion.[339] A total of 18 well-known Chinese intellectuals, including Ding Ling and Mao Dun, wrote an open letter to the writer Zhou Zuoren because of his cooperation with the Japanese occupants, calling him a "traitor" showing "evil behavior" in the fight between "civilisation" and "savagery".[340] The perception of a fight between good and evil was also accepted, believed and promoted by many ordinary people. The visitors' books in Soviet war museums are an example of this.[341]

To be sure, the Allies were not alone in their good-against-evil perspective. All sides in the war found their effort justified.[342] At the Tokyo summit of the Greater East-Asian Co-Prosperity Sphere in November 1943, Subhas Chandra Bose, Commander of the Indian National Army, stated that the East stood "for light and guidance ... in the creation of a new, free and prosperous world".[343] Japan maintained such a narrative to the end, with the emperor's declaration of August 14, 1945 that it had been "far from Our thought either to infringe upon the sovereignty of other nations or to embark on territorial aggrandizement".[344]

Genocide scholars, and experts on the murder of the Jews in particular, stress the important role that the dehumanization of the victims plays. In 1941, Stalin

---

335 Mukerjee, *Churchill's Secret War*, 20.
336 Quoted in Overy, *Blood*, 605, 609.
337 Mitter, *China's Good War*, 46.
338 Quoted in Darbara Singh, "1942", in Sharma, *Quit India*, 24.
339 See Raghavan, *India's War*, 227.
340 Quoted in Lary, *Chinese People*, 75–76 (quote 76).
341 Anne Hasselmann, *Wie der Krieg ins Museum kam: Akteure der Erinnerung in Moskau, Minsk und Tscheljabinsk, 1941–1956* (Bielefeld: Transcript, 2022), 329–351.
342 Overy, *Blood*, 596.
343 Quoted in Mitter, *China's War*, 307 (ommission by Mitter).
344 Quoted in Cook and Cook, *Japan*, 401. In reality, to my knowledge, Japan occupied many countries in World War II, but, unlike after earlier conquests, it did not annex any.

stated that the Germans were on the level of "wild beasts".[345] In 1937, Jiang Jieshi in his diary called the Japanese "dwarfs" and "dwarf bandits".[346] Officially, he spoke in 1943 of Japan as a "demon", the fight against whom was worth making sacrifices.[347] The wartime Soviet press spoke of Germans as vermin, including snails, scorpions, rats, dogs and bacteria.[348] As one film critic stated, U.S. movies during the war "robbed the enemy of any humanity and individuality".[349] Other intellectuals also drove the dehumanization forward. A.A. Milne called Hitler "the Devil" in 1940, and for U.S. theologian Reinhold Niebuhr, the Axis was "evil".[350] Adebajo Adedeji, then a schoolboy in British-Nigeria, remembered from the war: "We were not taught what Hitler did. We were taught to believe that he was the devil incarnate, and we had all sorts of school songs and plays that demonized Hitler."[351] On the other side, German propaganda, of course, dehumanized the enemy, especially if it was Soviet or Jewish.[352] Japanese newspapers and teachers portrayed U.S. Americans during the war as "demons" and "monsters".[353]

Again, people believed this themselves. Chinese used these words in their diaries, while Chinese prisoners held by the Japanese carved inscriptions about Japanese "devils" in the prison walls.[354] U.S. soldiers regarded their Japanese enemies as monkeys, apes, rats or dogs and the Germans as vampires,[355] and British bomber crews flew their missions targeting German and other cities "against an enemy now demonized as barbaric".[356] Marnie Seymour, the wife of a scientist employed in the Manhattan Project, remembered that the Japanese "were always evil in the movies [. . .]. You start to think of them not as human beings but as little yellow things to be eradicated."[357]

---

[345] Overy, *Blood*, 605. For demonization in war propaganda in general, see Morelli, Prinzipien, 35–44.
[346] Mitter, *China's War*, 84.
[347] Edgerton-Tarpley, "From 'Nourish the People'", 462.
[348] Lowe, *Der Wilde Kontinent*, 155.
[349] Account by Pauline Kael, Terkel, *"Good War"*, 123.
[350] Overy, *Blood*, 605.
[351] Interview with Adebajo Adedeji, 6 March 2001, found on the CD United Nations Intellectual History Project, *The Complete Oral History Transcripts from* UN Voices (New York: City University of New York, 2007), 2.
[352] For example, see posters in Johannes Schlootz, ed., *Deutsche Propaganda in Weissrussland 1941–1944* (Berlin: Freie Universität Berlin, 1996).
[353] Account by Hideo Sato, Cook and Cook, *Japan*, 239. See also Dower, *War*, 68.
[354] Schoppa, *In a Sea*, 100, 309; account by Shozo Tominaga, Cook and Cook, *Japan*, 466.
[355] Dower, *War*, 67–68.
[356] Overy, *Blood*, 791.
[357] Seymour's account is in Terkel, *"Good War"*, 520.

A fight with the devil meant, of course, that God was on the Allies' side, even if they murdered hundreds of thousands of civilians. U.S. President Franklin D. Roosevelt and other elites propagated this view,[358] and one day after the dropping of the Atomic bomb on Nagasaki, Roosevelt's successor Harry Truman said in a filmed statement on August 10, 1945: "It is an awful responsibility which has come to us. We thank God that it has come to us, instead of to our enemies, and we pray that He may guide us to use it in His ways and for His purposes."[359] However, the divine being was also invoked from an unlikely side, the Soviet Union, governed by communists. What they conceptualized as the country's "Great Patriotic War" they also called a holy war, among other things, in the most popular Soviet war song.[360]

The enemies of the Allies were often dehumanized and portrayed as diabolical, their reign was called hell, they were considered fascist beasts, or, in the case of the Japanese, racially inferior, and so depicted in official documents, films, books and comics. Thus, the war was necessary and everything needed for it was justified. For enemy prisoners and civilians, this meant that they deserved punishment collectively, as it was meted out with fire bombings, killings at the front even after surrendering, hard labor, rape and expulsion. A member of the U.S. prosecution team at the Nuremberg tribunal interrogating German mass murderer Otto Ohlendorf openly stated that "people resisting your tyranny stand on a higher moral level when they resort to the same horrible cruelties which you initiated in order to destroy your tyranny" in an exchange that involved references to Allied aerial attacks.[361] But what did these justifications of mass violence against non-combatants mean for people in Allied countries, Allied colonies and neutral countries occupied by the Allies, that is, the majority of those killed by the Allies?

It is significant that Allied leaders (and many citizens) did not reserve dehumanization for the enemy. As Churchill once confided to Leopold Amery, "I hate Indians. They are a beastly people with a beastly religion."[362] Nehru's arrest, Churchill's eruption and Jiang Jieshi's reference to sacrifices mentioned in this section are all important in this context.

---

358 Morelli, *Prinzipien*, 115–116.
359 Excerpts of Truman's speech are in the 1982 documentary film *The Atomic Cafe* (directors: Kevin Lafferty et al.), min. 6:29–6:45, https://www.youtube.com/watch?v=i9xQTJ-kbUk (last accessed August 21, 2023). Also quoted in Southard, *Nagasaki*, 66.
360 See Hasselmann, *Wie der Krieg*, 170; Isabelle de Keghel, "Glaube, Schuld und Erlösung: Religion im neuen russischen Kriegsfilm", *Osteuropa* 59, 1 (2009): 99.
361 James Heath during the examination of Otto Ohlendorf, October 8–15, 1947, in: *Trials of War Criminals before the Nuremberg Military Tribunals under Control Council Law No. 10, vol. IV* (Washington: U.S. Government Printing Office, 1949), 357. See Moses, Problems, 235. Thanks to Alexa Stiller for help concerning this document.
362 Quoted in Mukerjee, *Churchill's Secret War*, 78.

Concerning Allied mass violence *not* directed at enemies but their own citizens and colonial subjects, another aspect was crucial than those emphasized so far. It was that the Allies were posing as inherently good. This was a "good war" from a U.S., Soviet, Chinese and British perspective. Seeing oneself as good was needed as a counter-image to an evil enemy, but the implications went much further. In a good and necessary war, the military effort had to be prioritized, sacrifices could be demanded from the population, and those demanded from colonial subjects, illiterate peasants and ethnic minorities were especially great. Resistance against such efforts was declared criminal, as in the British suppression of the "Quit India!" movement. To stay in power, colonialists also smeared anti-colonial movements from Algeria to Indonesia as Axis collaborators.

In African colonies, this logic of rightful sacrifice led to conditions of violence characterized by the expansion of forced labor, enlarging war-related production and services, the growth of urban places and mining towns along with a rising demand for food and other materials, higher delivery quotas for peasants, white entrepreneurs making big profits, general inflation, and labor-deprived rural families exposed to famine with little to no help (because the war effort could not be compromised). Allied policies in Asia and the Pacific were not much different, leading to the death of millions in Bengal. Probably an equal number died in the famines in China, largely caused by Guomindang policies of forced recruitment, a high tax burden, confiscating grain and tardy, small relief efforts, all in the name of the war effort, just as the Yellow River flood was.

In this section, I have argued that the main point about Allied mass violence was not their perception that the enemy was evil. One has to go beyond this fairly conventional way of thinking as the main problem was that the Allies saw themselves as 'good'. It was this what made the Allies kill the greatest number of people, and they did so by imposing conditions of violence on certain groups.

It was not that all these events were denied completely, but they were marginalized in public memory, and little research was done about most of them. Marginalization was not possible for Hiroshima and Nagasaki, which, however, was said to have saved many U.S. soldiers' lives (at the cost of Japanese civilians), a post-war propaganda line. But marginalization was possible for mass expulsions or, outside India, for the Bengal famine, and Hiroshima has been largely written out of genocide studies.[363] To be sure, initially harsh censorship applied to both, the Indian press in the Bengal famine (through the British colonial government) and Japanese publication attempts in the first years after Hiroshima

---

363 See Moses, *Problems*, 457–460.

(through the U.S. military occupation administration in Japan).[364] This is another proof that the Allies wanted to marginalize their violence in public opinion. In the longer run, creating conditions of violence allowed for obscuring Allied mass violence, while posing as good allowed for marginalizing it; so, it was not even necessary to fully deny it.

Allied and Axis rationales for violence did not differ much. Both sides claimed to fight for civilization – Japan also for anti-racism – and fostered nationalism. It was not only the USA that aspired toward a world of nominally independent nation-states (then fostered by the post 1945 United Nations) – the Soviet Union did so, too, moving to the idea of a world system of independent socialist states, instead of merely incorporating states into the USSR; and so did Japan, resulting in six states being established under its occupation: Manchuria, Nanking-China, Burma, the Philippines, India and, belatedly, Indonesia. Even Germany supported the foundation of some states (Slovakia, Croatia and Albania), although it denied other nations statehood.

To this day, scholarship still treats substantial parts of Allied war propaganda as known truths. It also still uses their euphemistic terminology (for example, 'strategic bombing'). This tendency includes emphasizing the Axis having been the aggressors. This is like a sandbox kind of argument among little boys who are dragged away from a fight by their parents: 'But he started it . . . ! (and this is supposed to justify all that happened afterwards)'. If civilians have rights, then all of them do, regardless of whether they are from an 'aggressor' nation and a different skin color. Otherwise, these are not rights but privileges.

Those who might argue that they prefer the Allies over the Axis because the former killed fewer non-combatants than the latter echo Allied propaganda that the victory of the 'good' was necessary and required sacrifices. The widespread childish desire to identify with one side can move oneself close to justifying violence.

The fact that much of the existing historiography still argues that World War II was a fight between good and evil (represented by the Allies and the Axis, respectively) is closely connected with many liberal historians' lacking or deficient discussion of the war aims of Allied countries, except based on their propagandistic self-styling. A large part of the historiography of World War II, parroting wartime propaganda narratives, is a continuation of World War II with other means and, therefore, no critical scholarship.

---

364 See Siegel, *Hungry Nation*, 28–34; Collingham, *Taste*, 149; Braw, *Atomic Bomb Suppressed*.

Conclusion

World War II was an imperialist war from all sides. It was not just a binary conflict between two alliance systems and not a mere interstate war. Rather, there were multiple identifiable conflicts between men and women; capital and labor; urban and rural dwellers; among the leading classes; and between different ethno-racial groups. In many cases, these conflicts led to lethal conditions of violence that claimed the lives of millions belonging to identifiable groups. A different history of World War II should not stop at the fatalistic view that somehow all sides have skeletons in their cupboard.

The Allied treatment of colonies (and occupied countries such as Iran) and the reasons for it were not much different from the Axis countries' treatment of occupied countries. All imperialist countries involved extracted food and other resources from them with next to no regard for the survival of the local population, and many tried to block enemy countries' access to such resources. Usually, authorities and individuals in these countries (including Japan[365]) had no elaborate plans to starve populations to death, except for Germany and, to a degree, Romania.[366] But all of them were responsible for the population under their rule and its survival. Moreover, in all cases, famine was foreseeable, and there is a great deal of evidence suggesting that it was foreseen in the political circles of the powers involved.[367] A lesser degree of intentionality does not absolve those who created conditions of violence and, thus, caused premature mass death.

Jonathan Glover rates naval blockades and the systematic bombing of civilians as "killing at a distance", combined with a "fragmentation of responsibility".[368] Both mechanisms – being preferred ways of killing by liberal countries to this day – may help historical actors obscure things, deny that they kill, or make denialist historians maintain that nobody was killing in such situations. However, such specious reasoning is belied by arguments of inevitability at the time, that is, that sacrifices were necessary and the starvation or death of certain people could not be helped, if one takes the time to look at the manifest premises made –

---

[365] For Japan, see Collingham, *Taste*, 247.
[366] See Christian Gerlach, *Krieg, Ernährung, Völkermord: Forschungen zur deutschen Vernichtungspolitik im Zweiten Weltkrieg* (Hamburg: Hamburger Edition, 1998); Gerlach, *Extermination*, 215–260.
[367] On top of the examples mentioned before, Linlithgow, the British viceroy in India, told his successor Wavell in October 1943 that he had assumed for a long time that the Bengal famine would kill at least 1.5 million people. Mukherjee, *Hungry Bengal*, 213.
[368] Glover, *Humanity*, 64–112. In particular, Glover exemplified this with the British blockade of Germany in World War I (including food) and the Allied bombing of Germany and Japan in World War II.

which are often such that the supply of this or that group or groups *had* to have priority over those who died in the end, i.e., that there were people of lesser importance.

Again, nobody would deny that Jews who starved to death in the ghettos of Warsaw and Lodz or concentration camps were victims of violence, but so were Soviet and other POWs who died in masses and rural dwellers in Bengal and Henan. Forced labor and famines in Africa were mostly forgotten and are rarely mentioned in the scholarly literature, and the Henan famine was even systematically forgotten in China for decades until the 2000s. Like the Bengal famine by the British, the Guomindang had subjected it to an early postwar whitewashing exercise by an inquiry commission, which praised the sense of sacrifice of the people of Henan.[369]

There is no such thing as considerate imperialism, or imperialism without racism and exploitation. The Allies killed at least ten million non-combatants in World War II. Assertions that the Allies mainly took the lives of enemy soldiers, instead of civilians (and thus contrary to the Axis),[370] are false and need revision. Moreover, most non-combatants killed by Allied countries were *not even from the enemy side*. They were from their *own* side, being citizens or colonial subjects (and a sizable number also from neutral countries such as Iran). As philosopher Judith Butler has argued, "war is precisely an effort to minimize precariousness for some and maximize it for others", and "contemporary conditions of war" are characterized by a sense of belonging to one population group and identifying another population group "as a direct threat to my life", which leads to them being considered as having no life at all, as "ungrievable lives".[371] These are astute thoughts that also capture a sense of resource denial, but they seem to be based on the assumption that the violence is directed against people viewed as enemies. What can they possibly mean if this is not the case? Given that the bulk of Allied violence struck people on their own side, and considering who these victims were, how can one construct the argument that Allied violence was 'good'? The imaginable point that sacrifice was necessary for the victory of freedom and civilization is peculiar if most of those who were sacrificed happened to have dark skin.

One day encapsulates the story of World War II. Three things happened on May 8, 1945. In the Allied countries, Germany's capitulation was celebrated

---

[369] See Famine Inquiry Commission, *Report on Bengal* (n.p., 1945); Knight, *Food Administration*, 104; Mukherjee, *Hungry Bengal*, 289–294; Garnaut, "Quantitative Description", 2012, 2044.
[370] A recent example of this is Hedinger, *Achse*, 361–362.
[371] Judith Butler, *Frames of War: When Is Life Grievable?* (London and New York: Verso, 2016), 54 (first quote), 42 (second and third quotes), 43 (fourth quote). In a similar vein, see also Schoppa, *In a Sea*, 5.

with great rallies and parties, as is well known. During one of these rallies in Sétif, French-Algeria, Algerian nationalists waved Algerian (rather than French) flags, protesting colonial rule, were shot at, and the ensuing violence and counter-violence left thousands dead after a few days, most of them Algerians, as some know. On the very same day – May 8, 1945 – the British colonial authorities released their inquiry commission's report on the famine in Bengal which basically cleared the British authorities of responsibility, blaming it on Indian politicians, administrators and individuals, intentionally on that day to have little publicity – as very few know.[372] Victory, colonial oppression, exploitation, famine and lies were closely related.

This means that telling a different history of World War II is necessary. The existing historiography with its mainstream narratives, points of emphasis, marginalizations and omissions reflects, at least, a racist practice. A non-racist history of this war is needed. I will not write that history. This chapter only offers a research perspective. A different history of World War II should also include social history more broadly, explore the life of ordinary people in their own right and social changes through the war, whether they were temporary or long-lasting,[373] beyond single nations. Any research – and research programs, because a collective effort is necessary – would probably have to be designed and done by researchers from other parts of the world. One way or another, scholars from there will produce studies with more precision and a more complex understanding than the cursory treatment that this chapter can provide while also correcting possible racial-ethno-cultural biases that it may still contain. In comparison with those who have created the mainstream narratives of today and those who add ever new studies confirming their audiences' expectations again, producing for a market of white people who like to believe in the old good-against-evil stories (there is much money in this), these other scholars will produce for new markets. Moreover, by overcoming the logic of the enemy prevailing among contemporaries, historians could for once actually fulfill a mission of peace.

This chapter has several wider implications. First, recent historiographical debates about the comparison and relationship between the murder of the European Jews and colonialism have mainly referred to certain episodes of colonialism. They were primarily about older phases of colonialism (in particular, settler colonialism in the 19th and early 20th centuries) and secondarily about later decol-

---

372 See Planche, *Sétif*; Mukherjee, *Hungry Bengal*, 299.
373 One example for this is Cheah Boon Kheng, *Red Star Over Malaya: Resistance and Social Conflict During and After the Japanese Occupation of Malaya, 1941–1946* (Singapore: NUS Press, 2017), fourth ed., esp. 18–56.

onization conflicts (Vietnam, Algeria and others).³⁷⁴ But those who insist that colonial violence should not be forgotten, not be placed below the 'Holocaust' in terms of importance and/or that the latter had links to the former, have, for the most part, avoided pointing to colonial mass violence that happened *simultaneously* with gas chambers and mass shootings against Jews, during World War II. Writing and talking about the 'Holocaust' in particular – but not only that – often produces legitimatory ideology for liberal imperialism. However, there is no such thing as better imperialism.

Second, this chapter allows for insights concerning the current large international conflict. It is important to understand that the deeper exploitation that was so deadly during the Second World War was a near-worldwide system run by different states of various political models. In the current international conflict, imperialists will, as is already visible, try again to ruthlessly appropriate all the world's resources, claiming that they *are* mankind. Their reckless economic warfare will again harm not only the enemy side, but anybody who stands in the way of a certain side's victory. Again, both larger sides 'justify' their acts with the fight for a new world order. But at this point, more countries have been able to stay outside the war, also economically speaking (and so far, it is primarily an economic war). It remains to be seen how far and in which ways these countries, and societies, can protect themselves against this destructive imperialism in the years to come, including against liberal imperialism.

Third, the world order after 1945 was at no point legitimate and cannot draw legitimacy from World War II. The UN's one-sided condemnation of (alleged) wars of aggression, instead of war in general, founded on Allied propaganda in World War II, is a major part of the problem.³⁷⁵ This international order has led to the most critical current international situation. A stronger interest in the so-called global south during World War II is timely in a situation when it is primarily white-dominated countries that have chosen confrontation, which creates a whole array of dangers for all of mankind, including imminent nuclear warfare.

---

374 See Rothberg, *Multidirectional Memory*, 101–107; Böckmann et al., *Jenseits*; Jürgen Zimmerer, ed., *Erinnerungskämpfe: Neues deutsches Geschichtsbewusstsein* (Ditzingen: Reclam, 2022); Neiman and Wildt, *Historiker streiten*; Friedländer et al., *"Ein Verbrechen"*.

German and Israeli views on this topic are self-serving and not very illuminating but I refer to them here because they are indicative of certain ways of thinking and because they are being aggressively exported through channels like the International Holocaust Remembrance Alliance.

375 I am grateful to Alexa Stiller for sharing her insights on this with me. Moses, *Problems*, 20 argues that the fight against alleged wars of aggression stayed the centerpiece of Euro-American imperialism "not for long" after the Nuremberg Trials. I disagree.

This chapter has depicted conditions of violence, created by a near-global system of different competing imperialist and nationalist forces, leading to millions of deaths of non-combatants in World War II. However, given its macro-perspective and the strong involvement of governments at wartime, it could do relatively little to examine how ordinary individuals contributed to producing conditions of violence. This is what I attempt to do in the next chapter.

7 COVID-19 as Mass Violence

In this chapter, I propose to regard the COVID-19 epidemic as mass violence. I hold that hundreds of thousands, or even millions, have died unnecessarily during the pandemic because many people did not care whether they infected others. And I maintain that this view adds to our understanding of certain phenomena in the pandemic, and also to our understanding of social mechanisms involved in mass violence in general, and conditions of violence in particular. At least it has made *me* understand some of these mechanisms better.

Societies, and states, have dealt with the pandemic in different ways. Close to 700 million infections and 7 million deaths were registered worldwide. It is an important question how many members a society protects to the effect that they survive. In terms of COVID-related deaths per population, Europe (including Russia), the Americas (including the Caribbean) and parts of West Asia have a notably worse record than most of Africa, the rest of Asia and Oceania, with few exceptions.[1]

The biomedical scholarship on COVID-19 is vast and cannot and need not be covered here. Few scholars of any kind regard this pandemic as violence. If they do, there are mainly two discourses. The most common among them deals with gender or family violence within families or cohabitational partnerships because of the lockdowns, isolation and psychological pressures. The other strain consists of a small number of scholars who have applied Friedrich Engels' concept of "social murder" to the pandemic.[2] These people mainly blame governments for their policies and (in)action. This means that they do think that the violence has defin-

---

[1] See the continuously updated website https://www.worldometers.info/coronavirus/ (last retrieved May 4, 2023). However, the data do not include most of the over 99 million cases and close to 121,000 deaths in the People's Republic of China, according to WHO data: https://covid19.who.int/region/wpro/country/cn (last accessed May 4, 2023). Some reports in the Chinese press suggested significantly higher numbers of cases, though not of deaths, from December 2022 to February 2023. See various issues of the *China Daily*, esp. Wang Xiaoyu, "COVID-19 infections continue to decline in China", *China Daily*, February 15, 2023, https://www.chinadaily.com.cn/a/202302/15/WS63ec667aa31057c47ebaeef1.html, for 83,150 registered COVID-19 fatalities in the PRC from December 8, 2022 to February 9, 2023. See also "Coronawelle in China mit Millionen Neuinfektionen pro Woche", *Tagesspiegel* online, May 26, 2023. For a similar picture of how different world regions fared in the pandemic, see Karl Heinz Roth, *Blinde Passagiere: Die Coronakrise und die Folgen* (Munich: Antje Kunstmann, 2022), 213. Roth's differentiated and comprehensive account of a historian who is also trained as a physician is of high quality.

[2] See Elizabeth McGibbon, "The COVID-19 Pandemic: On the Everyday Mechanisms of Social Murder", *Critical Studies* 16, 1 (2021): 35–42; Kamran Abbasi, "Covid-19: social murder, they wrote – elected, unaccountable, and unrepentant", *British Medical Journal* 372, 3/4 (2021), Febru-

able originators – which would be in line with the concept of conditions of violence – but see only a narrow circle of people to be held responsible. Others also refer to Engels but see capitalist conditions at fault, for example working conditions in the U.S. meat packing industry, and link them to racial discrimination of minorities.[3] Elizabeth McGibbon too points to oppression, racial discrimination, stereotype and prejudice (and, so, by implication, social forces) and to "social murder" being "activated in a complex and hidden process" although her main focus remains state action.[4] In that, Judith Butler's analysis of the pandemic is similar, although she does not use the concept of 'social murder' and seems to be a bit in a class of her own among scholars linking events during COVID-19 to violence.[5]

Engels himself, who did not omit the role of the state, was with his concept closer to what I call 'conditions of violence' by his emphasis on society and "conditions", his reference to the near-inescapability for the victims and the predictability of their death for others, although he differed from my concept in staying abstract about actors and describing something very long-term: "But when society places hundreds of proletarians in such a position that they inevitably meet a too early and an unnatural death, one which is quite as much a death by violence as a sword or a bullet; when it deprives thousands of the necessities of life, places them under conditions in which they cannot live – forces them under the strong arm of the law [. . .] – knows that these thousands of victims must perish, yet permits these conditions to remain, its deed is murder [. . .]."[6]

This chapter treats the pandemic as participatory violence and combines the two research perspectives of this volume, conditions of violence and mass violence as social interaction. I concentrate on social interactions constituting conditions of violence and causing deaths rather than government policies and activities. The role of governments is important, and they will appear in this chapter because of their interaction with the population, but their role has already received more public attention than social actors, as usual, and for good reasons this book's focus is not on governments or state machineries.

---

ary 4, 2021, http://dx.doi.org/10.1136/bmj.n314; Joe Sim and Steve Tombs, "The failings behind the UK's abysmal death toll", letter to the editor, *The Guardian* online, January 27, 2021.
3 M. R. Greene-May [i.e., Ronald Walter Greene], "Living and Dying in the Age of COVID-19: Social Murder, Reproduction, and Rhetoric", *Cultural Critique* 120 (2023): 126–141.
4 McGibbon, "COVID-19 Pandemic", 35 (quote), 37.
5 Judith Butler, *What World Is This? A Pandemic Phenomenology* (New York: Columbia University Press, 2022).
6 Friedrich Engels, *The condition of the working class in England in 1844* (New York: Penguin, 2009 (first 1845)), quoted in McGibbon, "COVID-19 Pandemic", 35–36.

It is a truism that epidemics are about social interaction, but this pandemic is a reminder of the ways how many waves in epidemics come about: we are the wave, i.e., waves are caused by the interplay between social discipline (in part enforced by official measures) and the lack thereof (in part also facilitated by official measures) and by a myriad of individual acts.[7] It is necessary to ask who are the driving forces of the violence, how does the system function through which it works, and which people become endangered through this process.

There are special problems with the methodology here. The fact that the pandemic is a recent, arguably even ongoing, event (or process) implies that most official records about it are not yet accessible, that there is no established body of scholarship in the social sciences or at least a lack of systematic research, that maintaining an emotional distance to the topic under study is hard and making historical judgments is difficult. Moreover, the pandemic is a very controversial topic, and because, as I will try to show, the violence I describe is hegemonic in many societies, this author cannot rely on protection by courts and, thus, must discuss many things on a general level and in an anonymized manner. I will often refer to general knowledge about the pandemic and in addition draw on my experience as an eyewitness, which is highly problematic for a historian. My role as an eyewitness can be taken as the ultimate consequence of a book that heavily relies on accounts of people who lived through violence.

In this chapter, I first describe the violent practices in the pandemic and then the rationales for such action and denial of violence. This is followed by considerations about the role of states and courts, the influence of capitalism and contexts of (if not motives for) violence. Finally, I add some reflections on my personal experience during the pandemic and on European perceptions of it.

Violent Practices

The pandemic created a difficult situation for everybody, and many infections were inevitable. People had to work for a living, had to get to work by some means of transportation and had to go shopping for groceries and other essential goods in stores or at the market. Some essential services – medical, in nursing, teaching, public transportation and others – did necessitate close social contact. Workplaces needed reorganization to lower the infection risk, which was a prob-

---

7 See Sascha Karberg and Deike Diening, "Christian Drosten im Interview: 'Wir alle sind die Welle'", *Tagesspiegel* online, September 22, 2020 and, much more pronounced, Caroline Fetscher, "Wir sind die Kurve! Sich immer noch privat zu treffen, ist gefährlich egoistisch", *Tagesspiegel* online, April 4, 2021 (both retrieved on February 21, 2022).

lem for companies and public offices, and many workers were at risk for a long time. People living in crowded conditions in small apartments or other dwellings without their own gardens did need to get out into public spaces for recreation, which was sometimes outlawed. Families were another forum where many infections could not be avoided. Consequently, the most tragic situations ensued. None of this is what I call violent behavior.

But the fact remains that a large part of European societies did not care at all whether they infected others with a potentially deadly disease. One could expect that people would do a bit more than necessary to protect others, without holding any grudges about it, but this was often not the case. Even during high tides of the epidemic, 80 percent of the people who I saw kept no distance from others, whether strangers or acquaintances. Very many did not wear facemasks or did not cover their nose with them. Many refused to get vaccinated. Big and loud parties were organized. Scores of people *had* to go to bars and restaurants. Many went on leisure trips, also abroad, even during times when deaths from the virus were at their peak. At the same time, there were numerous hiking groups of people (often elderly) crowding together without facemasks. People went on shopping sprees as long as the stores were open, and as soon as they re-opened. All of these practices I call violent because they helped unnecessarily spread infections, always with the possibility that the virus would be passed on to vulnerable people. They added up to killing hundreds of thousands at least.

Then, there were the sucklers: people on the train who *had* to sip twenty times from their cup or bottle during a twenty-minute train ride and, therefore, wearing no facemasks. And there were those who reacted to, say, somebody wearing a facemask indoors by saying, "is it mandatory?" Even if such a person said this in a slight shock, it was still revealing that they would only – at best – follow instructions but not take their own measures. The main thing was to have fun, make profits, and not suffer any inconvenience.

Such behaviors were ways of expression of people for whom the most important thing was their personal freedom and interests. Individualism was looming large behind these actions. Large parts of the societies I saw are made up by 'Me-Me-Me' people for whom it seems to be difficult to think of anybody else and anything other than themselves. For them, wearing a facemask was an unbearable burden. (Infecting and killing other people was no unbearable burden.) Characteristically, the Austrian physician Peer Eifler issued certificates for hundreds of persons in 2020 to allow exemptions from wearing a facemask because it was "for medical reasons contraindicated, scientifically proven harmful to health and in terms of psychohygiene traumatizing and therefore unacceptable".[8] A court stripped Eifler of his approbation, but his rationale was that a facemask was a violation of any person's personal integrity, including mentally. This view was shared by many. The argument that the pandemic provided gateways for cyber control over individuals and their data[9] is a variation of the bourgeois freedom discourse.

The virus was also spread through exploitative, irresponsible practices in companies. This highlighted the state of global capitalism and exacerbated its 'normal' state, in which, according to Marx, "property is [. . .] also a kind of violence" if, as capital, it has dependent labor at its disposal.[10] There were firms where workers were forced to get into close contact, for example, in the Central European meat industry. Other examples could be cited. In some businesses, lowly paid workers employed under discriminatory terms were forced to live in crowded conditions in dormitories and similar dwellings where infections spread like wildfire. Often, they were migrant laborers – people from Eastern Europe in German agriculture, from Southeastern Europe or Africa in various economic sectors in Italy, South Asians in the boom state monarchies at the Persian Gulf, and South and Southeast Asians in Singapore or Malaysia.[11] Charmingly, for some time the daily "Straits Times" in Singapore distinguished between COVID-19 cases 'outside the community' (migrant workers) and 'within the community', initially noting with satisfaction that the number of the latter was low. As late as in March 2022, the government kept quotas for migrant workers residing in dorms in place to "visit the community" (i.e., Singaporeans).[12] The attempt at this segregation, which in Singapore would not be called racist, contributed to killing many Singaporean citizens because the dorms where many foreign workers were and are being housed in crowded conditions were first

---

8 Quoted in Tom Felber, "Maskenverweigerer halten die Richter auf Trab", *Neue Zürcher Zeitung*, January 31, 2022, 12.
9 See, for example, Andrea Komlosy, *Zeitenwende: Corona, Big Data und die kybernetische Zukunft* (Vienna: Promedia, 2022), esp. 10, 155, 222–240.
10 Quoted in Kurt Röttgers, "Andeutungen zu einer Geschichte des Redens über die Gewalt", in Otthein Rammstedt, ed., *Gewaltverhältnisse und die Ohnmacht der Kritik* (Frankfurt a.M.: Suhrkamp, 1974), 189 (my translation from German, "Das Eigentum ist jedenfalls auch eine Art Gewalt").
11 It should be added that the death figure in the Persian Gulf monarchies and Singapore remained low. This had to do with the fact that many migrant workers were young people, who coped better than others with the disease, but also with the high quality of medical services – also for migrants. In the monarchies at the Persian Gulf, it was many South Asian doctors and nurses who saved the lives of South Asian patients.
12 15,000 such workers were from then on permitted to "visit the community" on weekdays, compared to 3,000 before. "Covid-19 rules, community visit limits to be eased for migrant workers in dorms", *Straits Times*, March 11, 2022, https://www.straitstimes.com/singapore/covid-19-safety-measures-community-visits-for-migrant-workers-living-in-dorms (retrieved June 24, 2022).

excluded from some preventive measures and COVID-19 eventually leaped from there to the rest of the population.[13]

More cases can be mentioned of people creating conditions of violence for others, which endangered their lives as well as that of others. There were retirement homes where staff were instructed not to wear facemasks. In one Central European skiing resort, owners ignored the knowledge of many infections to continue making profits, thereby spreading the virus to northern Europe, among other areas. I heard from hotel staff in a holiday resort that they had been angrily urged by guests not to wear a facemask after the state had declared it was no longer mandatory as the sight probably inconvenienced them. Pharmaceutical companies from capitalist industrial countries made big profits and often denied non-industrialized countries deliveries, and these corporations had governments on their behalf veto the lifting of patent rights for vaccines. This is irreconcilable with the assumption that these firms' priority is saving lives.

Direct violence happened as well, but it has to be put into perspective. Compared with the millions who were unnecessarily infected with the Corona virus, and the many who died from it, the number of people beaten up or killed because they defended restrictive regulations was small (whether this was a bus conductor in France, a police guard in China or a shop assistant in Germany), and just a few public offices were attacked or torched. But these acts, and especially violent demonstrations, were important to intimidate others who supported responsible ways of action and, thus, attempts to establish a violent order. These acts were done openly, in public, because the murderers wanted to occupy and dominate the public space, as is done in many cases of mass violence.[14] As part of this, such direct killings found many supporters on the internet.[15] Individual acts of direct violence were mostly committed for one specific reason: when people (often men) were called upon wearing a facemask. No other issue triggered so much aggression, at least in Europe.

According to my observations, many people did not keep their distance, did not wear a facemask and joined groups and crowds without protection, regardless of whether they were men or women, young or old, of local or migrant background, resident or tourist, regardless also of their social class and level of education, as far as this was discernible. This distribution across social groups is remarkable even though the people that I saw may not have been representative

---

13 Roth, *Blinde Passagiere*, 97.
14 See also chapter 2 on Rwanda in this volume.
15 For example, see Sebastian Leber, "Nach Streit um Maskenpflicht: Rechte jubeln über Mord in Idar-Oberstein", *Tagesspiegel* online, September 21, 2021.

of society as a whole because they were the ones who went out into the public instead of staying away.

Karl Heinz Roth argues that these were small minorities (perhaps 20 percent of people) and that private precautions – wearing a facemask, refraining from hugs and handshakes, using disinfection, reducing traveling and contacts and avoiding going to events and restaurants – did more than public measures such as lockdowns and vaccinations to contain the disease and its effects. Of course, the impact of these precautions was very important, but he presents little evidence for his quantitative assessment.[16] I do not share my esteemed colleague's optimistic judgment, which is difficult to reconcile with my observations. If people showing careless behavior came from all walks of life in substantial numbers, this rather suggests that this was a mass phenomenon, encompassing more than a small minority. Some hints exist that indeed great numbers of people showed such a demeanor.[17]

The role of aggressive women is remarkable here. In virtually all other cases of mass violence that I have studied, men formed the vast majority of people committing violence, planning, organizing and justifying it. It was different during this epidemic. One reason for this was that the violence in the epidemic was indirect and concealed. However, countless women not only refused to protect others through their behavior as many men did, but many women were also active in – occasionally violent – protests against measures such as vaccinations, certificate requirements (related to vaccinations, recovery or COVID-19 tests) and regulations that prescribed wearing facemasks. When it became mandatory in one European country to wear a facemask in all stores and businesses that were open to customers, a network of thousands of business owners quickly emerged who vowed to violate this restriction, which was by a majority in the cosmetics, beauty and health product sectors, and obviously female-run. Andrea Komlosy has suggested that female opposition to COVID-19-related restrictions (which she sympathized with) may have to do with feminist ideas, including about priority of female control over their own body concerning pregnancy.[18] I should add that on the rare occasion that I had to stand indoors in a queue of about 100 people, the only three persons not to wear their facemask properly were muscular men who

---

16 Roth, *Blinde Passagiere*, 288–289, 399–400. Roth points to additional data but many of the studies cited are from institutions or authors with close relations to industry and thus suspicious of rejecting restrictions on business and events and of constructing evidence accordingly (ibid., 307–310). For practices of solidarity in terms of aid, charity and relief, see Marina Sitrin and Colectiva Sembrar, Pandemic Solidarity: Mutual Aid During the Covid-19 Crisis (London: Pluto, 2020).
17 For some evidence from Italy and Britain, see Noel Chellan, *F/Ailing Capitalism and the Challenge of COVID-19* (Boston: Brill, 2023), 104, 110.
18 Komlosy, *Zeitenwende*, in particular 224.

stood taller than 1.85 meters. But for all that I know, this was atypical. Usually, fewer people than seen in that queue showed such discipline, and women were as often participants in the violence as men actively, publicly, and unashamed.

Let me add that not everybody joined in these violent practices. This too was visible. Almost all students in my university courses acted responsibly. In the streets and parks, I saw young people meeting outside for (more or less) parties and drinking together, seeking ways to have fun without becoming a risk to others if they would meet in bars and clubs. There are some indicators that this, too, was a mass phenomenon.[19] There were vulnerable people who sealed themselves off from many social contacts, and some did it to protect close relatives who belonged to risk groups, while others who were in the position to do so moved to the countryside, including young families. All of this was encouraging. But I do not remember having seen any instance in which people acting responsibly confronted people who did not.

Denial of Violence, Rationales for Violence

There were myriads of justifications for the violence of carelessly infecting other people with the COVID-19 virus. These justifications were similar to genocide denial: the virus does not exist; it exists but is not lethal; or fatalities by the virus are just natural deaths.[20] For any of these reasons, the deniers found media warnings about the virus hysterical.

Like many 20th century mass murders, the spread of the COVID-19 virus was based on a complex division of labor, and, to a large extent, it worked in anonymous ways. Most people did not see the corpse they helped produce. Surveys in Central Europe found that in 40 to 50 percent of all cases, the source of the infection was not clear or not specified, according to the statements of those infected. Only 20 or 30 percent of transmissions occurred within families, and these reportings were likely to be accurate. Infections in public transport and restaurants, among others, were obviously understated.[21] Thus, those who infected others

---

[19] Fabian Baumgärtner and Nils Pfändler, "Der Gastro-Albtraum: Die Omikron-Welle zwingt Zürcher Restaurants und Klubs zu Schliessungen", *Neue Zürcher Zeitung,* January 14, 2022, https://www.nzz.ch/zuerich/corona-in-zuerich-clubs-und-restaurant-verlieren-sehr-viel-geld-ld.1664508 (retrieved April 12, 2023).

[20] Two other variants were the pseudo-argument that most people died with the virus, but not from it, and that many elderly victims would have died soon anyway.

[21] For one example, Andri Rostetter et al., "Jeder Fünfte steckt sich zu Hause an: Entscheidende Daten zu Infektionsketten fehlen", *Neue Zürcher Zeitung,* December 11, 2020: 1.

would almost invariably state that they did not kill anybody, an argument that scholars of mass violence know so well.

Like in other acts of mass violence, those who suffered and died were also regarded or portrayed as a dangerous threat. In the case of COVID-19, this argument was framed in a special manner: the victims seemed to threaten people's freedom and lifestyle. One journalist, who called those who acted responsibly "denouncers", argued that "Corona threatens Dionysian culture", making a positive reference to Friedrich Nietzsche.[22] Opponents of vaccinations, certificates and other measures presented themselves as victims, mostly victims of 'restrictions'. Many of them argued that they were threatened by genocide, as so many genocidaires in history have done. If one followed their line of argument, people vulnerable to the disease were unworthy of protection and, by default, of living.

One could expect that those who refused to get vaccinated at the time on the grounds that it did not prevent them from getting infected and infective (and those who use this argument in retrospect) used double caution in other ways not to infect others, but, generally, the contrary was the case. Those who rejected vaccinations often also rejected facemasks. This shows that they used this kind of argument not out of concern for their fellow humans.

In order to avoid further infections, those who caught the disease were at least isolated from society, if not externalized like so many victims of mass murder. Relatives and friends were not allowed to visit them in hospitals, and in some places and phases, even funeral ceremonies were prohibited. Close relatives were thrown into despair because they could not help their dying parents or spouses or say goodbye to them, but society as a whole showed a remarkable lack of consternation about the mass death. The lack of empathy with the victims, the easy acceptance of their death and a matter-of-fact kind of attitude toward them are also typical of mass violence.

Especially noteworthy were the murderers of the 'I-want-my-life-back' variety. They wanted to maintain their high quality of life. This was a special case of quality trumps quantity: the one side won back, or defended, a free life, while the number of lives of vulnerable people was reduced. The former were celebrating freedom days on the bones of their dead compatriots.[23]

This is what most of the arguments of the deniers and justifiers of violence boiled down to: freedom. This was so obvious that it does not need much elabora-

---

[22] Christian Saehrendt, "Corona bedroht die dionysische Kultur", *Neue Zürcher Zeitung*, January 13, 2022: 29.
[23] A similar reading is in Butler, *What World*, 47, 108. For the British example, see also Miray Caliscan, "Heute vor 2 Jahren: Als England beschloss, mit dem Coronavirus zu leben", *Tagesspiegel* online, July 19, 2023.

tion here. Letters to newspaper editors, blogs and other internet utterances were full of it. At their core, this is also what most political demonstrations against epidemic protection measures were about: the demonstrators said, or shouted, that they were defending their personal freedom.[24] Andrea Komlosy joined others in their rejection of mandatory protection measures against COVID-19 because it "prioritized life over human dignity" but 'forgot' to mention that this was about preserving ones *own* dignity by taking the life of *others*.[25] Many people wanted this personal freedom unconditionally, at the cost of others, regardless of the deaths it could cause.

As 'freedom' and individualism were so important for the violators of, and objectors to, protective restrictions, they rarely made reference to religious motivations (including when rejecting vaccination, which has historically sometimes been done on religious grounds). Religious festivals in India and church services in the USA contributed to spreading the disease in the early stages of the epidemic but this ebbed away. Funerals were a private concern but not a major point of contention in a collective sense. Infecting others was mostly justified with secular arguments.

Others have, to some degree, made similar points. Criticizing fanatics of freedom who went to beaches, barbecues and other gatherings for leisure, the South African Noel Chellan spoke of those who felt "free to infect others in society", linking their claim to the spirit of capitalism. In reference to India, he also saw this in a connection with the freedom of religion and the mass infections caused by Hinduist mass events.[26] More clearly, Judith Butler referred to those who insisted on their "right to get sick and make others sick, the right to spread death if that is one's wish, if spreading death is the expression of personal liberty", understood also as "furthering consumption and pleasure for the individual".[27]

But one needs to go a step further, as this point is of broader importance. The freedom to kill is an important political right and a basic one. The one who can exert the right to kill with impunity *is* somebody, politically speaking; "destruction is the sign of personal power, if not liberty", according to Butler.[28] I differ from her point where she links this to "rage" and then calls this rage and this understanding of liberty to be possibly in its "last gasps" before giving way to a

---

24 See also Chellan, *F/Ailing Capitalism*, 93–96.
25 The quote is in Komlosy, *Zeitenwende*, 224 ("Priorisierung des Lebens gegenüber der Würde des Menschen"), in positive reference to Ulrike Guerot.
26 Chellan, *F/Ailing Capitalism*, 93–95, quote 94.
27 Butler, *What World*, 108.
28 Butler, *What World*, 108.

solidary society and world.²⁹ This has a connection to her frequent, illusory and misleading use of the word "we" in her book about the pandemic.³⁰

By contrast, I am afraid that this reckless use of freedom will not be a thing of the past anytime soon. It is at the core of the capitalist order and a centerpiece of bourgeois ideology, and it is hard to see how it will go away as long as this order prevails. The pandemic was a time of self-empowerment like in other cases of mass violence, such as when Hutu nationalists went on killing sprees in Rwanda, during the mass murders of Jews and Armenians, and during crowd violence in Bangladesh in 1971–1972.³¹ The fact that the freedom to kill is a major political right also helps explain why so many women participated in this violence (and have played major roles in the current global conflict). This is because they claim equal political rights and a fair share of power.

It is no accident that the USA are the country where the highest number of people died from COVID-19. The right to kill is deeply enshrined there, which is illustrated by their gun laws. In the USA, owning a gun is a constitutional right, and in many U.S. states, citizens have far-reaching rights to use their guns against other people even in public spaces. The right to kill is an important part of their national identity and a marker of full citizenship. In practice, the admissable use of guns in the USA is highly racialized; it is mostly whites who get away with using them against people with darker skin. In the USA, the Second Amendment to the Constitution (the right to bear arms) was first introduced for killing indigenous people and later extensively used against runaway slaves. That country is built on mass violence. The existence of the USA would be unthinkable without the past murder of other peoples and taking their land, and in addition the country was built on slavery.

I must admit that I had neglected the importance of the right to kill for mass murder in general before living through this pandemic and thinking about it. It was also important in the murder of the European Jews, the destruction of Ottoman Armenians and the mass killings and destruction in the Soviet Union in the 1930s to 1950s, among others. Without being able to show all of its implications here, I should note that people claiming this right think that they do justice, or no injustice. Often, they defend a legal (often a colonial racist) order by exerting the right to kill; alternatively, they exert it for challenging, in the name of a majority, elites that are seen as acting unfairly; or they attack foreign rule. This also explains the "unshakable feeling of entitlement" felt by violent people in East

---

29 Butler, *What World*, 108–109, quotes 108.
30 Butler, *What World*. See ibid., 80 for a weak justification of this use of "we".
31 See chapters 2 and 4 in this volume.

Pakistan 1971–1972, regardless of whether they were pro-Bangladesh or pro-Pakistan.³² As in that case, the freedom to kill is often claimed as a political right in times of emergency during transitions from one order to another, or during wars.

In addition, the aggressors during the pandemic appeared so cool (and giving themselves airs of being individualistic was part of their coolness). Their hegemony was in part also produced on an aesthetic level. To wear a facemask was decidedly uncool; also therefore, coolly, those who refused to wear it let others die for their pleasure. I do not think that they did it with 'rage'.

This, too, can be related to other cases of mass violence. Some have already pointed to murderers' coolness, for example, in the Soviet war film "Come and See", which depicts German killers murdering Soviet civilians during 'anti-partisan warfare,' or one can point to photographs of U.S. soldiers in Vietnam.³³ Reflecting on his own deeds in Japanese-occupied China, Shōichi Kawano wrote about the soldier in war: "Without hesitation he kills women and children who implore him crying and with folded hands to spare them. And he does so coolly and with a triumphant face."³⁴ Further research on, for example, the dressing style and bodily poses of persecutors would probably lead to revealing results.³⁵

In the Corona crisis, those who did not join in the violence and objected were called too afraid, hysteric, party crashers,³⁶ misanthropists, or full of (inappropriate) distrust. These were strategies to delegitimize the objectors and deviants by shaming practices that were crucial to establish and then solidify the hegemony of violence. Low-threshold forms of such shaming included pitiful glances when some saw a minority still wearing a facemask, accompanied by questions like, 'Are you afraid?' With such remarks, their originators showed that they felt superior and looked down on others, including bystanders.

Of course, to deflect criticism, the usual suspects were also blamed: communists and Jews. According to one narrative, the virus leaked out from a Chinese epidemiological research laboratory in Wuhan, which triggered the epidemic. Accusers either charged that this had happened because of illicit research (possibly for biological weapons), because of an irresponsible cover-up of the outbreak by

---

32 See chapter 4, p. 108 in this volume.
33 See chapter 5 (on Soviet war movies) in this volume.
34 Account by Shōichi Kawano in Siegfried Schaarschmidt, ed., *Schrei nach Frieden: Japanische Zeugnisse gegen den Krieg* (Düsseldorf and Vienna: Econ, 1984), 75.
35 A recent attempt to interpret poses of a German-Austrian deporter of Jews from Vienna on photographs is in Markus Brosch, *Zur Geschichte einer Wiener Institution: Das Sammellager an der Kleinen Sperlgasse*, Ph.D dissertation, University of Vienna, 2021, 215–239.
36 In German, an equivalent term is 'Spassbremse' (literally, a brake on fun).

Chinese authorities,[37] or because the Chinese state wanted to undermine 'Western' societies by distributing the virus. Another story goes that the virus is either a scam (i.e., it does not exist), or that it was intentionally distributed, by conspiring shady and powerful capitalists in the IT and finance sectors, such as Bill Gates and George Soros, and Jews in general, to get control over people either by injecting unknown substances into their bodies during vaccination or by close supervision of their movements and activities through measures restricting the spread of the epidemic.

In some English-speaking countries, there have been some who refer to those refusing to take measures to protect others from being infected as 'covidiots'.[38] This is misleading. The murderers were not thoughtless. On the contrary, many people were exasperated by the amount of online texts by opponents of COVID-related restrictions. The experience from this pandemic shows how much reasoning, how many thoughts, how many rationales existed in the media, on the internet, in the streets and in private conversations to justify behavior resisting protecting others. The many arguments that erupted among families, friends, colleagues and neighbors point in the same direction (while simultaneously showing that many people did care not to infect others). If I have learned one thing in my thirty years of researching mass violence, it is this: never call the perpetrators mere idiots. Not only because it belittles what they do, but also because they do reflect on their actions.

And the denial and the rationales were successful in the case of the pandemic. They were crucial in facilitating deaths. Like other cases of mass violence, this one happened because it was socially widely accepted. Was it such a big deal that this or that person did not cover his or her nose with a facemask? Was it really necessary to check the certificate? In Switzerland, authorities observed that the number of people reported as contacts of newly infected people to the COVID tracing service was minimal. Obviously, people wanted to spare friends and relatives from the hassle of being quarantined. This was a mass phenomenon, one that caused deaths.

---

37 A relatively balanced account is Roth, *Blinde Passagiere*, 35–38. To those using this 'China virus' argument, it did not matter that later outbreaks of the disease were denied or belittled by politicians and authorities in many other countries in the early phase of the pandemic, as it had happened in the PRC, nor did the fact matter that the transnational spread of such a contagious virus could hardly be prevented in any case.
38 In German-speaking countries, an equivalent term was used ('Covidioten').

Complicit Politicians and States

Some will say that it cannot be true that killing was involved in the COVID-19 pandemic because in many affected countries there is democracy and a rule of law. Therefore, I present a few thoughts about the role of the state, politicians and courts.

Everybody knows about the policies of the Trumps, the Bolsonaros, the Lukashenkos and the Magafulis during the pandemic and how they belittled the virus, refused to take measures against it, delayed or obstructed such measures (except for xenophobic responses), disseminated obvious falsehoods and encouraged the irresponsible parts of society. By mentioning these names, I do not want to exaggerate individuals' influence on the course of history; instead, I am suggesting that they embody a whole range of political figures acting in similar ways, in their countries and others. And even in their countries, there were notable successes in the fight for lives and against the dissemination of the disease: many regions in Brazil have great achievements in terms of vaccinating the vast majority of people, and registered deaths from the virus per population in Belarus have been much lower than in most other European countries at the time of this writing. This points to the existence of conflicts between different population groups in these countries as well as between different elite groups.

Everybody knows that many governments were slow and hesitant to respond to the threat of the Corona virus and that many shied away from enacting restrictions because they were afraid of their citizens. Further, it is well-known that many governments judged the situation not by how many people died from COVID-19 but by whether hospitals' intensive care units were overwhelmed or not. This points to a management-oriented approach that showed little concern for saving lives, and there was much politics involved in state responses. This managerial attitude also explains governments' strong emphasis on vaccinations which, rather than protecting people from infections, served to greatly reduce the risk of a severe course of the disease for those vaccinated and, thus, hospitals from overflowing with patients.

The spread of the epidemic and many deaths were also caused by dysfunctional institutions, badly equipped hospitals with underpaid staff to facilitate profitmaking or reducing the costs of public health, underfunded and inapt health offices, useless pre-existing plans for the control of epidemics, useless websites and web applications – for example, in the country where I live, which boasts of being technically advanced, looking so much down on others. Unreachable phone numbers and incapable bureaucrats were also part of the story. Additionally, many official regulations were full of loopholes, and intentionally so.

The official lack of transparency added to the calamity. In a lecture on the contemporary history of South Asia in the spring of 2020, I shocked my students in Bern by pointing them to the fact that I could track in the Indian media the daily development of the COVID-19 epidemic in Asia's supposedly biggest slum – Dharavi in Mumbai – but not in my town of residence in Switzerland (which is sizable enough to have its own daily newspaper). Evidently, the authorites made much greater efforts to contain the disease in the former place than in the latter.[39]

However, Dharavi was a place where the state concentrated its resources (unlike elsewhere in India, and even in the city of Mumbai, for that matter). More generally, governments' influence during the pandemic was low. If the pandemic showed one thing, then it is that governments were incapable of exercising tight control over their population. States – whether 'democracies' or dictatorships – depend on large population groups, even if these are ready to use violence. Officials were also under direct pressure; for example, in a 2021 survey, 20 percent of German communal civil servants and 11 percent of the mayors reported having been physically attacked in office, with the requirement to wear a facemask being the biggest source of aggression.[40] In Europe, Latin America, the USA and West Asia, where so many died of the disease, many local and national governments suffered from an obvious lack of legitimacy in the view of large sections of the populace, which has also been highlighted by decreasing voting turnouts in recent years.

Mass murder is the crime that goes unpunished. There has not been a single case of mass violence in the 20th century or afterwards, after which the majority of perpetrators and organizers were sentenced by courts. The COVID-19 pandemic is no exception. In many countries, such as Vietnam, Ghana, Germany and Austria, spreading a dangerous disease is a punishable offense.[41] In some countries, this is theoretically assessed as causing serious bodily harm, which could lead to imprisonment. But it has been very rare that people are actually put on trial for that, as it was sometimes done for spreading HIV in earlier times. In German law, there is the concept of conditional intent, but to my knowledge, it has not been

---

[39] For Dharavi, see also Natalie Mayroth, "'Virus unter Kontrolle', meldet ausgerechnet Indiens grösster Slum", *Neue Zürcher Zeitung*, July 6, 2020: 4.
[40] Fabian Löhe, "Durchsetzung der Maskenpflicht: Kommunalpolitiker immer öfter beleidigt, bespuckt, geschlagen", *Tagesspiegel* online, April 27, 2021.
[41] See Lisa Breuer, "Gefängnis, Liegestütze oder Probeliegen im Sarg: Das sind die skurrilsten Strafen für Regelbrecher in der Corona-Pandemie", *Tagesspiegel* online, September 7, 2021; for Austria, see "Nach Tod des Nachbarn: Ermittlungen nach mutmasslichem Verstoss gegen Corona-Quarantänepflicht", *Der Spiegel* online, February 8, 2022.

used in this case. Internationally, courts leave the vast majority of willful or grossly negligent spreaders of COVID-19 alone, and they would not have the power to do otherwise – even if they wanted – because the violence is socially hegemonic.

This social hegemony is also the reason why I cannot say many things here in more detail. Courts will hardly prosecute people who spread the virus willfully and negligently, but I am convinced that they would protect the former's interests in a libel suit.

COVID-19 and Capitalism

In most countries, the pandemic happened under capitalist conditions. The violent behavior during the COVID-19 pandemic was shaped by capitalism, which influenced conditions and ways of life in a general sense. This is true for hyperindividualism and the problems with bourgeois democracy. It is also true for the roots of the claim to the 'right to kill' in that bourgeois order.

I have already mentioned some extremes of doing business during the pandemic and their consequences, but the problems with the capitalist system were not only about a few excesses. Of course, the fight against the pandemic was, for the most part, going on in a capitalistic system, and, in many cases, in oligopolistic capitalism at that. Therefore, it is not surprising that capitalist enterprises attempted to make profits and expand their business in sectors like digital communication, biotech, online trade and surveillance technology. This was inevitable unless one argues for the overthrow of capitalism, which, however, not all of the critics of the pandemic business do.[42] Big pharma made huge profits, often publically financed, during the pandemic, although some firms were more successful than others in getting support. Corruption was obvious and sometimes charged by courts.

IT and biotech are lead sectors in the economy of the current Kondratieff cycle, and some speculate that they may have received a new technological impulse for further innovation and growth in the pandemic.[43] Other capital groups (representative of older industries) were championing the lifting of restrictions, with variable influence on governments but certainly not a negligible one. Without a doubt, arguments to 'save the economy' had a major impact.

---

42 For example, see Komlosy, *Zeitenwende*, esp. 8.
43 See Komlosy, *Zeitenwende*.

But the hyperindividualism that I mentioned before does not prevail everywhere where there is capitalism, which is also indicated by the statistics about COVID-related fatalities. In other words, liberal capitalism and the societies it shapes are especially grave problems, which do not prevail in Subsaharan Africa and South and Southeast Asia.[44]

However, the employment conditions of workers hardly changed through the pandemic. Nurses usually continue to be underpaid despite verbal lip service in honor of them; conditions for agricultural laborers or workers in the meat industry have not improved; and foreign workers in the Persian Gulf region and Southeast Asia are mostly working in the same way as they were before 2019. The ones who could arguably improve their condition as a result of the pandemic were office workers who gained more chances for home office activities.[45]

For some time, countries with many migrant workers abroad (many of whom were sent home) and/or depending on international tourism (which dried out temporarily) were thrown into a crisis, but it rarely had a lasting effect as in Sri Lanka. In that sense, COVID-19 brought little systemic change, although it put a heavy economic burden on many families. On another level, it probably contributed to some capital concentration.

Contexts

It is difficult to speak about motivations for violence during the COVID-19 pandemic because this violence was so obscure and the damage so collateral. However, I think it is possible and necessary to place it in some contexts, namely, generational conflicts and gender conflicts.

Most of those who died of COVID-19 were elderly people, and two-thirds of the dead were men. Some analysts have stressed the fact that authorities left people in retirement homes and nursing homes unprotected and deaths in such institutions represented a large part of COVID-19 fatalities in countries such as Canada, Belgium, Italy and Germany.[46] Repeatedly, old people were rejected in

---

[44] For the reasons why I consider conditions in Subsaharan Africa, South and Southeast Asia capitalistic, but not liberal capitalistic, see Christian Gerlach, *How the World Hunger Problem Was Not Solved* (London: Routledge, 2024).
[45] The pros and cons of home office are under debate, and more time must pass for a conclusive picture, but many office workers do consider it an improvement.
[46] See Roth, *Blinde Passagiere*, 205, 292. Roth cites Japan as a positive exception among industrialized nations (318).

hospitals or sent back from there to retirement homes to brighten up these hospitals' statistics.⁴⁷

The role of old people in industrial societies is contested. They – especially men – are said to have immense power, as part of the electorate and as dominant part of elites. But in increasing numbers, they are also sent off, or retreat by themselves, to retirement institutions in relative isolation from family and larger society, instead of living with their descendants as was often done in earlier times. One of the biggest long-term problems in European capitalist societies is the funding of retirement insurance. In this situation, weak measures to protect old people against early death are noteworthy, although it should be added that the percentage of the entire generation of the elderly who died from COVID-19 was so low that it did not have a large impact on pension insurance funds and it is most unlikely that governments or big business had plans to weed out the elderly.⁴⁸ However, in a sense, deaths in retirement homes were perfect deaths at the time from a government's point of view as they caused little cost in terms of public money and did not crowd hospitals. At least as important is the economization of retirement homes in industrial societies since the 1990s, which became subject to investment by profit-seekers and shareholders, and the resulting cheap solutions (also fueled by families having problems paying for a place in a higher-quality home), low pay for and, often, low qualification and motivation of their staff created relative neglect and, thus, deadly conditions in the decisive months.⁴⁹ This is in contrast with societies like those in South Asia where care for the elderly is rarely institutionally outsourced, few retirement homes exist, and most old people stay with the family, usually with that of the oldest son (in this context, this was, or is, a superior form of social organization); but it matches Christoph Keller's point that, for example, Swiss society considered the "weakest" as "useless" and expendable, sacrificing them in the name of profit.⁵⁰

Furthermore, inheritance is an important way to transfer wealth, and, in some countries (with low home ownership rates), it is currently the only way through which young families can hope to afford their own house. Men in particular leave much wealth to their descendants. I am not saying that people intentionally infected their relatives to acquire their assets, but a general atmosphere

---

47 Roth, *Blinde Passagiere*, 344–345.
48 It is remarkable that in East Asian countries where the retirement of many old people is also a big financial problem, like China and Japan, old people were comparatively well protected against the epidemic.
49 See Roth, *Blinde Passagiere*, 319–320, 329–330, 346–347.
50 Christoph Keller, "Das ist Sozialdarwinismus nach Schweizer Art", *Neue Zürcher Zeitung am Sonntag*, January 16, 2022: 17.

characterized by a lack of concern about the danger that old people were in may have influenced their fate. And I see few indications that families took close relatives out of retirement homes – which were dangerous places during the epidemic – to protect them. That said, the lack of sympathy caused by the death of old people is a phenomenon also observed in other cases of mass violence.[51] More research about this topic as a whole is necessary.

The majority of those who died were men. This is interesting in times when male hegemony is being challenged and a considerable section of public opinion holds men, and purported male properties and values, in low esteem. More than half of all deaths were registered in Europe and the Americas, which means that a large part of the victims were 'old white men', who have been under fierce criticism in general in recent times. Even if this says nothing about straightforward intentional action, it will be interesting to see whether the epidemic influences the future social position of men.

Often those opposed to protective measures were from the political right. In the fall of 2021, two of three German adults not vaccinated against COVID-19 stated that they voted for far-right parties.[52] For some time, the rate of infections per capita in Germany correlated with the strongholds of a far-right party, the Alternative für Deutschland (AfD). Hungary, which is among the world's top three countries in terms of the rate of COVID-19 deaths per capita,[53] has also perhaps the most right-wing politics, with two far-right parties drawing almost 70 percent of votes in general elections. Widespread survival of the fittest-kind of arguments about the epidemic are consistent with the ideas of the political far right. However, vocal resistance against vaccinations and other protective measures came also from many on the political left, for example in Italy.[54] To reiterate, I argue that this meant advocating for violence against innocents, and doing so was far more widespread than being just confined to one political faction.

The Me-Me-Me attitude mentioned above indicated a maximal degree of alienation.[55] The attempt to maintain their own high level of consumption determined many people's behavior in the pandemic. Nothing less was acceptable to

---
51 For example, see Christian Gerlach, *The Extermination of the European Jews* (Cambridge et al.: Cambridge University Press, 2016), 428–429.
52 "Umfrage unter Wählern: Zwei von drei Ungeimpften wählen AfD oder 'Die Basis'", *Tagesspiegel* online, November 11, 2021.
53 See Worldometer Coronavirus, https://www.worldometers.info/coronavirus/ (retrieved April 12, 2023).
54 Stefano Azzarà, "Der Weg nach unten: Gegen Impfung und 'Green Pass': Die italienische Linke auf Abwegen", *Junge Welt*, November 27/28, 2021: 12–13.
55 This applies even though one argument not to reduce contacts was loneliness and needing company (Komlosy, *Zeitenwende*, 139). The basic argument behind it was personal well-being.

them. Radical individualism and hedonism were at the root of the violence, and they were pursued by people from virtually all parts of the political spectrum.

My experience

I lived through this case of mass violence rather than being a distant contemporary and, therefore, would like to briefly reflect on it. During this time, I recognized several phenomena that I had previously merely studied academically. There was the perplexing feeling caused by the fact that everyday life continued despite the horrors going on. Part of my experience was that I was powerless. I saw many things coming, but they were inevitable. There were no authorities to turn to with any prospect for success, and no organized groups either. I am not innocent here. There was nothing that I did against this mass violence, or next to nothing. I could not help other people, or so I thought.

I was also unable to protect my little daughter from being infected. We were caught up in institutions that were guided by, as one mother from the same region called it, a policy of viral contamination. When she told the authorities that she wanted to take her daughter out of school because of the danger she was in, the school confronted her, according to her statement, with the threat of informing the KESB, a Swiss institution known for having deprived many parents of custody for their children, in a country with a long record of official child abduction.[56] After the summer holidays in 2021, the school authorities in the Swiss Canton of Bern stopped conducting the regular mass COVID-19 tests of all students once per week precisely at the moment when these tests found many positive results for infections.[57] The person who signed the announcement regarding the discontinuation had incidentally, in an earlier publication, failed to keep sufficient distance from denial of the shoah.[58] Be that as it may, Judith Butler argues: "Schools and universi-

---

[56] Camille Kündig and Danny Schlumpf, "Corona-Chaos an Berner Schulen: 'Regierungsrat Schnegg durchseucht unsere Kinder mit Gewalt'", *Blick*, November 21, 2021, https://wwwmsn.com/de-ch/nachrichten/politik/corona-chaos-an-berner-schulen-%c2%abregierungsrat-schnegg-durchseucht-unsere-kinder-mit-gewalt%c2%bb/ar-AAQXJwa?ocid_se, retrieved November 22, 2021.

[57] Kanton Bern, Gesundheits-, Sozial- und Integrationsdirektion, Gesundheitsamt, "Coronatests an Volksschulen", signed Raphael Ben Nescher, Corona Sonderstab GSI, August 30, 2021.

[58] See Raphael Ben Nescher, *Holocaust-Revisionismus: Ideologie oder Wissenschaft* (Borsdorf: edition winterwork, 2011, second, revised edition). Ben Nescher's publication is contradictory in content and, thus, in its assessment of revisionism, and suffers from a narrow source basis, but on p. 11 it contains the following sentences: "Documents which would prove a mass murder [of Jews] are far from being as numerous as one might think. Strictly speaking, there are none."

ties have opened during pandemic peaks based on a calculation that only so many will fall ill and so many will die. There is always a dispensable population factored into such equations. There are always people who can be sacrificed to make such equations work."[59]

However, this does not mean one should put the entire blame on the state. All of this happened in an atmosphere of irresponsibility, recklessness and lack of concern that permeated society. It was against this background that authorities could act that way, and it was this atmosphere that made living through this crisis a constant struggle in which everyday encounters took a lot of energy.

Europe

Europeans confronted the disease largely with methods of the 14th century: quarantine, xenophobic measures against incoming travelers, facemasks, keeping distance from others, and/or moving to the countryside.[60] For the most part, contact tracing based on digital methods did not work in European societies, unlike in some East Asian countries.

Once there were times when the European bourgeoisie embodied discipline, but those times are over. However, as I have shown, this does not mean that the behavior in the pandemic was a perversion of bourgeois values; some of the latter prevailed over others.

Europe has been among the world's regions with the highest rate of COVID-19-related deaths per capita. On that count, Europe is fairly united. Other areas with similarly high levels are the Americas and parts of West Asia. Compared to countries' population sizes, considerably fewer people died in the rest of Asia,[61] Africa and the Pacific nations.

These marked differences can, in part, be explained by considering the natural-social conditions. Among the factors that were advantageous to Africa and parts of Asia were the age structure of the population (i.e., fewer elderly people

---

("Dokumente, die einen Massenmord beweisen würden, sind bei weitem nicht so zahlreich, wie man glaubt. Eigentlich gibt es gar keine.") This obviously wrong statement is one of the most far-reaching examples of denial known to me.
59 Butler, *What World*, 28.
60 For the 14th century, see Giovanni Boccaccio, *Das Dekameron* (Bochum: Deutscher Buchklub, n.y. [first 1353]), 13–28. For some xenophobic policies and popular attitudes outside Europe during the COVID-19 pandemic, see Sitrin and Colectiva Sembrar, Pandemic Solidarity, 12, 59, 67–68, 91, 154, 177 (examples from Autonomous Northeastern Syria, Taiwan and India).
61 This excludes Siberia.

as percent of the population⁶², a lower urbanization rate, a higher home ownership rate and warmer climate, which allowed people to stay outside while keeping some distance from others. But some factors were also disadvantageous for Africa and those parts of Asia, such as crowded housing conditions, often a lack of access to clean water and bad hygienic conditions. Nevertheless, this chapter argues that all of these influences, and state policies, explain the disparity between death rates only to a degree and that the behavior and attitude of the population mattered.

In ten European countries that were once in Nazi Germany's sphere of influence, such as France and Italy, the number of people who died of COVID-19 surpasses that of the Jews deported from there and murdered by the Germans in World War II (in absolute figures). Furthermore, in the USA, substantially more citizens died in this pandemic than in the Spanish flu (1918–1920) – which, by the way, should be called the U.S. flu because it probably originated from Kansas.

The entire world has witnessed what happened in Europe: the recklessness, the dysfunctional states and the technological backwardness. The emperor is without clothes. There are many societies of irresponsibility in Europe. European politicians and intellectuals, however, have kept their robust self-confidence, which is not backed up by facts. Politicians here like to boast that 'we have coped well with the crisis'. Upon his re-election in February 2022, German president Frank-Walter Steinmeier said that no authoritarian state had made it better through the pandemic than Germany.[63] In fact, some dozen such countries immediately come to mind (measured by deaths per capita, or cases per capita, through COVID-19). It should be no surprise that one of the most aggressive imperialists among German politicians is also a racist, but in its counterfactuality, his ignorance of large parts of the world and their achievements borders on a denial that they exist, which, however, is not atypical of Europeans' behavior nowadays.

In the racist mindset of many Europeans, the numbers reported from other world regions, especially Africa, just cannot be true because Europe is the best by definition. While it may be correct that not all deaths from COVID-19 in Africa have been officially registered, attempts to 'prove' that it was worse there than in Europe or North America are unpersuasive.[64] Europeans and North Americans

---

62 Some examples are in Roth, *Blinde Passagiere*, 124.
63 "Aber man zeige mir ein autoritäres System, das besser durch die Pandemie gekommen wäre!" Der Bundespräsident, "Wiederwahl zum Bundespräsidenten durch die 17. Bundesversammlung", February 13, 2022, https://www.bundespraesident.de/SharedDocs/Reden/DE/Frank-Walter-Steinmeier/Reden/2022/02/220213-Bundesversammlung.html (retrieved April 25, 2022).
64 Among other things, evidence for such claims is patchy, mostly related to urban areas, and the arguments made rest partially on mere assumptions. WHO estimates about excess mortality

do their best to use their epistemic power to demonstrate their alleged supremacy.[65] But their best is not good enough.

Conclusions

This chapter argues, like the entire book, that mass violence is to a great extent participatory in character. Much of the violence comes from the people. A variety of population groups are active in it, and social groups are forceful actors. Rather than being the work of a few sinister governments, the COVID-19 disaster was based on close interrelationships between states and social groups.

Moreover, this chapter, like others in this volume, shows that violence, or its justification, is often socially hegemonic. Aside from the COVID-19 pandemic, this is also the case for the 1994 mass murders in Rwanda and for European and North American narratives of World War II, which have deep roots in people's minds (and not only in propaganda; see chapters 2 and 6 in this volume). Studying mass violence and persecution through sound history in particular demonstrates how persecutors try to dominate the public sphere and establish their hegemony, and how their opponents are forced to speak in a low voice and avoid making noises.

The COVID-19 pandemic exemplifies how conditions of violence are created as well as what effects they can have. This was a different type of conditions of violence than those described for World War II, i.e., less tightly regulated by states, to no small extent occurring in violation of official regulations, and though it was certainly not unrelated to economic factors and worldviews influenced by capitalism, there was more than that to the violent process. Myriad everyday practices consti-

---

in addition to officially registered deaths from COVID-19 show no fundamental change of the magnitude of impact in international comparison. This is to say, the share of deaths in African and Asian countries of the world total did not disproportionately increase over what was known from the registered data, although 14.83 million additional deaths were found worldwide. See William Msemburi et al., "The WHO estimates of excess mortality associated with the COVID-19 pandemic", *Nature* 613 (January 5, 2023), particularly 130–133. For statistical problems and questionable statistics in some countries, see Roth, *Blinde Passagiere*, 117–119, 192–200.

65 Indirectly and involuntarily, even an analyst of COVID society as critical as Judith Butler appears to reproduce this perception ("A large part of pandemic pain is clustered in some parts of the subjugated and colonized world"; Butler, What World, 4). For another example, see Andreas Malm, *Corona, Climate, Chronic Emergency: War Communism in the Twenty-First Century* (London and New York: Verso, 2020), 20.

tuted these conditions. People insisting on their freedom created conditions of violence, which seemed rightful to them (and their supporters), and even imperative because it was in defense of a higher virtue. They were no outsiders and created basic social facts. That such behavior was so widespread, at least in certain countries, made these conditions hard to fight and almost inescapable.

8 Conclusion

This book has applied two concepts, 'mass violence as social interaction' and 'conditions of violence' as new elements in the effort to demystify violence. Both have led to inconvenient findings. This final chapter will synthesize some of these findings, discuss overarching patterns and add some concluding reflections. It also suggests some possible avenues for future research. In this chapter, I consider the two core concepts one after the other and finally offer some further perspectives.

Mass Violence as Social Interaction

The approach to observing mass violence as social interaction through individual accounts and views from below (and participant observation to a limited extent) has shown how widespread violence was and pointed to the phenomenon of multipolar violence. First, here are some thoughts about the former. This volume argues that violence is made by the people, as chapter 4 on crowd violence in Bangladesh, chapter 2 on Rwanda in 1994 and chapter 7 on COVID-19 illustrate. It is not by accident that all of these deal with intrasocietal conflict in which, as I argue, many claimed the freedom to kill as a political right (which I would not have grasped without examining the COVID-19 pandemic). Indirectly, I also argue (in chapter 5) that non-violence can be made by the people: many war films in the Soviet Union, about which there were heated debates at the time, generated a peace message by constructing narratives of wartime suffering, pain and tragedy (instead of victory and heroism), and millions flocked to the cinemas to watch them.

Sound history employed for studying mass violence as social interaction brings out, inter alia, the emotions and the degree of personal involvement on all sides of conflicts (and in particular, feelings of loss by survivors who tell the story). While I have concentrated on overarching patterns, sound violence also shows the individuality of action related to violence on all sides.

As I said, my approach serves to take everybody involved in mass violence seriously and understand them as autonomous agents under certain man-made conditions (capitalism, war, civil war and epidemic). Among other things, this also means analyzing the ideologies of those targeted. A theme that stood out in this respect was religion, the role of which differed between the cases. For persecutors, religion or spirituality do not seem to have played a big role in mass violence. In Rwanda, attackers made few claims to religious values, and the same goes for objectors to protective restrictions in the COVID-19 pandemic. During the massacre at Chuknagar, the Pakistani soldiers killed in a shallow instrumentalization of religion (as group distinction), and Bihari crowds in East Pakistan possibly made claims to maintaining the unity of an Islamic state but with little obvious spirituality (see chapters 2, 7, 3 and 4, respectively). Those under attack had their religion silenced and repressed at Chuknagar, which was, in part, replaced by elementary pain and loss, along with being reduced to bodily markers and knowledge of songs or language. In the Soviet Union after World War II, religion in anti-war films resurged to a limited extent in invoking a general notion of the humane and was often expressed on a symbolic plain for depicting the sacrifice of the innocent. Only in Rwanda did religion play a massive role, was becoming louder, declergyized, autonomous and personalized among those who were persecuted (see chapters 2, 3 and 5).

Multipolar violence against non-combatants, which surfaced in this volume, is an inconvenient finding because its existence is often denied or belittled and it undermines simplistic, heroic and Manichean interpretations of history. It is not rare; historically, it could be observed in Azerbaijan/Armenia, Israel/Palestine, Serbia/Kosovo, in Myanmar and many other areas; in this volume, it is represented in cases in East Pakistan/Bangladesh, Rwanda, the Soviet Union, and World War II in general.

One implication of multipolar violence is that it often involves racism from various sides when violence is being fueled by collective ascriptions, for example, between many Pakistanis, Bangladeshis and 'Biharis' in 1971, perceived Hutus and Tutsis, and citizens of Axis and Allied states (see chapters 2, 4 and 6).[1] This, of course, is also to say that non-white racism exists, a notion that some authors dispute.[2] And it is in conflict with those who try to monopolize the status of a victim of racism by arguing that only black people, only people of color, only Jews, or only members of a certain other group suffer from racism, whereas in other cases one can only speak of prejudice and discrimination. Those who argue that only those in power can be racist and those without power cannot,[3] overlook that power hierarchies are not immutable, can shift and, consequently, "victims [can]

---

[1] I do not call this mutual racism because this would obscure that many people in societies in conflict were probably not racist, including many victims.
[2] See Reni Eddo-Lodge, *Why I'm No Longer Talk to White People about Race* (London et al.: Bloomsbury, 2017), 98.
[3] Ibid., 2, 89. Eddo-Lodge's book, which has been influential among scholars, is a scathing criticism of white racism in Britain. She justifies her argument that there can be only white, and no anti-white, racism mainly by saying that whites form the vast majority in society (and hold almost all positions of power), which is a British perspective that does not apply to many other countries. However, I do concur with Eddo-Lodge's argument that few things are more repulsive than to talk to white racists who say that they are not and that it may not make much sense to talk to them about this issue.

become killers".[4] That said, keeping asymmetric power relations in mind remains important. This is a profoundly racist world, and white racism is its biggest problem. In any case, particularly concerning racism, the belief is not plausible that it is only produced by the state or a few propagandists.

A key conclusion that can be drawn from the existence of multiple collective ascriptions and multiple racisms is that one needs to soberly analyze violence (and not mystify it), including on a low level of action, to not use collective prejudice oneself and fight the conditions of violence and its causes rather than perpetuate it.

Here is another inconvenient thought. Often, suffering from violence does not make people better. There is plenty of evidence to support this. This volume's findings come close to those by the Polish historian Adam Leyszczynski, who stated in his "People's History of Poland": "People who lived in material distress and in a state that contemporaries often compared to slavery can be brutal and cruel, not only in moments of their rebellion, but also among themselves. Victims are only rarely likeable. Violence and oppression do not make for good manners. It would be a great mistake to idealize the heroes and heroines of this book."[5] To say so, and contradict the widespread belief that suffering violence ennobles people, results from the effort to take all sides in violence seriously and scrutinize their action.

Conditions of Violence

Conditions of violence cause many deaths. The concept builds on an understanding of violence as participatory. Attention to the existence of conditions of violence and their genesis highlights once again how deep and entangled roots violence can have in society. These conditions had a lot to do with imperialism, as the two case studies in this volume suggest (World War II and the COVID-19 pandemic). Creating conditions of violence is the preferred weapon of liberal imperialism, elegant and near-invisible as they are if one controls the media. Creating

---

[4] See Mahmood Mamdani, *When Victims Become Killers: Colonialism, Nativism, and the Genocide in Rwanda* (Princeton: Princeton University Press, 2001); Nicholas Robins and Adam Jones, eds., *Genocides by the Oppressed* (Bloomington and Indianapolis: Indiana University Press, 2009). For some examples of intellectuals justifying what was arguably counter-violence by the oppressed against civilians, see Dirk Moses, *The Problems of Genocide: Permanent Security and the Language of Transgression* (Cambridge et al.: Cambridge University Press, 2021), 256–260.

[5] Adam Leszczynski, *Ludowa historia Polski*, quoted in Reinhard Lauterbach, "Ausbeutung und Renitenz", *Junge Welt*, February 17, 2021, 11 (my translation from German).

these conditions is perfect for those who conduct economic war from their sofa and strangle a lot of people while saying, 'hopefully there will be no war' (i.e., no war that reaches them). This also is to say that conditions of violence are not only created by small elite groups but by large though identifiable collectives who act through mechanisms that prevail in capitalism (and sometimes, actually, market mechanisms in socialism). As an effect of these mechanisms, most of those who die under conditions of violence are poor and vulnerable (but this can include people impoverished by force, displacement and internment).

That said, one chapter in this book that analyzes conditions of violence is focused on economic warfare while the other is not (see chapters 6 and 7 on World War II and on COVID-19, respectively). Although many threads connected patterns of behavior in the Corona crisis to the inner workings of capitalist economy and society (and to imperialism), that case also differs from economic warfare in terms of a lower degree and different forms of political organization and an even greater impact of individual decisions and reasoning. It is a reminder of the questions that should be asked related to conditions of violence: who is it who creates them; what characterizes the system through which conditions of violence work; and what directions does the violence take?

This book often refers to capitalism but is not totally silent on violence in socialism. The Soviet Union and Soviet citizens imposed conditions of violence on various groups, foreign and domestic, in World War II, and the removal of COVID-19 related restrictions in the People's Republic of China in December 2022 was clearly enforced by political pressure from out of the population (see chapters 6 and 7). Both facts point once again to the importance of agency from below. And they say that conditions of violence are not solely a problem of capitalism.

The participatory character of creating conditions of violence also encompasses rationales for violence. As conditions of violence in World War II and in the COVID-19 pandemic demonstrate, these rationales were not only elite-driven and certainly not only provided and distributed by the state. This was also true for crowd violence in East Pakistan/Bangladesh in 1971–1972 and, indirectly, the mass murder in Rwanda in 1994. There is more conscious behavior in the populations than many assume.

This participatory character raises questions about the relationships between rationales, denial of violence and violence itself in conditions of violence. The case of the current world conflict, in which parts of the northern hemisphere are drifting toward comprehensive nuclear war, is insightful. Large parts of the intelligentsia play a big role there. If, when the rubble is cleared up in the end, they will claim that they were only followers and unwilling executioners, don't believe them! People from the intelligentsia (on different sides) are a driving force of war, not fellow travelers; drivers of repression; their own censors and the censors of others. In other words, they are manipulators, not manipulated. This goes in particular for people presented in the mass media as 'experts'. This is the time to question the ideology of liberal imperialists, the people who assert that everybody else is ideological, except for them.

The concept of conditions of violence allows to shed light on the inner workings of destructive liberalism. In the case of this book, I hope to have done so in regard to the previous world conflict and the COVID-19 pandemic (chapters 6 and 7).

Mystification in the mass media and scholarship involves completely delegitimating certain incidences or forms of violence and its carriers (for example, violence for decolonization or revolution), which they call 'terrorism', 'genocide' and bestiality, allegedly driven by an absurd ideology (this is for dehumanizing the 'perpetrators' or depicting them as insane); and that serves, in turn, to legitimate and demand different forms or incidences of violence which they give other names such as 'sanctions', 'self-defense', 'air strikes' and 'soft power'.[6] They deny that this is violence at all or that it claims victims. Scandalizing some kinds of violence is used, and essential, to produce other violence. The misuse of the study of past mass violence for legitimizing war in different national political contexts has recently reached new peaks.

Accordingly, there will be criticism that this book simply declares everything violence and that one needs to keep apart different kinds (methods) of violence, some of which are allegedly more severe, repulsive and intentional. Presumably, among such critics will be some war intellectuals who have called the loudest for arms shipments, aerial attacks, invasion or economic warfare.

Bourgeois scholarship serves to stabilize and optimize capitalism, bourgeois rule, and the international rule of certain groups of the bourgeoisie. System-preserving 'experts' work, therefore, in close cooperation with courts, including international courts, which maintain the existing order. Make the laws, man the courts. And write the history. This is also a question of class. After all, violence is often regarded as a disturbance of the bourgeois order, and this perspective is also derived from feelings of moral, political and cultural superiority in relation to lower class, uneducated or colonized people. The 'haves' determine the rules legally as well

---

6 For great imperialist (naval) powers and their legal scholars keeping their starvation blockades out of international law for about a century, see Mulder and van Dijk, "Why".The connection between narratives of violence suffered, allegedly or actually, and using violence is also discussed in the psychological literature about competitive victimhood. Two examples are Masi Noor et al., "When Suffering Begets Suffering: The Psychology of Competitive Victimhood Between Adversarial Groups in Violent Conflict", *Personality and Social Psychology Review* 16, 4 (2012): 351–374; Isaac Young and Daniel Sullivan, "Competitive victimhood: a review of the theoretical and empirical literature", *Current Opinion in Psychology* 11 (2016): 30–34.

as they do in economic warfare: both are neat and veiled. Few of these well-paid intellectuals have any regard for the 'have-nots', against which the kinds of war they support are often directed, and often they do not even see them. Their rules-based world order has violent rules. Others have said so too. Through his concept of structural violence, Johan Galtung referred in particular to imperialism, finding the two almost identical.[7] I just suggest considering other forms of indirect violence than him, violence that has a direction and kills somewhat more quickly.

All of this does not mean to omit, belittle or glorify severe forms of decolonial or revolutionary violence against unarmed people (like killing, rape and expulsion). One can resist the temptation to identify with one side without being politically 'balanced' in a bourgeois sense. However, to take this violence seriously, one should soberly analyze it, and not on system-stabilizing 'experts' terms. In this volume, I have tried to do so with regard to the violence by Bengalis in 1971-1972 and, arguably, Soviet mass violence against non-combatants in World War II, arguing that it was not necessarily distinct from other violence at the time in terms of forms and justifications. The conviction that one's own side was 'good' also played a momentous role in these cases.

By combining the two research concepts of mass violence as social interaction and conditions of violence, this book describes how violence can become hegemonic, especially in chapter 7, and that many people derive from this social hegemony the claim to a *right* to kill. Examining the COVID-19 epidemic made me understand this. Chapter 7 also shows how conditions of violence can be produced through everyday practices. I argue that propaganda and indoctrination play some role in violence becoming hegemonic but not a primary one, while the main problem is that violence becomes a dominant social practice. It is not by accident that violent masses repeatedly appear in different forms and with different ways of action in this volume: in East Pakistan/Bangladesh in 1971–1972, in the COVID-19 pandemic and in the mass killings in Rwanda of 1994 (see chapters 2, 4 and 7). Racism is a case in point: it is a social practice, and that it is being deeply engrained this way may be a worse problem than racist ideology.[8]

---

7 Johan Galtung, "A Structural Theory of Imperialism", *Journal of Peace Research* 8, 2 (1971): 85.
8 This is not to say that racism is the only problem depicted in this book, which also talks about violent discrimination according to age, religion and sometimes gender and class.

Further Perspectives

A conditions of violence perspective can be applied to other cases. Such conditions are also imposed by the economic warfare euphemistically – and arrogantly – called 'sanctions', and could be examined accordingly. In the 1990s, when this practice intensified, researchers pointed to the many deaths it caused, especially among the poor.[9] A recent, more comprehensive study allows for a more far-reaching argument. It shows, based on a large country sample, that "sanctions" on average reduce the life expectancy of the population in the target country significantly (0.4 to 0.5 years in the case of unilateral adoption by the USA, and 1.2 to 1.4 years in the case of UN "sanctions") and that 98 mostly non-industrialized countries were subject to "sanctions" 1977–2012. Under certain conditions, the life expectancy of women is cut short more than that of men.[10] In other words, this economic warfare *usually* kills non-combatant non-elites en masse, and most countries in the world have suffered from this or must expect that they can become targets. The organizers, promoters and defenders of the economic warfare called 'sanctions' usually claim emphatically that they pursue 'values' through them; these statistics show what values they actually represent. The decrease in life expectancy is especially grave when 'sanctions' are adopted by the United Nations. Today's United Nations, founded in 1942 as another name for the anti-Axis coalition, based on the Atlantic Charter, are worthy of their origins.[11] Conditions of violence have also been imposed through 'humanitarian' interventions (a temporary label of modern imperialism) and through 'development' policies.[12] This is evidence for the fact that liberal imperialism is now the main threat to mankind.

---

9 For example, see John Mueller and Karl Mueller, "Sanctions of Mass Destruction", *Foreign Affairs* 78, 3 (1999): 43–53; Joy Gordon, "A Peaceful, Silent, Deadly Remedy: The Ethics of Economic Sanctions", *Ethics and International Affairs* 13, 1 (1999): 123–142; Anthony Arnove, ed., *Iraq Under Siege: The Deadly Impact of Sanctions and War* (Cambridge: Southend, 2002, updated ed.).- Galtung already observed much earlier that "[e]conomic sanctions occupy [an] interesting middle position" between direct and structural violence, although he trivialized it as being driven by good hopes. Johan Galtung, "Violence, Peace, and Peace Research", *Journal of Peace Research* 6, 3 (1969): 188 note 17.
10 Jerg Gutmann et al., *Sanctioned to Death? The Impact of Economic Sanctions on Life Expectancy and Its Gender Gap*, working paper (Munich: CESifo, 2019).
11 See United Nations website, https://www.un.org/en/about-us/history-of-the-un/preparatory-years (last accessed April 19, 2024).
12 For development policies, see for example Patrick Barron et al., *Contesting Development: Participatory Projects and Local Conflict Dynamics in Indonesia* (New Haven and London: Yale University Press, 2011), 36–43; Christian Gerlach, "Indonesian strategic resettlement and development policies

That said, liberal imperialism is unfortunately not mankind's only problem. The concept of conditions of violence could also be applied to the treatment of nature by humans. After all, some of the same sources of aggression as in the COVID-19 pandemic are at work in the human destruction of, if not the planet, then at least of animals and plants. The main reason is the refusal to change one's lifestyle even though it is destructive. It is not comfortable to live in harmony with nature. One piece of evidence is fundamental to describing the relationship between humans and nature: the biomass of all humans (390 million tons) exceeds by far the estimated biomass of all wild mammals, terrestrial and marine combined, on Earth (61 million tons). The biomass of humans is only surpassed by that of livestock, that is, mammals in human captivity (often intended to be killed at some point; 630 million tons).[13] Man does not only kill the big mammals (and fish[14]); man has not only *displaced* mammals; it has *replaced* them. *This* is humanity. It shows to which degree humans monopolize life, based on boundless arrogance and a merely instrumental relationship to nature.[15] The 'right' to kill and torture animals – and plants –, to regulate and dominate them and decide their fate, is derived from an alleged moral, cultural and intellectual superiority (although empirical evidence has increasingly shown how baseless such assumptions are), which leads to a "global commodification of living organisms" and their exploitation. At the core of this is simply a lack of respect.[16]

---

in East Timor", in Martin Thomas and Gareth Curless, eds., *The Oxford Handbook of Late Colonial Insurgencies and Counter-Insurgencies* (Oxford: Oxford University Press, 2023), 584–599.

13 See Lior Greenspoon et al., "The global biomass of wild mammals", *PNAS* 120, 10, 2023 (February 27, 2023), https://doi.org/10/1073/pnas.2204892120.

14 For freshwater fish, see Stefan Lovgren, https://www.spektrum.de/news/riesenfische-die-letzten-giganten-der-fluesse/2143479 May 22, 2023 (last accessed June 5, 2023).

15 Humans' capacity to monopolize life in the oceans seems to be more restricted. Thus, estimates of the total biomass of fish globally are not only higher than the biomass of humans (ranging between 1 and 5 billion tons) but also vary greatly, indicating (fortunately) a lack of control. See figure 1 in Daniele Bianchi et al., "Estimating global biomass and biogeochemical cycling of fish and without fishing", *Science Advances* 7, 41 (October 8, 2021), https://www.science.org/doi/10.1126/sciadv.abd7554 (last accessed November 18, 2023).

16 A recent philosophical effort for a non-hierarchical ethics of human-nature relationships is Rosi Braidotti, *The Posthuman* (Cambridge and Malden: Polity, 2013), quote: 8. Less far-reaching, Martha Nussbaum, *Justice for Animals* (New York et al.: Simon and Schuster, 2022) is a liberal reformist kind of study.

How does the knowledge about intellectual, cultural and social qualities of animals, as well as about the existence and (near-)extinction of species, come about? Often through humans holding animals in captivity, doing animal trials, killing animals, controlling and 'regulating' species.

Personal Reflections

My efforts to demystify violence through sober inquiry have stretched over 30 years, with limited effect. In a sense, this may be true for most scholarship in the social sciences. However, it is difficult and intellectually limiting to operate in a public sphere, and a scholarly sphere, that consistently reward the mystification of violence that aggressive liberals need for the violence imposed by their side – for their structural violence, for conditions of violence, and at times for direct violence against civilians as well. This problem is highlighted in a situation of world conflict and an atmosphere of repression.

Some time ago, a former students from Pittsburgh wrote to me. In her view, the USA are an extremely violent society, which was the topic of a course of mine that she was reminded of due to current events more than a decade later. I felt ashamed. Was it only this that my teaching is memorable for? Is there nothing inspiring in what I teach?

The COVID-19 pandemic, for one, has revealed societies of recklessness. Mercilessly, it has shown that other forms of social order are needed that could be called societies of solidarity and responsibility. It is research on such societies, or the possibility thereof, to which I should turn.

Acknowledgments

It took several years to complete this volume. As usual, research has, to some extent, been a collective effort, and I owe thanks to many people. First of all, what would historians do without archivists and librarians? I am grateful to the staff of all archives that I worked in for this publication, including the archive of the Food and Agriculture Organisation of the UN in Rome (Giuliano Fregoli in particular), the National Archive of Australia at Canberra, the German Bundesarchiv at Koblenz and the Politisches Archiv des Auswärtigen Amtes at Berlin. I also thank the staff at the University of Bern library system, especially Therese Meier-Salzmann and the librarians at the Basisbibliothek Unitobler.

Financial support for publishing this book open access, for which I am grateful, came from the University of Bern's professorship for contemporary history in a global perspective. That said, the views expressed in this book are mine and not those of the University of Bern.

Martin Thomas was so kind to read the entire manuscript, and Andreas Stucki read large parts of it. I am most grateful to both of them for their many helpful critical comments and hints. Early versions of single chapters received critical feedback by Frank Jacob, Axel Paul, Benjamin Schwalb and two anonymous reviewers, which I gratefully acknowledge. Thanks to Clemens Six for his special help! Moreover, inputs made by many people in various contexts influenced my ideas, including those by Susanne Buckley-Zistel, Fabian Christl, Richard Derderian, Tomislav Dulić, Moritz Feichtinger, Julian Flückiger, Daniel Gammenthaler, Dario Gomes Caliandro, Gerhard Hirschfeld, Nikita Hock, Andrej Kotljarchuk, Dirk Moses, Patrick Neveling, Vladimir Petrović, Julia Richers, Michael Schmocker, Anna Shternshis, Alexa Stiller, Max Sury, Catherine Tighe, Gregor Thum, Felix Wemheuer, David Whyte, Andreas Zeman and Aleksei Zhbanov. Thanks to all of them, and to Gabriele Jordan for technical assistance. Of course, all remaining errors and misconceptions are mine.

Early versions of parts of this book were presented at several conferences. I thank all the organizers and panel organizers, including Juliane Prade-Weiss, Dominik Markl and Vladimir Petrović (at a conference in Amsterdam), Luis Velasco-Pufleau and Marion Uhlig (Fribourg), Alon Confino, Andrea Graziosi and Frank Sysyn (at a conference in Toronto), Günter Riederer and Lydia Meißner (Stuttgart), Susanne Buckley-Zistel (Marburg), Bart Luttikhuis (Leiden) and Yehonatan Alsheh (then in Bloemfontein).

Many thanks go to the collaborators of Paper True for the language editing and to Julia Brauch from De Gruyter Oldenbourg publishers as well as to Vithya Ramalingam from Integra Software Services.

Chapter 4 of this volume was, in a slightly different form, published earlier as "Crowd Violence in East Pakistan/Bangladesh 1971/72" in Frank Jacob, ed., *Genocide and Mass Violence in Asia* (Berlin and Boston: De Gruyter Oldenburg, 2019), 15–39. Thanks to De Gruyter Oldenbourg publishers for permitting to use it here. An early version of a section of chapter 6 of this volume was published before as "Hunger in den besetzten Gebieten im Zweiten Weltkrieg – deutsch und global" in: Haus der Geschichte Baden-Württemberg, eds., *Hunger: Zur Geschichte einer existentiellen Bedrohung* (Ubstadt-Weiher: Verlag Regionalkultur, 2019), 149–164 and 253–257. Thanks to Verlag Regionalkultur and Haus der Geschichte Baden-Württembergs for the permission.

This volume would not have been possible without the support of my family, which is the greatest inspiration. I stay indebted to Magdi, Emilia and Nina.

Bibliography

Abayomi, Disu Oleyemisi, and Raheem Oluwafunminiyi. "Fighting for Britain: Examining British Recruitment Strategies in Nigeria". *Unknown Conflicts of the Second World War: Forgotten Fronts*, ed. Chris Murray. London and New York: Routledge, 2019: 8–22.

Abbasi, Kamran. "Covid-19: social murder, they wrote – elected, unaccountable, and unrepentant". *British Medical Journal* 372, 3/4 (2021), February 4, 2021, http://dx.doi.org/10.1136/bmj.n314.

Abelshauser, Werner. *Wirtschaftsgeschichte der Bundesrepublik Deutschland*. Frankfurt a. M.: Suhrkamp, 1980.

Adamovich, Ales, et al., *Out of the Fire*. Moscow: Progress, 1980.

Adamowitsch, Ales. "Chatyn berichtet über sich selbst". *Kunst und Literatur* 28 (1980): 451–467.

Adamowitsch, Ales. *Henkersknechte*. Berlin [East] and Weimar: Aufbau, 1982.

Adamowitsch, Ales. „Über das neue Denken und das adäquate Wort". *Kunst und Literatur* 35 (1987): 707–712.

Adamowitsch, Ales, and Daniil Granin. *Das Blockadebuch*. Berlin: Volk und Welt, vol. I 1987, vol. II 1984.

Adams, Michael. *The Best War Ever: America and World War II*. Baltimore and London: Johns Hopkins University Press, 1994.

Adekunle, Julius. *Culture and Customs of Rwanda*. Westport and London: Greenwood, 2007.

African Rights. *Rwanda: Death, Despair and Defiance*. London: African Rights, 1995, second rev. ed.

Ahmed, Hasina, et al. „Compilers' Note". *1971 Chuknagar Genocide*, ed. Muntasir Mamoon. Dhaka: University Press Publishers, 2014, second ed.: 19–20.

Akhtar, Shaheen et al., eds. *Rising from the Ashes: Women's Narratives of 1971*. Dhaka: Ain O Salish Kendra and University Press, 2014.

Akhtar, Shaheen. "Ferdousi Priyobhashini: A Hidden Chapter". *Rising from the Ashes: Women's Narratives of 1971*, eds. Shaheen Akhtar et al. Dhaka: Ain O Salish Kendra and University Press, 2014: 135–156.

Akizuki, Tatsuichiro. *Nagasaki 1945*. London et al.: Quartet, 1981.

Alamgir, Mohiuddin. *Famine in South Asia*. Cambridge, MA: Oelgeschlager, Gunn & Hain, 1980.

Ali, Imam. *Hindu-Muslim Community in Bangladesh*. Delhi: Kanisha, 1992.

Allen, Matthew. *Greed and Grievance: Ex-Militants' Perspective on the Conflict in the Solomon Islands, 1998–2003*. Honolulu: University of Hawai'i Press, 2013.

Aly, Götz. *Hitlers Beneficiaries: Plunder, Racial War and the Nazi Welfare State*. New York: Metropolitan Books, 2006.

Aly, Götz, ed. *Volkes Stimme: Skepsis und Führervertrauen im Nationalsozialismus*. Frankfurt a.M.: Fischer, 2006.

Anderson, Benedict. *Java in a Time of Revolution: Occupation and Resistance, 1944–1946*. Ithaca and London: Cornell University Press, 1972.

Angrick, Andrej. *Besatzungspolitik und Massenmord: Die Einsatzgruppe D in der Sowjetunion 1941–1943*. Hamburg: Hamburger Edition, 2003.

Antognini, Timeo. *Geschichte der Tuwinischen Volksrepublik*. Masters thesis, University of Bern, 2022.

Aras, Ramazan. *The Wall: The Making and Unmaking of the Turkish-Syrian Border*. Cham: Palgrave Macmillan, 2020.

Arendt, Hannah. *Eichmann in Jerusalem: A Report on the Banality of Evil*. New York: Viking, 1965, revised ed.

Armingeon, Florian. *Organisationen von Besatzungskindern des Zweiten Weltkrieges im Vergleich.* Master's thesis, University of Bern, 2023.
Arnold, Sabine. *Stalingrad im sowjetischen Gedächtnis: Kriegserinnerung und Geschichtsbild im totalitären Staat.* Bochum: Projekt, 1998.
Arnove, Anthony, ed. *Iraq Under Siege: The Deadly Impact of Sanctions and War.* Cambridge: Southend, 2002, updated ed.
"Atlantic Charter", August 14, 1941. https://avalon.law.yale.edu/wwii/atlantic.asp.
Aziz, Qutubuddin. *Blood and Tears.* Karachi: United Press of Pakistan, 1974.
Azzarà, Stefano. „Der Weg nach unten: Gegen Impfung und ‚Green Pass': Die italienische Linke auf Abwegen". *Junge Welt,* November 27/28, 2021: 12–13.
Bachir Diagne, Souleymane and Jean-Loup Amselle. *In Search of Africa(s): Universalism and Decolonial Thought.* Cambridge and Medford: Polity, 2020.
Bacque, James. *Crimes and Mercies: The Fate of German Civilians under Allied Occupation, 1944–1950.* Toronto: Little, Brown & Co, 1997.
Bagilishya, Déogratias. "Mourning and Recovery from Trauma: In Rwanda, Tears Flow Within". *Transcultural Psychology* 37, 3 (2000): 337–353.
Bakhtin, Mikhail. *Problems of Dostoevski's Poetics.* No place: Ardis, 1973.
Bakonyi, Jutta and Berit Bliesemann de Guevara, "The Mosaic of Violence – An Introduction". *A Macro-Sociology of Violence: Decyphering patterns and dynamics of collective violence,* eds. Bakonyi and Bliesemann de Guevara. London and New York: Routledge, 2012: 1–17.
Bangla Desh Documents. Delhi: Ministry of External Affairs n.y. [1971].
Barrea, Giulia. "Wrestling with Race at the Eve of Human Rights: The British Management of the Color Line in Post-Fascist Eritrea". *Africa and World War II,* eds. Judith Byfield et al. New York: Cambridge University Press, 2015: 259–275.
Barron, Patrick, et al. *Contesting Development: Participatory Projects and Local Conflict Dynamics in Indonesia.* New Haven and London: Yale University Press, 2011.
Baumgärtner, Fabian, and Nils Pfändler. "Der Gastro-Albtraum: Die Omikron-Welle zwingt Zürcher Restaurants und Klubs zu Schliessungen". *Neue Zürcher Zeitung,* January 14, 2022, https://www.nzz.ch/zuerich/corona-in-zuerich-clubs-und-restaurant-verlieren-sehr-viel-geld-ld.1664508.
Bayly, Christopher, and Tim Harper. *Forgotten Armies: The Fall of British Asia, 1941–1945.* Cambridge: Belknap, 2005.
Beevor, Antony. *Der Zweite Weltkrieg.* Munich: Bertelsmann, 2014.
Begum, Suraiya. "Introduction". *Rising from the Ashes: Women's Narratives of 1971,* eds. Shaheen Akhtar et al. Dhaka: Ain O Salish Kendra and University Press, 2014: 105–106.
Begum, Suraiya. "Binapani Saha: The Many Faces of 1971". *Rising from the Ashes: Women's Narratives of 1971,* eds. Shaheen Akhtar et al. Dhaka: Ain O Salish Kendra and University Press, 2014: 261–284.
Beidler, Philip. *The Good War's Greatest Hits: World War II and American Remembering.* Athens and London: University of Georgia Press, 1998.
Belaja, G. „Ales Adamowitsch über Kriegsprosa". *Kunst und Literatur* 30 (1982).
Ben Nescher, Raphael. *Holocaust-Revisionismus: Ideologie oder Wissenschaft.* Borsdorf: edition winterwork, 2011, second, revised edition.
Benda, Richard. *The Test of Faith: Christians and Muslims in the Rwandan Genocide.* Ph.D dissertation, University of Manchester, 2012.
Bergholz, Olga. *Tagessterne.* Berlin [East]: Kultur und Fortschritt, 1963.
Berkhoff, Karel. "'Total Annihilation of the Jewish Population': The Holocaust in the Soviet Media, 1941–1945". *Kritika* 10, 11 (2009): 61–105.

Bessel, Richard. "Unnatural deaths". *The Oxford Illustrated History of World War II*, ed. Richard Overy. Oxford: Oxford University Press, 2015: 322–343.

Bezborodova, Evgenia. *Die Rolle des Imaginären in sowjetischen Kriegsfilmen*. Ph.D dissertation, Ludwig-Maximilians-Universität München, 2018.

Bianchi, Daniele, et al. "Estimating global biomass and biogeochemical cycling of fish and without fishing". *Science Advances* 7, 41 (October 8, 2021), https://www.science.org/doi/10.1126/sciadv.abd7554.

Bigagaza, Jean, et al. "Land Scarcity, Distribution and Conflict in Rwanda". *The Ecology of Africa's Conflicts*, eds. J. Lind and K. Sturmon. Pretoria: Institute for Security Studies, 2004: 51–82.

Blood, Archer. *The Cruel Birth of Bangladesh: Memoirs of an American Diplomat*. Dhaka: University Press, 2002.

Boccaccio, Giovanni. *Das Dekameron*. Bochum: Deutscher Buchklub, n.y. [first 1353].

Böckmann, Matthias, et al., eds. *Jenseits von Mbembe: Geschichte, Erinnerung, Solidarität*. Berlin: Metropol, 2022.

Bogomolow, Wladimir. *Leuchtspur über den Strom*. Berlin [East]: Kultur und Fortschritt, 1960.

Bogosian Ash, Catherine. "Free to Coerce: Forced Labour during and after the Vichy Years in French West Africa". *Africa and World War II*, eds. Judith Byfield et al. New York: Cambridge University Press, 2015: 109–126.

Bonwetsch, Bernd. „Der ‚Grosse Vaterländische Krieg': Vom öffentlichen Schweigen unter Stalin zum Heldenkult unter Breshnew". *„Wir sind die Herren dieses Landes": Ursachen, Verlauf und Folgen des deutschen Überfalls auf die Sowjetunion*, ed. Babette Quinkert. Hamburg: VSA, 2002: 166–187.

Bonwetsch, Bernd. "'Ich habe an einem völlig anderen Krieg teilgenommen': Die Erinnerung an den Grossen Vaterländischen Krieg in der Sowjetunion". *Krieg und Erinnerung*, ed. Helmut Berding. Göttingen: Vandenhoeck & Ruprecht, 2000: 145–168.

Bose, Sarmila. *Dead Reckoning: Memories of the 1971 Bangladesh War*. London: Hurst, 2011.

Bose, Sugata. "Starvation amidst Plenty: The Making of Famine in Bengal, Honan and Tonkin, 1942–45". *Modern Asian Studies* 24, 4 (1990): 699–727.

Braidotti, Rosi. *The Posthuman*. Cambridge and Malden: Polity, 2013.

Braw, Monica. *The Atomic Bomb Suppressed: American Censorship in Occupied Japan*. Armonk and London: M.E. Sharpe, 1991.

Brennan, Lance, et al. "War and Famine around the Indian Ocean during the Second World War". *Ethics of the Global South* 18 (2017): 5–70.

Breuer, Lisa. „Gefängnis, Liegestütze oder Probeliegen im Sarg: Das sind die skurrilsten Strafen für Regelbrecher in der Corona-Pandemie". *Tagesspiegel* online, September 7, 2021.

Brosch, Markus. *Zur Geschichte einer Wiener Institution: Das Sammellager an der Kleinen Sperlgasse*. Ph. D dissertation, University of Vienna, 2021.

Brown, Carolyn. "African Labor in the Making of World War II". *Africa and World War II*, eds. Judith Byfield et al. New York: Cambridge University Press, 2015: 43–68.

Brown, Sara. *Gender and Genocide in Rwanda: Women as Rescuers and Perpetrators*. New York: Routledge, 2018.

Browning, Christopher. *Ordinary Men*. New York: HarperCollins, 1993.

Buchanan, Andrew. "Globalizing the Second World War". *Past & Present* 258 (2023): 246–281.

Bùi Minh Dũng. "Japan's Role in the Vietnamese Starvation of 1944–1945". *Modern Asian Studies* 29, 3 (1995): 573–618.

Bulgakowa, Oksana, and Dietmar Hochmuth, eds. *Der Krieg gegen die Sowjetunion im Spiegel von 36 Filmen: Eine Dokumentation*. Berlin: Freunde der Deutschen Kinemathek e.V., n.y. [1992].

Burnet, Jeannie. *Genocide Lives in Us: Women, Memory, and Silence in Rwanda*. Madison: University of Wisconsin Press, 2012.
Butler, Judith. *Frames of War: When Is Life Grievable?* London and New York: Verso, 2016 [first 2010].
Butler, Judith. *What World Is This? A Pandemic Phenomenology*. New York: Columbia University Press, 2022.
Byfield, Judith. "Preface". *Africa and World War II*, eds. Judith Byfield et al. New York: Cambridge University Press, 2015: xvii-xxiii.
Byfield, Judith. "Producing for the War". *Africa and World War II*, eds. Judith Byfield et al. New York: Cambridge University Press, 2015: 24–42.
Bykau, Wassil. *Romane und Novellen*. Cologne: Pahl-Rugenstein, 1985.
Caliscan, Miray. "Heute vor 2 Jahren: Als England beschloss, mit dem Coronavirus zu leben". *Tagesspiegel* online, July 19, 2023.
Cantier, Jacques. *L'Algérie sous le régime de Vichy*. Paris: Odile Jacob, 2002.
Card, Claudia. *The Atrocity Paradigm: A Theory of Evil*. Oxford et al.: Oxford University Press, 2002.
Carlson, Amanda, and Courtnay Micots. "Carnival in Africa: Join the Party!" *African Arts* 55, 4 (2022): 6–17.
Carlton, Eric. *Massacres: An historical perspective*. Aldershot and Brookfield: Scholar Press, 1994.
Césaire, Aimé. *Discourse on Colonialism*. New York: Monthly Review Press, 1972.
Chandra, Prabodh. *Bloodbath in Bangla Desh*. Delhi: Adarsh, n.y. [1971].
Chapman, Adam, and Chris Kempshall. "Battlefield 1: Can The Great War Be a Great Game?" *The Ontological Geek*, 16 February 2017, ontologicalgeek.com/battlefield-1-can-the-great-war-be-a-great-game/.
Chaudhuri, Kalyan. "Across the Border: The Masses Are Active". *Frontier*, 1 May 1971. Printed in: *Media and the Liberation War of Bangladesh*, vol. 2, ed. Muntassir Mamoon. Dhaka: Centre for Bangladesh Studies, 2002: 107–111.
Chaudhuri, Kalyan. *Genocide in Bangladesh*. Bombay et al.: Orient Longman, 1972.
Chaumont, Jean-Michel. *La concurrence des victimes*. Paris: Éditions la Découverte, 1997.
Cheah Boon Kheng. *Red Star Over Malaya: Resistance and Social Conflict During and After the Japanese Occupation of Malaya, 1941–1946*. Singapore: NUS Press, 2017, fourth ed.
Chellan, Noel. *F/Ailing Capitalism and the Challenge of COVID-19*. Boston: Brill, 2023.
Chossudowsky, Michel. "Economic Genocide in Rwanda". *Economic and Political Weekly* 31, 15 (1996): 938–941.
Chowdhury, M. A. Taiyeb. *Dimensions of Development and Change in Bangladesh, 1960–1980*. Ph.D dissertation, University of Western Ontario, 1988.
Chowdhury, Nusrat Sabina. *Paradoxes of the Popular: Crowd Politics in Bangladesh*. Stanford: Stanford University Press, 2019.
Chowdhury, Shahid Kader. "Age, Gender and Religion of the Victims of the Bangladesh Genocide". *Jagannath University Journal of Arts* 11, 1 (2021).
Churchill, Winston. *The Second World War: The Gathering Storm*. New York: Houghton Mifflin, 1948.
Churchill, Winston. *The Second World War, vol. IV: The Hinge of Fate*. London et al.: Cassell, 1951.
Clarence-Smith, Gervase. "The Impact of the Spanish Civil War and the Second World War on Portuguese and Spanish Africa". *Journal of African History* 26, 4 (1985): 309–326.
Clarence-Smith, William G. *The Battle for Rubber in the Second World War: Cooperation and Resistance*. Working paper, London: School of Oriental and African Studies, 2009.
Clarke, Thurston. *The Last Caravan*. New York: Putnam, 1978.
Coates, Oliver. "The Indian Ocean". *Unknown Conflicts of the Second World War: Forgotten Fronts*, ed. Chris Murray. London and New York: Routledge, 2019: 73–95.

Coe, Charles. *Food for now or coffins for later; the meaning of the world food crisis*. New York: Farm Research, 1946.
Cohen, Stephen. *The Pakistan Army*. Oxford et al.: Oxford University Press, fourth ed. 2002.
Collingham, Lizzie. *The Taste of War: World War II and the Battle for Food*. New York: Penguin, 2012.
Conrad, Sebastian. "Erinnerung im globalen Zeitalter". *Merkur* 75, 867 (2021): 5–17.
Cook, Haroko Taya, and Theodore Cook, eds. *Japan at War: An Oral History*. New York: New Press, 1992.
Corbin, Alain. *Village Bells: Sound and Meaning in the Nineteenth-Century French Countryside*. New York: Columbia University Press, 1998.
"Coronawelle in China mit Millionen Neuinfektionen pro Woche". *Tagesspiegel* online, May 26, 2023.
"Covid-19 rules, community visit limits to be eased for migrant workers in dorms". *Straits Times*, March 11, 2022, https://www.straitstimes.com/singapore/covid-19-safety-measures-community-visits-for-migrant-workers-living-in-dorms.
Crepeau, Pierre. *Parole et sagesse: Valeurs sociales dans les proverbes du Rwanda*. [Brussels:] Musée Royal de l'Afrique Centrale, 1985.
Cribb, Robert. *Gangsters and Revolutionaries: The Jakarta People's Militia and the Indonesian Revolution 1945–1949*. Sydney: Allen and Unwin, 1991.
Crowley, Daniel. "The Sacred and the Profane in African and African-Derived Carnivals". *Western Folklore* 58, 3–4 (1999): 223–228.
Dackweiler, Regina-Maria, and Reinhild Schäfer, eds. *Gewaltverhältnisse: Feministische Perspektiven auf Geschlecht und Gewalt*. Frankfurt a.M. and New York: Campus, 2002.
Dahinden, Philippe. "Information in Crisis Areas as a Tool for Peace: the Hirondelle Experiment". *The Media and the Rwandan Genocide*, ed. Allan Thompson. New York et al.: Pluto, 2007: 381–388.
de Keghel, Isabelle. „Ungewöhnliche Perspektiven: Der Zweite Weltkrieg in neuen russländischen Filmen". *Osteuropa* 55, 4–6 (2005): 337–346.
de Keghel, Isabelle. "Glaube, Schuld und Erlösung: Religion im neuen russischen Kriegsfilm". *Osteuropa* 59, 1 (2009): 97–108.
de Waal, Alex. "Writing Human Rights and Getting It Wrong". *Boston Review*, June 6, 2016, http://bostonreview.net/world/alex-de-waal-writing-human-rights/.
del Arco Blanco, Miguel Ángel. "The famine that 'never' existed: Causes of the Spanish famine". *Franco's Famine: Malnutrition, Disease and Starvation in Post-Civil War Spain*, eds. Miguel Ángel del Arco Blanco and Peter Anderson. London et al.: Bloomsbury, 2022: 19–35.
del Arco Blanco, Miguel Ángel, and Peter Anderson. "Introduction: Famine, not hunger?" *Franco's Famine: Malnutrition, Disease and Starvation in Post-Civil War Spain*, eds., in Miguel Ángel del Arco Blanco and Peter Anderson. London et al.: Bloomsbury, 2022: 1–16.
Des Forges, Alison. *Kein Zeuge darf überleben: Der Genozid in Ruanda*. Hamburg: Hamburger Edition, 2002.
Des Forges, Alison. "Call for Genocide: Radio in Rwanda, 1994". *The Media and the Rwandan Genocide*, ed. Allan Thompson. New York et al.: Pluto, 2007: 41–54.
Devereux, Stephen, ed. *The New Famines*. London: Routledge, 2006.
Diner, Dan. "Über kognitives Entsetzen". *"Ein Verbrechen ohne Namen": Anmerkungen zum neuen Streit über den Holocaust*, eds. Saul Friedländer et al. Munich: Beck, 2022: 69–86.
Dixon, Thomas. *Weeping Britannia*. Oxford et al.: Oxford University Press, 2015.
Doughty, Kristin, and David Moussa Ntambara. *Resistance and Protection: Muslim Community Actions During the Rwandan Genocide*. Cambridge, 2005.
Dower, John. *War Without Mercy: Race and Power in the Pacific War*. New York: Pantheon, 1986.

Dumas, Hélène. "Enfants victimes, enfants tueurs: Expériences infantines (Rwanda, 1994)". *Vingtième Siècle* 122 (2014): 75–86.
Dumas, Hélène. *Le génocide au village: Les massacres des Tutsi au Rwanda*. Paris: Seuil, 2014.
Dunn, James. *Timor: A People Betrayed*. Gladesville et al.: Jacaranda Press, 1983.
Dwyer, Philip, and Lyndall Ryan. "The Massacre and History". *Theatres of Violence: Massacre, Mass Killing and Atrocity throughout History*, eds. Philip Dwyer and Lyndall Ryan. New York and Oxford: Berghahn, 2012: xi-xxv.
Eddo-Lodge, Reni. *Why I'm No Longer Talk to White People about Race*. London et al.: Bloomsbury, 2017.
Eckmann, Monique, and Gottfried Kössler. "Polarisierungen verweigern: Spanungsfelder in der pädagogischen Auseinandersetzung mit dem Antisemitismus". *Jenseits von Mbembe: Geschichte, Erinnerung, Solidarität*, eds. Matthias Böckmann et al. Berlin: Metropol, 2022: 125–140.
Edele, Mark. *Stalinism at War: The Soviet Union in World War II*. London et al.: Bloomsbury, 2021.
Edgerton-Tarpley, Kathryn Jean. "From 'Nourish the People' to 'Sacrifice for the Nation': Changing Responses to Disaster in Late Imperial and Modern China". *Journal of Asian Studies* 73, 2 (2014): 447–469.
Edgerton-Tarpley, Kathryn. "Between War and Water: Farmer, City, and State in China's Yellow River Flood of 1938–1947". *Agricultural History* 90, 1 (2016): 94–116.
El Kenz, David. „Présentation: le massacre, objet d'histoire". *Le massacre, objet d'histoire*, ed. David El Kenz. Paris: Gallimard, 2005: 7–23.
Ellman, Michael. "The 1947 Soviet famine and the entitlement approach to famine". *Cambridge Journal of Economics* 24 (2000): 603–630.
Elphinston, W. G. "The Kurdish Question". *International Affairs* 22, 1 (1946): 91–103.
Engel, Christine, et al., eds. *Geschichte des sowjetischen und russischen Films*. Stuttgart and Weimar: Metzler, 1999.
Engel, Christine. „60 Jahre danach: Neue Sichtweisen auf den 'Grossen Vaterländischen Krieg' im Film Polumgla". *Kriegsbilder: Mediale Repräsentationen des 'Grossen Vaterländischen Krieges'*, eds. Beate Fieseler and Jörg Ganzenmüller. Fulda: Fuldaer Verlagsanstalt, 2010: 96–110.
Erlinghagen, Helmut. *Hiroshima und wir*. Frankfurt a.M.: Fischer, 1982.
Fair, C. Christine. *Fighting to the End: The Pakistan Army's Way of War*. Oxford et al.: Oxford University Press, 2014.
Falgout, Suzanne. "From Passive Pawns to Political Strategists: Wartime Lessons for the People of Pohnpei". *The Pacific Theatre; Island Representations of World War II*, eds. Geoffrey White and Lamont Lindstrom. Honolulu: University of Hawaii Press, 1989: 279–297.
Falgout, Suzanne. "Lessons from Wartime Pohnpei", *Remembering the Pacific War*, ed. Geoffrey White. Honolulu: University of Hawaii, 1991: 126–134.
Fall, Babacar. *Le travail forcé en Afrique occidentale française (1900–1945)*. Paris: Karthala, 1993.
Feichtinger, Moritz. *"Villagization": A People's History of Strategic Resettlement and Violent Transformation: Kenya and Algeria 1952–1962*. Ph.D dissertation, University of Bern, 2016.
Felber, Tom. „Maskenverweigerer halten die Richter auf Trab". *Neue Zürcher Zeitung*, January 31, 2022: 12.
Feltz, Gaëtan, and Jean-Étienne Bidou. "La famine Manori au Burundi 1943–1944". *Revue française d'histoire d'outre-mer* 81, 304 (1994): 265–304.
Fetscher, Caroline. „Wir sind die Kurve! Sich immer noch privat zu treffen, ist gefährlich egoistisch". *Tagesspiegel* online, April 4, 2021.

Fieseler, Beate. „Der Kriegsinvalide in ausgewählten sowjetischen Spielfilmen der Kriegs- und Nachkriegszeit (1944 bis 1964)". *Krieg und Militär im Film des 20. Jahrhunderts*, eds. Bernhard Chiari et al. Munich: Oldenbourg, 2003: 199–222.

Fieseler, Beate. "Keine Leidensbilder: Der Invalide des 'Grossen Vaterländischen Krieges' in sowjetischen Spielfilmen". *Kriegsbilder: Mediale Repräsentationen des 'Grossen Vaterländischen Krieges'*, eds. Beate Fieseler and Jörg Ganzenmüller. Fulda: Fuldaer Verlagsanstalt, 2010: 77–94.

Fieseler, Beate, and Jörg Ganzenmüller, „Einführung". *Kriegsbilder: Mediale Repräsentationen des 'Grossen Vaterländischen Krieges'*, eds. Beate Fieseler and Jörg Ganzenmüller. Fulda: Fuldaer Verlagsanstalt, 2010: 7–12.

Filtzer, Donald. "Die Auswirkungen der sowjetischen Hungersnot im Jahr 1947 auf die Industriearbeiter". *Hunger, Ernährung und Rationierungssysteme unter dem Staatssozialismus (1917–2006)*, eds. Matthias Middell and Felix Wemheuer. Frankfurt am Main et al.: Peter Lang, 2011: 59–85.

Donald Filtzer, "Starvation Mortality in Soviet Home-Front Industrial Regions during World War II". *Hunger and War: Food Provisioning in the Soviet Union during World War II*, eds. Wendy Goldman and Donald Filtzer. Bloomington and Indianapolis: Indiana University Press, 2015: 265–338.

Fleischer, Hagen. *Im Kreuzschatten der Mächte: Griechenland 1941–1944*. Frankfurt a.M. et al.: Peter Lang, 1986.

Fletcher, Mary. "Famine in Arabia, 1943–1947", https://www.britishempire.co.uk/article/faminearabia/htm.

Firdousi, Ishrat, ed. *The Year That Was*. Dhaka: Bastu Prakashan, 1996.

Firth, Shirley. *Dying, Death and Bereavement in a British Hindu Community*. Leuven: Peeters, 1997.

Foreign Relations of the United States, 1969–1976, vol. XI. Washington: United States Government Printing Office, 2005.

Franco, Robert. "Samoan Representations of World War II and Military Work: The Emergence of International Movement Networks". *The Pacific Theatre; Island Representations of World War II*, eds. Geoffrey White and Lamont Lindstrom. Honolulu: University of Hawaii Press, 1989: 373–394.

Franda, Marcus. *Bangladesh: The First Decade*. New Delhi: South Asian Publishers, 1982.

Frederick, William. *Visions and Heat: The Making of the Indonesian Revolution*. Athens: Ohio University Press, 1989.

Frederick, William. "The Man Who Knew Too Much: Ch.O. van der Plas and the Future of Indonesia, 1927–1950". *Imperial Policies and Southeast Asian Nationalism 1930–1957*, eds. Hans Antlöv and Stein Tønnesson. Richmond: Curzon Press, 1995: 34–62.

Fujii, Lee Ann. *Killing Neighbors: Webs of Violence in Rwanda*. Ithaca and London: Cornell University, 2009.

Fujii, Lee Ann. *Show Time: The Logic and Power of Violent Display*. Ithaca and London: Cornell University Press, 2021.

Furuta, Motoo. "A Survey of Village Conditions during the 1945 Famine in Vietnam". *Food Supplies and the Japanese Occupation in South-East Asia*, ed. Paul Kratoska. Basingstoke: Macmillan, 1998: 227–237.

Gado, Boureima Alpha. *Une histoire des famines au Sahel*. Paris: L'Harmattan, 1993.

Galtung, Johan. "Violence, Peace and Peace Research". *Journal of Peace Research* 6, 3 (1969): 167–191.

Galtung, Johan. "A Structural Theory of Imperialism". *Journal of Peace Research* 8, 2 (1971): 81–117.

Ganson, Nicholas. *The Soviet Famine of 1946–47 in Global and Historical Perspective*. New York and Basingstoke: Palgrave Macmillan, 2009.

Ganzenmüller, Jörg. *Das belagerte Leningrad 1941–1944*. Paderborn et al.: Schöningh, 2005.

Ganzer, Christian, and Alena Paškovič. „'Heldentum, Tragik, Tapferkeit': Das Museum der Verteidigung der Brester Festung". *Osteuropa* 60, 12 (201): 81–96.

Garnaut, Anthony. "A Quantitative Description of the Henan Famine of 1942". *Modern Asian Studies* 47, 6 (2013): 2007–2045.

Gebhardt, Miriam. "Eine Frage des Schweigens? Forschungsthesen zur Vergewaltigung deutscher Frauen nach Kriegsende". *Besatzungskinder: Die Nachkommen alliierter Soldaten in Österreich und Deutschland*, eds. Barbara Stelzl-Marx and Slike Satjukow. Vienna et al.: Böhlau, 2015: 62–90.

Gerlach, Christian. *Krieg, Ernährung, Völkermord: Forschungen zur deutschen Vernichtungspolitik im Zweiten Weltkrieg*. Hamburg: Hamburger Edition, 1998.

Gerlach, Christian. "The Wannsee Conference, the Fate of German Jews, and Hitler's Decision in Principle to Exterminate All European Jews". *Journal of Modern History* 70, 4 (1998): 759–812.

Gerlach, Christian. *Kalkulierte Morde: Die deutsche Wirtschafts- und Vernichtungspolitik in Weissrussland 1941–1944*. Hamburg: Hamburger Edition, 1999.

Gerlach, Christian. "The Eichmann Interrogations in Holocaust Historiography". *Holocaust and Genocide Studies* 15, 3 (2001): 428–452.

Gerlach, Christian, and Nicolas Werth. "State Violence – Violent Societies". *Beyond Totalitarianism: Stalinism and Nazism Compared*, eds. in Michael Geyer and Sheila Fitzpatrick. Cambridge et al.: Cambridge University Press, 2009: 133–179.

Gerlach, Christian. *Extremely Violent Societies: Mass Violence in the Twentieth-Century World*. Cambridge et al.: Cambridge University Press, 2010.

Gerlach, Christian. *The Extermination of the European Jews*. Cambridge et al.: Cambridge University Press, 2016.

Gerlach, Christian. „Echoes of persecution: Sounds in early post-liberation Jewish memories", *Holocaust Studies* 24, 1 (2018): 1–25.

Gerlach, Christian. "Hunger in den besetzten Gebieten im Zweiten Weltkrieg – deutsch und global". *Hunger: Zur Geschichte einer existenziellen Bedrohung*, ed. Haus der Geschichte Baden-Württembergs. Ubstadt-Weiher: Verlag Regionalkultur, 2019: 151–164.

Gerlach, Christian and Clemens Six, eds. *The Palgrave Handbook of Anti-Communist Persecutions*. Cham: PalgraveMacmillan, 2020.

Gerlach, Christian. "Indonesian Narratives of Survival in and after 1965 and Their Relation to Societal Persecution". *The Palgrave Handbook of Anti-Communist Persecutions*, eds. Christian Gerlach and Clemens Six. Cham: PalgraveMacmillan, 2020: 441–458.

Gerlach, Christian, ed. *On the Social History of Persecution*. Berlin and Boston: De Gruyter Oldenbourg, 2023.

Gerlach, Christian. "Indonesian strategic resettlement and development policies in East Timor". *The Oxford Handbook of Late Colonial Insurgencies and Counter-Insurgencies*, eds. Martin Thomas and Gareth Curless. Oxford: Oxford University Press, 2023: 584–599.

Gerlach, Christian. *How the World Hunger Problem Was Not Solved*. London: Routledge, 2024.

Gershenson, Olga. „Les Insoumis (1945) ou comment un roman soviétique et devenue un film juif". *Kinojudaica: les représentations des Juifs dans le cinéma de Russie et d'Union soviétique des années 1910 aux années 1980*, eds. Valérie Pozner and Natacha Laurent. Paris: Nouveau monde, 2012: 341–364.

Gershenson, Olga. "The Missing Links of Holocaust Cinema: Evacuation in Soviet Films". *Post Script* 32, 2 (2013): 53–62.

Gershenson, Olga. *The Phantom Holocaust: Soviet Cinema and Jewish Catastrophe*. New Brunswick et al.: Rutgers University Press, 2013.

Gerwarth, Robert, and Erez Manela, *Empires at War, 1911–1923*. Oxford: Oxford University Press, 2014.

Gholi Majd, Mohammad. *Iran under Allied Occupation in World War II*. Lanham et al.: University Press of America, 2016.

Gholi Majd, Mohammad. "The Three Famines and the Makings of a Malthusian Catastrophe in Iran (1869–1944)". *Quarterly Journal of the Iranian Islamic Period History* 12, 27 (2021): 75–105.

Ghulam Kabir, Muhammad. *Minority Politics in Bangladesh*. Delhi: Vikas, 1980.

Gilbert, Martin. *The Routledge Atlas of the Second World War*. London and New York: Routledge, 2008.

Ginio, Ruth. *French Colonialism Unmasked: The Vichy Years in French West Africa*. Lincoln and London: University of Nebraska Press, 2006.

Glover, Jonathan. *Humanity: A Moral History of the Twentieth Century*. London: Pimlico, 2001.

Goldhagen, Daniel. *Hitler's Willing Executioners*. New York: Vintage Books, 1997.

Goodman, Steve. *Sonic Warfare: Sound, Affect, and the Ecology of Fear*. Cambridge and London: MIT Press, 2010.

Gorbatov, Boris. *Die Unbeugsamen*. Stockholm: Neuer Verlag, 1944.

Gordon, Joy. "A Peaceful, Silent, Deadly Remedy: The Ethics of Economic Sanctions". *Ethics and International Affairs* 13, 1 (1999): 123–142.

Gouda, Frances, with Thijs Brocades Zaalberg. *American Visions of the Netherlands East Indies/ Indonesia: US Foreign Policy and Indonesian Nationalism, 1920–1949*. Amsterdam: Amsterdam University Press, 2002.

Government of Pakistan. *White Paper on the Crisis in East Pakistan*. N.p. [Rawalpindi]: Government of Pakistan, August 5, 1971.

Grant, Andrea Mariko. "Noise and Silence in Rwanda's Postgenocide Religious Soundscape". *Journal of Religion in Africa* 48 (2018): 35–64.

Greene-May, M. R. "Living and Dying in the Age of COVID-19: Social Murder, Reproduction, and Rhetoric". *Cultural Critique* 120 (2023): 126–141.

Greengrass, Mark. „Hidden Transcripts: Secret Histories and Personal Testimonies of Religious Violence in the French Wars of Religion". *The Massacre in History*, eds. Mark Levene and Penny Roberts. New York and Oxford: Berghahn, 1999: 69–88.

Greenspoon, Lior, et al. "The global biomass of wild mammals". *PNAS* 120, 10, 2023 (February 27, 2023), https://doi.org/10/1073/pnas.2204892120.

Grigg, David. *The World Food Problem*. Oxford and New York: Basil Blackwell, 1986.

Gross, Jan. *Revolution from Abroad: The Soviet Conquest of Poland's Western Ukraine and Western Belorussia*. Princeton: Princeton University Press, 1988.

Grundlingh, Louis. "The Military, Race and Resistance: The Conundrums of Recruiting Black South African Men during the Second World War". *Africa and World War II*, eds. Judith Byfield et al. New York: Cambridge University Press, 2015: 71–88.

Grüter, Balthasar. *Aufstachelung zum Massenmord? Das Radioprogramm von Radio Télévision Libre des Mille Collines in Ruanda von Juli 1993 bis Juli 1994*. Master's thesis, University of Bern, June 2016.

Gudkov, Lev. "Die Fesseln des Sieges: Russlands Identität aus der Erinnerung an den Krieg". *Osteuropa* 55, 4–6 (2005): 56–73.

Gudkov, Lev. "The fetters of history: How the war provides Russia with its identity", 2005, www.eurozine.com/articles/2005-05-03-gudkov.en.html.

Guha, Ranajit. *History at the Limits of World-History*. New York: Columbia University Press, 2002.

Gunn, Geoffrey. "The Great Vietnamese Famine of 1944–45 Revisited". *Asia-Pacific Journal*, no date [2011], japanfocus.org/-geoffrey-gunn/3483/article.htlm.

Gunn, Geoffrey. *Rice Wars in Colonial Vietnam: The Great Famine and the Viet Minh Road to Power*. Lanham et al.: Rowman and Littlefield, 2014.

Gutmann, Jerg, et al. *Sanctioned to Death? The Impact of Economic Sanctions on Life Expectancy and Its Gender Gap*. Munich: CESifo working paper, 2019.
Haak, Sebastian. *The Making of* The Good War: *Hollywood, das Pentagon und die amerikanische Deutung des Zweiten Weltkriegs 1945–1962*. Paderborn: Schöningh, 2013.
Hachiya, Michihiko. *Hiroshima Diary*. Chapel Hill: University of North Carolina Press, 1985, tenth ed.
Haider, Zaglul. "Repatriation of the Biharis Stranded in Bangladesh: Diplomacy and Development". *Asian Profile* 31, 6 (2003): 525–541.
Harerimana, Prosper. "Death and Life after Death in Rwandan Culture", 2009. https://deathinafrica.wordpress.com/2009/05/02/death-and-life-after-death-in-rwandan-culture-by-prosper-harerimana-hareprosyahoofr/.
Hart, Nicki. "Famine Maternal Nutrition and Infant Mortality: A Re-Examination of the Dutch Hunger Winter". *Population Studies*, 47, 1 (1993): 27–46.
Hartmann, Betsy, and James Boyce. *A Quiet Violence: View from a Bangladesh Village*. London: Zed, 1983.
Hasselmann, Anne. *Wie der Krieg ins Museum kam: Akteure der Erinnerung in Moskau, Minsk und Tscheljabinsk, 1941–1956*. Bielefeld: Transcript, 2022.
Hatzfeld, Jean. *Nur das nackte Leben: Berichte aus den Sümpfen Ruandas*. Giessen: Haland & Wirth and Psychosozial-Verlag, 2004.
Hatzfeld, Jean. *Zeit der Macheten: Gespräche mit den Tätern des Völkermords in Ruanda*. Giessen: Haland & Wirth and Psychosozial-Verlag, 2004.
Haridas, G.[opal]. "Infantile Beri-beri in Singapore in the Latter Part of the Japanese Occupation". *Archives of Disease in Childhood* 22, 1947: 23–33.
Hausmann, Guido. "Die unfriedliche Zeit: Politischer Totenkult im 20. Jahrhundert". *Gefallenengedenken im globalen Vergleich*, eds. Manfred Hettling and Jörg Echternkamp. Munich: Oldenbourg, 2013: 413–438.
Häusser, Alexander, and Gordon Maugg. *Hungerwinter: Deutschlands humanitäre Katastrophe 1946/47*. Berlin: List, 2009.
Hearman, Vannessa. "Hearing the 1965–66 Indonesian Anti-Communist Repression". *A Cultural History of Sound, Memory and the Senses*, eds. Joy Darmousi and Paula Hamilton. New York and London: Routledge, 2017: 142–156.
Hedinger, Daniel. *Die Achse: Berlin – Tokio – Rom 1919–1946*. Munich: Beck, 2021.
Hefley, James und Marti Hefley. *Christ in Bangladesh*. New York et al.: Harper and Row, 1973.
Helal, Emad Ahmed. "Egypt's Overlooked Contribution to World War II". *The World in World Wars: Experiences, Perceptions and Perspectives from Africa and Asia*, eds. Heike Liebau et al. Leiden and Boston: Brill, 2010: 217–247.
Hemetsberger-Koller, Hildegard. "Unternehmen Bergius "Nahrung aus Holz": Prestigeprojekt der Hungerjahre 1945/46". *Zeitgeschichte* 26, 2 (1999): 108–126.
Henebury, Anja, and Yehonatan Alsheh, eds. *Silence after violence*, special issue, *Acta Academica* 47, 1 (2015).
Hénia, Latifa. "Les grandes sécheresses en Tunisie au cours de la dernière période séculaire". *Eau et environnement: Tunisie et milieux méditerranéens*, eds. Paul Arnoult and Micheline Hotyat. Lyon: ENS, 2003: 25–36.
Herbert, Ulrich. "Arbeiterschaft im 'Dritten Reich': Zwischenbilanz und offene Fragen". *Geschichte und Gesellschaft* 15 (1989): 320–360.
Hess, Peter. *Bangladesh: Tragödie einer Staatsgründung*. Frauenfeld and Stuttgart: Huber, 1972.
Hicks, Jeremy. "Confronting the Holocaust: Mark Donskoi's *The Unvanquished*". *Studies in Russian and Soviet Cinema* 3, 1 (2009): 33–51.

Hicks, Jeremy. *First Films of the Holocaust: Soviet Cinema and the Genocide of the Jews*. Pittsburgh: University of Pittsburgh Press, 2012.
Hida, Shuntaro. *Der Tag, an dem Hiroshima verschwand: Erinnerungen eines japanischen Militärarztes*. Bremen: Donat, 1986.
Hilberg, Raul. *Perpetrators, Victims, Bystanders: The Jewish Catastrophe 1933–1945*. New York: Harper Perennial, 1992.
Hinton, Alexander Laban, ed. *Annihilating Difference: The Anthropology of Genocide*. Berkeley et al.: University of California Press, 2002.
Hionidou, Violetta. *Famine and Death in Occupied Greece, 1941–1944*. Cambridge et al.: Cambridge University Press, 2006.
Hionidou, Violetta. „Relief and Politics in Occupied Greece, 1941–4". *Journal of Contemporary History* 48 (2013): 761–783.
Hoffmann, Martin. "Der Zweite Weltkrieg in der offiziellen sowjetischen Erinnerungskultur". *Krieg und Erinnerung*, ed. Helmut Berding. Göttingen: Vandenhoeck & Ruprecht, 2000: 129–143.
Horne, Alistair. *A Savage War of Peace: Algeria, 1954–1962*. New York: Macmillan, 1977.
Huff, Gregg. "The Great Second World War Vietnam and Java Famines". *Modern Asian Studies* 54, 2 (2020): 1–36.
Huff, Gregg, and Gillian Huff. "Urban growth and change in 1940s Southeast Asia". *Economic History Review* 68, 2 (2015): 522–547.
Huff, Gregg, and Gillian Huff. "The Second World War Japanese Occupation of Singapore". *Journal of Southeast Asian Studies* 51, 1–2 (2020): 243–270.
Huff, Gregg, and Shinobu Majima. "Financing Japan's World War II Occupation of Southeast Asia". *Journal of Economic History* 73, 4 (2013): 937–977.
Huff, Gregg, and Shinobu Majima, eds. *World War II Singapore: The Chosabu Reports on Syonan*. Singapore: NUS Press, 2018.
Huq, M. Ameerul, ed. *Exploitation and the Rural Poor*. Comilla: Bangladesh Academy for Rural Development, 1976.
Hutchins, Francis. *India's Revolution: Gandhi and the Quit India Movement*. Cambridge: Harvard University Press, 1973.
Ihde, Don. *Listening and Voice: Phenomenologies of Sound*. Albany: State University of New York, 2007, second rev. ed.
Imam, Jahanara. *Of Blood and Fire*. New Delhi: Sterling, 1989.
Imhasly, Patrick. "Wo ist das Gewusel Afrikas?" *Neue Zürcher Zeitung*, July 17, 2022: 14.
Ingrao, Christian. *Hitlers Elite*. Berlin: Propyläen, 2012.
Irvin-Erickson, Douglas. *Raphaël Lemkin and the Concept of Genocide*. Philadelphia: University of Pennsylvania Press, 2017.
Irlye, Akira. *The Origins of the Second World War in Asia and the Pacific*. Abingdon and New York: Routledge, 2013 [first 1987].
Isaacs-Martin, Wendy. "Political and Ethnic Identity in Violent Conflict: The Case of Central African Republic". *International Journal of Conflict and Violence* 10 (2016): 25–39.
Islam, Rafiq ul. *A Tale of Millions*. Dacca: Bangladesh Books International, 1981.
Ito, Narihiko, et.al., eds. *Seit jenem Tag: Hiroshima und Nagasaki in der japanischen Literatur*. Frankfurt a.M.: Fischer, 1984.
Jackson, Ashley. *Botswana 1939–1945: An African Country at War*. Oxford: Clarendon, 1999.
Jackson, Ashley. *War and Empire in Mauritius and the Indian Ocean*. Basingstoke: Palgrave, 2001.
Jackson, Ashley. *The British Empire and the Second World War*. London and New York: Continuum, 2006.

Jackson, Ashley. "Ceylon's Home Front during the Second World War". *Home Fronts: Britain and the Empire at War, 1939–1945*, eds. Mark Crowley and Sandra Trudgen Dawson. Rochester: Boydell, 2017: 111–129.

Jahan, Rounaq. "Genocide in Bangladesh." *Genocide in the Twentieth Century*, eds. Samuel Totten and William S. Parsons. New York/London: Garland, 1995: 371–402.

Jahn, Peter. „Patriotismus, Stalinismuskritik und Hollywood: Der ‚Grosse Vaterländische Krieg' in russischen TV-Serien der Gegenwart". *Kriegsbilder: Mediale Repräsentationen des ‚Grossen Vaterländischen Krieges'*, eds. Beate Fieseler and Jörg Ganzenmüller. Fulda: Fuldaer Verlagsanstalt, 2010: 115–130.

Jastrząb, Mariusz. "Rationierungspolitik in Polen zwischen 1945 und 1953. *Hunger, Ernährung und Rationierungssysteme unter dem Staatssozialismus (1917–2006)*, eds. Matthias Middell and Felix Wemheuer. Frankfurt am Main et al.: Peter Lang, 2011: 183–211.

Jennings, Eric. *Vichy sous les tropiques: La Révolution nationale à Madagascar, en Guadeloupe, en Indochine 1940–1944*. Paris: Bernard Grasset, 2004.

Jones, Adam. "On the Genocidal Aspects of Certain Subaltern Uprisings". *Genocides by the Oppressed*, eds. Nicholas Robins and Adam Jones. Bloomington and Indianapolis: Indiana University Press, 2009: 47–57.

Jones, Adam, and Nicholas Robins. "Introduction: Subaltern Genocide in Theory and Practice". *Genocides by the Oppressed*, eds. Nicholas Robins and Adam Jones. Bloomington and Indianapolis: Indiana University Press, 2009: 1–24.

Jose, Ricardo. "The Rice Shortage and Countermeasures during the Occupation". *The Philippines under Japan: Occupation Policy and Reaction*, eds. Setsuho Ikehata and Ricardo Troba Jose. Manila: Ateneo de Manila Press, 1999: 197–214.

Kabir, Shariar, ed. *Tormenting Seventy One: An account of Pakistan army's atrocities during Bangladesh liberation war of 1971*. Dhaka: Nirmul Committee, 1999.

Kahin, George McT. "The Crisis and Its Aftermath". *Far Eastern Survey* 17, 22 (17 November 1948): 261–264.

Kahin, George McTurnan. *Nationalism and Revolution in Indonesia*. Ithaca: Cornell University Press, 2003 [first 1952].

Kammen, Douglas. *Three Centuries of Conflict in East Timor*. New Brunswick and London: Rutgers University Press, 2015.

Kamtekar, Indivar. "A Different War Dance: State and Class in India 1939–1945". *Past & Present* 176 (2002): 187–221.

Kannapin, Detlef. „Avantgarde, Agonie und Anpassung: Die ideologischen Grundlagen des sowjetischen Kinos nach 1945". *Leinwand zwischen Tauwetter und Frost: Der osteuropäische Spiel- und Dokumentarfilm im Kalten Krieg*, ed. Lars Karl. Berlin: Metropol, 2007: 21–36.

Kapchan, Deborah. "The Splash of Icarus: Theorizing Sound Writing/Writing Sound Theory", *Theorizing Sound Writing*, ed. Deborah Kapchan. Middletown: Wesleyan University Press, 2017: 1–22.

Kapchan, Deborah. "Listening Acts: Witnessing the Pain (and Praise) of Others". *Theorizing Sound Writing*, ed. Deborah Kapchan. Middletown: Wesleyan University Press, 2017: 277–293.

Karberg, Sascha, and Deike Diening. „Christian Drosten im Interview: ‚Wir alle sind die Welle'". *Tagesspiegel* online, September 22, 2020.

Karl, Lars. „Von Helden und Menschen: Der Zweite Weltkrieg im sowjetischen Spielfilm (1941–1965)". *Osteuropa* 52, 1 (2002): 67–82.

Karl, Lars. „Zwischen politischem Ritual und kulturellem Dialog: Die Moskauer Internationalen Filmfestspiele im Kalten Krieg 1959–1971". *Leinwand zwischen Tauwetter und Frost: Der osteuropäische Spiel- und Dokumentarfilm im Kalten Krieg*, ed. Lars Karl. Berlin: Metropol, 2007: 279–298.

Keller, Christoph. „Das ist Sozialdarwinismus nach Schweizer Art". *Neue Zürcher Zeitung am Sonntag*, January 16, 2022: 17.

Kenez, Peter. *Cinema and Soviet Society, 1917–1953*. Cambridge: Cambridge University Press, 1992.

Kessler, Mario. "Postkolonialismus und Internationalismus". *Historiker streiten*, eds. Susan Neiman and Michael Wildt. Berlin: Propyläen, 2023: 155–170.

Khenouf, Mohamed, and Michael Brett. "Algerian Nationalism and the Allied Military Strategy and Propaganda during the Second World War". *Africa and the Second World War*, eds. David Killingray and Richard Rathbone. Basingstoke and London: Macmillan, 1986: 258–274.

Killingray, David. "Labour Mobilisation in British Colonial Africa for the War Effort, 1939–1946". *Africa and the Second World War*, eds. David Killingray and Richard Rathbone. Basingstoke and London: Macmillan, 1986: 68–96.

Killingray, David, and Richard Rathbone, eds. *Africa and the Second World War*. Basingstoke and London: Macmillan, 1986.

Killingray, David, and Richard Rathbone. "Introduction". *Africa and the Second World War*, eds. David Killingray and Richard Rathbone. Basingstoke and London: Macmillan, 1986: 1–19.

Kimoni, Mary. "RTLM: the Medium That Became a Tool for Mass Murder". *The Media and the Rwandan Genocide*, ed. Allan Thompson. New York et al.: Pluto, 2007: 110–124.

Kimonyo, Jean-Paul. *Rwanda's Popular Genocide*. Boulder and London: Lynne Rienner, 2016.

Kinder von Hiroshima. Frankfurt a.M.: Röderberg, 1981, fourth ed.

Kleinen, John. *Facing the Future, Reviving the Past: A Study of Social Change in a Northern Vietnamese village*. Singapore: ISEAS, 1999.

Klöss, Erhard, ed. *Der Luftkrieg über Deutschland 1939–1945*. Munich: dtv, 1964.

Knight, Henry. *Food Administration in India 1939–1947*. Stanford: Stanford University Press, 1954.

Komlosy, Andrea. *Zeitenwende: Corona, Big Data und die kybernetische Zukunft*. Vienna: Promedia, 2022.

Kratoska, Paul. "Introduction". *Asian Labor in the Wartime Japanese Empire*, ed. Paul Kratoska. Armonk and London: M. E. Sharpe, 2005: xv–xviii.

Kratoska, Paul. *The Japanese Occupation of Malaya and Singapore: A Social and Economic History*. Singapore: NUS Press, 2018, second ed.

Kubai, Anne. "Post-Genocide Rwanda: The Changing Religious Landscape". *Exchange* 36 (2007): 198–214.

Kucherenko, Olga. *Little Soldiers: How Soviet Children Went to War, 1941–1945*. Oxford et al: Oxford University Press, 2011.

Kukulin, Ilja. "Schmerzregulierung: Zur Traumaverarbeitung in der sowjetischen Kriegsliteratur". *Osteuropa* 55, 4–6 (2005): 235–255.

Kündig, Camille, and Danny Schlumpf, "Corona-Chaos an Berner Schulen: 'Regierungsrat Schnegg durchseucht unsere Kinder mit Gewalt'". *Blick*, November 21, 2021, https://wwwmsn.com/de-ch/nachrichten/politik/corona-chaos-an-berner-schulen-%c2%abregierungsrat-schnegg-durchseucht-unsere-kinder-mit-gewalt%c2%bb/ar-AAQXJwa?ocid_se.

Kurasawa, Aiko. "Transportation and Rice Distribution in South-East Asia during the Second World War". *Food Supplies and the Japanese Occupation in South-East Asia*, ed. Paul Kratoska. Basingstoke: Macmillan, 1998: 32–66.

Laakkonen, Simo, et al. *The Long Shadows: A Global Environmental History of the Second World War*. Corvallis: Oregon State University Press, 2017.

Laakkonen, Simo, et al. "The Long Shadows". *The Long Shadows: A Global Environmental History of the Second World War*, eds. Simo Laakkonen et al. Corvallis: Oregon State University Press, 2017: 3–13.

Labrousse, Henri. *L'Océan Indien dans le Seconde Guerre Mondiale*. Paris: Economica, 2007.

Lange, Katharina. "Peripheral Experiences: Everyday Life in Kurd Dagh (Northern Syria) During the Allied Occupation in the Second World War". *The World in World Wars: Experiences, Perceptions and Perspectives from Africa and Asia*, eds. Heike Liebau et al. Leiden and Boston: Brill, 2010: 401–428.

Láníček, Jan, and Jan Lambertz, eds. *More Than Parcels: Wartime Aid for Jews in Nazi-Era Camps and Ghettos*. Detroit: Wayne State University Press, 2022.

Lary, Diana. "Drowned Earth: The Strategic Breaching of the Yellow River Dyke, 1938". *War in History* 8, 2 (2001): 191–207.

Lary, Diana. *The Chinese People at War: Human Suffering and Social Transformation, 1937–1945*. Cambridge and New York: Cambridge University Press, 2010.

Lastra, James. „Reading, Writing and Representing Sounds". *Sound Theory, Sound Practice*, ed. Rick Altman. London and New York: Routledge, 1992: 65–86.

Laur, Ernst. "Die Beschlüsse der Internationalen Lebensmittel- und Agrarkonferenz der Vereinigten Nationen in Hot Springs (U.S.A.)". *Beiträge zum Ausbau der schweizerischen Wirtschaft*, ed. Ernst Laur. Brugg: Verlag des Schweizerischen Bauernsekretariats, 1943.

Laurie, Emma, and Ian Shaw. "Violent conditions: The injustices of being". *Political Geography* 65 (2018): 8–16.

Lauterbach, Reinhard. "Ausbeutung und Renitenz". *Junge Welt*, February 17, 2021: 11.

Lovering, Timothy. "Military Service, Nationalism and Race: The Experience of Malawians in the Second World War". *The World in World Wars: Experiences, Perceptions and Perspectives from Africa and Asia*, eds. Heike Liebau et al. Leiden and Boston: Brill, 2010: 107–129.

Le Joubioux, Hervé. "L'île de la Réunion dans le Seconde Guerre mondiale". *Revue historique des armées* 263 (2011): 81–92.

Leber, Sebastian. „Nach Streit um Maskenpflicht: Rechte jubeln über Mord in Idar-Oberstein". *Tagesspiegel* online, September 21, 2021.

Lemkin, Raphael. *Axis Rule in Occupied Europe*. Washington: Carnegie Endowment for International Peace, 1944.

Leonard, Thomas, and John Bratzel, eds. *Latin American during World War II*. Lanham et al.: Rowman and Littlefield, 2007.

Levene, Mark. „Introduction". *The Massacre in History*, eds. Mark Levene and Penny Roberts. New York and Oxford: Berghahn, 1999: 1–38.

Levisse-Touzé, Christine. *L'Afrique du nord dans la guerre 1939–1945*. Paris: Albin Michel, 1998.

Li, Darryl. "Echoes of violence: considerations on radio and genocide in Rwanda". *Journal of Genocide Research* 6, 1 (2004): 9–27.

Liebau, Heike, et al. "Introduction". *The World in World Wars: Experiences, Perceptions and Perspectives from Africa and Asia*, eds. Heike Liebau et al. Leiden and Boston: Brill, 2010: 1–25.

Lieser, Jürgen *"Unser Reichtum hat immer unsere Armut hervorgebracht": Zur Geschichte und Gegenwart wirtschaftlicher Abhängigkeit und politischer Unterdrückung in Bolivien*. Bonn and Trier: Informationsstelle Lateinamerika and Bolivienhilfe, 1982, second ed.

Lilly, Robert. *Taken by Force: Rape and American GIs in Europe during World War II*. Basingstoke and New York: Palgrave Macmillan, 2007.

Lindstrom, Lamont. "Working Encounters: Oral Histories of World War II Labor Corps from Tanna, Vanuatu". *The Pacific Theatre; Island Representations of World War II*, eds. Geoffrey White and Lamont Lindstrom. Honolulu: University of Hawaii Press, 1989: : 395–417.

Lindstrom, Lamont, and Geoffrey White. "War Stories". *The Pacific Theatre; Island Representations of World War II*, eds. Geoffrey White and Lamont Lindstrom. Honolulu: University of Hawaii Press, 1989: 3–40.

Lindstrom, Lamont, and Geoffrey White. *Island Encounters: Black and White Memories of the Pacific War*. Washington and London: Smithsonian Institution Press, 1990.

Lloyd, E. M. H. *Food and Inflation in the Middle East 1940–1945*. Stanford: Stanford University Press, 1956.

Lockerbie, Jeannie. *On Duty in Bangladesh*. Grand Rapids: Zondervan, 1976.

Löhe, Fabian. „Durchsetzung der Maskenpflicht: Kommunalpolitiker immer öfter beleidigt, bespuckt, geschlagen". *Tagesspiegel* online, April 27, 2021.

Longman, Timothy. *Christianity and Genocide in Rwanda*. Cambridge: Cambridge University Press, 2010.

Lonsdale, John. "The Depression and the Second World War in the Transformation of Kenya". *Africa and the Second World War*, eds. David Killingray and Richard Rathbone. Basingstoke and London: Macmillan, 1986: 97–142.

Loshak, David. *Pakistan Crisis*. New York et al.: McGraw Hill, 1971.

Lovgren, Stefan. "Die letzten Giganten der Flüsse". https://spektrum.de/news/riesenfische-die-letzten-giganten-der-fluesse/2143479, May 22, 2023.

Lowe, Keith. *Der wilde Kontinent: Europa in den Jahren der Anarchie 1943–1950*. Stuttgart: Klett Cotta, 2014.

Lu Xun. "Wartime collaborations in rural North China". *Unknown Conflicts of the Second World War: Forgotten Fronts*, ed. Chris Murray. London and New York: Routledge, 2019: 171–192.

Lutz, Tom. Crying: *The Natural and Cultural History of Tears*. New York and London: W.W. Norton, 1999.

MacKenzie, S. P. "The treatment of prisoners of war in World War II". *Journal of Modern History* 66 (1994): 487–520.

MacPherson, Neil. "Death Railway Movements", n.d. http://www.mansell.com/pow_resources/camp lists/death_rr/movements_1.html.

Maddox, Gregory. "Food Disruption and Agricultural Policy in Tanganyika". *The Long Shadows: A Global Environmental History of the Second World War*, eds. Simo Laakkonen et al. Corvallis: Oregon State University Press, 2017: 231–249.

Malkki, Liisa. *Purity and Exile: Violence, Memory, and National Cosmology among Hutu Refugees in Tanzania*. Chicago and London: University of Chicago Press, 1995.

Malm, Andreas. *Corona, Climate, Chronic Emergency: War Communism in the Twenty-First Century*. London and New York: Verso, 2020.

Mamdani, Mahmood. *When Victims Become Killers: Colonialism, Nativism, and the Genocide in Rwanda*. Princeton: Princeton University Press, 2001.

Mamoon, Muntassir, ed. *1971 Chuknagar Genocide*, second ed. Dhaka: University Press Publishers, 2014.

Mandel, Ernest. *Der Zweite Weltkrieg*. Frankfurt am Main: ISP, 1991.

Maniruzzaman, Talukder. *The Bangladesh Revolution and Its Aftermath*. Dacca: Bangladesh Books International, 1980.

Manley, Rebecca. "The Perils of Displacement: The Soviet Evacuee between Refugee and Deportee". *Contemporary European History* 16, 4 (2007): 495–509.

Mann, Michael. *The Dark Side of Democracy*. Cambridge et al.: Cambridge University Press, 2005.

Mark, Ethan. *Japan's Occupation of Java in the Second World War*. London: Bloomsbury, 2018.
Marr, David. *Vietnam 1945: The Quest for Power*. Berkeley et al.: University of California Press, 1995.
Marr, David. *Vietnam: State, War, and Revolution (1945–1946)*. Berkeley et al.: University of California Press, 2013.
Marx, Karl. *The Eighteenth Brumaire of Louis Bonaparte*. https://www.marxists.org/archive/marx/works/1852/18th-brumaire/ch01.htm.
Mascarenhas, Anthony. *The Rape of Bangla Desh*. Delhi et al.: Vikas, n.y. [1971].
Massa, François. *Bengale: Historie d'un conflit*. Paris: Éditions Alain Moreau, 1972.
Mater, Nadire, ed. *Voices from the Front: Turkish Soldiers on the War with the Kurdish Guerrillas*. New York and Basingstoke: Palgrave Macmillan, 2005.
Mawdsley, Evan. *World War II: A New History*. Cambridge et al.: Cambridge University Press, 2009.
Mawdsley, Evan. "World War II: A Global Perspective". *The Long Shadows: A Global Environmental History of the Second World War*, eds. Simo Laakkonen et al. Corvallis: Oregon State University Press, 2017: 37–52.
Mayall, James, and Ricardo Soares de Oliveira, eds. *The New Protectorates*. New York: Hurst, 2011.
Mayroth, Natalie. „'Virus unter Kontrolle', meldet ausgerechnet Indiens grösster Slum". *Neue Zürcher Zeitung*, July 6, 2020: 4.
Mazimpaka, Jean Louis. "I survived the Rwandan genocide". *Guardian* online, July 18, 2009.
Mazower, Mark. *Inside Hitlers Greece*. New Haven and London: Yale University Press, 2001.
Mazower, Mark. *No Enchanted Palace: The End of Empire and the Ideological Origins of the United Nations*. Princeton and Oxford: Princeton University Press, 2009.
Mazzali, Francesca. *The Kremlin's Propaganda for Patriotic Education and Russian War Movies (2000–2010)*. Ph.D. dissertation, Charles University, Prague, 2016.
Mbembe, Achille. *Ausgang aus langer Nacht: Versuch über ein entkolonialisiertes Afrika*. Frankfurt a.M.: Suhrkamp, 2016.
McDoom, Omar Shahabudin. "The Psychology of Threat in Intergroup Conflict: Emotions, Rationality, and Opportunity in the Rwandan Genocide". *International Security* 37, 2 (2012): 119–155.
McDowell, David. *A Modern History of the Kurds*. London et al.: I.B. Tauris, 2021, fourth ed.
McFarland, Stephen. "Anatomy of an Iranian Political Crowd: The Tehran Bread Riot of December 1942". *International Journal of Middle East Studies* 17, 1 (1985): 51–65.
McGibbon, Elizabeth. "The COVID-19 Pandemic: On the Everyday Mechanisms of Social Murder". *Critical Studies* 16, 1 (2021): 35–42.
McKinley, Jim. *Death to Life: Bangladesh as Experienced by a Missionary Family*. Louisville: Highview Baptist Church, n.y.
Melber, Takuma. *Zwischen Kollaboration und Widerstand: Die japanische Besatzung in Malaya und Singapur (1942–1945)*. Frankfurt a.M. and New York: Campus, 2017.
Merridale, Catherine. *Nights of Stone: Death and Memory in Russia*. London: Granta, 2000.
Metcalf, Peter, and Richard Huntington. *Celebrations of Death: The Anthropology of Mortuary Ritual*. New York et al.: Cambridge University Press 1991: 43–61.
Michaels, Axel. *Der Hinduismus*. Munich: Beck, 1998.
Mironko, Charles. "'Ibitero': Means and Motive in the Rwandan Genocide". *Genocide in Cambodia and Rwanda: New Perspectives*, ed. Susan Cook. New Brunswick and London: Transaction, 2006: 163–189.
Mironko, Charles. "The Effect of RTLM's Rhetoric of Ethnic Hatred in Rural Rwanda". *The Media and the Rwandan Genocide*, ed. Allan Thompson. New York et al.: Pluto, 2007: 125–135.
Missfelder, Jan-Friedrich. „Period Ear: Perspektiven einer Klanggeschichte der Neuzeit". *Geschichte und Gesellschaft* 38, 1 (2012): 21–47.

Missfelder, Jan-Friedrich. „Der Klang der Geschichte: Begriffe, Traditionen und Methoden der sound history". *Geschichte in Wissenschaft und Unterricht* 66, 11/12 (2015): 633–649.

Mitter, Rana. *China's War with Japan, 1937–1945*. London et al.: Penguin, 2013.

Mitter, Rana. *China's Good War: How World War II Is Shaping a New Nationalism*. Cambridge and London: Belknap, 2020.

Mokopakgosi III., Brian. "The Impact of the Second World War: the Case of Kareneng in the then Bechuanaland Protectorate, 1939–1950". *Africa and the Second World War*, eds. David Killingray and Richard Rathbone. Basingstoke and London: Macmillan, 1986: 160–180.

Mookherjee, Nayanika. *The Spectral Wound: Sexual Violence, Public Memory and the Bangladesh War of 1971*. Durham and London: Duke University Press, 2015.

Moore, Aaron William. *Bombing the City: Civilian Accounts of the Air War in Britain and Japan, 1939–1945*. Cambridge et al.: Cambridge University Press, 2018.

Morelli, Anne. *Die Prinzipien der Kriegspropaganda*. Springe: zu Klampen, 2021, third ed. [French 2004].

Moses, Dirk. *The Problems of Genocide: Permanent Security and the Language of Transgression*. Cambridge et al.: Cambridge University Press, 2021.

Msemburi, William, et al. "The WHO estimates of excess mortality associated with the COVID-19 pandemic". *Nature* 613 (January 5, 2023).

Mueller, John, and Karl Mueller. "Sanctions of Mass Destruction". *Foreign Affairs* 78, 3 (1999): 43–53.

Muhith, A. M. A. *Bangladesh: Emergence of a Nation*. Dacca: Bangladesh Books International, 1978.

Mukerjee, Madusree. *Churchill's Secret War: The British Empire and the Ravaging of India during World War II*. New York: Basic Books, 2010.

Mukherjee, Janam. *Hungry Bengal: War, Famine, Riots, and the End of Empire 1939–1946*. Ph.D dissertation, University of Michigan, 2011.

Mukherji, Partha. "The Great Migration of 1971. I – Exodus". *Economic and Political Weekly* 9, 9 (March 2, 1974): 365–369.

Mulder, Nicholas, and Boyd van Dijk. "Why Did Starvation Not Become the Paradigmatic War Crime in International Law?" *Contingency in International Law,* eds. Kevin Heller and Ingo Venzke. Oxford: Oxford University Press, 2021: 370–388.

Müller, Rolf-Dieter, ed. *Die deutsche Wirtschaftspolitik in den besetzten sowjetischen Gebieten: Der Abschlussbericht des Wirtschaftsstabes Ost und Aufzeichnungen eines Angehörigen des Wirtschaftskommandos Kiew*. Boppard: Harald Boldt, 1991.

Müller, Rolf-Dieter. *Der Bombenkrieg 1939–1945*. Berlin: Christoph Links, 2004.

Müller, Rolf-Dieter. *Der Zweite Weltkrieg*. Darmstadt: Wissenschaftliche Buchgesellschaft, 2015.

Muqeem Khan, Fazal. *Pakistan's Crisis in Leadership*. Islamabad et al.: National Book Foundation, 1973.

Murray, Chris, ed. *Unknown Conflicts of the Second World War: Forgotten Fronts*. London and New York: Routledge, 2019.

Murray, Chris. "Introduction: Forgotten fronts". *Unknown Conflicts of the Second World War: Forgotten Fronts*, ed. Chris Murray. London and New York: Routledge, 2019: 1–7.

Muscolino, Micah. "Violence Against People and the Land: The Environment and Refugee Migration from China's Henan Province, 1938–1945". *Environment and History* 17 (2011): 291–311.

Muscolino, Micah. "Conceptualizing Wartime Flood and Famine in China". *The Long Shadows: A Global Environmental History of the Second World War*, eds. Simo Laakkonen et al. Corvallis: Oregon State University Press, 2017: 97–115.

Mustafa, Sami. "Who Is Conducting a Genocide?" *Pakistan Forum* 3, 4 (1973): 15–16.

Muzaini, Hamzah, and Brenda Yeoh. *Contested Memoryscapes: The Politics of Second World War Commemoration in Singapore*. London and New York: Routledge, 2016.

„Nach Tod des Nachbarn: Ermittlungen nach mutmasslichem Verstoss gegen Corona-Quarantänepflicht". *Der Spiegel* online, February 8, 2022.

Nagai, Paul Takashi. *Die Glocken von Nagasaki*. Luzern: Schweizer Volk-Buchgemeinde, 1955, fourth ed.

Nakahara Michiko. "Malayan Labor on the Thailand-Burma Railway". *Asian Labor in the Wartime Japanese Empire*, ed. Paul Kratoska. Armonk and London: M. E. Sharpe, 2005: 249–265.

Nakamura, Takafusa. "The Age of Turbulence: 1937–54". *The Economic History of Japan: 1600–1990, vol. 3: Economic History of Japan 1914–1955: A Dual Structure*, eds. Takafusa Nakamura and Kônôsuke Odaka. Oxford et al.: Oxford University Press, 2003: 55–110.

Nancy, Jean-Luc. *Zum Gehör*. Zurich: diaphanes, 2010.

Nandi, Gouranga. „ Killing Fields in Khulna". *Tormenting Seventy One: An Account of Pakistany army's atrocities during Bangladesh liberation war of 1971*, ed. Shahriar Kabir. Dhaka: Nirmul Committee, 1999, www.mukto-mona.com/Special_Event_126-march/shahriar_kabir/Tormenting71_1.pdf.

Nero, Karen. "Time of Famine, Time of Transformation: Hell in the Pacific, Palau". *The Pacific Theatre; Island Representations of World War II*, eds. Geoffrey White and Lamont Lindstrom. Honolulu: University of Hawaii Press, 1989: 117–147.

Newitt, Malyn. "The Portuguese African Colonies during the Second World War". *Africa and World War II*, eds. Judith Byfield et al. New York: Cambridge University Press, 2015: 238–258.

Ngô Viñh Long. *Before the Revolution: The Vietnamese Peasants under the French*. New York: Columbia University Press, 1991 [first 1973]).

Niazi, A. A. K. *The Betrayal of East Pakistan*. Karachi et al.: Oxford University Press, 1998.

Nicholls, Lucius. "The State of Nutrition in Singapore before, during and after the Japanese Occupation". *British Medical Journal*, supplement, March 6, 1948.

Noman, Omar. *Pakistan: A Political and Economic History Since 1947*. London/New York: Kegan Paul International, 1988.

Noor, Masi, et al. "When Suffering Begets Suffering: The Psychology of Competitive Victimhood Between Adversarial Groups in Violent Conflict". *Personality and Social Psychology Review* 16, 4 (2012): 351–374.

Nussbaum, Martha. *Justice for Animals*. New York et al.: Simon and Schuster, 2022.

O'Grada, Cormac. *Famine: A Short History*. Princeton and Oxford: Princeton University Press, 2009.

Ogot, Bethwell. "Mau Mau and Nationhood: The untold story". *Mau Mau & Nationhood: Arms, Authority & Narration*, eds. E. S. Atieno Odhiambo and John Lonsdale. Oxford et al.: Ohio University Press, 2003: 8–36.

Ogura, Toyofumi. *Letters from the End of the World*. Tokio et.al.: Kodamsha International, 2001.

Olson, Marian. Bangladesh: *Tears and Laughter*. Willmar, MN: Willmar Assembly of God, 2002.

„Over one lakh killed in Khulna alone". *Bangladesh Observer*, February 4, 1972.

Overy, Richard. *Why the Allies Won*. New York and London: W.W. Norton, 1996.

Overy, Richard. "Front Line II: Civilians at War". *The Oxford Illustrated History of World War II*, ed. Richard Overy. Oxford: Oxford University Press, 2015: 293–321.

Overy, Richard. *Blood and Ruins: The Great Imperial War, 1931–1945*. London: Allan Lane, 2021.

Palairet, Michael. *The Four Ends of the Greek Hyperinflation of 1941–1946*. Copenhagen: Museum Tusculanum Press, 2000.

Palomo, Tony. "Island in Agony: The War in Guam". *Remembering the Pacific War*, ed. Geoffrey White. Honolulu: University of Hawaii, 1991: 133–144.

Parsons, Timothy. "The Military Experiences of Ordinary Africans in World War II". *Africa and World War II*, eds. Judith Byfield et al. New York: Cambridge University Press, 2015: 3–23.

Patton, Kimberley Christine, and John Stratton Hawley, eds. *Holy Tears: Weeping in the Religious Imagination*. Princeton and Oxford: Princeton University Press, 2005.
Paul, Axel, and Benjamin Schwalb, eds. *Gewaltmassen: Über Eigendynamik und Selbstorganisation kollektiver Gewalt*. Hamburg: Hamburger Edition, 2015.
Payne, Robert. *Massacre*. New York: Macmillan, 1973.
Peschanski, Denis. *La France des camps: L'internement 1938–1946*. Paris: Gallimard, 2002.
Petry, Erik. "Die erkenntnistheoretische falsche Frage: Was ist Antisemitismus?" *Jenseits von Mbembe: Geschichte, Erinnerung, Solidarität*, eds. Matthias Böckmann et al. Berlin: Metropol, 2022: 107–116.
Pika-don über Japan. Cologne: Maximilian, 1955.
Piton, Florent. *Le génocide des Tutsi du Rwanda*. Paris: La Découverte, 2018.
Planche, Jean-Louis. *Sétif 1945: Histoire d'un massacre annoncé*. Paris: Perrin, 2006.
Polewoi, Boris. *Der wahre Mensch*. Berlin [East] and Weimar, 1975.
Poljan, Pavel. "Westarbeiter: Reparation durch Arbeitskraft: Deutsche Häftlinge in der UdSSR". *Lager, Zwangsarbeiter, Vertreibung und Deportation: Dimensionen der Massenverbrechen in der Sowjetunion und in Deutschland 1933 bis 1945*, eds. Dittmar Dahlmann and Gerhard Hirschfeld. Essen: Klartext, 1999: 337–367.
Pollock, Nancy. "Nauruans during World War II". *Remembering the Pacific War*, ed. Geoffrey White. Honolulu: University of Hawaii, 1991: 91–107.
Power, Samantha. *"A Problem from Hell": America and the Age of Genocide*. New York: HarperCollins, 2003.
Poyer, Lin. "Micronesian Experiences of the War in the Pacific". *Remembering the Pacific War*, ed. Geoffrey White. Honolulu: University of Hawaii, 1991: 79–89.
Pozner, Valérie, and Natacha Laurent, eds. *Kinojudaica: les représentations des Juifs dans le cinéma de Russie et d'Union soviétique des années 1910 aux années 1980*. Paris: Nouveau monde, 2012.
"Preparatory Years: UN Charter History". https://www.un.org/en/about-us/history-of-the-un/preparatory-years.
Privitelli, Tobias. *Irredentism, Expansion and the Liberation of the European Proletariat: Stalin's Considerations on how to Bring Communism to the Western Neighbors of the Soviet Union, 1920–1941*. Ph.D dissertation, University of Bern, 2008.
Prunier, Gérard. *The Rwanda Crisis: History of a Genocide*. London: Hurst & Company, 1995.
Quader Quaderi, Fazlul, ed. *Bangladesh Genocide and World Press*. Dacca: Begum Dilafroz Quaderi, 1972.
Qureshi, Hakeem Arshad. *The 1971 Indo-Pak War: A Soldier's Narrative*. Oxford et al.: Oxford University Press, 2002.
Raghavan, Srinath. *India's War*. New York: Basic Books, 2016.
Rammstedt, Otthein, ed. *Gewaltverhältnisse und die Ohnmacht der Kritik*. Frankfurt a.M.: Suhrkamp, 1974.
Rashid, Saifur. "Meaning and Rituals of Death: An Insight into Selected Ethnic and Religious Communities of Bangladesh". *Vietnam Social Sciences* 5, 193 (2019): 75–92.
Rawls, John. *The Law of Peoples*. Cambridge and London: Harvard University Press, 1999.
Reid, Anthony. *The Indonesian National Revolution 1945–1950*. Westport: Greenwood, 1974.
Reinwald, Brigitte. "Zwischen Imperium und Nation: Westafrikanische Veteranen der französischen Armee am Beispiel des spätkolonialen Obervolta". Gerhard Höpp and Brigitte Reinwald, eds., *Fremdeinsätze: Afrikaner und Asiaten in europäischen Kriegen, 1914–1945*. Berlin: Das Arabische Buch, 2000: 227–252.
Republic of Rwanda, Parliament, The Senate. *Rwanda: Genocide Ideology and Strategies for Its Eradication*. Kigali: Senate, 2006.

Reydams, Luc. "NGO Justice: African Rights as Pseudo-Prosecutor of the Rwandan Genocide". *Human Rights Quarterly* 38, 3 (2016): 547–588.

Reydams, Luc. "Protesting Too Much: A Response to Linda Melvern et al." *Human Rights Quarterly* 40 (2018): 466–473.

Rheinisches JournalistInnenbüro. *"Unsere Opfer zählen nicht": Die Dritte Welt im Zweiten Weltkrieg.* Berlin and Hamburg: Assoziation A, 2005.

Robins, Nicholas, and Adam Jones, eds. *Genocides by the Oppressed.* Bloomington and Indianapolis: Indiana University Press, 2009.

Roorda, Eric Paul. "The Dominican Republic: The Axis, the Allies, and the Trujillo Dictatorship". *Latin America during World War II*, eds. Thomas Leonard and John Bratzel. Lanham et al.: Rowman and Littlefield, 2007: 75–91.

Roshwald, Aviel. *Occupied: European and Asian Resonses to Axis Conquest, 1937–1945.* Cambridge: Cambridge University Press, 2023.

Rossy, Katherine. "The UN search for stolen and hidden Polish children (1944–47)". *Unknown Conflicts of the Second World War: Forgotten Fronts*, ed. Chris Murray. London and New York: Routledge, 2019: 218–229.

Rostetter, Andri, et al., „Jeder Fünfte steckt sich zu Hause an: Entscheidende Daten zu Infektionsketten fehlen". *Neue Zürcher Zeitung*, December 11, 2020: 1.

Roth, Karl Heinz. *Blinde Passagiere: Die Coronakrise und die Folgen.* Munich: Antje Kunstmann, 2022.

Rothberg, Michael. *Multidirectional Memory: Remembering the Holocaust in the Age of Decolonization.* Stanford: Stanford University Press, 2009.

Röttgers, Kurt. "Andeutungen zu einer Geschichte des Redens über die Gewalt". *Gewaltverhältnisse und die Ohnmacht der Kritik*, ed. Otthein Rammstedt. Frankfurt a.M.: Suhrkamp, 1974: 157–234.

Roy, A. *Genocide of Hindus and Buddhists in East Pakistan/Bangladesh.* Delhi: Kranti Prakashan, 1981.

Roy, Beth. *Some Trouble With Cows: Making Sense of Social Conflict.* Berkeley et al.: University of California Press, 1994.

Rushbrook Williams, L.F. *The East Pakistan Tragedy.* New York: Drake, 1972.

Rwanda Youth & Children's Testimonies, University of Southern Florida, http://genocide.lib.usf.edu/taxonomy/term/1435.

Ryklin, Michail, et al. "Deutscher auf Abruf: Vom *Schwarzbuch* zur *Jungen Garde*". *Osteuropa* 55, 4–6 (2005): 165–177.

Saehrendt, Christian. „Corona bedroht die dionysische Kultur". *Neue Zürcher Zeitung*, January 13, 2022: 29.

Saikia, Yasmin. "Beyond the Archive of Silence: Narratives of the 1971 Liberation War of Bangladesh". *History Workshop Journal* 58 (2004): 275–287.

Saikia, Yasmin. *Women, War, and the Making of Bangladesh: Remembering 1971.* Durham, NC/London: Duke University Press, 2011.

Saikia, Yasmin. "Insāniyat for peace: survivors' narrative of the 1971 war of Bangladesh". *Journal of Genocide Research* 13, 4 (2011): 475–501.

Salik, Siddiq. *Witness to Surrender.* Karachi: Lancer, 1998, third ed.

Sato, Shigeru. *War, Nationalism and Peasants: Java and the Japanese Occupation 1942–1945.* Armonk and London: M. E. Sharpe, 1984.

Sato, Shigeru. "Economic life in villages and towns". *The Encyclopedia of Indonesia in the Pacific War*, eds. Peter Post et al. Leiden and Boston: Brill, 2010: 267–279.

Schaarschmidt, Siegfried, ed. *Schrei nach Frieden: Japanische Zeugnisse gegen den Krieg.* Düsseldorf and Vienna: Econ, 1984.

Schafer, R. Murray. *The Soundscape: Our Sonic Environment and the Tuning of the World*. Rochester: Destiny, 1994, second ed.

Schanberg, Sydney. „East Pakistan: An ‚Alien Army' Imposes Its Will". *New York Times*, July 4, 1971.

Schlootz, Johannes, ed. *Deutsche Propaganda in Weissrussland 1941–1944*. Berlin: Freie Universität Berlin, 1996.

Schmidt, Elizabeth. "Popular Resistance and Anticolonial Mobilization: The War Effort in French Guinea". *Africa and World War II*, eds. Judith Byfield et al. New York: Cambridge University Press, 2015: 441–461.

Scholochow, Michail. *Ein Menschenschicksal*. Frankfurt a.M.: Büchergilde, 2009 [1957].

Scholochow, Michail. *Sie kämpften für die Heimat*. Berlin [East]: Kultur und Fortschritt, 1960.

Schoppa, R. Keith. *In a Sea of Bitterness: Refugees during the Sino-Japanese War*. Cambridge and London: Harvard University Press, 2011.

Schulze, Holger. „Bewegung Berührung Übertragung". *Sound Studies*, ed. Holger Schulze. Bielefeld: Transcript, 2008: 143–165.

Schuman, Howard. "A Note on the Rapid Rise of Mass Bengali Nationalism in East Pakistan". *American Journal of Sociology* 28, 2 (1972): 290–298.

Schwartz, Michael. "Ethnische „Säuberung" als Kriegsfolge". *Das Deutsche Reich und der Zweite Weltkrieg*, vol. 10/2: *Der Zusammenbruch des Deutschen Reiches 1945 und die Folgen des Zweiten Weltkrieges*, sub-volume 2: *Die Auflösung der Wehrmacht und die Auswirkungen des Krieges*, ed. Rolf-Dieter Müller. Munich: Deutsche Verlags-Anstalt, 2008: 509–656.

Schweighauser, Philip. *The Noises of American Literature, 1890–1985*. Gainesville: University of Florida Press, 2006.

Scott, James. *Domination and the Arts of Resistance: Hidden Transcripts*. New Haven and London: Yale University Press, 1990.

Secretariat of the International Commission of Jurists. *The Events in East Pakistan, 1971: A Legal Study*. Geneva: International Commission of Jurists, 1972, http://nsm1.nsm.imp.edu/sanwar/Bangla desh%20Genocide.htm.

Segesser, Daniel Marc. *Recht statt Rache oder Rache durch Recht? Die Ahndung von Kriegsverbrechen in der internationalen wissenschaftlichen Debatte 1972–1945*. Paderborn: Ferdinand Schöningh, 2010.

Seikaly, Sherene. "A Nutritional Economy: The Calorie, Development and War in Mandate Palestine". *Home Fronts: Britain and the Empire at War, 1939–1945*, eds. Mark Crowley and Sandra Trudgen Dawson. Rochester: Boydell, 2017: 37–58.

Semelin, Jacques. "In consideration of massacres". *Journal of Genocide Research* 3, 3 (2001): 377–389.

Sémelin, Jacques. „Analyser le massacre: Reflexions comparatives". *Questions de Recherche* no. 7, 2012: 1–42.

Sen, Amartya. *Poverty and Famines*. Oxford: Clarendon, 1981.

Sen, Sumit. "Stateless Refugees and the Right to Return: The Bihari Refugees of South Asia, part I". *International Journal of Refugee Law* 11, 4 (1999): 625–645.

Sharif, Ahmed et al., eds., *Genocide '71: An Account of the Killers and Collaborators*. Dhaka: Muktijuddha Chetana Bikash Kendra, 1988.

Sharma, S. K., ed. *Quit India Movement*. New Delhi: Mittal, 2009.

Shimizu Hiroshi and Hitoshi Hirakawa. *Japan and Singapore in the World Economy: Japan's Advance into Singapore 1870–1965*. London: Routledge, 1999.

Shlapentokh, Dmitri, and Vladimir Shlapentokh. *Soviet Cinematography 1918–1991: Ideological Conflict and Social Reality*. New York: Aldine de Gruyter, 1993.

Shrader, Charles. *The Withered Vine: Logistics and the Communist Insurgency in Greece, 1945–1949*. Westport and London: Praeger, 1999.

Shub, Boris. *Starvation over Europe (Made in Germany)*. N.p. [New York]: Institute of Jewish Affairs, 1943.

Siddiqi, Kalim. *Conflict, Crisis and War in East Pakistan*. New York: Praeger, 1972.

Siegel, Benjamin. *Hungry Nation: Food, Famine and the Making of Modern India*. Cambridge et al.: Cambridge University Press, 2018.

Siemes, P. T. "The Atomic Bomb on Hiroshima: An Eye-Witness Account". *The Irish Monthly* 74, 873 (1946): 93–104 and 74, 874 (1946): 148–154.

Sim, Joe, and Steve Tombs. "The failings behind the UK's abysmal death toll", letter to the editor. *The Guardian* online, January 27, 2021.

Simatupang, T. B. *Report from Banaran: Experiences During the People's War*. Ithaca: Cornell University, 1972.

Simonow, Joana. "Der Hungertod in Bildern: Fotografie in der öffentlichen Debatte um Hungerhilfe in Bengalen 1943". *Zeithistorische Forschungen* 18 (2021): 346–362.

Simonow, Konstantin. *Die Lebenden und die Toten*. Berlin [East]: Kultur und Fortschritt, 1975 [1960].

Simonow, Konstantin. *Wie lang vergessene Träume*. Berlin [East]: Volk und Welt, 1975.

Singiza, Dantès. *La famine Ruzagayura (Rwanda, 1943–1944)*. Tervuren: Musée royale de l'Afrique centrale, 2011.

Sisson, Richard, and Leo Rose. *War and Secession: Pakistan, India, and the Creation of Bangladesh*. Berkeley et al.: University of California Press, 1990.

Sitrin, Marina, and Colectiva Sembrar. *Pandemic Solidarity: Mutual Aid During the Covid-19 Crisis*. London: Pluto, 2020.

Smail, John. *Bandung in the Early Revolution 1945–1946: A Study in the Social History of the Indonesian Revolution*. Singapore: Equinox, 2009 [first 1964].

Smillie, Ian. *Freedom from Want: The Remarkable Story of BRAC, the Global Grassroots Organization That's Winning the Fight Against Poverty*. Sterling: Kumarian, 2009.

Smith, Mark. *Listening to Nineteenth-Century America*. Chapel Hill and London: University of North Carolina Press, 2001.

Sofsky, Wolfgang. *Traktat über die Gewalt*. Frankfurt a.M.: Fischer, 1996.

Southard, Susan. *Nagasaki: Life After Nuclear War*. New York: Viking, 2015.

Spencer, Ian. "Settler Dominance, Agricultural Production and the Second World War in Kenya". *Journal of African History* 21, 4 (1980): 497–514.

Sperling, Carrie. "Mother of Atrocities: Pauline Nyiramasuhuko's Role in the Rwandan Genocide". *Fordham Urban Law Journal* 33, 2 (2006): 101–127.

Staub, Ervin. *The Roots of Evil: The Origins of Genocide and Other Group Violence*. Cambridge et al.: Cambridge University Press, 1989.

Stokke, Olav, ed. *Aid and Political Conditionality*. London: Frank Cass, 1995.

Stratton Hawley, John. „The Gopis' Tears". *Holy Tears: Weeping in the Religious Imagination*, eds. Kimberley Christine Patton and John Stratton Hawley. Princeton and Oxford: Princeton University Press, 2005: 94–111.

Straus, Scott. *The Order of Genocide: Race, Power and War in Rwanda*. Ithaca and London: Cornell University Press, 2006.

Straus, Scott. "What Is the Relationship between Hate Radio and Violence? Rethinking Rwanda's 'Radio Machete'". *Politics and Society* 35, 4 (2007): 609–637.

Südkamp, Holger. "Ich war neunzehn: Zur filmischen und politischen Bedeutung von Konrad Wolfs DEFA-Film". *Europäische Geschichtsdarstellungen – Diskussionspapiere* 2, 3 (2005): 2–17.

"Summary Judgment of the Media Trial" (ICTR-99-52-T, 3 December 2003). *The Media and the Rwandan Genocide*, ed. Allan Thompson. New York et al.: Pluto, 2007: 277–306.

Swift, Ann. *The Road to Madiun: The Indonesian Communist Uprising of 1948*. Ithaca: Cornell University, 1989.

Tamina, Qurratul Ain. "Zabunessa Begum: A Mother's Struggle for Her Family". *Rising from the Ashes: Women's Narratives of 1971*, eds. Shaheen Akhtar et al. Dhaka: Ain O Salish Kendra and University Press, 2014: 9–32.

Tauger, Mark. "The Indian Famine Crises of World War II". *British Scholar* 1, 2 (2009): 166–196.

Taylor, Christopher. *Milk, Honey, and Money: Changing Concepts in Rwandan Healing*. Washington and London: Smithsonian Institution Press, 1992.

Taylor, Christopher. "The Cultural Face of Terror in the Rwandan Genocide of 1994". *Annihilating Difference: The Anthropology of Genocide*, ed. Alexander Laban Hinton. Berkeley et al.: University of California Press, 2002: 137–178.

Tejel, Jordi. "The Kurds and World War II: Some Considerations for a Social History Perspective". *Kulturní Studia* 21 (2), 2023: 3–17.

Tembo, Alfred. *The Impact of the Second World War on Northern Rhodesia (Zambia), 1939–1953*. Ph.D dissertation, Bloemfontein: University of the Free State, 2015.

Terkel, Studs. *"The Good War": An Oral History of World War II*. New York: Pantheon, 1984.

Tewary, I.N. *War of Independence in Bangla Desh: A Documentary Study*. New Delhi: Navachetna Prakashan, 1971.

"The Joint Declaration of the Greater East Asia Conference in Tokyo, November 6, 1943". https://en.wikisource.org/wiki/Joint_Declaration_of_the_Greater_East_Asia_Conference.

"The Problem of Rice: Stenographic Notes on the Fourth Session of the Sanyo Kaigi, January 8, 2605, 10:00 A.M." *Indonesia* 2 (October 1966): 77–123.

Thibon, Christian. *Histoire démographique du Burundi*. Paris: Karthala, 2004.

Thomas, Martin. "Resource War, Civil War, Rights War: Factoring Empire into French North Africa's Second World War". *War in History* 18, 2 (2011): 225–248.

Thompson, Allan, ed. The Media and the Rwandan Genocide. New York et al.: Pluto, 2007.

Thompson, E. P. *The Making of the English Working Class*. New York: Penguin, 1968.

Thompson, Elizabeth. "The Climax and Crisis of the Colonial Welfare State in Syria and Lebanon during World War II". *War, Institutions and Social Change in the Middle East*, ed. Steven Heydemann. Berkeley et al.: University of California Press, 2000: 59–99.

Thousand My Lais: World Bank Study on Bangladesh. N.p., n.y. [1971].

Thrane, Susan. „Hindu End of Life: Death, Dying, Suffering, and Karma". *Journal of Hospice and Palliative Nursing* 6, 12 (2010): 337–342.

Tischler, Carola. „ Der Krieg als Komödie: Die Wiederkehr der sowjetischen Filmgroteske während des Zweiten Weltkrieges". *Kriegsbilder: Mediale Repräsentationen des ‚Grossen Vaterländischen Krieges'*, eds. Beate Fieseler and Jörg Ganzenmüller. Fulda: Fuldaer Verlagsanstalt, 2010: 63–76.

Tønnesson, Stein. *The Vietnamese Revolution of 1945: Roosevelt, Ho Chi Minh and de Gaulle in a World at War*. London: Sage and PRIO, 1991.

Totten, Samuel, and Rafiki Ubaldo, eds. *We Cannot Forget: Interviews with Survivors of the 1994 Genocide in Rwanda*. New Brunswick: Rutgers University Press, 2011.

Trials of War Criminals before the Nuremberg Military Tribunals under Control Council Law No. 10, vol. IV. Washington: U.S. Government Printing Office, 1949.

Tripathi, Salil. *The Colonel Who Would Not Repent: The Bangladesh War and Its Unquiet Legacy*. New Delhi: Aleph, 2014.

Tripathi, Salil. „Blood in the water: The contested history of one of Bangladesh's worst wartime massacres". *The Caravan*, November 1, 2014, https://caravanmagazine.in/essay/blood-water.

Tsu, Timothy, et al. "The Second World War in postwar Chinese and Japanese film". *Chinese and Japanese Films on the Second World War*, eds. King-fai Tam et al. London and New York: Routledge, 2015: 1–11.

Tubiana, Jerôme, Victor Tanner and Musa Adam Abdul-Jalil. *Traditional Authorities' Peacemaking Role in Darfur*. Washington: United States Institute for Peace, 2012.

Tumarkin, Nina. *The Living and the Dead: The Rise and Fall of the Cult of World War II in Russia*. New York, Basic Books, 1994.

Turnbull, C. M. *A History of Modern Singapore*. Singapore: NUS Press, 2016.

Turner, Michele. *Telling: East Timor: Personal Memories, 1942–1992*. Kensington: New South Wales University Press, 2003.

Twagilimana, Aimable, ed. *Teenage Refugees From Rwanda Speak Out*. New York: Rosen, 1997.

„Umfrage unter Wählern: Zwei von drei Ungeimpften wählen AfD oder ‚Die Basis'". *Tagesspiegel* online, November 11, 2021.

United Nations Intellectual History Project. *The Complete Oral History Transcripts from* UN Voices. New York: City University of New York, 2007.

Unruh, Jon, and Musa Adam Abdul-Jalil. "Constituencies of conflict and opportunity: Land rights, narratives and collective action in Darfur". *Political Geography* 42 (2016): 104–116.

Uvin, Peter. *Aiding Violence: The Development Enterprise in Rwanda*. West Hartford: Kumarian, 1998.

Vail, Leroy, and Landeg White. *Capitalism and Colonialism in Mozambique: A Study of Quelimane District*. London: Heineman, 1980.

van der Eng, Pierre. "Regulation and Control: Explaining the Reduction of Food Production in Java, 1940–6". *Food Supplies and the Japanese Occupation in South-East Asia*, ed. Paul Kratoska. Basingstoke: Macmillan, 1998: 187–207.

van der Eng, Pierre. *Food Supply in Java During War and Decolonization, 1940–1950* (no place, 2008), http://mpra.ub.unibe.uni-muenchen.de/8852/.

van der Zee, Henri. *The Hunger Winter: Occupied Holland 1944–5*. London: Jill Norman & Hobhouse, 1982.

van Hoyweghen, Saskia. "The Urgency of Land and Agrarian Reform in Rwanda". *African Affairs* 98, 392 (1999): 353–372.

van Schendel, Willem. *A History of Bangladesh*. Cambridge et al.: Cambridge University Press, 2009.

van't Spijker, Gerard. *Les usages funéraires et la mission de l'église: Une étude anthropologique et theologique des rites funéraires au Rwanda*. Kampen: Uitgeversmaatschappij, 1990.

Venkataramani, M. S. *Bengal Famine of 1943: The American Response*. Delhi et al.: Vikas, 1973.

Verhey, Jeffrey. *Der "Geist von 1914" und die Erfindung der Volksgemeinschaft*. Hamburg: Hamburger Edition, 2000.

Verwimp, Philip. "Development ideology, the peasantry and genocide: Rwanda represented in Habyarimana's speeches". *Journal of Genocide Research* 2, 3 (2000): 325–361.

Verwimp, Philip. "Death and survival during the 1994 genocide in Rwanda". *Population Studies* 58, 2 (2004): 233–245.

Verwimp, Philip. "An economic profile of peasant perpetrators of genocide: Micro-level evidence from Rwanda". *Journal of Development Economics* 77 (2005): 297–323.

Verwimp, Philip. *Peasants in Power: The Political Economy of Development and Genocide in Rwanda*. Heidelberg et al.: Springer, 2013.

Vidal, Claudine. *Sociologie des passions: Côte d'Ivoire, Rwanda*. Paris: Karthala, 1991.

Vincent-Buffault, Anne. *The History of Tears: Sensibility and Sentimentality in France*. Basingstoke and London: Macmillan, 1991.

Vinke, Hermann, ed. *Als die erste Atombombe fiel . . . : Kinder aus Hiroshima berichten*. Ravensburg: Otto Maier, 1982.

Vitalis, Robert, and Steven Heydemann. "War, Keynesianism, and Colonialism". *War, Institutions and Social Change in the Middle East*, ed. Steven Heydemann. Berkeley et al.: University of California Press, 2000: 100–147.

Vogel, Christine. „ Einleitung". *Bilder des Schreckens: Die mediale Inszenierung von Massakern seit dem 16. Jahrhundert*, ed. Christine Vogel. Frankfurt a.M. and New York: Campus, 2006: 7–14.

Volkov, I. M. "The Drought and Famine 1946–47". *Russian Studies in History* 31, 2 (1992): 31–60.

von Trotha, Trutz, ed. *Soziologie der Gewalt*. Opladen: Westdeutscher Verlag, 1997.

Vu, Tuong. "Of rice and revolution: The politics of provisioning and state-society relations on Java, 1945–49". *South-East Asia Research* 11 (3), 2003: 237–267.

Waller, James. *Becoming Evil: How Ordinary People Commit Genocide and Mass Violence*. Oxford et al.: Oxford University Press, 2002.

Wang Xiaoyu. "COVID-19 infections continue to decline in China". *China Daily*, February 15, 2023, https://www.chinadaily.com.cn/a/202302/15/WS63ec667aa31057c47ebaeef1.html.

Watts, Michael. *Silent Violence: Food, Famine and Peasantry in Northern Nigeria*. Berkeley et al.: University of California Press, 1987.

Wenzel, Eric. „Introduction: Le massacre dans les méandres de l'histoire du droit". *Le massacre, objet d'histoire*, ed. David El Kenz. Paris: Gallimard, 2005: 25–45.

Wenzel, Horst. *Hören und Sehen, Schrift und Bild: Kultur und Gedächtnis im Mittelalter*. Munich, 1995.

Weinberg, Gerhard. *A World at Arms: A Global History of World War II*. Cambridge et al.: Cambridge University Press, 1994.

Weinberg, Gerhard. "Total War: The Global Dimensions of Conflict". *A World at Total War: Global Conflict and the Politics of Destruction, 1937–1945*, eds. Roger Chickering et al. Cambridge: Cambridge University Press, 2005: 19–31.

Weiner, Amir. *Making Sense of War: The Second World War and the Fate of the Bolshevik Revolution*. Princeton and Oxford: Princeton University Press, 2001.

Werner, Hans. *Soundscape-Dialog: Landschaften und Methoden des Hörens*. Göttingen: Vandenhoeck & Ruprecht, 2006.

Westcott, Nicholas. "The Impact of the Second World War on Tanganyika, 1939–49". *Africa and the Second World War*, eds. David Killingray and Richard Rathbone. Basingstoke and London: Macmillan, 1986: 143–159.

Whitaker, Ben et al., *The Biharis in Bangladesh*. London: Minority Rights Group, n.y. [1977].

Wiedemann, Charlotte. *Das Leid der anderen verstehen: Holocaust und Weltgedächtnis*. Berlin: Propyläen, 2022.

Woll, Josephine. *Real Images: Soviet Cinema and the Thaw*. London and New York: I. B. Tauris, 2000.

Wong, Diana. "Memory Suppression and Memory Production: The Japanese Occupation of Singapore". *Perilous Memories: Asia-Pacific War(s)*, eds. T. Fujitani et al. Durham and London: University of North Carolina Press, 2003: 218–238.

Wong Hong Suen. *Wartime Kitchen: Food and Eating in Singapore 1942–1950*. Singapore: Editions Didier Millet and National Museum of Singapore, 2009.

Xi Jinping, *The Governance of China*, vol. II. Beijing: Foreign Language Press, 2017.

Yablonka, Hanna. *The State of Israel vs. Adolf Eichmann*. New York: Schocken, 2004.

Young, Isaac, and Daniel Sullivan. "Competitive victimhood: a review of the theoretical and empirical literature". *Current Opinion in Psychology* 11 (2016): 30–34.

Youngblood, Denise. "*Ivan's Childhood* (USSR, 1962) and *Come and See* (1985): Post-Stalinist Cinema and the Myth of World War II". *World War II, Films, and History*, eds. John Whiteclay Chambers II and David Culbert. New York and Oxford: Oxford University Press, 1996: 85–95.

Youngblood, Denise. *Russian War Films: On the Cinema Front, 1914–2005*. Lawrence: University Press of Kansas, 2007.

Zachariah, Benjamin. "The Creativity of Destruction: Wartime Imaginings of Development and Social Policy, c. 1942–1946". *The World in World Wars: Experiences, Perceptions and Perspectives from Africa and Asia*, eds. Heike Liebau et al. Leiden and Boston: Brill, 2010: 547–578.

Zeiler, Thomas. *Annihilation: A Global Military History of World War II*. New York and Oxford: Oxford University Press, 2011.

Zhao Tingyang. *Alles unter einem Himmel: Vergangenheit und Zukunft der Weltordnung*. Frankfurt a.M.: Suhrkamp, 2020.

Zhurzhenko, Tatiana. "Heroes into victims: The Second World War in post-Soviet memory politics", 2012. www.eurozine.com/articles/2012-10-31-zhurzhenko-en.html.

Zimmerer, Jürgen, ed. *Erinnerungskämpfe: Neues deutsches Geschichtsbewusstsein*. Ditzingen: Reclam, 2022.

Zorkaja, Neja. "Kino in Zeiten des Krieges: Visualisierungen von 1941 bis 1945". *Osteuropa* 55, 4–6 (2005): 328–334.

Zorkaya, Neya. *The Illustrated History of the Soviet Cinema*. New York: Hippocrene, 1989.

Index

abduction 34, 46, 75, 92, 98, 103, 105, 108, 242
Adamovich, Ales 133, 140–142
Africa 9, 13–14, 25–63, 152, 156, 162, 170, 177–180, 182–183, 191–194, 196–198, 201–202, 205, 208–210, 215, 219, 223 227, 239, 243–245
Algeria 146, 170, 177, 182, 204, 216, 220–221
Armenians 15, 164, 233, 248
Asia 2, 11, 12–14, 64–110, 152, 155–157, 160, 163, 176, 178, 187, 195, 198, 207, 209, 213, 216, 223, 227, 237, 239–240, 243–245
Atlantic Charter 210–212, 253
Atlantic Ocean 156, 185, 203
animals 36–37, 172, 208, 254
anti-guerrilla warfare 48, 73, 140, 234
Australia 156, 163, 170, 185, 188–189, 191, 194, 204–205
Austria 170, 176, 187, 226, 234, 237
Awami League 68–69, 73, 90, 93–97, 100, 103, 108

Bangladesh (see also: Bengal) 15–16, 19–20, 64–110, 233–234, 247–248, 250, 252
Belarus 12, 15–16, 48, 124, 136, 138, 140–141, 143, 236
Belgium 26, 165, 170, 177, 180, 191, 199, 210, 239
Bengal 6, 156–157, 170–171, 176, 184–186, 195–201, 205–206, 216–220
Berggolts, Olga 140, 145
Berlin 120–121, 134–135, 137, 141
Biharis (non-Bengalis) 68–69, 83, 90, 92, 95–109, 248
black market 172, 181, 190, 196, 205, 208–209
bombing 4, 12, 18, 67, 69, 119, 132, 146, 165–166, 169, 203–204, 210, 214–215, 217–218
Bondarchuk, Sergei 122, 131–132, 141–142
Botswana 177–178, 194, 197, 205
Brest 119–120, 123, 134, 138
Brezhnev, Leonid 113–114, 119–120, 130, 144–145
Britain 11–13, 152, 156–158, 161–170, 173, 176–177, 179–180, 182–186, 188, 191–197, 199–206, 208, 210–214, 216, 218–220, 229, 248
Bulgaria 145, 175, 203

Burma 151, 163, 170, 176, 178, 184–185, 193, 198, 217
Burundi 27, 29, 36, 39, 52, 61, 170–171, 177–178
Butare 38–39, 55, 57–59
Butler, Judith 2, 4, 219, 224, 232, 242–243, 245
Bykau, Vasil 122, 140–142

Calcutta 69, 109, 185–186, 207, 213
Canada 185, 212, 239
Cape Verde 177–178, 193, 203
capitalism 11, 151, 178, 197, 218, 224–225, 227–228, 232–233, 235, 238–240, 245, 247, 250
cash crops 26, 38, 179, 181–182, 186, 193, 209
Ceylon 179, 193
children 6, 17, 28, 34, 42–44, 46–47, 49–50, 69–72, 74–76, 78–79, 81, 92, 98, 101, 103–109, 113, 117–124, 127–130, 132–135, 137–138, 140–141, 143, 145, 158–159, 167–169, 172, 179, 186, 199, 203, 207, 214, 234, 242
China 12, 138, 151–152, 156–158, 160, 162, 166–170, 173, 176–178, 186–187, 192–193, 198–199, 203, 206, 211, 213, 216–217, 219, 223, 228, 234–235, 240, 250
Chittagong 96, 98–99, 101–102, 104
Christians/Christianity 28, 33–34, 40, 43–44, 48–52, 62, 92, 118, 122–123, 125–126, 140, 153, 170, 232
Chuknagar 48, 62, 64–87, 110, 247–248
Churchill, Winston 157, 162, 185, 196, 202, 211, 215
civil war 9, 26–27, 29, 60, 62, 110, 137, 163, 169, 247
class 4, 6–8, 14, 17, 44–45, 52, 54, 59, 67, 102, 161–163, 171, 184, 193, 208, 218, 228, 251
communists 111, 118, 122–125, 128–129, 137, 139–141, 168–169, 178, 186–187, 190, 209, 215, 234
conditions of violence 1, 3–9, 17, 20–21, 151–246
Congo/Zaïre 25, 27, 47, 199
coolness 3, 62, 75, 234
courts 9–10, 12–13, 28, 55, 167, 225, 227, 236–238, 251

COVID-19 2, 4–5, 15, 20, 62, 223–247, 249–252, 254–255
crowds 17, 19–20, 31–34, 40–42, 47–49, 53–54, 58, 64, 70–71, 78, 80, 83, 88–110, 121, 128, 132, 140, 169, 226, 228, 233, 247–248, 250
crying 44–48, 62, 72, 78–79, 84, 119–120, 234
Cyangugu 34, 57
Czechoslovakia 154, 165, 167, 187, 211

Dacca 69–70, 93–94, 97, 99, 101–103, 105
dehumanization 8, 35, 107, 133–135, 160, 213–215, 251
Djibouti 179, 204
Donskoi, Mark 126, 140–141
Dreyfus, Louis 199–200

East Pakistan 15, 19–20, 48, 64–110, 248, 250, 252
East Timor 170, 176, 204–205
Engels, Friedrich 223–224
epidemics 5, 153, 163, 181–182, 184, 200, 205, 207–208, 223–247, 252
Ethiopia 163, 202
ethnicity 11, 15–16, 26–27, 29, 52, 107, 152, 161–162, 164, 167–168, 171, 178, 190, 201, 205, 208, 216
Europe 2, 10–11, 14–15, 79, 105, 111–146, 152–153, 155–156, 160, 163, 166–167, 175–176, 178, 180, 182–183, 187–188, 190–197, 201–203, 209–210, 212, 220, 223, 225–230, 233, 235–237, 240–241, 243–245
'evil' 2, 6–10, 134–135, 145–146, 151, 158–161, 213–217, 220
exploitation 6, 162, 168, 170, 172, 180, 182–184, 186, 190–192, 194, 196, 199, 201, 205–206, 209–210, 216, 219–221, 226–227, 236, 240, 254

food 6, 83–84, 90, 97, 132–133, 161, 172, 179–209, 212, 216, 218
forced labor 4–5, 117, 132, 134, 152, 163, 167, 170, 179–181, 183, 186, 191–194, 209–210, 216, 219
France 11–12, 60, 145–146, 152, 165–168, 170, 176, 179–182, 191–192, 194, 197–198, 202, 204–205, 210, 220, 228, 244
freedom to kill 3, 232–234, 247

Galtung, Johan 6–7, 252–253
Gerasimov, Sergei 140–141
Germany 4–5, 12, 16, 26, 48, 65, 69, 73, 75, 111–112, 117–143, 146, 151–152, 154–155, 159–160, 162–163, 165–171, 175–176, 180–181, 187, 191, 194–196, 199–203, 208, 210–215, 217–219, 221, 227–228, 234, 237, 239, 241, 244
Göring, Hermann 162, 199
Greece 175, 180, 190, 185, 195, 198, 203, 206, 209, 211
guerrilla war 69, 88, 90, 103, 105, 119–120, 122, 132, 136–137, 140
Gulag 139, 168, 170–171

Habyarimana, Juvenal 27, 59
Henan 170, 173, 176, 186, 190, 192–193, 195, 198–199, 206, 219
Hindus/Hinduism 14, 64, 67, 69–86, 90, 92–93, 95, 102–104, 106–109, 232
Hiroshima 48, 67, 141, 146, 159, 165, 170, 210, 216
Hitler, Adolf 128, 134–137, 153, 162, 214
Hope, Victor alias Linlithgow 185, 212
Hunan 176–177
Hungary 15, 166–167, 241
hunger 5–6, 20, 26, 41, 47, 69, 79, 90, 92, 109, 111, 119, 130, 132–133, 146, 153–158, 163, 172–210, 216, 218–220
Hutus 9, 14, 25–63, 210, 233, 248

India 5, 64, 68–73, 77, 86, 90–93, 104–105, 107, 151, 156–157, 168–170, 176–177, 185–188, 190, 193, 196–197, 200–201, 203, 205–207, 210, 212–213, 215–218, 220, 232, 237, 243
Indian Ocean 185, 203–204, 208
Indonesia 15, 48, 73, 163, 177, 181, 188–190, 197, 216–217
industry 85, 92, 102–103, 129, 154, 161, 185–187, 196, 205, 209, 224, 227–229, 238–239
inflation 6, 172, 181–185, 190–191, 195, 197–200, 206, 208–209, 216
intelligentsia 12–13, 30–31, 54, 67, 135, 163, 250
intimidation 18, 31–32, 34–35, 37, 46, 54–55, 62–63, 77, 79, 89, 94, 108, 228, 242
Iran 152, 170, 176, 183–184, 193, 198–200, 202, 206, 218–219
Iraq 11–12, 152, 176, 179

Israel 14, 145, 221, 245
Italy 151–152, 159, 163, 166–167, 202–203, 211–212

Japan 12, 152, 155–163, 165–170, 173, 176–178, 181–182, 184, 186–188, 197–199, 203–205, 207–208, 210–218, 234, 239–240
Java 177, 181, 188–190
Jessore 69–70, 98, 100
Jews 5, 15, 48, 65, 73, 79, 81, 111, 118, 125–129, 140, 143, 145, 158, 163–164, 168, 175, 178–181, 196, 202–203, 213–214, 219–221, 233–235, 241–242
Jiang Jieshi (Chiang Kaishek) 213–215

Kenya 170, 177, 182, 192–194, 201–202, 205
Khulna 64, 67, 69–70, 73, 96, 98–99, 102, 105
Kibeho 38, 49, 60
Kibuye 44, 57
Kigali 27, 38, 40, 57–60
Klimov, Elem 77, 136, 141–142
Korea 152, 167
Kurdistan 176, 179

land conflicts 6, 9, 26, 28–29, 36–37, 41, 62, 69, 85, 91, 172, 185–186, 202, 233
landlessness 26, 29, 179, 198, 206, 209
Latin America 13–14, 156, 198, 210, 237
Leningrad 119–120, 132–133, 140–141, 171, 175, 203
looting 28, 36–37, 40–42, 61–62, 69–70, 77, 83–85, 92, 95, 99, 101, 104–105, 109, 134, 170, 172, 196, 208–209

Malaysia/Malaya 198, 227
Manchuria 137, 163, 167, 178–179, 217
Marx, Karl 4, 227
Marxism 125, 134–135, 154
massacres 20, 25, 28, 33–38, 42–44, 47–49, 51, 57, 62, 64–87, 90, 92, 98, 101, 103–105, 121, 127, 136–137, 140, 167, 208, 247
MDR 33, 36, 60
Mexico 12, 202
Moscow 118, 130, 139, 142
Mozambique 179, 193
MRND 27, 29, 48, 53
Mujibur Rahman 90, 93–95, 99

Mumbai 176, 237
Murambi 46, 51
music 18–19, 31–33, 35–36, 40–41, 45, 48–49, 51–52, 55, 59–62, 80, 118–119, 126–129, 139, 147, 214–215, 248
Muslims/Islam 14, 50, 67, 69, 71–72, 74–76, 80–86, 90, 92–93, 103–104, 106–109, 182, 193, 210, 248
Mymensingh 98–103

Nagasaki 48, 67, 165, 204, 210, 215–216
naval warfare 156, 166, 172, 179, 190, 195, 202–204, 212, 218
Nehru, Jawarlahal 212–213
neighbors 6, 31, 34–35, 41, 61, 63, 69, 90, 104, 108, 130, 235
Netherlands 176–177, 180–181, 188–190, 197
neutrality 170, 178, 183, 193, 199, 204, 212, 215, 219
New Guinea 191–192
Niger 177, 205
Nigeria 170, 177, 192, 194, 197, 214
North America 2, 11, 244–245
Nuremberg trials 167, 210, 215, 221
Nyamata 43, 49, 52

Pacific Ocean 152, 156, 159, 170, 190, 204, 211, 216, 243
Pakistan 16, 20, 64–110, 234, 247–248
Palau 177, 211
Palestine 14, 179, 193, 248
peasants 4, 6, 26–27, 29, 31, 36, 39, 41, 50, 53, 55, 85, 90, 93, 100, 109, 171, 185–186, 190, 201, 205, 209, 216
Philippines 177, 198, 217
Poland 65, 81, 137, 145, 167, 175, 181, 187, 202, 211, 249
political misuse of the study of violence 4, 10–12, 164–165, 241, 251
Portugal 170, 177–179, 191–193, 203–204
poverty 4–6, 26, 28–30, 41, 62, 67–69, 85–86, 90, 107, 179, 181, 183, 185, 197–198, 205–206, 208, 250, 253
Power, Samantha 8, 11–12
POWs 5, 14, 103, 120–122, 128–130, 132, 135–137, 142, 151–152, 159, 163, 166, 168, 171–172, 175–176, 180, 199, 202–203, 214–215, 219

propaganda 27, 29, 42, 53, 55, 57–58, 61, 73, 77, 86, 90, 98, 113, 116, 159–161, 165, 206, 210–217, 221, 245, 249, 252

Quit India movement 107, 169–170, 216

racism 2–3, 13–14, 16, 107, 151, 153–155, 158–159, 164–167, 170–171, 193, 201–202, 209, 219–220, 227, 233, 240, 244, 248–249, 252
radio 29, 36–37, 51–52, 55–62, 73, 99, 108, 123, 199, 212
rape 34, 42, 46, 51, 68–69, 75, 77, 90, 92, 99, 105, 108, 112, 137–138, 167–168, 171–172, 205, 215, 252
rations 6, 179–181, 184, 189–190, 192, 198, 201–202
Rawls, John 13–14
refugees 5, 26–28, 31, 34, 36, 39, 46–50, 54, 58, 60–61, 64, 67–74, 76–77, 80, 82–83, 86, 90, 92, 101, 103–104, 108, 132, 135, 139, 151–152, 169, 184, 186, 190–191, 198, 202, 206–208, 250
retirement homes 228, 239–241
Réunion 179, 204
riots 68, 85, 87–110, 220, 228
Romania 152, 166–167, 211, 218
Romm, Mikhail 127, 135–136, 140, 142
Roosevelt, Franklin 211, 213, 215
RPF 25, 27, 31, 56, 58, 60, 62
Russia 12–13, 114, 116, 120, 123–124, 127, 129, 134, 137, 154, 158, 200, 223
Rwanda 9, 12, 15, 17, 20, 25–63, 164, 170, 177, 233, 245, 247–248, 250, 252

'sanctions' (economic) 6, 13, 212, 251, 253
Senegal 191, 202
shoah 5, 9–10, 12, 15, 48, 65, 73, 79, 81, 118, 125–129, 140, 145, 159, 163–165, 175, 180–181, 213, 219–221, 233, 242, 244
Sholokhov, Mikhail 128, 131, 140
Shostakovich, Dmitri 118–119, 140
Siddqi, Kader 105–106
silence 15, 33, 37, 43–45, 49–50, 52, 63, 79–81, 84–85, 114–115, 128, 208, 248
Simonov, Konstantin 129, 135, 140, 143

Singapore 176, 203, 207–208, 227
social mobility 6, 26, 29–30, 41, 62, 90, 107, 187, 190, 192, 195, 205–206, 208, 216, 250
socialism 114–115, 119, 154–155, 178, 217, 250
Somalia 180, 193, 211
sounds 16–20, 25–87, 121, 128, 131, 234, 245, 247–248
South Africa 159, 175, 177, 232
Soviet Union 2, 5, 15–16, 20, 81, 111–148, 152, 154, 158–160, 163, 165–168, 171, 175–176, 178, 180–184, 187, 199–203, 209, 211–219, 233–234, 247–248, 250, 252
Spain 11, 163, 168, 175–176, 188, 191–192
Stalin, Joseph 114–115, 120–121, 125, 129, 134–135, 139–140, 162, 213–214
Stalinism 119, 12–122, 124, 134, 136, 138–139, 142
Stalingrad 120–121, 136, 140–142
structural violence 6–7, 252–253, 256
Switzerland 235, 237, 240, 242
Syria 12, 152, 179

Tanganyika 27, 61, 170, 177, 180, 182, 192–194, 197
Tarkovsky, Andrei 118, 122, 141, 143, 145
television 59, 105, 113, 143
tenancy 206, 209
Thailand 152, 163, 179, 198, 204
Tokyo 204, 210, 212–213
torture 34, 44–46, 48, 103, 105, 117, 127, 134, 136, 169, 205, 254
traders 6, 185, 205–206, 209
trials 13, 55–56, 137, 145, 167, 210, 215, 221, 237
Turkey 12, 15, 179, 210
Tutsis 14, 25–63, 164, 248

Ukraine 5, 12, 125–126, 143, 187
United Nations 11–12, 156, 187–188, 211–212, 217, 221, 244–245, 253
UNRRA 167, 187–188
USA 10–13, 16, 69, 85, 93–94, 98, 125, 152, 155, 158, 161, 163, 166–171, 176–177, 183–185, 187, 194, 196, 198–199, 202, 204, 210–217, 224, 232–234, 237, 244, 253, 255

Vietnam 177, 181–182, 188, 190, 198–199, 202, 209, 221, 234, 237

The original version of this chapter was revised. The index entry for "Roosevelt, Franklin" has been corrected. We apologize for the mistake.

women 14, 17, 28, 34, 42, 46–47, 62–63, 67, 69–71, 74–76, 78, 80, 82, 85, 91–92, 98–99, 101, 103–105, 107, 109, 118–120, 122, 128–131, 133–134, 137, 162, 167–168, 171, 190, 218, 228–230, 233–234, 253
workers 4, 55, 85, 93, 96, 102, 109, 117, 125, 130, 134–136, 180–187, 191–194, 198, 202–203, 206, 209, 226–227, 239

Yahya Khan 68, 94–95
Yellow River (Huang He) 169–170, 186, 216
Yemen 12, 176
Yugoslavia 11, 161, 165, 167, 211

Zambia 192–194, 197, 201, 206
Zimbabwe 180, 192

www.ingramcontent.com/pod-product-compliance
Lightning Source LLC
LaVergne TN
LVHW042251070526
838201LV00089B/107